PRENTICE HALL

Teacher's SCIENCE EXPLORER **Edition**

Electricity and Magnetism

PRENTICE HALL
Needham, Massachusetts
Upper Saddle River, New Jersey

ISBN 0-13-434566-5
3 4 5 6 7 8 9 10   03 02 01 00 99

PRENTICE HALL
SCIENCE EXPLORER
GET READY FOR A CONTENT-RICH, HANDS-ON EXPLORATION!
PRENTICE HALL SCIENCE EXPLORER Earth's Waters
PRENTICE HALL SCIENCE EXPLORER Motion, Forces and Energy
PRENTICE HALL SCIENCE EXPLORER Animals
15 Books In All

Chart your own course.

15 motivational hardcover books make it easy for you to create your own curriculum; meet local, state, and national guidelines; and teach your favorite topics in depth.

Prepare your students with rich, motivating content...

Science Explorer is crafted for today's middle grades student, with accessible content and in-depth coverage of all the important concepts.

...and a wide variety of inquiry activities.

Motivational student- and teacher-tested activities reinforce key concepts and allow students to explore science concepts for themselves.

Check your compass regularly.

Science Explorer gives you more ways to regularly check student performance than any other program available.

Utilize a variety of tools.

Integrated science sections in every chapter and Interdisciplinary Explorations in every book allow you to make in-depth connections to other sciences and disciplines. Plus, you will find a wealth of additional tools to set your students on a successful course.

Chart the course you want with 15 motivating books that easily match your curriculum.

Each book in the series contains:
- Integrated Science sections in every chapter
- Interdisciplinary Explorations for team teaching at the end of each book
- Comprehensive skills practice and application—assuring that you meet the National Science Education Standards and your local and state standards

For custom binding options, see your local sales representative.

EXPLORATION TOOLS: BASIC PROCESS SKILLS

Observing

Measuring

Calculating

Classifying

Predicting

Inferring

Graphing

Creating data tables

Communicating

LIFE SCIENCE TITLES

From Bacteria to Plants
1 Living Things
2 Viruses and Bacteria
3 Protists and Fungi
4 Introduction to Plants
5 Seed Plants

Animals
1 Sponges, Cnidarians, and Worms
2 Mollusks, Arthropods, and Echinoderms
3 Fishes, Amphibians, and Reptiles
4 Birds and Mammals
5 Animal Behavior

Cells and Heredity
1 Cell Structure and Function
2 Cell Processes and Energy
3 Genetics: The Science of Heredity
4 Modern Genetics
5 Changes Over Time

Human Biology and Health
1 Healthy Body Systems
2 Bones, Muscles, and Skin
3 Food and Digestion
4 Circulation
5 Respiration and Excretion
6 Fighting Disease
7 The Nervous System
8 The Endocrine System and Reproduction

Environmental Science
1 Populations and Communities
2 Ecosystems and Biomes
3 Living Resources
4 Land and Soil Resources
5 Air and Water Resources
6 Energy Resources

Integrated Science sections in every chapter

EXPLORATION TOOLS: ADVANCED PROCESS SKILLS

Posing questions

Forming operational definitions

Developing hypotheses

Controlling variables

Interpreting data

Interpreting graphs

Making models

Drawing conclusions

Designing experiments

EARTH SCIENCE TITLES

Inside Earth
1 Plate Tectonics
2 Earthquakes
3 Volcanoes
4 Minerals
5 Rocks

Earth's Changing Surface
1 Mapping Earth's Surface
2 Weathering and Soil Formation
3 Erosion and Deposition
4 A Trip Through Geologic Time

Earth's Waters
1 Earth: The Water Planet
2 Fresh Water
3 Freshwater Resources
4 Ocean Motions
5 Ocean Zones

Weather and Climate
1 The Atmosphere
2 Weather Factors
3 Weather Patterns
4 Climate and Climate Change

Astronomy
1 Earth, Moon, and Sun
2 The Solar System
3 Stars, Galaxies, and the Universe

PHYSICAL SCIENCE TITLES

Chemical Building Blocks
1 An Introduction to Matter
2 Changes in Matter
3 Elements and the Periodic Table
4 Carbon Chemistry

Chemical Interactions
1 Chemical Reactions
2 Atoms and Bonding
3 Acids, Bases, and Solutions
4 Exploring Materials

Motion, Forces, and Energy
1 Motion
2 Forces
3 Forces in Fluids
4 Work and Machines
5 Energy and Power
6 Thermal Energy and Heat

Electricity and Magnetism
1 Magnetism and Electromagnetism
2 Electric Charges and Current
3 Electricity and Magnetism at Work
4 Electronics

Sound and Light
1 Characteristics of Waves
2 Sound
3 The Electromagnetic Spectrum
4 Light

Integrated Science sections in every chapter

Place your students in the role of science explorer through a variety of inquiry activities.

Motivational student- and teacher-tested activities reinforce key concepts and allow students to explore science concepts for themselves. More than 350 activities are provided for each book in the Student Edition, Teacher's Edition, Teaching Resources, Integrated Science Lab Manual, Inquiry Skills Activity Book, Interactive Student Tutorial CD-ROM, and *Science Explorer* Web Site.

STUDENT EDITION ACTIVITIES

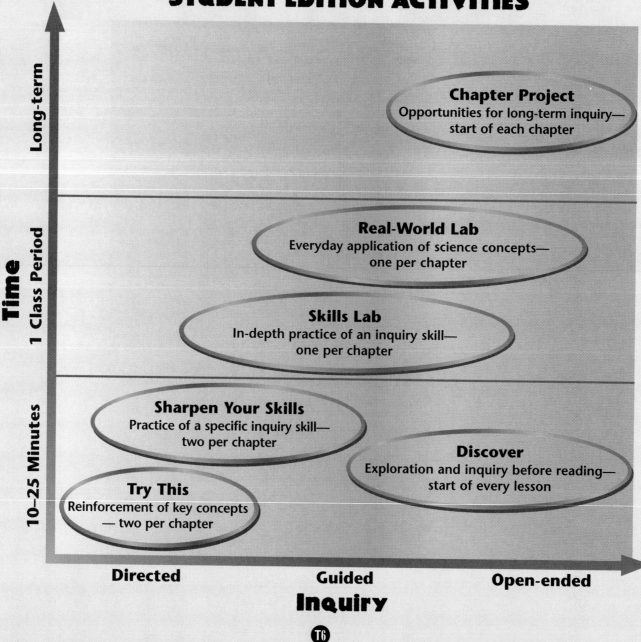

Time

Long-term

1 Class Period

10–25 Minutes

Chapter Project
Opportunities for long-term inquiry—start of each chapter

Real-World Lab
Everyday application of science concepts—one per chapter

Skills Lab
In-depth practice of an inquiry skill—one per chapter

Sharpen Your Skills
Practice of a specific inquiry skill—two per chapter

Discover
Exploration and inquiry before reading—start of every lesson

Try This
Reinforcement of key concepts—two per chapter

Directed   Guided   Open-ended

Inquiry

Check your compass regularly with integrated assessment tools.

Prepare for state exams with traditional and performance-based assessment.

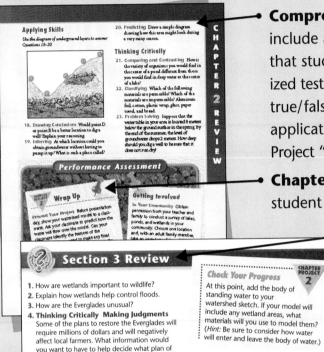

- **Comprehensive Chapter Reviews** include a wide range of question types that students will encounter on standardized tests. Types include multiple choice, enhanced true/false, concept mastery, visual thinking, skill application, and critical thinking. Also includes Chapter Project "Wrap Up."

- **Chapter Projects** contain rubrics that allow you to easily assess student progress.

- **Section Reviews** provide "Check your Progress" opportunities for the Chapter Project, as well as review questions for the section.

Additional *Science Explorer* assessment resources:

- **Assessment Resources with CD-ROM**
- **Resource Pro® with Planning Express® CD-ROM**
- **Standardized Test Practice Book**
- **On-line review activities** at www.phschool.com
  See page T9 for complete product descriptions.

Self-assessment opportunities help students keep themselves on course.

- **Caption Questions** throughout the text assess critical thinking skills.

- **Checkpoint Questions** give students an immediate content check as new concepts are presented.

- **Interactive Student Tutorial CD-ROM** provides students with electronic self-tests, review activities, and Exploration activities.

- **Got It! Video Quizzes** motivate and challenge students with engaging animations and interactive questions.

- **www.science-explorer.phschool.com** provides additional support and on-line test prep.

Utilize a wide variety of tools.

Easy-to-manage, book-specific teaching resources

15 Teaching Resource Packages, each containing a Student Edition, Teacher's Edition, Teaching Resources with Color Transparencies, Guided Reading Audiotape, Materials Kit Order form, and Correlation to the National Science Education Standards.

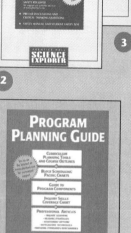

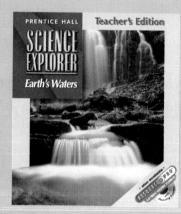

15 Teacher's Editions with a three-step lesson plan—*Engage/Explore, Facilitate,* and *Assess*—that is ideal for reaching all students. Chapter planning charts make it easy to find resources, as well as to plan for block scheduling and team teaching.

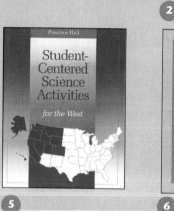

15 Teaching Resource Books with Color Transparencies offer complete support organized by chapter to make it easy for you to find what you need—when you need it.

15 Guided Reading Audiotapes (English and Spanish) provide section summaries for students who need additional support.

15 Explorer Videotapes allow students to explore concepts through spectacular short videos containing computer animations. Available in Spanish.

1. **Materials Kits**—Prentice Hall and Science Kit, Inc. have collaborated to develop a Consumable Kit and Nonconsumable Kit for each book. Ordering software makes it easy to customize!

2&3. **Integrated Science Laboratory Manual with Teacher's Edition**—74 in-depth labs covering the entire curriculum, with complete teaching support.

4. **Inquiry Skills Activity Book**—additional activities to teach, practice, and assess a wide range of inquiry skills.

5. **Student-Centered Science Activities**—five activity books for the Northeast, Southeast, Midwest, Southwest, and West.

6. **Program Planning Guide**—course outlines, block scheduling pacing charts, correlations, and more.

7. **Product Testing Activities by *Consumer Reports***—19 student-oriented testing activities turn students into real-world explorers.

Additional print resources...

8. **Reading in the Content Area**—with Literature Connections

9. **Standardized Test Practice**—review and self-tests to prepare for statewide exams.

10. **15 Prentice Hall Interdisciplinary Explorations**

11. **How to Assess Student Work**

12. **How to Manage Instruction in the Block**

13. ***Cobblestone, Odyssey, Calliope,* and *Faces* Magazines**

Program-wide technology resources

1. **Resource Pro® CD-ROM**—the ultimate management tool with easy access to blackline masters and lab activities for all 15 books. Planning Express® software lets you customize lesson plans by day, week, month, and year. Also includes Computer Test Bank software.

2. **Assessment Resources with CD-ROM**—*Computer Test Bank* software with Dial-A-Test® provides you with unparalleled flexibility in creating tests.

3. ***Science Explorer* Web Site**—activities and teaching resources for every chapter at www.science-explorer.phschool.com

4. **Interactive Student Tutorial CD-ROMs**—provide students with self-tests, helpful hints, and Explorations. Tests are scored instantly and provide complete explanations to all answers.

5. **An Odyssey of Discovery CD-ROMs**—interactive labs encourage students to hypothesize and experiment. (Life and Earth Science).

6. **Interactive Earth CD-ROM**—explore global trends, search the media library, and zoom in on a 3-D globe.

7. **Mindscape CD-ROMs**—*The Animals!™, Oceans Below,* and *How Your Body Works* bring science alive with compelling videoclips, 3-D animations, and interactive databases.

8. **A.D.A.M. The Inside Story**—take an entertaining tour of each body system, designed for middle grades students.

9. **Interactive Physics**—explore physics concepts with computer simulations that encourage what-if questions.

10. **Explorer Videotapes and Videodiscs**—explore and visualize concepts through spectacular short documentaries containing computer animations (Spanish audio track).

11. **Event-Based Science**—series of NSF-funded modules that engage students with inquiry-based projects. Includes video.

Options for Pacing *Electricity and Magnetism*

The Pacing Chart below suggests one way to schedule your instructional time. The **Science Explorer** program offers many other aids to help you plan your instructional time, whether regular class periods or **block scheduling.** Refer to the Chapter Planning Guide before each chapter to view all program resources with suggested times for Student Edition activities.

Pacing Chart

	Days	Blocks		Days	Blocks
Nature of Science: An Electrical Engineer in Outer Space	1	$\frac{1}{2}$	**2** Generating Electric Current	4	2
Chapter 1 Magnetism and Electromagnetism			**3** Using Electric Power	$3\frac{1}{2}$	1–2
Chapter 1 Project Electromagnetic Fishing Derby	Ongoing	Ongoing	**4** Integrating Chemistry: Batteries	4	2
			Chapter 3 Review and Assessment	1	$\frac{1}{2}$
1 The Nature of Magnetism	5	$2\frac{1}{2}$	**Chapter 4 Electronics**		
2 Integrating Earth Science: Magnetic Earth	3	$1\frac{1}{2}$	Chapter 4 Project Bits and Bytes	Ongoing	Ongoing
			1 Electronic Signals and Semiconductors	4	2
3 Electric Current and Magnetic Fields	4	2	**2** Electronic Communication	4	2
4 Electromagnets	$1\frac{1}{2}$	$\frac{1}{2}$–1	**3** Computers	5	$2\frac{1}{2}$
Chapter 1 Review and Assessment	1	$\frac{1}{2}$	**4** Integrating Technology: The Information Superhighway	$2\frac{1}{2}$	1–2
Chapter 2 Electric Charges and Current			Chapter 4 Review and Assessment	1	$\frac{1}{2}$
Chapter 2 Project Cause for Alarm	Ongoing	Ongoing	Interdisciplinary Exploration: Edison–Genius of Invention		
1 Electric Charge and Static Electricity	5	$2\frac{1}{2}$			
2 Circuit Measurements	4	2			
3 Series and Parallel Circuits	2	1			
4 Integrating Health: Electrical Safety	$2\frac{1}{2}$	1–2			
Chapter 2 Review and Assessment	1	$\frac{1}{2}$			
Chapter 3 Electricity and Magnetism at Work					
Chapter 3 Project Electrical Energy Audit	Ongoing	Ongoing			
1 Electricity, Magnetism, and Motion	3	$1\frac{1}{2}$			

RESOURCE PRO®

The Resource Pro® CD-ROM is the ultimate scheduling and lesson planning tool. Resource Pro® allows you to preview all the resources in the *Science Explorer* program, organize your chosen materials, and print out any teaching resource. You can follow the suggested lessons or create your own, using resources from anywhere in the program.

Thematic Overview of *Electricity and Magnetism*

The chart below lists the major themes of *Electricity and Magnetism.* For each theme, the chart supplies a big idea, or concept statement, describing how a particular theme is taught in a chapter.

	Chapter 1	Chapter 2	Chapter 3	Chapter 4
Scale and Structure	Every magnet has two poles where the magnetic effects are the strongest.			
Unity and Diversity			Electric motors and generators use electromagnets to convert one form of energy into another. Electric motors convert electrical energy into mechanical energy; electric generators convert mechanical energy into electrical energy.	Solid state electronic devices include simple diodes and transistors, and complex integrated circuits with millions of separate transistors and other elements. All depend on the same basic principles of solid state electronics.
Systems and Interactions	Properties of the atoms of a substance determine whether it will conduct electricity or not. The opposition to the movement of charges flowing through a material is called resistance. A magnetic field will exert a force on a wire that is carrying current.	Electrons flow from an area of high potential energy to an area of lower potential energy. Electrons in a series circuit stop flowing when any part of the circuit is broken; electrons in a parallel circuit continue flowing through remaining closed paths when a single path is broken.	When a loop of wire spins in a magnetic field, current is generated. Electric current can be alternating or direct, depending on the type of generator that produces the current. Wet and dry cells pass electrons from a positive to a negative terminal; a cell is made up of two electrodes with an electrolyte between them.	Analog and digital signals can be sent through wires or carried by electromagnetic waves to operate telephones, fax machines, radios, and televisions. Computers are electronic devices that process information. Computer systems can be connected in wide area networks so that information can travel great distances.
Energy		Electricity is a form of energy in which electrons flow. Interactions between electric fields can cause electrons to flow. Voltage, resistance, and current are properties of electrical energy. In the human body, energy from a high current can disrupt normal electrical activity.	Electricity can be converted into many other forms of energy. A magnetic field can induce electric current. Electrical energy can be generated from many sources. Transformers can increase or decrease the voltage of electrical energy. Electrochemical cells store energy chemically and convert it into electricity.	Electronics use electrical energy to carry information. Semiconductors are substances that transfer energy better than insulators but not as well as conductors.
Stability	Conductors are materials through which electric charges flow. A magnetic field will always exist around a magnet and a wire that carries current.		A magnetic field always exists around a current-carrying wire.	
Modeling				Students model how a computer uses binary numbers to count and add.

Inquiry Skills Chart

The Prentice Hall *Science Explorer* program provides comprehensive teaching, practice, and assessment of science skills, with an emphasis on the process skills necessary for inquiry. The chart lists the skills covered in the program and cites the page numbers where each skill is covered.

Basic Process SKILLS

	Student Text: Projects and Labs	Student Text: Activities	Student Text: Caption and Review Questions	Teacher's Edition: Extensions
Observing	22–23, 36–37, 44–45, 54–55, 62–63, 76–77, 110–111, 119	14, 16, 20, 24, 30, 34, 38, 46, 48, 50, 56, 64, 66, 78, 84, 86, 92, 95, 99, 120, 152	31	16–17, 28, 32, 34, 47–48, 50, 52, 57, 59, 69, 71, 117
Inferring	22–23, 36–37, 54–55, 82–83	16, 24, 30, 46, 50, 56, 64, 66, 78, 112, 120, 128, 138, 152	43, 109	17, 20, 27–28, 66, 70–71, 81, 87, 103, 117, 121, 125
Predicting	22–23, 54–55, 62–63	34, 66, 152	40, 43, 75, 101, 109, 145	15, 27, 50, 59, 66, 70, 86–87, 101–102, 122, 131
Classifying	110–111	34, 87, 120, 153	15, 75, 109, 135, 145	49, 90, 113
Making Models	12–13, 36–37, 82–83, 119, 136–137	20, 59, 153	58, 75	18–19, 39, 49, 57–58, 115, 122, 126, 129, 134
Communicating	12–13, 44–45, 110–111	28, 59, 70, 80, 87, 97, 106, 112, 114, 117, 128, 133, 140, 142, 153	42, 74, 108, 144–145	30, 32, 39–40, 56, 58, 65, 85, 97, 101, 114, 123, 129, 139
Measuring	76–77	25, 27, 56, 128, 154		26, 58, 60, 85, 114
Calculating	76–77, 136–137	60, 128, 130, 155	61, 145	60, 94
Creating Data Tables	54–55, 76–77	138, 162		
Graphing		162–164		

Advanced Process SKILLS

Posing Questions		92, 156		97
Developing Hypotheses	54–55	29, 68, 84, 156		39, 100, 133
Designing Experiments	12–13, 44–45, 54–55, 62–63, 82–83, 104–105, 110–111, 119	157	43	65, 85, 101, 123
Controlling Variables	12–13, 62–63	86, 157	43, 75	16, 59, 65, 86
Forming Operational Definitions		38, 157	138	

Advanced Process SKILLS (continued)

	Student Text: Projects and Labs	Student Text: Activities	Student Text: Caption and Review Questions	Teacher's Edition: Extensions
Interpreting Data	76–77	86, 157		
Drawing Conclusions	22–23, 54–55, 62–63, 82–83, 104–105	27, 48, 157	43	50, 52, 123

Critical Thinking SKILLS

	Student Text: Projects and Labs	Student Text: Activities	Student Text: Caption and Review Questions	Teacher's Edition: Extensions
Comparing and Contrasting	36–37, 110–111, 119	25, 158	19, 39, 43, 53, 67, 75, 91, 95, 109, 145	25–26, 69, 71, 86, 114
Applying Concepts	22–23, 44–45, 62–63, 82–83, 119, 136–137	138, 158	18, 20–21, 43, 65, 71–72, 75, 86, 103, 109, 113, 116, 118, 125, 145	20, 69, 94, 96, 101, 115, 122, 126, 140
Interpreting Diagrams, Graphs Photographs, and Maps		158	16, 26, 47, 67, 79, 81, 85, 90, 114, 121	26, 33, 51, 79, 88, 95, 116, 124, 130
Relating Cause and Effect	44–45	28, 159	35, 43, 53, 61, 69, 81	39, 124
Making Generalizations		159	127	65
Making Judgments		106, 142, 159		93
Problem Solving	22–23, 36–37, 136–137	159	43, 75, 93, 98, 109, 141, 145	

Information Organizing SKILLS

	Student Text: Projects and Labs	Student Text: Activities	Student Text: Caption and Review Questions	Teacher's Edition: Extensions
Concept Maps		160	42, 108	138
Compare/ Contrast Tables		160		
Venn Diagrams		161	74	84
Flowcharts		161	144	40, 88, 120
Cycle Diagrams		161		

The *Science Explorer* program provides additional teaching, reinforcement, and assessment of skills in the Inquiry Skills Activities Book and the Integrated Science Laboratory Manual.

Throughout the *Science Explorer* program, every effort has been made to keep the materials and equipment *affordable, reusable,* and *easily accessible.*

The *Science Explorer* program offers an abundance of activity options so you can pick and choose those activities that suit your needs. To help you order supplies at the beginning of the year, the Master Materials List cross-references the materials by activity. If you prefer to create your list electronically, use the electronic order forms at:
www.science–explorer.phschool.com

There are two kits available for each book of the *Science Explorer* program, a Consumable Kit and a Nonconsumable Kit. These kits are produced by **Science Kit and Boreal Laboratories,** the leader in providing science kits to schools. Prentice Hall and Science Kit collaborated throughout the development of *Science Explorer* to ensure that the equipment and supplies in the kits precisely match the requirements of the program activities.

The kits provide an economical and convenient way to get all of the materials needed to teach each book. For each book, Science Kit also offers the opportunity to buy equipment and safety items individually. For a current listing of kit offerings or additional information about materials to accompany *Science Explorer*, please, contact Science Kit at:
1-800-828-7777
or at their Internet site at:
www.sciencekit.com

Master Materials List

Consumable Materials

*	Description	Quantity per class	Textbook Section(s)	*	Description	Quantity per class	Textbook Section(s)
C	Aluminum Foil, Roll, 12" × 25'	1	1-3 (SYS) 1-3 (Lab) 2-1 (Lab)	C	Lead (Graphite Rod) 4", Pkg/6	2	1-3 (SYS) 2-2 (Lab)
SS	Apples	10	3-4 (Lab)	SS	LED, Bicolor (Optional)	5	4-1 (Lab)
C	Balloons, Blue, Round, 9", Pkg/16	1	2-1 (DIS)	C	LED, Red, Diffused, 1.5 V	5	4-1 (Lab)
				SS	Metal Polish	1	3-4 (DIS)
C	Battery, Size D	10	1-3 (DIS) 1-3 (SYS) 1-3 (Lab) 1-4 (DIS) 2-2 (DIS) 2-2 (Lab) 2-3 (DIS) 2-3 (SYS) 2-4 (DIS) 3-1 (DIS) 3-1 (Lab) 4-1 (DIS) 4-1 (Lab)	SS	Newspaper	5	4-4 (DIS)
				SS	Paper Towel Roll (120 sheets)	1	3-4 (DIS)
				SS	Paper, Sheet	15	1-2 (TT) 2-1 (Lab) 4-3 (Lab)
				C	Paper, Tissue, Assorted Colors/20, 20" × 30"	1	2-1 (SYS)
				SS	Pencil	5	1-1 (SYS) 1-1 (Lab) 2-1 (Lab)
C	Cardboard, White, 8-1/2" × 11"	5	1-1 (Lab)	C	Plates, Styrofoam, 9", Pkg/35	1	2-1 (TT) 2-1 (Lab)
C	Clay, Modeling (Cream), lb (water-resistant)	2	2-2 (DIS) 3-1 (Lab) 3-2 (DIS) 3-4 (Lab)	C	Salt, Non-Iodized, 737 g	1	3-4 (DIS)
				C	Sandpaper, Medium, 9 × 11" Sheet	5	3-1 (Lab)
C	Cup, Paper, 200 mL	5	1-3 (Lab)	C	Tape, Duct, 10 yds	1	1-3 (Lab)
C	Cup, Styrofoam, 6 oz	10	1-1 (SYS) 2-1 (Lab)	SS	Tape, Masking, 3/4" × 60 yd	1	1-1 (Lab) 1-2 (SYS) 2-1 (TT) 2-2 (DIS) 4-1 (Lab)
C	Detergent, Household, 14.7 oz (dish detergent)	1	1-2 (DIS)				
SS	Foam	5	1-3 (SYS)	C	Wax Paper, Roll, 75 sq ft	1	1-3 (SYS)
C	Lamp, Miniature, #14 (2.47 V)	20	1-3 (DIS) 1-3 (SYS) 1-3 (Lab) 2-2 (DIS) 2-2 (Lab) 2-3 (DIS) 2-3 (SYS) 2-4 (DIS) 3-3 (DIS) 3-4 (DIS) 4-1 (Lab)				

KEY: **DIS**: Discover; **SYS**: Sharpen Your Skills; **TT**: Try This; **Lab**: Lab **Quantities are based on 5 lab groups per class.**
* Items designated **C** are in the Consumable Kit, **NC** are in the Nonconsumable Kit, and **SS** are School Supplied.

Master Materials List

Nonconsumable Materials

*	Description	Quantity per class	Textbook Section(s)	*	Description	Quantity per class	Textbook Section(s)
NC	Alligator Clip with 3/8" Jaw	10	1-3 (SYS) 2-2 (Lab) 2-4 (DIS) 4-1 (Lab)	SS	Glass	5	3-4 (DIS)
				NC	Iron Filings (Shaker Top) 8 oz	2	1-1 (TT)
SS	Aluminum Can, Empty	5	2-1 (DIS)	SS	Key	5	1-3 (SYS)
SS	Appliances, Electrical	5	3-3 (SYS)	NC	Light Socket, Mini w/Fahn. Clips	20	1-3 (DIS) 1-3 (SYS) 2-2 (DIS) 2-2 (Lab) 2-3 (DIS) 2-3 (SYS) 2-4 (DIS) 3-3 (DIS) 3-4 (DIS) 4-1 (Lab)
NC	Ball, Styrofoam, 1"	5	1-2 (DIS)				
NC	Battery Holder w/Fahnestock Clips, D-Cell	10	1-3 (DIS) 1-3 (SYS) 1-4 (DIS) 2-2 (DIS) 2-2 (Lab) 2-3 (DIS) 2-3 (SYS) 2-4 (DIS) 3-1 (DIS)				
				NC	Magnet, Bar, Alnico w/Marked Poles, 3"	5	1-1 (DIS) 1-1 (TT) 1-1 (Lab) 1-2 (DIS) 1-2 (TT) 3-1 (Lab) 3-2 (TT)
NC	Beaker, Pyrex Low Form, 400 mL, Double Scale	5	2-2 (TT)				
NC	Bolt, Long, Round Head, 10–32, 4"	10	1-4 (DIS) 3-1 (DIS) 3-4 (Lab)	NC	Magnet, Donut, 3 cm OD, 1 cm ID	10	1-1 (SYS)
SS	Books	30	3-1 (DIS)	NC	Magnet, Horseshoe, 7.5 cm	5	1-1 (DIS) 3-1 (DIS) 3-2 (DIS)
NC	Canister, Film Type w/Snap Cap	5	3-1 (Lab)				
SS	Clock or Watch	1	4-3 (DIS)	NC	Magnet, Steel Bar (pair in box) 150 mm × 19 mm × 7 mm, both poles marked	1	3-2 (TT)
NC	Cloth, Wool, 12 × 24"	1	2-1 (Lab)				
NC	Clothespin, Spring Type, Pkg/18	2	3-4 (Lab)	NC	Magnifying Glass, 3x, 6x	5	4-2 (DIS)
SS	Coins, Various	30	1-1 (Lab)	SS	Map, Local	5	1-2 (DIS) 1-2 (SYS)
NC	Comb, Plastic, 15 cm	5	2-1 (SYS)				
NC	Compass, Pocket, 40 mm	15	1-2 (SYS) 1-2 (TT) 1-3 (DIS) 2-2 (DIS)	NC	Needles, Metal, Blunt, Pkg/7	1	1-2 (DIS)
				NC	Pan, Aluminum Foil, 22.5 cm Diam	5	2-1 (TT)
SS	Dimes	25	3-4 (DIS)	NC	Paper Clips, Box/100	2	1-1 (DIS) 1-3 (SYS) 1-4 (DIS)
SS	Dish	5	1-2 (DIS)				
NC	Flashlight, Plastic (Size D)	5	4-1 (DIS) 4-1 (Lab)	NC	Paper Clips, Jumbo, Box/100	1	3-1 (Lab)
NC	Funnel, Plastic, 3.25"	5	2-2 (TT)	SS	Pennies	75	3-4 (DIS) 4-3 (Lab)

KEY: **DIS**: Discover; **SYS**: Sharpen Your Skills; **TT**: Try This; **Lab**: Lab
* Items designated **C** are in the Consumable Kit, **NC** are in the Nonconsumable Kit, and **SS** are School Supplied.

Nonconsumable Materials (cont.)

*	Description	Quantity per class	Textbook Section(s)
SS	Pliers	5	3-1 (Lab)
SS	Protractor, 6", Plastic, 180 degrees	5	1-1 (Lab) 1-2 (SYS)
SS	Ruler, Plastic, 12"/30 cm	5	3-1 (DIS) 1-1 (Lab) 4-3 (Lab)
SS	Scissors	5	1-3 (Lab) 2-1 (Lab) 3-4 (DIS)
NC	Steel Wool Pads, Pkg/6	1	2-4 (DIS)
NC	Sticks, Craft, Pkg/30	1	1-1 (Lab)
NC	Switch, Single Pole, Single Throw, Plastic	10	2-2 (DIS) 2-3 (DIS) 2-3 (SYS) 3-1 (DIS)
NC	Test Tube, Plastic w/Cap, 16 × 125 mm, Polystyrene	5	1-1 (TT)
NC	Tube, Cardboard, 13 × 5.5 cm OD	5	1-3 (Lab)
NC	Tubing, Rubber, Black, 1/8" × 1/16", Foot	2	2-2 (Lab)
NC	Tubing, Vinyl Plastic, 3/8" × 1/16", Foot	5	2-2 (TT)
NC	Washer, Metal, 3/4"OD × 5/16"ID, Zinc Plated, Flat	20	1-1 (Lab)
NC	Wire, Copper, Bare, 16 Gauge, 4 oz	1	2-2 (Lab) 3-4 (Lab)
NC	Wire, Enameled Copper, 24 Gauge, 4 oz (Approx. 200 ft)	1	3-1 (Lab)

*	Description	Quantity per class	Textbook Section(s)
NC	Wire, Insulated Copper, 22 Gauge, 25 m	2	1-3 (DIS) 1-3 (SYS) 1-3 (Lab) 1-4 (DIS) 2-2 (DIS) 2-2 (Lab) 2-3 (DIS) 2-3 (SYS) 2-4 (DIS) 3-1 (DIS) 3-1 (Lab) 3-2 (DIS) 3-2 (TT) 3-4 (DIS) 3-4 (Lab) 4-1 (Lab)

Equipment

*	Description	Quantity per class	Textbook Section(s)
SS	Calculator	5	3-4 (Lab) 4-3 (DIS)
SS	Galvanometer	5	3-2 (DIS) 3-2 (TT)
SS	Goggles, Chemical Splash - Class Set	1	1-3 (Lab)
SS	Hand Generator	10	3-2 (SYS) 3-3 (DIS)
SS	Ring Stand with Clamp	5	2-2 (TT)
SS	Stopwatch	5	2-2 (TT)
SS	Voltmeter	5	3-4 (DIS)

KEY: **DIS**: Discover; **SYS**: Sharpen Your Skills; **TT**: Try This; **Lab**: Lab
* Items designated **C** are in the Consumable Kit, **NC** are in the Nonconsumable Kit, and **SS** are School Supplied.

PRENTICE HALL
SCIENCE EXPLORER

Electricity and Magnetism

Program Resources
Student Edition
Annotated Teacher's Edition
Teaching Resources Book with Color Transparencies
Electricity and Magnetism Materials Kits

Program Components
Integrated Science Laboratory Manual
Integrated Science Laboratory Manual, Teacher's Edition
Inquiry Skills Activity Book
Student-Centered Science Activity Books
Program Planning Guide
Guided Reading English Audiotapes
Guided Reading Spanish Audiotapes and Summaries
Product Testing Activities by Consumer Reports™
Event-Based Science Series (NSF funded)
Prentice Hall Interdisciplinary Explorations
Cobblestone, Odyssey, Calliope, and *Faces* Magazines

Media/Technology
Science Explorer Interactive Student Tutorial CD-ROMs
Odyssey of Discovery CD-ROMs
Resource Pro® (Teaching Resources on CD-ROM)
Assessment Resources CD-ROM with Dial-A-Test®
Internet site at www.science-explorer.phschool.com
Life, Earth, and Physical Science Videodiscs
Life, Earth, and Physical Science Videotapes

Science Explorer Student Editions

From Bacteria to Plants

Animals

Cells and Heredity

Human Biology and Health

Environmental Science

Inside Earth

Earth's Changing Surface

Earth's Waters

Weather and Climate

Astronomy

Chemical Building Blocks

Chemical Interactions

Motion, Forces, and Energy

Electricity and Magnetism

Sound and Light

Staff Credits

The people who made up the *Science Explorer* team—representing editorial, editorial services, design services, field marketing, market research, marketing services, on-line services/multimedia development, product marketing, production services, and publishing processes—are listed below. Bold type denotes core team members.

Kristen E. Ball, **Barbara A. Bertell,** Peter W. Brooks, **Christopher R. Brown, Greg Cantone,** Jonathan Cheney, **Patrick Finbarr Connolly,** Loree Franz, Donald P. Gagnon, Jr., **Paul J. Gagnon, Joel Gendler,** Elizabeth Good, Kerri Hoar, **Linda D. Johnson,** Katherine M. Kotik, Russ Lappa, Marilyn Leitao, David Lippman, **Eve Melnechuk, Natania Mlawer,** Paul W. Murphy, **Cindy A. Noftle,** Julia F. Osborne, Caroline M. Power, Suzanne J. Schineller, **Susan W. Tafler,** Kira Thaler-Marbit, Robin L. Santel, Ronald Schachter, **Mark Tricca,** Diane Walsh, Pearl B. Weinstein, Beth Norman Winickoff

ISBN 0-13-434485-5
3 4 5 6 7 8 9 10   05 04 03 02 01 00 99

Cover: The powerful magnets that move this maglev train give it a much higher speed than ordinary trains.

Teacher's Edition ISBN 0-13-434566-5

Program Authors

Michael J. Padilla, Ph.D.
Professor
Department of Science Education
University of Georgia
Athens, Georgia

Michael Padilla is a leader in middle school science education. He has served as an editor and elected officer for the National Science Teachers Association. He has been principal investigator of several National Science Foundation and Eisenhower grants and served as a writer of the National Science Education Standards.

As lead author of *Science Explorer,* Mike has inspired the team in developing a program that meets the needs of middle grades students, promotes science inquiry, and is aligned with the National Science Education Standards.

Ioannis Miaoulis, Ph.D.
Dean of Engineering
College of Engineering
Tufts University
Medford, Massachusetts

Martha Cyr, Ph.D.
Director, Engineering
   Educational Outreach
College of Engineering
Tufts University
Medford, Massachusetts

Science Explorer was created in collaboration with the College of Engineering at Tufts University. Tufts has an extensive engineering outreach program that uses engineering design and construction to excite and motivate students and teachers in science and technology education.

Faculty from Tufts University participated in the development of *Science Explorer* chapter projects, reviewed the student books for content accuracy, and helped coordinate field testing.

CHAPTER PROJECT

Book Author

Camille L. Wainwright, Ph.D.
Professor of Science Education
Pacific University
Forest Grove, Oregon

Contributing Writers

Edward Evans
Former Science Teacher
Hilton Central School
Hilton, New York

Mark Illingworth
Teacher
Hollis Public Schools
Hollis, New Hampshire

Thomas L. Messer
Science Teacher
Cape Cod Academy
Osterville, Massachusetts

Thomas R. Wellnitz
Science Teacher
The Paideia School
Atlanta, Georgia

Reading Consultant

Bonnie B. Armbruster, Ph.D.
Department of Curriculum
   and Instruction
University of Illinois
Champaign, Illinois

Interdisciplinary Consultant

Heidi Hayes Jacobs, Ed.D.
Teacher's College
Columbia University
New York City, New York

Safety Consultants

W. H. Breazeale, Ph.D.
Department of Chemistry
College of Charleston
Charleston, South Carolina

Ruth Hathaway, Ph.D.
Hathaway Consulting
Cape Girardeau, Missouri

Tufts University Program Reviewers

Behrouz Abedian, Ph.D.
Department of Mechanical
    Engineering

Wayne Chudyk, Ph.D.
Department of Civil and
    Environmental Engineering

Eliana De Bernardez-Clark, Ph.D.
Department of Chemical Engineering

Anne Marie Desmarais, Ph.D.
Department of Civil and
    Environmental Engineering

David L. Kaplan, Ph.D.
Department of Chemical Engineering

Paul Kelley, Ph.D.
Department of Electro-Optics

George S. Mumford, Ph.D.
Professor of Astronomy, Emeritus

Jan A. Pechenik, Ph.D.
Department of Biology

Livia Racz, Ph.D.
Department of Mechanical Engineering

Robert Rifkin, M.D.
School of Medicine

Jack Ridge, Ph.D.
Department of Geology

Chris Swan, Ph.D.
Department of Civil and
    Environmental Engineering

Peter Y. Wong, Ph.D.
Department of Mechanical Engineering

Content Reviewers

Jack W. Beal, Ph.D.
Department of Physics
Fairfield University
Fairfield, Connecticut

W. Russell Blake, Ph.D.
Planetarium Director
Plymouth Community
    Intermediate School
Plymouth, Massachusetts

Howard E. Buhse, Jr., Ph.D.
Department of Biological Sciences
University of Illinois
Chicago, Illinois

Dawn Smith Burgess, Ph.D.
Department of Geophysics
Stanford University
Stanford, California

A. Malcolm Campbell, Ph.D.
Assistant Professor
Davidson College
Davidson, North Carolina

Elizabeth A. De Stasio, Ph.D.
Associate Professor of Biology
Lawrence University
Appleton, Wisconsin

John M. Fowler, Ph.D.
Former Director of Special Projects
National Science Teacher's Association
Arlington, Virginia

Jonathan Gitlin, M.D.
School of Medicine
Washington University
St. Louis, Missouri

Dawn Graff-Haight, Ph.D., CHES
Department of Health, Human
    Performance, and Athletics
Linfield College
McMinnville, Oregon

Deborah L. Gumucio, Ph.D.
Associate Professor
Department of Anatomy and Cell Biology
University of Michigan
Ann Arbor, Michigan

William S. Harwood, Ph.D.
Dean of University Division and Associate
    Professor of Education
Indiana University
Bloomington, Indiana

Cyndy Henzel, Ph.D.
Department of Geography
    and Regional Development
University of Arizona
Tucson, Arizona

Greg Hutton
Science and Health
    Curriculum Coordinator
School Board of Sarasota County
Sarasota, Florida

Susan K. Jacobson, Ph.D.
Department of Wildlife Ecology
    and Conservation
University of Florida
Gainesville, Florida

Judy Jernstedt, Ph.D.
Department of Agronomy and Range Science
University of California, Davis
Davis, California

John L. Kermond, Ph.D.
Office of Global Programs
National Oceanographic and
    Atmospheric Administration
Silver Spring, Maryland

David E. LaHart, Ph.D.
Institute of Science and Public Affairs
Florida State University
Tallahassee, Florida

Joe Leverich, Ph.D.
Department of Biology
St. Louis University
St. Louis, Missouri

Dennis K. Lieu, Ph.D.
Department of Mechanical Engineering
University of California
Berkeley, California

Cynthia J. Moore, Ph.D.
Science Outreach Coordinator
Washington University
St. Louis, Missouri

Joseph M. Moran, Ph.D.
Department of Earth Science
University of Wisconsin–Green Bay
Green Bay, Wisconsin

Joseph Stukey, Ph.D.
Department of Biology
Hope College
Holland, Michigan

Seetha Subramanian
Lexington Community College
University of Kentucky
Lexington, Kentucky

Carl L. Thurman, Ph.D.
Department of Biology
University of Northern Iowa
Cedar Falls, Iowa

Edward D. Walton, Ph.D.
Department of Chemistry
California State Polytechnic University
Pomona, California

Robert S. Young, Ph.D.
Department of Geosciences and
    Natural Resource Management
Western Carolina University
Cullowhee, North Carolina

Edward J. Zalisko, Ph.D.
Department of Biology
Blackburn College
Carlinville, Illinois

Teacher Reviewers

Stephanie Anderson
Sierra Vista Junior
    High School
Canyon Country, California

John W. Anson
Mesa Intermediate School
Palmdale, California

Pamela Arline
Lake Taylor Middle School
Norfolk, Virginia

Lynn Beason
College Station Jr. High School
College Station, Texas

Richard Bothmer
Hollis School District
Hollis, New Hampshire

Jeffrey C. Callister
Newburgh Free Academy
Newburgh, New York

Judy D'Albert
Harvard Day School
Corona Del Mar, California

Betty Scott Dean
Guilford County Schools
McLeansville, North Carolina

Sarah C. Duff
Baltimore City Public Schools
Baltimore, Maryland

Melody Law Ewey
Holmes Junior High School
Davis, California

Sherry L. Fisher
Lake Zurich Middle
    School North
Lake Zurich, Illinois

Melissa Gibbons
Fort Worth ISD
Fort Worth, Texas

Debra J. Goodding
Kraemer Middle School
Placentia, California

Jack Grande
Weber Middle School
Port Washington, New York

Steve Hills
Riverside Middle School
Grand Rapids, Michigan

Carol Ann Lionello
Kraemer Middle School
Placentia, California

Jaime A. Morales
Henry T. Gage Middle School
Huntington Park, California

Patsy Partin
Cameron Middle School
Nashville, Tennessee

Deedra H. Robinson
Newport News Public Schools
Newport News, Virginia

Bonnie Scott
Clack Middle School
Abilene, Texas

Charles M. Sears
Belzer Middle School
Indianapolis, Indiana

Barbara M. Strange
Ferndale Middle School
High Point, North Carolina

Jackie Louise Ulfig
Ford Middle School
Allen, Texas

Kathy Usina
Belzer Middle School
Indianapolis, Indiana

Heidi M. von Oetinger
L'Anse Creuse Public School
Harrison Township, Michigan

Pam Watson
Hill Country Middle School
Austin, Texas

Activity Field Testers

Nicki Bibbo
Russell Street School
Littleton, Massachusetts

Connie Boone
Fletcher Middle School
Jacksonville Beach, Florida

Rose-Marie Botting
Broward County
    School District
Fort Lauderdale, Florida

Colleen Campos
Laredo Middle School
Aurora, Colorado

Elizabeth Chait
W. L. Chenery Middle School
Belmont, Massachusetts

Holly Estes
Hale Middle School
Stow, Massachusetts

Laura Hapgood
Plymouth Community
    Intermediate School
Plymouth, Massachusetts

Sandra M. Harris
Winman Junior High School
Warwick, Rhode Island

Jason Ho
Walter Reed Middle School
Los Angeles, California

Joanne Jackson
Winman Junior High School
Warwick, Rhode Island

Mary F. Lavin
Plymouth Community
    Intermediate School
Plymouth, Massachusetts

James MacNeil, Ph.D.
Concord Public Schools
Concord, Massachusetts

Lauren Magruder
St. Michael's Country
    Day School
Newport, Rhode Island

Jeanne Maurand
Glen Urquhart School
Beverly Farms, Massachusetts

Warren Phillips
Plymouth Community
    Intermediate School
Plymouth, Massachusetts

Carol Pirtle
Hale Middle School
Stow, Massachusetts

Kathleen M. Poe
Kirby-Smith Middle School
Jacksonville, Florida

Cynthia B. Pope
Ruffner Middle School
Norfolk, Virginia

Anne Scammell
Geneva Middle School
Geneva, New York

Karen Riley Sievers
Callanan Middle School
Des Moines, Iowa

David M. Smith
Howard A. Eyer Middle School
Macungie, Pennsylvania

Derek Strohschneider
Plymouth Community
    Intermediate School
Plymouth, Massachusetts

Sallie Teames
Rosemont Middle School
Fort Worth, Texas

Gene Vitale
Parkland Middle School
McHenry, Illinois

Zenovia Young
Meyer Levin Junior
    High School (IS 285)
Brooklyn, New York

PRENTICE HALL
SCIENCE EXPLORER

Contents

Electricity and Magnetism

Prepare your students with rich, motivating content

Science Explorer is crafted for today's middle grades student, with accessible content and in-depth coverage. **Integrated Science Sections** support every chapter and the **Interdisciplinary Exploration** provides an engaging final unit.

Check your compass— regularly assess student progress.

Self-assessment tools are built right into the student text and **on-going assessment** is woven throughout the Teacher's Edition. You'll find a wealth of **assessment technology** in the Resource Pro®, Interactive Student Tutorial, and Assessment Resources CD-ROMs.

Activities

Inquiry Activities

CHAPTER PROJECT

Opportunities for long-term inquiry

DISCOVER

Exploration and inquiry before reading

Sharpen your Skills

Practice of specific science inquiry skills

TRY THIS

Reinforcement of key concepts

Skills Lab

In-depth practice of inquiry skills

Real-World Lab

Everyday application of science concepts

Interdisciplinary Activities

Science and History

Science and Society

Connection

An Electrical Engineer in Outer Space

Focus on Engineering

This four-page feature introduces the process of scientific inquiry by involving students in a high-interest article about a working scientist, astronaut Dr. Ellen Ochoa. Using Dr. Ochoa's varied engineering work in the space program as an example, the feature focuses on persistence, determination, and a passion for science as key elements of scientific inquiry.

Generating an electric current is presented in Section 3-2 of this book. However, students need not have any previous knowledge of that chapter's content to understand and appreciate this feature.

Scientific Inquiry

◆ Before students read the article, let them read the title, examine the pictures, and read the captions on their own. Then ask: **What questions came into your mind as you looked at these pictures?** (*Students might suggest questions such as "Who determines which astronauts get to fly on a mission? What is the RMS? Why did Ellen take her flute? Is it more difficult to play a flute in weightlessness?"*) Point out to students that just as they had questions about what they were seeing, scientists too have questions about what they observe.

AN ELECTRICAL ENGINEER IN OUTER SPACE

Ellen Ochoa was born and raised in California. She earned a doctorate in electrical engineering from Stanford University and became an astronaut in 1991. She has flown on two space-shuttle missions. Currently she is a Spacecraft Communicator, an astronaut at Mission Control who talks with other astronauts while they are in space. She is a talented flute player who has taken her flute with her on the shuttle. She hopes to be aboard more missions in space soon.

When she was studying electricity in school science classes, Ellen Ochoa didn't know that some day her studies would help take her into space. "I just always liked math and science," the California-born Dr. Ochoa says. Today she is an astronaut and has flown on two space-shuttle missions. Trained as an electrical engineer, she is an expert in the uses of electricity. This is the important skill she brings to the astronaut team.

Astronaut Ochoa has worked in the testing and training process for robotics — humanlike machines that can carry out complicated tasks in space. On her shuttle flights, Ellen had the key job of controlling one of these machines, the Remote Manipulator System, or RMS. "The RMS is a robotic arm that reaches out of the spacecraft," she explains. "We use electricity to operate it. The RMS is about 50 feet long. On my flights, we used it to pick up a satellite that was in the shuttle payload bay and put it in orbit. Then a few days later, we'd come back and retrieve the satellite and put it back in the spacecraft cargo area." One of the satellites was used by scientists to gather information about the sun and its effects on Earth. Another was used to study Earth's atmosphere.

"We have a work station with two hand controllers. One is sort of like a joystick on a kid's game. The other is like a square knob that you hold. You push and pull, or move up and down or left and right, to move the electrical RMS arm to the correct position."

Background

Engineering is the application of math and science knowledge to the effective use of materials and forces in nature. There are numerous branches of engineering; however, because the branches are interrelated, an engineer specializing in any field needs to have some understanding of the other fields and how they relate.

Electrical engineering is divided into four fields: electric power, electronics, communications, and computers. Engineers studying the generation of electricity, like Ellen Ochoa, design and operate systems that generate, transmit, and distribute electrical power.

Talking with Dr. Ellen Ochoa

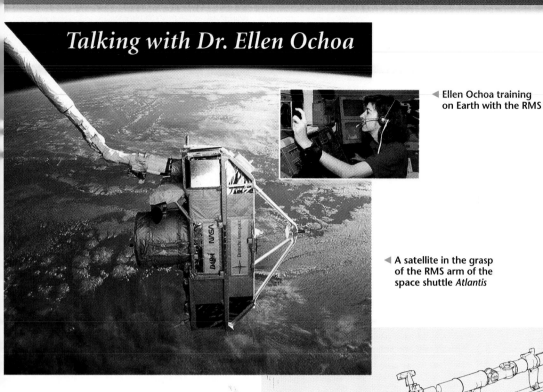

◀ Ellen Ochoa training on Earth with the RMS

◀ A satellite in the grasp of the RMS arm of the space shuttle *Atlantis*

This diagram of the RMS arm shows its three joints and mechanical hand (at the right). The arm is about 15 meters long.

Q *How did you become interested in science?*

A I got into science because I liked math. I always enjoyed math and did well at it. I was interested in finding out about all the ways that people could use math. So I studied physics at college. I didn't know until then that I would have a career in science.

Q *Did you follow the space program when you were young?*

A Oh sure. It was a very big thing in the 1960s when I was in elementary school. At the time, the Apollo program was sending astronauts to the moon. But it wasn't until I was in graduate school in electrical engineering that I learned how to apply for the space program and what they were looking for in selecting astronauts.

Q *What happened when you applied to the space program?*

A The first time I applied in 1985 I was not selected. So I tried again in 1990 and was chosen. That's been the case with many astronauts. Persistence is one of our qualities.

Q *How do astronauts use electricity in the space shuttle?*

A We use electrical power for many of the systems on board the shuttle. It's used for the computers and for the sensors and detectors to make sure

---

♦ Ask: **What qualifications do you think you need to be an astronaut?** *(Answers will vary. Samples: a doctorate in the sciences)* Ask students how many of them want to be astronauts and why. If students want to know more about astronaut program requirements, share with them the background information below. Also suggest that they consult library books to learn more about the space shuttle. (See Further Reading, page 11).

♦ Challenge interested students to research more about what the satellites were studying.

♦ Ask: **What skills do you think you need to operate the RMS?** *(Good coordination, good concentration, patience)* **Why is it important to be careful while operating the RMS?** *(If you were careless, you could damage the RMS, the satellite, or maybe even the shuttle.)*

♦ Ask students who follow the space program closely to share the latest news from the space program with the class. Ask them about Mars explorations as well as developments on the International Space Station.

♦ Ask: **Why did Ellen reapply after she was turned down?** *(She was determined to be admitted to the program. Perhaps she already knew that it was common to be turned down the first time you applied.)*

Background

The minimum requirements to be an astronaut are: excellent physical condition, a bachelor's degree in engineering, science, or mathematics, and usually some years of related experience beyond the degree. Preference is given to applicants with advanced degrees.

There are about 20 job openings every two years. NASA typically receives about 4,000 applications for those 20 openings.

- ◆ Ask: **The shuttle uses electricity. Where does the electricity come from?** *(Answers may vary. Samples: solar panels, generated by the engine, batteries)* Point out that there is not room in the shuttle for huge numbers of batteries, so astronauts have to generate their own electricity once they get into space.
- ◆ Ask: **What does the life-support system do?** *(Answers may vary. Samples: Keeps the astronauts warm. Keeps fresh air inside the shuttle and removes the stale air.)* If students want to know more about some of the systems on the shuttle, share with them the background information below.
- ◆ Ask: **Why do they use very cold oxygen and hydrogen?** *(Students may or may not know enough chemistry to answer this question. Very cold gases usually take up far less room than warm gases.)* Point out that students will learn how batteries work in Chapter 3 of this book.
- ◆ Explain that in this book students will learn about Earth's magnetic field. They will also learn that when an electric current passes through a wire, it creates a small magnetic field around the wire. Scientists have also found out that if you pull a wire through a magnetic field, you generate an electric current in the wire. Astronauts used this discovery to experiment with generating current for the shuttle.

that the life-support systems are working correctly. Many of our instruments for research use other forms of energy related to electricity, like light or radio waves. We can use these instruments, for instance, to measure the chemicals in the atmosphere that affect climate and weather. And, of course, we use radio for communicating with the ground crew.

Ellen Ochoa at the controls of the RMS arm with astronaut Donald R. McMonagle

Q *Where does the electricity you use come from?*

A We have fuel cells on board. We bring up cryogenic (very cold) oxygen and hydrogen. Then we allow the two chemicals to mix together in the fuel cells. Fuel cells use chemical reactions, like batteries. The chemical reactions in fuel cells produce both electricity and water, which we use on board. We would like to carry up more oxygen and hydrogen fuel cells, to make more electric power. But more fuel cells would mean we could carry less of other things, such as the equipment for the scientific experiments we do.

Q *Are you studying other ways to make electricity?*

A We've had two shuttle flights that experimented with tethered satellites. Basically, the idea was to drag a satellite through space on a tether—a long conducting cable. As the conductor passes through Earth's magnetic field, electric current is generated. Tethered satellites are just at the research stage now.

Ellen Ochoa entertains other crew ▶ members during a flight.

Background

The space shuttle is equipped with as many of the tools and systems that astronauts might need as is possible. Astronauts heat up meals in a kitchen area similar to that on an aircraft. Minor illnesses and injuries can be treated using the onboard medical system. Radiation from solar flares is a concern, so astronauts have to monitor how much radiation they are subjected to. Sleeping bags with restraints keep astronauts from colliding with equipment and each other while trying to sleep. Temporary and permanent foot restraints, handholds, ladders, and rails help astronauts stay in place or move around. To stay in shape, astronauts work out on a specially designed treadmill.

Students with Internet access can read about the shuttle in detail at **http://shuttle.nasa.gov.**

An artist's concept of the space shuttle and tethered satellite

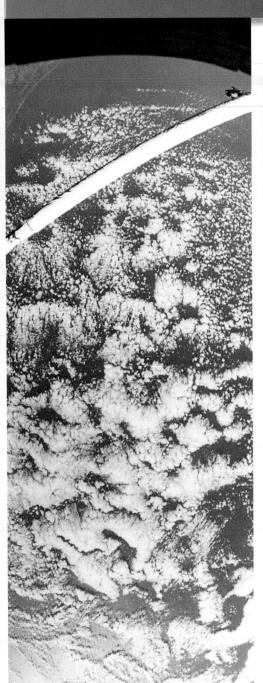

A view of the atmospheric satellite and RMS arm from a 1994 flight

But eventually, we'd like to use power from tethers to move satellites up and down in orbit without using up precious fuel.

Q *What parts of working as an astronaut do you enjoy?*

A I think the whole flight is fun— the launch, viewing Earth from space, and living in weightlessness, although that can be frustrating, too. Doing the activities we've been trained for is hard work, but it's really enjoyable as well. There are a lot of interesting, exciting careers for people with backgrounds in science and math. Being an astronaut is just one of them.

In Your Journal

Ellen talks about persistence, a quality that helped her become an astronaut. Think of a time when you succeeded in doing something after many attempts. Describe what happened. How did persistence and determination help you? Why would these qualities be important for scientists to have?

◆ Ask students: **Do you think NASA would let you take any musical instrument into space?** (*No; they would probably only let you take something small, like Ellen's flute.*)

◆ Ask: **What do you think could be frustrating about living in weightlessness?** (*Accept all reasonable answers. Sample: when you drop something, it floats away; you have to tie yourself to your bed*)

◆ Ask: **Did Ellen intend being an astronaut when she was young?** (*No; she was interested in science but didn't apply for the space program until after she was in college.*)

In Your Journal To prompt student thinking, ask students why they kept trying. As an alternative, suggest that students write a letter to a friend who gives up quickly, giving them advice about why they should be more persistent.

Introducing Electricity and Magnetism

Have students look through the table of contents and the book to find the parts that relate most closely to this article. (*Chapter 3, Electricity and Magnetism at Work, particularly Section 3-2, Generating Electric Current, and Section 3-4, Batteries.*) Ask: **Besides electricity and magnetism, what else is this book about?** (*safety, electronics, computers, the Internet*) **What kinds of things do you think you will be learning about?** (*Accept all responses without comments.*)

READING STRATEGIES

Further Reading

◆ Joels, Kerry Mark and Gregory P. Kennedy. *The Space Shuttle Operators Manual.* Ballantine Books, 1988.

◆ Bondar, Barbara and Roberta Bondar. *On the Shuttle: Eight Days in Space.* Owl Communications, 1993.

◆ Brown, Robert A. *Endeavour Views the Earth.* Cambridge University Press, 1996.

Magnetism and Electromagnetism

Sections	Time	Student Edition Activities	Other Activities	
CHAPTER PROJECT 1 **Electromagnetic Fishing Derby** p. 12	Ongoing (3 weeks)	Check Your Progress, pp. 21, 35, 40 Wrap Up, p. 43	TE	Chapter 1 Project Notes, pp. 12–15
1 **The Nature of Magnetism** pp. 14–23 ◆ Define magnetic poles and describe the interaction between like and unlike magnetic poles. ◆ Define magnetic fields and describe magnetic field lines. ◆ Define magnetic domain and state how magnetic domains are lined up in magnetized material.	5 periods/ $2\frac{1}{2}$ blocks	**Discover** What Do All Magnets Have in Common?, p. 14 **Sharpen Your Skills** Observing, p. 16 **Try This** How Attractive!, p. 20 **Real-World Lab: You Solve the Mystery** Detecting Fake Coins, pp. 22–23	TE TE TE IES	Building Inquiry Skills: Predicting, p. 15 Building Inquiry Skills: Observing, p. 16 Including All Students, p. 19 "The Power of Patterns," pp. 28–29
2 ⬤ **INTEGRATING EARTH SCIENCE** **Magnetic Earth** pp. 24–29 ◆ Identify the magnetic properties of Earth and compare the magnetic and geographic poles. ◆ Describe some of the effects of Earth's magnetic fields.	3 periods/ $1\frac{1}{2}$ blocks	**Discover** Can You Use a Needle to Make a Compass?, p. 24 **Sharpen Your Skills** Measuring, p. 25 **Try This** Spinning in Circles, p. 27	TE TE IES IES	Including All Students, p. 26 Demonstration, p. 28 "The Wreck of the Henrietta Marie," pp. 15–16 "Wagons West," p. 41
3 **Electric Current and Magnetic Fields** pp. 30–37 ◆ Describe the relationship between electric current and a magnetic field. ◆ Define and give examples of conductors and insulators. ◆ Identify the characteristics of an electric circuit.	4 periods/ 2 blocks	**Discover** Are Magnetic Fields Limited to Magnets?, p. 30 **Sharpen Your Skills** Classifying, p. 34 **Real-World Lab: How It Works** Build a Flashlight, pp. 36–37	TE TE	Demonstration, p. 32 Integrating Technology, p. 34 ⬤
4 **Electromagnets** pp. 38–40 ◆ Identify characteristics and cite uses of an electromagnet.	$1\frac{1}{2}$ periods/ $\frac{1}{2}$–1 block	**Discover** How Do You Turn a Magnet On and Off?, p. 38	TE TE TE ISLM	Building Inquiry Skills: Making Models, p. 39 Inquiry Challenge, p. 39 Integrating Technology, p. 40 ⬤ N-1, "Electromagnetism"
Study Guide/Chapter Review pp. 41–43	1 period/ $\frac{1}{2}$ block		ISAB	Provides teaching and review of all inquiry skills

 For Standard or Block Schedule The Resource Pro® CD-ROM gives you maximum flexibility for planning your instruction for any type of schedule. Resource Pro® contains Planning Express®, an advanced scheduling program, as well as the entire contents of the Teaching Resources and the Computer Test Bank.

CHAPTER PLANNING GUIDE

Program Resources	Assessment Strategies	Media and Technology
TR Chapter 1 Project Teacher Notes, pp. 6–7 TR Chapter 1 Project Overview and Worksheets, pp. 8–11 TR Chapter 1 Project Scoring Rubric, p. 12	SE Performance Assessment: Chapter 1 Project Wrap Up, p. 43 TE Check Your Progress, pp. 21, 35, 40 TE Performance Assessment: Chapter 1 Project Wrap Up, p. 43 TR Chapter 1 Project Scoring Rubric, p. 12	Science Explorer Internet Site
TR 1-1 Lesson Plan, p. 13 TR 1-1 Section Summary, p. 14 TR 1-1 Review and Reinforce, p. 15 TR 1-1 Enrich, p. 16 TR Chapter 1 Real-World Lab, pp. 29–31 SES Book K, *Chemical Building Blocks,* Chapter 3	SE Section 1 Review, p. 21 SE Analyze and Conclude, p. 23 TE Ongoing Assessment, pp. 15, 17, 19 TE Performance Assessment, p. 21 TR 1-1 Review and Reinforce, p. 15	Audiotapes: English-Spanish Summary 1-1 Transparency 1, "Magnetic Fields" Transparency 2, "Dividing Magnets" Interactive Student Tutorial CD-ROM, N-1
TR 1-2 Lesson Plan, p. 17 TR 1-2 Section Summary, p. 18 TR 1-2 Review and Reinforce, p. 19 TR 1-2 Enrich, p. 20 SES Book F, *Inside Earth,* Chapter 1 SES Book J, *Astronomy,* Chapter 2	SE Section 2 Review, p. 29 TE Ongoing Assessment, pp. 25, 27 TE Performance Assessment, p. 29 TR 1-2 Review and Reinforce, p. 19	Exploring Physical Science Videodisc, Unit 5 Side 1, "The Northern Lights" Audiotapes: English-Spanish Summary 1-2 Transparency 3, "The Magnetosphere" Interactive Student Tutorial CD-ROM, N-1
TR 1-3 Lesson Plan, p. 21 TR 1-3 Section Summary, p. 22 TR 1-3 Review and Reinforce, p. 23 TR 1-3 Enrich, p. 24 TR Chapter 1 Real-World Lab, pp. 32–33 SES Book O, *Sound and Light*, Chapter 3	SE Section 3 Review, p. 35 SE Analyze and Conclude, p. 37 TE Ongoing Assessment, pp. 31, 33 TE Performance Assessment, p. 35 TR 1-3 Review and Reinforce, p. 23	Exploring Physical Science Videodisc, Unit 5 Side 1, "What Is Electricity?" Audiotapes: English-Spanish Summary 1-3 Transparency 4, "Exploring Electric Circuits" Interactive Student Tutorial CD-ROM, N-1
TR 1-4 Lesson Plan, p. 25 TR 1-4 Section Summary, p. 26 TR 1-4 Review and Reinforce, p. 27 TR 1-4 Enrich, p. 28	SE Section 4 Review, p. 40 TE Ongoing Assessment, p. 39 TE Performance Assessment, p. 40 TR 1-4 Review and Reinforce, p. 27	Audiotapes: English-Spanish Summary 1-4 Transparency 5, "Electromagnetism" Transparency 6, "Doorbell" Interactive Student Tutorial CD-ROM, N-1
TR Chapter 1 Performance Assessment, pp. 130–132 TR Chapter 1 Test, pp. 133–136	SE Chapter Review, pp. 41–43 TR Chapter 1 Performance Assessment, pp. 130–132 TR Chapter 1 Test, pp. 133–136 CTB Test N-1	Computer Test Bank, Test N-1 Interactive Student Tutorial CD-ROM, N-1

Key: **SE** Student Edition **TE** Teacher's Edition **TR** Teaching Resources
CTB Computer Test Bank **SES** Science Explorer Series Text **ISLM** Integrated Science Laboratory Manual
ISAB Inquiry Skills Activity Book **PTA** Product Testing Activities by *Consumer Reports* **IES** Interdisciplinary Explorations Series

Meeting the National Science Education Standards and AAAS Benchmarks

National Science Education Standards	Benchmarks for Science Literacy	Unifying Themes
Science as Inquiry (Content Standard A) ◆ **Ask questions that can be answered by scientific investigations** How can you use a magnet to tell the difference between real and fake coins? (*Real-World Lab*) ◆ **Communicate scientific procedures and explanations** Students build a flashlight that works. Students build an electromagnet. (*Real-World Lab; Chapter Project*) **Physical Science** (Content Standard B) ◆ **Transfer of energy** An electric current is the flow of charge through a material. (*Section 3*) An electromagnet is a magnet that can be turned on and off. (*Section 4*) **Earth Science** (Content Standard D) ◆ **Structure of the earth system** Earth is surrounded by an immense magnetic field that is similar to the magnetic field around a bar magnet. (*Section 2*)	**1C The Scientific Enterprise** Students learn about the development of the electric light bulb and the different materials that Edison used in its development. (*Section 3*) **4G Forces of Nature** Magnetism is the attraction of a magnet for iron. A magnet has two ends called magnetic poles where the magnetic effect is the strongest. The magnetic force around a magnet is known as its magnetic field. Earth's magnetic poles differ from Earth's geographic north and south. (*Sections 1, 2*) **8C Energy Sources and Use** Electric currents flow though metal wires. The charges of electric currents move freely through materials called *conductors*. Charges are not able to move freely through materials called *insulators*. (*Section 2*)	◆ **Stability** Conductors are materials through which electric charges flow; electric charges do not flow through insulators. A magnetic field will always exist around a magnet and a current. (*Sections 1, 3*) ◆ **Scale and Structure** Every magnet regardless of size or shape has two poles where the magnetic effects are usually the strongest. (*Sections 2, 3, 4*) ◆ **Systems and Interactions** Properties of the atoms in a substance determine whether it will conduct electricity or not. The opposition to the movement of charges flowing through a material is called resistance. A magnetic field will exert a force on a wire that is carrying current. (*Sections 1, 2, 3*)

Media and Technology

Exploring Physical Science Videodisc

◆ **Section 2** "The Northern Lights" focuses on the concept of magnetism and shows the bands of colored lights, or aurora borealis, that appear near the poles of Earth.

◆ **Section 3** "What Is Electricity?" introduces electricity and explains its atomic structure by modeling electrical charges.

Interactive Student Tutorial CD-ROM

◆ **Chapter Review** Interactive questions help students to self-assess their mastery of key chapter concepts.

Student Edition Connection Strategies

◆ **Section 2 Integrating Earth Science,** p. 24
   Language Arts Connection, p. 28

◆ **Section 3 Integrating Technology,** p. 34

◆ **Section 4 Integrating Technology,** p. 40

USING THE INTERNET

www.science-explorer.phschool.com

Visit the Science Explorer Internet site to find an up-to-date activity for Chapter 1 of *Electricity and Magnetism.*

Student Edition Activities Planner

ACTIVITY	Time (minutes)	Materials Quantities for one work group	Skills
Section 1			
Discover, p. 14	15	**Nonconsumable** bar magnet, horseshoe magnet, paper clips	Observing
Sharpen Your Skills, p. 16	10	**Nonconsumable** pencil, foam cup, 2 circular magnets	Observing
Try This, p. 20	20	**Nonconsumable** clear plastic tube, iron filings, strong bar magnet	Making Models
Real-World Lab, pp. 22–23	45	**Consumable** popsicle stick; tape; thin, stiff cardboard, about 25 cm × 30 cm **Nonconsumable** various coins; metric ruler; pencil; protractor; coin-sized steel washers; small bar magnet, about 2 cm wide	Predicting, Inferring
Section 2			
Discover, p. 24	20	**Consumable** water, dishwashing soap **Nonconsumable** large needle, strong bar magnet, dish, cork or foam ball, pliers	Observing
Sharpen Your Skills, p. 25	15	**Nonconsumable** local map, compass, protractor	Measuring
Try This, p. 27	20	**Consumable** sheet of paper **Nonconsumable** bar magnet, compass, centimeter ruler	Drawing Conclusions
Section 3			
Discover, p. 30	25	**Nonconsumable** 2 wires (20 cm long insulation stripped from ends), light bulb, bulb holder, 3 compasses, D cell (1.5 volt)	Inferring
Sharpen Your Skills, p. 34	20	**Nonconsumable** 3 10-cm wires with insulation stripped from ends; 2 alligator clips; light bulb; battery; conductors and insulators to test such as keys, foam, erasers, pencil lead, foil, wax paper, paper clips	Classifying
Real-World Lab, pp. 36–37	40	**Consumable** one cardboard tube, aluminum foil, paper cup, duct tape **Nonconsumable** one D cell; flashlight bulb; scissors; 2 lengths of wire about 10 cm, with the insulation stripped off about 2 cm at each end; 1 length of wire, 15–20 cm, with the insulation stripped off each end	Making Models, Observing, Inferring
Section 4			
Discover, p. 38	20	**Nonconsumable** 1 m bell wire or magnet wire, iron nail, D cell, paper clips	Forming Operational Definitions

A list of all materials required for the Student Edition activities can be found on pages T14–T15. You can order Materials Kits by calling 1-800-828-7777 or by accessing the Science Explorer Internet site at **www.science-explorer.phschool.com.**

Electro-magnetic Fishing Derby

Electromagnets can be turned on and off using the switch of an electric circuit. This allows electromagnets to perform complicated tasks such as lifting and releasing objects.

Purpose In this project, students will apply concepts about magnetism and electricity from the chapter to design a circuit and build electromagnetic fishing rods. They will use their fishing rods to lift paper clips and move them to another container.

Skills Focus After completing the Chapter 1 Project, students will be able to
- make model fishing rods using permanent magnets;
- design a switch for an electric circuit;
- identify and experiment with variables that affect the strength of an electromagnet.

Project Time Line This project will take about three weeks. Spend the first day discussing magnetism and electro-magnetic devices. Students should spend the next two or three days designing their model fishing rods using permanent magnets. Allow three or four days for students to experiment with electric circuits and develop a working switch. By the end of the second week, students should begin testing their electromagnets and incorporating them into their devices. At the end of the project, allow one class period for students to practice and fine-tune their fishing techniques. On the final day, allow students to present their fishing rods and "fish" for one minute. Before beginning the project, see Chapter 1 Project Teacher Notes on pages 6–7 in Teaching Resources for more details on carrying out the project. Also distribute to students the Chapter 1 Project Overview, Worksheets, and Scoring Rubric on pages 8–12 in Teaching Resources.

Possible Shortcuts This project can be completed in class by groups of four students rather than by individuals. Give each group a dowel, 12 m of wire, paper clips, a large nail, and tape. Two group

CHAPTER 1
Magnetism and Electromagnetism

WHAT'S AHEAD

Integrating Earth Science

SECTION 1 The Nature of Magnetism
Discover **What Do All Magnets Have in Common?**
Sharpen Your Skills **Observing**
Try This **How Attractive!**
Real-World Lab **Detecting Fake Coins**

SECTION 2 Magnetic Earth
Discover **Can You Use a Needle to Make a Compass?**
Sharpen Your Skills **Measuring**
Try This **Spinning in Circles**

SECTION 3 Electric Current and Magnetic Fields
Discover **Are Magnetic Fields Limited to Magnets?**
Sharpen Your Skills **Classifying**
Real-World Lab **Build a Flashlight**

members can make the electromagnet while the other two devise a switch mechanism to be mounted on the fishing rod's handle. Students in a group can fish in relay style—they take turns lifting a batch of "fish" out of the pond and then pass the rod to the next person.

Possible Materials
- Each student will need 12–15 m of thin insulated wire and one fresh 1.5-volt D cell.
- Students can use meter sticks, dowels, broom handles, or plain sticks for the 1-m fishing rods.
- Students will use string for suspending the electromagnets and masking or electrical tape for connecting wires or attaching parts to the rod.
- Provide one large plastic container to serve as a fishing "pond." Provide an additional container for each group (Note: up to three groups at a time) to serve as "catch" basins. The pond should contain 50 paper clips for each group.

Electromagnetic Fishing Derby

If you went fishing for cars, what kind of hook would you use—a ship's anchor? Though they resemble giant fishing rods, the cranes used in junkyards to move scrap cars don't use hooks—they use electromagnets.

In this chapter, you will learn what magnets are and how they are used. You will learn about electric current. And you will find out how electric current can be used to produce strong magnets, called electromagnets, that can be turned on and off. As you read the chapter, you will use what you learn to construct an electromagnetic fishing rod. Now go fish!

Your Goal To build an electromagnetic fishing rod that can lift paper clips from one container and drop them into another.

To complete your project you must
- ♦ make a model of a fishing rod that has a magnet as its hook
- ♦ design an on-off switch for an electromagnet suspended by string from the end of the rod and powered by a single D cell
- ♦ modify variables so you can move as many paper clips as possible from one container to another in one minute
- ♦ follow the safety guidelines in Appendix A

Get Started Think about fishing rods. Discuss some of their features. Then think about how you could catch and let go of a paper clip with a similar fishing device. Brainstorm ideas for using a magnet as a "hook."

Check Your Progress You'll be working on this project as you study this chapter. To keep your project on track, look for Check Your Progress boxes at the following points.

Section 1 Review, page 21: Make an initial model with a permanent magnet.
Section 3 Review, page 35: Design a switch.
Section 4 Review, page 40: Construct and improve your electromagnet by experimenting with variables.

Wrap Up At the end of the chapter (page 43), you will use your rod to fish alongside classmates in an electromagnetic fishing derby.

A crane uses an electromagnet to move iron and steel in a junkyard.

SECTION
4 **Electromagnets**

Discover **How Do You Turn a Magnet On and Off?**

Program Resources

- ♦ **Teaching Resources** Chapter 1 Project Teacher Notes, pp. 6–7; Chapter 1 Project Overview and Worksheets, pp. 8–11; Chapter 1 Project Scoring Rubric, p. 12

Launching the Project

Electromagnetism is discussed in Section 1-4, but you should give students a preview of this topic before introducing the Chapter Project. Build and demonstrate a basic electromagnet: Wrap about 100 turns of insulated wire around a large nail, and tape one bare end of the wire to one end of a 1.5-volt battery. Demonstrate how touching the other end of the wire to the other end of the battery produces an electromagnet that can be used to pick up small pieces of metal such as staples or paper clips.

Pass out copies of the Chapter 1 Project Overview and Worksheets on pages 8–11 in Teaching Resources for students to review. Allow time for students to read the description of the project in their text and in the Chapter Project Overview. Then encourage discussions on electric circuits and electromagnetism, materials that could be used, and any initial questions students may have.

Performance Assessment

The Chapter 1 Project Scoring Rubric on page 12 of Teaching Resources will help you evaluate how well students complete the Chapter 1 Project. Students will be assessed on
- ♦ how well they apply chapter concepts to their design of a fishing rod, electric circuit, and switch;
- ♦ how well they identify and experiment with variables and how well they apply the results of their tests to improve the strength of their electromagnets;
- ♦ how well their electromagnetic fishing rod works in an electromagnetic fishing derby;
- ♦ the thoroughness and organization of their presentation.

By sharing the Chapter 1 Scoring Rubric with students at the beginning of the project, you will make it clear to them what they are expected to do.

Objectives

After completing the lesson, students will be able to

◆ define magnetic poles and describe the interaction between like and unlike magnetic poles;

◆ define magnetic fields and describe magnetic field lines;

◆ define magnetic domain and state how magnetic domains are lined up in magnetized material.

Key Terms magnetism, magnetic pole, magnetic field, magnetic field line, atom, element, nucleus, proton, electron, magnetic domain, ferromagnetic material, permanent magnet

1 Engage/Explore

Activating Prior Knowledge

Challenge students to think how magnets are used in the kitchen. Ask: **What keeps cabinet, refrigerator, and freezer doors tightly closed? What holds a can to an electric can opener?** (*Students should infer magnets do these functions.*)

· · · · · · DISCOVER · · · · · ·

Skills Focus observing
Materials *bar magnet, horseshoe magnet, paper clips*
Time 15 minutes
Tips Tell students they will observe how two different types of magnets attract materials.
Expected Outcome Most paper clips will be attracted to the magnets' poles. Few or none will be attracted to the middle of the bar magnet, or to the curved part of the horseshoe magnet.
Think It Over Students should note that most of the magnetic pull comes from the poles, or ends, of each magnet.

DISCOVER ·ACTIVITY· · ·

What Do All Magnets Have in Common?

1. Obtain a bar magnet and a horseshoe magnet.
2. See how many paper clips you can make stick to different parts of each magnet.
3. Draw a diagram showing the number and location of paper clips on each magnet.

Think It Over

Observing Where does each magnet hold the greatest number of paper clips? What similarities do you observe between the two magnets?

GUIDE FOR READING

◆ How do magnetic poles interact?

◆ What is the shape of magnetic lines of force?

◆ How are the domains of a magnet arranged?

Reading Tip As you read, use the headings to make an outline of the main ideas and supporting details about magnetism and electricity.

I magine zooming along in a train that glides without even touching the ground. You feel no vibration and hear no noise from solid steel tracks. You can just sit back and relax as you speed toward your destination at nearly 400 kilometers per hour.

Are you dreaming? No, you are not. Although you have probably not ridden on such a train, experimental trains capable of floating a few centimeters in air do exist. What makes them float? Believe it or not, magnets make them float.

Figure 1 This Japanese high-speed train is moved by strong magnets instead of wheels. It is called a magnetically levitating train, or maglev train.

READING STRATEGIES

Reading Tip Outline the information under the first section heading as a class, as shown in the example. Suggest students modify the headings and subheadings as necessary to create phrases or sentences.

I. Magnets
  A. Magnetic rocks found in Magnesia 2,000 years ago
  B. Magnetic rocks contain magnetite
  C. Magnetic rocks known as lodestones

Study and Comprehension Before students begin reading, have them preview the section by reading the headings, subheadings, and captions and by looking at the pictures and diagrams. Invite students to ask questions they may have about the nature of magnets, magnetic poles, and magnetic fields. Write the questions on the board. After students read the section, have them work as a class to answer the questions on the board.

Magnets

When you think of magnets, you might think about the magnets that hold notes on your refrigerator. But magnets can also be found in many familiar devices, such as doorbells, televisions, and computers.

Magnets have many modern uses, but they are not new. More than 2000 years ago, people living in a region known as Magnesia discovered an unusual rock. (Magnesia is in Greece.) The rock attracted materials that contained iron. It contained a mineral that we call magnetite. Both the word *magnetite* and the word *magnet* come from the name "Magnesia." **Magnetism** is the attraction of a magnet for another object.

About a thousand years ago, people in other parts of the world discovered another interesting property of magnets. If they allowed the magnetic rock to swing freely from a string, one part of the rock would always point in the same direction. That direction was toward a certain northern star, called the leading star, or lodestar. For this reason, magnetic rocks also became known as lodestones.

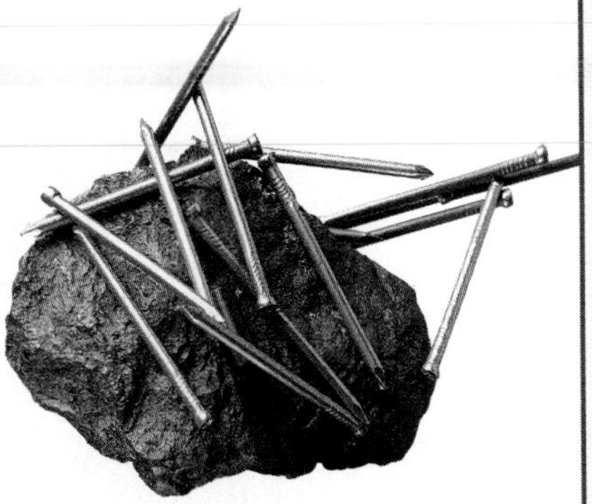

Figure 2 Magnetic rocks contain the mineral magnetite.

Magnetic Poles

The magnets with which you are familiar are not found in nature, but they are made to have the same properties as lodestone. Any magnet, no matter what its shape, has two ends, each one called a **magnetic pole.** A pole is the area of a magnet where the magnetic effect is strongest. Just as one end of a piece of magnetite always points toward the north star, one pole of a magnet will also point north and is labeled the north pole. The other pole is labeled the south pole. Two north poles or two south poles are a pair of like poles. A north pole and a south pole are a pair of unlike, or opposite poles.

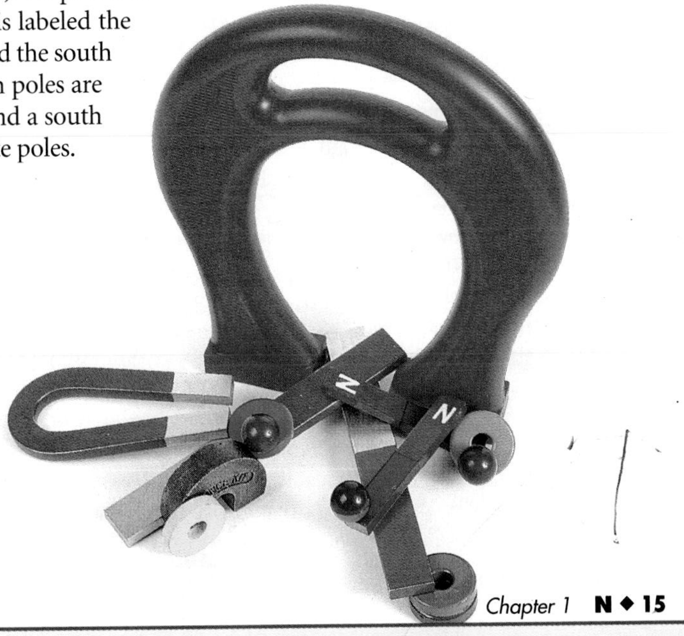

Figure 3 Modern magnets come in a variety of shapes and sizes. *Classifying How many different shapes of magnets can you identify in the photograph?*

---

2 Facilitate

Magnets

Building Inquiry Skills: Predicting

Materials *bar magnets, items for testing (assorted materials including nails, screws, coins, paper, plastic, plastic foam packing, cans)* **Time** 20 minutes

ACTIVITY

Have students predict which materials will be attracted to the magnets. Then have students test their predictions. Objects that contain the element iron will be attracted. Students might be surprised to find that most coins are not magnetic. Note that a "tin" can is attracted to a magnet because it is made of steel, not tin. Any nails attracted to a magnet have iron in them. Some nails are made of brass or aluminum and are not attracted to magnets. **learning modality: kinesthetic**

Magnetic Poles

Using the Visuals: Figure 3

Have students identify the poles of each magnet shown in the figure. Ask: **Where are the poles on the circular magnets? How can you tell?** *(The flat sides, or the top and bottom, of the circular magnets are the poles. These sides are where the magnets are attracted to the other magnets in the photo.)* **learning modality: visual**

Program Resources

◆ **Teaching Resources** 1-1 Lesson Plan, p. 13; 1-1 Section Summary, p. 14

Media and Technology

🎧 **Audiotapes** English-Spanish Summary 1-1

Answers to Self-Assessment

Caption Question

Figure 3 Students should be able to see horseshoe, bar, spherical, semicircular, and circular magnets.

Ongoing Assessment

Writing Have students define magnetism in their own words.

Building Inquiry Skills: Observing

Materials *2 bar magnets*
Time 5 minutes

Have students place the magnets on their desks. Then slide the poles of the magnets together until the students can first feel the attraction between the magnets and then the repulsion. Encourage students to find out how close they can put the magnets before they are "pulled" together and how close together before they are "pushed apart." **limited English proficiency**

Observing

Materials *pencil, foam cup, 2 circular magnets*
Time 10 minutes
Tips Have students predict what will happen when they place the two magnets together on the pencil.
Expected Outcome In the first case, the top magnet will levitate. The levitation is caused by the repulsion between like poles. In the second case, the top magnet will be pulled down. This is caused by the attraction of unlike poles.
Extend Have students use more magnets to increase the height of the levitating magnet. Ask: **What happens when more magnets are used?** (*Adding more magnets increases the strength of the field.*)

Figure 4 Two bar magnets suspended by strings are brought near each other. *Interpreting Photographs What force is acting between the magnets in each photograph?*

Sharpen your Skills

Observing ACTIVITY

1. Use a pencil to poke a hole in the bottom of a foam cup. Turn the cup upside-down and stand the pencil in the hole.
2. Place two circular magnets on the pencil, so that their like sides are together.
3. Remove the top magnet. Flip it over and replace it on the pencil.

What happens to the magnets in each case? Explain your observations.

Interactions Between Magnetic Poles What happens if you bring two magnets together? The answer depends on how you hold the poles of the magnets. If you bring two north poles together, the magnets push away from each other. The same is true if two south poles are brought together. However, if you bring the north pole of one magnet near the south pole of another, the two magnets attract one another. **Magnetic poles that are alike repel each other and magnetic poles that are unlike attract each other.** Figure 4 shows how two bar magnets interact.

The force of attraction or repulsion between magnetic poles is magnetism. Any material that exerts magnetic forces is considered a magnet.

The maglev train you read about earlier depends on magnetism. Magnets in the bottom of the train and in the guideway on the ground have like poles. Since like poles repel, the two magnets push each other away. The result is that the train car is lifted up, or levitated. Other magnets push and pull the train forward.

Paired Poles What do you think happens if you break a magnet in two? Will you have a north pole in one hand and a south pole in the other? The answer is no. Rather than two separate poles, you will have two separate magnets. Each smaller magnet will be complete with its own north pole and south pole. And if you break those two halves again, you will then have four magnets.

✓ *Checkpoint* **What is a magnetic pole?**

Background

Facts and Figures Both Germany and Japan have worked on maglev prototypes since the early 1970s.

The first successful test of levitation and propulsion was made on a 200-meter track in 1975. By the mid 1980s, maglev trains were making demonstration runs and carrying passengers. In March 1989, the HSST-05, a two-car, 158-passenger maglev train operated at the Yokohama Expo in Japan. Currently, projects for developing intra-urban and inter-city trains are underway. Using maglev technology, these trains could reach speeds of up to 200 to 300 kilometers per hour.

Magnetic Fields

The magnetic force is strongest at the poles of a magnet, but it is not limited to the poles. Magnetic forces are exerted all around a magnet. The region of magnetic force around a magnet is known as its **magnetic field.** Magnetic fields allow magnets to interact without touching.

Figure 5A shows the magnetic field of a bar magnet. The lines, called **magnetic field lines,** map out the magnetic field around a magnet. **Magnetic field lines spread out from one pole, curve around a magnet, and return to the other pole.** The lines form complete loops from pole to pole and never cross.

Although you can't actually see a magnetic field, you can see its effects, as shown in Figure 5B. This photograph shows iron filings sprinkled on a sheet of plastic over a magnet. The magnetic forces act on the iron filings so that they point toward the poles of the magnet. The result is that the iron filings form a pattern similar to the magnetic field lines in Figure 5A.

The iron filings and the diagram are both on flat surfaces. But a magnetic field exists in three dimensions. You can see in Figure 5C that the magnetic field completely surrounds the magnet.

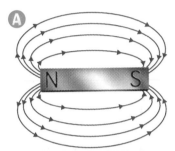

Figure 5 A magnetic field surrounds a magnet. **A.** In this diagram, magnetic field lines are shown in red. **B.** You can see the same magnetic field mapped out by iron filings. **C.** Iron filings also show that a magnetic field has three dimensions.

Building Inquiry Skills: Inferring

Ask students to observe the magnetic field lines in the photos in Figure 5. Have students describe where the field seems to be the strongest. *(Around the poles)* Ask them to explain the evidence for this. *(The lines of iron filings are densest near the poles.)* Have students use their fingers to trace the field lines in the photo. Challenge students to explain why the lines curve between the two poles. Prompt them by asking: **Find an iron filing that is on the curve about halfway between the two poles. Describe the forces acting at that point.** *(At that point, the filing is equally attracted to both poles.)* **learning modality: logical/ mathematical**

Addressing Naive Conceptions

Students may be confused by the concept of a magnetic field. Explain that scientists recognize two kinds of forces, contact forces and field forces. Contact forces act when two objects are in physical contact, but field forces can act without physically touching. Ask: **If the filings were not present around the magnet in Figure 5B, would the field forces still be present around the poles of the magnet?** *(Yes, the field forces are always present. The iron filings are used to make the effects of the field visible.)* **learning modality: verbal**

Program Resources

- **Science Explorer Series** *Chemical Building Blocks,* Chapter 3, describes atomic structure.
- ◆ **Interdisciplinary Exploration Series** "The Power of Patterns," pp. 28–29

Media and Technology

- **Transparencies** "Magnetic Fields" Transparency 1

Answers to Self-Assessment

Caption Question

Figure 4 In the first photo, unlike poles attract each other. In the second photo, the like poles repel each other.

✓ Checkpoint

A magnetic pole is one of the two ends of the magnet where the magnetic effect is the strongest.

Ongoing Assessment

Drawing Challenge students to draw how iron filings would make a pattern around the poles of a bar magnet and a horseshoe magnet. *(Note: The lines of force in their drawings of the horseshoe magnet should be closer together than those lines around the poles of a bar magnet because the poles of the horseshoe magnet are close together.)*

Magnetic Fields,
continued

Using the Visuals: Figure 6

Have students compare the magnetic fields created by placing bar magnets near each other. Ask: **When like poles are placed near each other, where is the field weakest? Explain.** (*At the point exactly between the two magnets; there are no field lines there.*) **When unlike poles are placed near each other, where is the field strongest?** (*At the center point between the poles*) Discuss the field lines and have students determine where a compass needle would point at different places in the magnetic field. **learning modality: logical/mathematical**

Inside a Magnet

Building Inquiry Skills: Making Models

Encourage students to read the description of atomic structure in the text and use the description to diagram an atom. You may wish to refer students to a model of the atom that includes protons and electrons. Have students label the parts of the atom and indicate positive and negative charges. Ask: **How can an atom become a tiny magnet?** (*Because the motion of the electrons produces a magnetic field.*) **learning modality: visual**

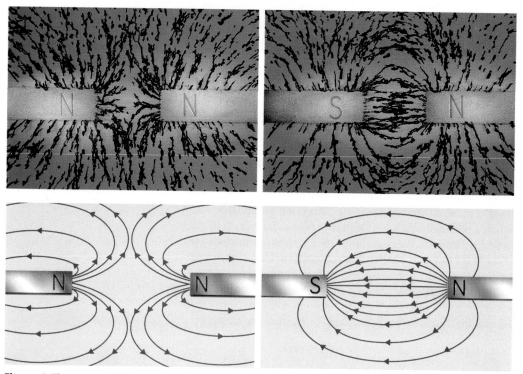

Figure 6 The magnetic field of each bar magnet is altered when two bar magnets are brought together.
Applying Concepts What do these photos and diagrams show about the interaction between magnetic poles?

When the magnetic fields of two or more magnets overlap, the result is a combined field. Figure 6 shows the magnetic fields produced when the poles of two bar magnets are brought near each other.

Inside a Magnet

What happens if you bring a piece of wood, glass, or plastic near a pile of paper clips? Nothing happens. These materials have no effect on the paper clips. But if you bring a bar magnet near the same pile, the paper clips will cling to the magnet. Why do some materials have strong magnetic fields while others do not?

Electron Spin The magnetic properties of a material depend on the structure of its atoms. All matter is made up of atoms. An **atom** is the smallest particle of an element that has the properties of that element. An **element** is one of about 100 basic materials that make up all matter.

The center of every atom is called a **nucleus.** The nucleus contains particles within it. **Protons** are nuclear particles that carry a positive charge. Orbiting the nucleus are other tiny particles called **electrons,** which carry a negative charge. All of the

---

Background

History of Science When scientists first discovered the relationship between the electric charge on electrons and magnetic fields, they began searching for a single particle with a magnetic charge. These particles, called monopoles because they would have only one magnetic pole, have never been found. Physicists continue to look for monopoles. When a new source of matter is discovered, as in 1969 when astronauts brought back moon rocks, physicists examine it to look for monopoles.

Magnetic monopoles are consistent with certain theories. In 1931, P.A.M. Dirac, an English physicist, stated that if there were only one monopole in the universe, it would explain why electric charge only occurs in multiples of the charge on an electron. Theories to explain the origin of the universe also involve monopoles.

electrons in an atom spin as they orbit the nucleus. A moving electron produces a magnetic field. The spinning and orbiting motion of the electrons make each atom a tiny magnet.

Magnetic Domains In most materials the magnetic fields of the atoms point in random directions. The result is that the magnetic fields cancel one another almost entirely. The magnetism of most materials is so weak that you cannot usually detect it.

In certain materials, the magnetic fields of the spinning electrons of many atoms are aligned with one another. A cluster of billions of atoms that all have magnetic fields that are lined up in the same way is known as a **magnetic domain.** The entire domain acts like a bar magnet with a north pole and a south pole.

In a material that is not magnetized, the domains point in random directions as shown in Figure 7. The magnetic fields exerted by some of the domains cancel the magnetic fields exerted by other domains. The result is that the material is not a magnet. **In a magnetized material all or most of the domains are arranged in the same direction.** In other words, the domains are aligned.

Magnetic Materials A material can be a strong magnet if it forms magnetic domains. A material that shows strong magnetic effects is said to be a **ferromagnetic material.** The word *ferromagnetic* comes from the Latin *ferrum*, which means "iron." Iron, nickel, and cobalt are the common ferromagnetic materials. Others include the elements samarium and neodymium, which can be made into magnets that are extremely powerful. Some very strong magnets are also made from mixtures, or alloys, of several metals.

Checkpoint How is magnetism related to domains?

Figure 7 The arrows represent the domains of a material. The arrows point toward the north pole of each domain. *Comparing and Contrasting* How does the arrangement of domains differ between magnetized iron and unmagnetized iron?

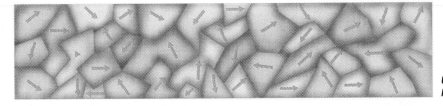

Unmagnetized Iron

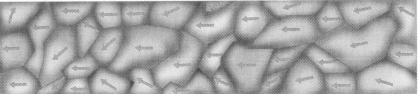

Magnetized Iron

Answers to Self-Assessment

Caption Questions

Figure 6 Field lines are pushed apart for like poles and pulled together for unlike poles.

Figure 7 Unmagnetized iron—domains arranged at random; magnetized iron—domains are arranged in mostly the same direction.

Answers to Self-Assessment

Checkpoint

The domains of magnetized materials are aligned in mostly the same direction.

Media and Technology

Transparencies "Dividing Magnets" Transparency 2

Ongoing Assessment

Writing Have students explain what causes a material to have magnetic properties. Then have them name one ferromagnetic material.

Making Magnets

Skills Focus making models

Materials *clear plastic tube, iron filings, strong bar magnet*

Time 20 minutes

Tips Make sure students rub their plastic tubes in one direction. Suggest they start at the top of the tube and rub down to the bottom, then begin again at the top.

Expected Outcome When the tube is rubbed, the filings become aligned and point in the same direction.

Making Models The iron filings model the magnetic domains by becoming arranged in the way domains are in a magnet.

Extend Have students repeat the experiment with paper clips in a large clear bottle or test tube and compare the results. *(All the paper clips will point in the same direction.)* **learning modality: kinesthetic**

Destroying Magnets

Building Inquiry Skills: Applying Concepts

Tell students that the temperature above which a magnetic material loses its ferromagnetic properties is called the Curie temperature. This temperature is named for Pierre Curie, a French physicist who discovered the relationship between magnetic properties and changes in temperature. Each magnetic material loses its ferromagnetism at a different Curie temperature. Ask students: **What happens to a ferromagnetic material above its Curie temperature?** *(The domains lose their alignment and the material loses its magnetic properties.)* Ask students to infer what happens when the material cools to below its Curie temperature. *(The domains realign, and the material becomes magnetic again.)* **learning modality: verbal**

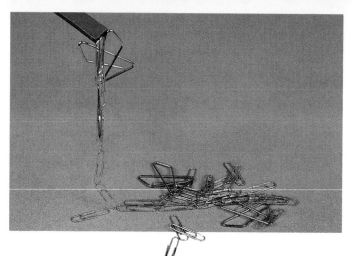

Figure 8 The magnet attracts the metal paper clips. *Applying Concepts How can a paper clip be attracted to a magnet?*

How Attractive!

You can use iron filings to find out how materials become magnetic.

1. Fill a clear plastic tube about two-thirds full with iron filings. Seal the tube.

2. Observe the arrangement of the filings.

3. Rub the tube lengthwise about 30 times in the same direction with one end of a strong magnet.

4. Again observe the arrangement of the filings.

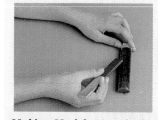

Making Models How do the iron filings in the tube model magnetic domains?

Making Magnets

You know that magnetite exists in nature. The magnets you use everyday, however, are made by people. A magnet can be made from a ferromagnetic material. This is done by placing the unmagnetized material in a strong magnetic field or by rubbing it with one pole of a strong magnet.

If the magnetic field is strong enough, two processes take place. First, the domains that point in the direction of the magnetic field become larger by lining up the fields of neighboring domains. Second, domains that are not pointing in the same direction as the magnetic field rotate toward the magnetic field. The result is that the majority of domains line up in the same direction. With its domains aligned, the material is a magnet.

The ability to make a magnet explains why an unmagnetized object, such as a paper clip, can be attracted to a magnet. Paper clips are made of steel, which is mostly iron. The magnet's field causes domains in the paper clip to line up slightly so that the clip becomes a magnet. Its north pole faces the south pole of the magnet. The paper clip can attract other paper clips for the same reason. After the magnet is removed, however, the domains of the paper clips return to their random arrangements. Thus the paper clips are no longer magnetic.

Some metals, such as the ordinary steel that paper clips are made of, are easy to magnetize but lose their magnetism quickly. Magnets made from these materials are called temporary magnets. Harder metals, such as other types of steel, are more difficult to magnetize but tend to stay magnetized. A magnet made of a material that keeps its magnetism is called a **permanent magnet.**

✓ *Checkpoint* *How does a magnet attract another object?*

Background

Facts and Figures The scientific study of magnetism appears in many fields. For example, measuring the magnetic fields of stars and other astronomical bodies gives astronomers clues to their structure and origin. In the field of medicine, magnetic resonance imaging (MRI), allows physicians to view images of the human body including the brain, heart, liver, kidneys, spleen, pancreas, and breast. MRI images can differentiate between normal tissues and abnormal ones and can show tumors, blood-starved tissues, and other diseased or distressed areas of the body.

Destroying Magnets

Just as paper clips lose their magnetism when their domains become randomly arranged, a permanent magnet can also become unmagnetized. One way is to drop it or strike it hard. If a magnet is hit hard, its domains can be knocked out of alignment. Heating a magnet will also destroy its magnetism. When an object is heated, its particles move faster and more randomly. This makes it more difficult for all the domains to stay lined up. In fact, above a certain temperature a material loses the property of ferromagnetism. The temperature depends on the material.

Breaking Magnets

Now that you know about domains, you can understand why breaking a magnet in half does not result in two pieces that are individual poles. Within the original bar magnet shown in Figure 9, there are many north and south poles facing each other. These poles balance each other.

At the ends of the magnet, there are many poles that are not facing an opposite pole. This produces strong magnetic effects at the north and south poles. If the magnet is cut in half, the domains will still be lined up in the same way. So the shorter pieces will still have strong ends made up of many north or south poles. Figure 9 shows the results of dividing a magnet into four pieces.

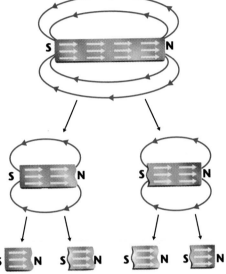

Figure 9 No matter how many times a magnet is cut in half, each piece retains its magnetic properties.

Chapter 1 **N ◆ 21**

Section 1 Review

1. What happens if you bring together two like poles? Two unlike poles?
2. How are magnetic domains arranged in a magnet? How are they arranged in an unmagnetized object?
3. What parts of an atom produce magnetism?
4. How is a magnet made?
5. **Thinking Critically Applying Concepts** Iron filings align with the magnetic field of a bar magnet. What must be happening to the domains in the iron filings in the magnetic field?

Check Your Progress

CHAPTER PROJECT 1

Gather materials for the different parts of your fishing rod. Consider such items as a broom handle, dowel, or meter stick for the rod. You'll also need a string. Draw a basic design for your fishing rod. Make a model of the rod with a permanent magnet. Test how easily you can maneuver your model.

Program Resources

◆ **Teaching Resources** 1-1 Review and Reinforce, p. 15; 1-1 Enrich, p. 16

Media and Technology

Interactive Student Tutorial CD-ROM N-1

Answers to Self-Assessment

Caption Question

Figure 8 A paper clip has its magnetic domains arranged in the same direction by the magnetic field so that the clip too becomes a magnet that is attracted to the larger magnet.

☑ *Checkpoint*

The magnet's field causes the object to become a magnet.

Breaking Magnets

Using the Visuals: Figure 9

Point out that each new magnet has a north and a south pole. Explain that this process can continue until the magnets are extremely small. Ask students to infer what is the smallest thing that has the properties of the larger magnet. (*A domain or an atom*) **learning modality: visual**

3 Assess

Section 1 Review Answers

1. Two like poles repel each other. Two unlike poles attract each other.
2. Most of the domains in a magnet are aligned. In an unmagnetized material, they are not aligned.
3. The spinning motions of electrons produce magnetism.
4. A magnet is made when an unmagnetized ferromagnetic material is placed in a strong magnetic field or rubbed in one direction with one pole of a magnet.
5. Most of the domains in the filings are moving into alignment.

Check Your Progress

CHAPTER PROJECT 1

Provide small permanent magnets so students can test the designs of their rods to make sure they will work when the electromagnet is attached. If possible, set up a sample showing the containers of paper clips that will be used to test the rods at the end of the project.

Performance Assessment

Drawing Have students draw a bar magnet and label its poles. Then have students sketch the magnetic fields around the poles and indicate the alignment of the domains in the magnet.

Detecting Fake Coins

Preparing for Inquiry

Key Concept In the United States, coins are made of nonmagnetic metals. They can be separated from magnetic metal slugs using a magnet.

Skills Objectives Students will be able to

♦ predict how different metals will react to the presence of a magnetic field;

♦ make inferences about the content of metallic objects based on their reaction to a magnetic field.

Time 45 minutes

Advance Planning You will need the type of cardboard used to make file folders, as well as popsicle sticks, washers of various sizes, and small bar magnets. Make sure the washers are attracted to the magnet. Supply coins or have students bring in their own.

Alternative Materials The magnet can be replaced with an electromagnet made by wrapping 50 loops of insulated wire around a nail and connecting the ends of the wire to a battery. If students use electromagnets, do not allow them to close the circuit for more than a few seconds in order to avoid overheating.

Guiding Inquiry

Invitation Ask students if they have ever wondered how a vending machine can tell the difference between a real coin and a fake coin or slug. Discuss different ways that a machine might be able to distinguish between one coin and another. (*Students may list properties of metals or of coins, such as size and shape, mass or density, magnetic properties.*)

Introducing the Procedure
Place a pile of coins and washers mixed together on a desk. Move a magnet around the top of the pile and pick up the magnet. The washers will stick to the magnet and the coins will be left behind.

Troubleshooting the Experiment
The effectiveness of students' devices can

Detecting Fake Coins

Suppose there has been a rash of fake steel coins used in vending machines. The machines may be removed by the owners unless someone can prevent the fake coins from being used. What can you do?

Problem
How can you use a magnet to tell the difference between real and fake coins?

Skills Focus
predicting, inferring

Materials

various coins	popsicle stick	tape
metric ruler	pencil	protractor

coin-sized steel washers
small bar magnet, about 2 cm wide
thin, stiff cardboard, about 25 cm × 30 cm

Procedure

1. Mark a piece of cardboard to show its front, back, top, and bottom.
2. Draw a line lengthwise down the middle of both sides of the cardboard.
3. On the back of the cardboard, draw a line parallel to the first and about 2 cm to the right.
4. Place a magnet vertically about a third of the way down the line you drew in Step 3. Tape the magnet in place.
5. Place a popsicle stick on the front of the cardboard. The stick's upper end should be about 1 cm to the left of the center line and about 8 cm from the bottom of the cardboard.
6. Tape the stick at an angle, as shown in the photograph.
7. Prop the cardboard against something that will hold it at an angle of about 45°. Predict what will happen when you slide a coin down the front of the cardboard.
8. Place a coin on the center line and slide the coin down the front of the cardboard. (*Hint:* If the coin gets stuck, slowly increase the angle.)
9. Predict what will happen when you slide an iron washer.
10. Test your prediction by sliding a washer down the cardboard. Again, if the washer gets stuck, slowly increase the angle and try again.
11. Once you have reached an angle at which the objects slide easily, send down a randomly mixed group of coins and washers.

be affected by several factors. Probably the easiest for students to control is the angle of the inclined cardboard. When the angle of the incline is increased, the coins and washers will move down more quickly, decreasing a washer's chance of becoming stuck at the magnet. The other factor is the strength of the magnet. If a strong magnet is used, a steeper angle of incline or placing the magnet farther from the center line will allow coins and washers to slide down.

Expected Outcome
Coins should slide straight down the center line on the cardboard and be deposited in a pile. Washers should be pulled to the side by the magnet, then slide down along the popsicle stick and be deposited in a separate pile.

Analyze and Conclude

1. What was your prediction from Step 7? Explain your reasoning.
2. What was your prediction from Step 9? Explain your reasoning.
3. Describe how observations made during the lab either supported or did not support your predictions.
4. What is the role of the magnet in this lab?
5. What is the role of the popsicle stick?
6. Why did you have to use thin cardboard?
7. What can you conclude about the metals from which the coins are made? About the metals in the washers?
8. Why does the steepness of the cardboard affect how the coin separating device works?

9. **Apply** Some Canadian coins contain metals that are attracted to magnets. Would this device be useful in Canada to detect fake coins? Explain your answer.

Getting Involved

Go to a store that has vending machines. Find out who owns the vending machines. Ask the owners if they have a problem with counterfeit coins (sometimes called "slugs"). Ask how they or the makers of the vending machines solve the problem. How is their solution related to the device you built in this lab?

Analyze and Conclude

1. Students' predictions will vary. Sample: The coins will slide straight down.
2. Sample: The washers will be deflected and will slide along the stick.
3. Answers will depend on students' predictions. When the coins and washers slid down the incline, the coins slid straight down and the washers were deflected.
4. The magnet attracts any iron or magnetic materials in the objects as they slide down the incline.
5. The popsicle stick served to separate the two groups into piles at the bottom of the incline.
6. Other materials such as thick cardboard or wood increase the distance from the magnet so that the objects would be in a weaker part of the field.
7. The coins did not contain detectable amounts of magnetic metals. The washers contained a significant amount of magnetic metal.
8. The angle of the incline affects the speed of the objects sliding down the incline. When they are moving slowly, washers may stick to the magnet.
9. The device would not be useful in Canada because some Canadian coins are magnetic and would be deflected from the straight path.

Extending the Inquiry

Getting Involved This device is similar to the device that was used in many vending machines long ago. Today, magnetic fields are set up using electromagnets and the size and mass of the coins are analyzed very closely to differentiate real coins from fake coins.

Program Resources

◆ **Teaching Resources** Chapter 1 Real-World Lab, pp. 29–31

SECTION 2 Magnetic Earth

Objectives

After completing the lesson, students will be able to
- identify the magnetic properties of Earth and compare the magnetic and geographic poles;
- describe some of the effects of Earth's magnetic fields.

Key Terms compass, magnetic declination, Van Allen belts, solar wind, magnetosphere, aurora

1 Engage/Explore

Activating Prior Knowledge

Ask students which way is north. Some students may be able to point in the correct direction. Encourage students to discuss different ways to determine direction. Students may mention using the location and motion of the sun or using a compass. Challenge students to explain how to use a compass.

DISCOVER

Skills Focus observing
Materials *large needle, strong bar magnet, dish, water, dishwashing soap, cork or foam ball, pliers*
Time 20 minutes
Tips CAUTION: *Warn students to handle the needle carefully.* Students should rub the needle in only one direction. Have students use pliers to hold the needles when pushing them through the foam. Objects in the room may be magnetized and may attract the needle. Use a compass to find areas in the classroom where the compass needle will point north.
Expected Outcome The needle will point north.
Think It Over The needle will always point north, because Earth has a magnetic field.

SECTION 2 Magnetic Earth

DISCOVER .... ACTIVITY

Can You Use a Needle to Make a Compass?

1. Magnetize a large needle by rubbing it several times in the same direction with one end of a strong bar magnet. Push the needle through a ball of foam or tape it to a small piece of cork.

2. Place a drop of dishwashing soap in a dish of water. Then float the foam or cork in the water. Adjust the needle until it floats horizontally.

3. Allow the needle to stop moving. Which way does it point?

4. Use a local map to determine the direction in which it points.

Think It Over

Observing In what direction did the needle point? Will it always point in the same direction? What does this tell you about Earth?

GUIDE FOR READING

- What are the magnetic properties of Earth?
- What are the effects of Earth's magnetic field?

Reading Tip As you read, make a table that compares the magnetic fields of Earth and a bar magnet.

When Christopher Columbus sighted land in 1492, he didn't really know what he had found. He was trying to find a shortcut from Europe to India. Where he landed, however, was on an island in the Caribbean Sea just south of the present-day United States. He had no idea that such an island even existed.

In spite of his error, Columbus had successfully followed a course west to the Americas without the help of an accurate map. Instead, Columbus used a compass for navigation. A **compass** is a device that has a magnetized needle that can spin freely. The compass needle usually points north, and as you read you'll find out why.

Figure 10 In 1492, Columbus set sail across the Atlantic Ocean. He and his crews navigated using compasses like these.

READING STRATEGIES

Reading Tip After students prepare their tables comparing Earth to a bar magnet, invite volunteers to write the tables on the board and explain the information in them. Students should ask questions and have discussions to clarify any differences between their tables.

Vocabulary As students read, have them write boldfaced terms on note cards, one term per card. Instruct them to write definitions on the other side of the cards. After students have finished reading, have partners quiz each other, using the note cards as flashcards.

Figure 11 William Gilbert demonstrates his research to Queen Elizabeth I.

Earth As a Magnet

In the late 1500s, the English physician Sir William Gilbert became interested in compasses. He spoke with several navigators and experimented with his own compass. Gilbert confirmed that a compass always points in the same direction, no matter where you are. But no one knew why.

Gilbert suggested that a compass behaves as it does because Earth acts as a giant magnet. Although many educated people of his time laughed at this idea, Gilbert turned out to be correct. **Earth has an immense magnetic field surrounding it, just as there is a magnetic field around a bar magnet.**

Gilbert believed that Earth contains magnetic rock. Scientists now believe that this is not the case, since Earth's core is too hot for the rock to be solid. Earth's magnetism is still not completely understood. Scientists do know that it is due to the circulation of molten metal (iron and nickel) within Earth's core.

The fact that Earth has a magnetic field explains why a compass works as it does. The poles of the magnetized needle on the compass align themselves with Earth's magnetic field.

☑ *Checkpoint* *What was Gilbert's new idea about Earth?*

Magnetic Declination

Earth's magnetic poles are not the same as the geographic poles. For example, the magnetic north pole (in northern Canada) is about 1,250 kilometers from the geographic north pole. The geographic north pole is sometimes called true north. The magnetic south pole is located near the coast of Antarctica.

Sharpen your Skills

Measuring ACTIVITY

1. Use a local map to locate geographic north relative to your school. Mark the direction on the floor with tape or chalk.
2. Use a compass to find magnetic north. Again mark the direction.
3. Use a protractor to measure the number of degrees between the two marks.

Compare the directions of magnetic and geographic north. Is magnetic north to the east or west of geographic north?

2 Facilitate

Earth As a Magnet

Cultural Diversity

Note for students that compasses were used by Chinese navigators as early as A.D. 1100. By the 1300s, they were used by western European, Arabic, and Scandinavian sailors as well. Early compasses were magnetized needles floating with a piece of wood or reed on water. Ask students: **Why can people all over the world use compasses of the same design?** (*Because Earth's magnetic field surrounds Earth.*) Encourage some students to prepare a class report on how various cultures built and used compasses. **cooperative learning**

Magnetic Declination

Sharpen your Skills

Measuring

Materials *local map, compass, protractor* ACTIVITY
Time 15 minutes
Tips If possible, do this activity outdoors, away from power lines or other magnetic materials.
Expected Outcome Students should find that the compass needle points at an angle to true north.
Extend Have students identify the direction the compass points on a local map and compare it to true north. Encourage students to identify landmarks in each direction.

Program Resources

◆ **Teaching Resources** 1-2 Lesson Plan, p. 17; 1-2 Section Summary, p. 18
◆ **Interdisciplinary Exploration Series** "The Wreck of the Henrietta Marie," pp. 15–16

Media and Technology

🎧 **Audiotapes** English-Spanish Summary 1-2

Answers to Self-Assessment

☑ *Checkpoint*
Gilbert suggested that Earth acted as a giant magnet.

Ongoing Assessment

Writing Have students explain why the needle of a compass always points in the same direction.

Including All Students

Materials *world map, compass*

Time 15 minutes

To reinforce the concept of magnetic declination, give students flat maps of the world. Have students find and mark true north on the maps. If the map has a compass "rose," suggest they use this to find true north. Then have students place the marked end of their maps toward true north for your location. Have each student place a compass on the map and mark the position of the needle. Students should be able to see the difference between true north and the position of the needle on the compass. **limited English proficiency**

Building Inquiry Skills: Interpreting Diagrams

Have students examine the map in Figure 13. Ask: **Does the compass needle always point to the same place? Where?** *(Yes, to the magnetic north pole.)* Then ask: **Does the compass needle always point in the same direction? Explain.** *(No, it depends where you are in relation to the pole. If you were standing at the geographic north pole, it would point south.)* **learning modality: logical/mathematical**

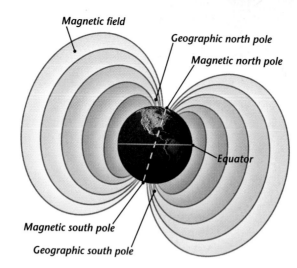

Figure 12 The magnetic poles are not located exactly at the geographic poles.

You can see the difference between the magnetic and geographic poles more clearly by imagining lines that connect each set of poles together. Figure 12 shows that the line connecting Earth's magnetic poles is tipped slightly from Earth's axis—the imaginary line around which Earth rotates.

If you use a compass you have to account for the fact that the geographic and magnetic poles are different. Suppose you could draw a line between you and the geographic north pole. The direction of this line is geographic north. Then imagine a second line between you and the magnetic pole. The angle between these two lines is the angle between geographic north and the north to which a compass needle points. This angle is known as **magnetic declination.**

Magnetic declination differs depending on where you are. Figure 13 shows magnetic declination in various locations in the United States. In North Carolina, for example, a hiker must head about 8 degrees east of the compass reading to get to a place that

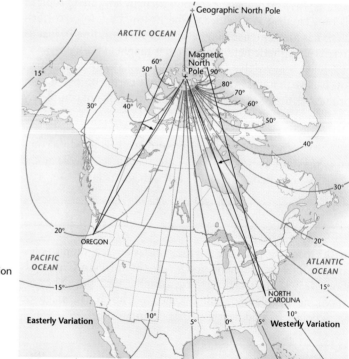

Figure 13 Magnetic declination varies with location.
Interpreting Maps What is the magnetic declination where you live?

Background

Facts and Figures Because Earth's magnetic field is generally detected with a horizontally mounted compass, it would seem that Earth's magnetic field lies only along the surface. The magnetic field is actually three-dimensional and extends throughout Earth and into space around Earth. A vertically mounted compass shows the angle Earth's magnetic field makes with the surface, called magnetic "dip." The instrument used to measure magnetic dip is called a "dipping needle." If a dipping needle were used directly over Earth's magnetic pole, the needle would point straight down. Locating the precise position of the north magnetic pole using this technique is complicated because the pole is located far below Earth's surface. The dipping needle would point straight down over an area in northeastern Canada.

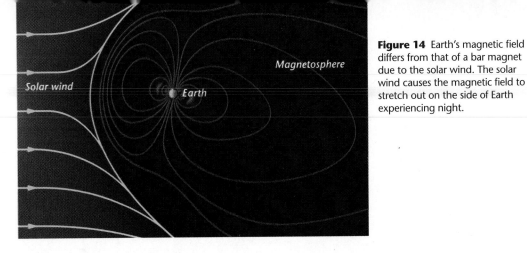

Figure 14 Earth's magnetic field differs from that of a bar magnet due to the solar wind. The solar wind causes the magnetic field to stretch out on the side of Earth experiencing night.

is directly north on a map. A hiker in Oregon would have to head about 20 degrees west of the compass reading.

Magnetic declination changes over time because the magnetic poles move slowly. Between 1580 and 1820, for example, the direction of magnetic north in London changed by 35 degrees.

Checkpoint What is magnetic declination?

The Magnetosphere

Earth's magnetic field extends into space, which contains electrically charged particles. **Earth's magnetic field affects the movements of electrically charged particles in space. Charged particles also affect Earth's magnetic field.**

Between 1,000 and 25,000 kilometers above Earth's surface are two doughnut-shaped regions called the **Van Allen belts.** They are named after their discoverer, J. A. Van Allen. These regions contain electrons and protons traveling at very high speeds. At one time it was feared the particles would be dangerous for spacecraft passing through them, but this has not been the case.

Other electrically charged particles in space come from the sun. Earth and the other planets experience a solar wind. The **solar wind** is a stream of electrically charged particles flowing at high speeds from the sun. The solar wind pushes against Earth's magnetic field, and surrounds the field, as shown in Figure 14. The region of Earth's magnetic field confined by the solar wind is called the **magnetosphere.** The solar wind constantly reshapes the magnetosphere as Earth rotates on its axis.

Although most particles in the solar wind cannot penetrate Earth's magnetic field, some particles do. They follow the lines of Earth's magnetic field to the magnetic poles. At the poles the magnetic field lines dip down to Earth's surface.

Spinning in Circles

Which way will a compass point?

1. Place a bar magnet in the center of a sheet of paper.
2. Place a compass about 2 cm beyond the north pole of the magnet. Draw a small arrow showing the direction of the compass needle.
3. Repeat Step 2 at 20 to 30 different positions around the magnet.
4. Remove the magnet and observe the pattern of arrows you drew.

Drawing Conclusions What does your pattern of arrows represent? Do compasses respond only to Earth's magnetic field?

Using the Visuals: Figure 14

Have students compare the magnetosphere shown in Figure 14 to the magnetic field of a bar magnet. (*The bar magnet's field has a regular shape, but the magnetosphere is compressed on one side and spread out on the other.*) Make sure students understand that the shape of the magnetosphere depends on the solar wind. **learning modality: visual**

Building Inquiry Skills: Inferring

Ask students: **Where do the auroral lights occur?** (*Almost exclusively at latitudes near the magnetic poles of Earth*) Ask students to infer why there would be more activity at these places than at others. (*Because the magnetic force is stronger at the poles, the charged particles cluster near the poles.*) **learning modality: verbal**

TRY THIS

Skills Focus drawing conclusions
Materials *bar magnet,* *sheet of paper, compass, centimeter ruler*
Time 20 minutes
Tips Use a bar magnet that is much larger than the compass to give the most accurate results.
Drawing Conclusions The pattern of arrows represents the magnetic field. Compasses also respond to magnetic material near them.
Extend Students can repeat the activity using a horseshoe magnet. Before they begin, ask students to predict how the arrows will appear around the horseshoe magnet based on their results with the bar magnet. **learning modality: kinesthetic**

Program Resources

- **Science Explorer Series** *Inside Earth,* Chapter 1
- ◆ **Interdisciplinary Exploration Series** "Wagons West," p. 41

Media and Technology

- **Transparencies** "The Magnetosphere," Transparency 3

Answers to Self-Assessment

Caption Question
Figure 13 Students should use the map to find the magnetic declination at their location.

Checkpoint
Magnetic declination is the angle between a line pointing at the magnetic north pole and a line pointing at the geographic north pole.

Ongoing Assessment

Drawing Have students make captioned sketches to explain why a compass does not point to true north. Students can save their sketches in their portfolios.

Language Arts
CONNECTION

If possible, show students images or read a description of the auroral lights. Ask volunteers who have seen the lights to describe them. Encourage students to imagine living with the people described in the feature and hearing stories about the aurora.

In Your Journal Students' stories should be creative and descriptive. Encourage students to speculate on what could be the result of whistling at the aurora. **learning modality: verbal**

Effects of Earth's Magnetic Field

Demonstration

Materials *metal filing cabinet or other large metal object that has been in one place for a long time, such as a locker; compass*

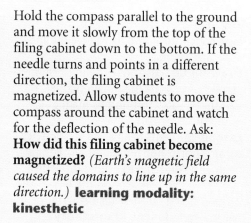

Time 5 minutes

Hold the compass parallel to the ground and move it slowly from the top of the filing cabinet down to the bottom. If the needle turns and points in a different direction, the filing cabinet is magnetized. Allow students to move the compass around the cabinet and watch for the deflection of the needle. Ask: **How did this filing cabinet become magnetized?** *(Earth's magnetic field caused the domains to line up in the same direction.)* **learning modality: kinesthetic**

Figure 15 A band of colors called an aurora appears in the sky near the magnetic poles. *Relating Cause and Effect What causes an aurora?*

Language Arts
CONNECTION

From ancient times, people have sought to explain what they observe in nature. Imagine trying to explain the auroras without knowing that Earth is magnetic.

The Fox people in Wisconsin feared that the aurora was made up of the ghosts of their dead enemies.

A common belief among Eskimos in the Hudson Bay area of North America is that the aurora can be attracted by whistling to it. A hand clap will cause it to move away.

In Your Journal

Imagine that the aurora could really be attracted by whistling to it. Write a story about what might happen. Before you write the story, plan who the characters will be and what events will happen.

When charged particles get close to Earth's surface, they interact with atoms in the atmosphere. This causes the atoms to give off light. The result is one of Earth's most spectacular displays—a curtain of shimmering bright light in the atmosphere. A glowing region caused by charged particles from the sun is called an **aurora**. In the northern hemisphere, an aurora is called the Northern Lights, or aurora borealis. In the southern hemisphere, it is called the Southern Lights, or aurora australis.

Effects of Earth's Magnetic Field

You learned that a material such as iron can be made into a magnet by a strong magnetic field. **Since Earth produces a strong magnetic field, Earth itself can make magnets.**

Earth as a Magnet Maker Suppose you leave an iron bar lying in a north-south direction for many years. Earth's magnetic field may attract the domains strongly enough to cause them to line up in the same direction. (Recall that a strong magnetic field can cause the magnetic domains of a ferromagnetic material to increase in size or to line up in the same direction.) To speed the process, you could gently tap on the bar with a hammer. This vibrates the domains and they can then be aligned by the magnetic field.

What objects might be lying in Earth's magnetic field for many years? Consider metal objects or appliances that are left in the same position for many years, such as filing cabinets in your school. Even though no one has tried to make them into magnets, Earth might have done so anyway.

Background

Integrating Science Where magnetic lines of force break through the sun's surface, the temperature of the surface gases is lowered somewhat. These cooler areas appear as dark areas known as sunspots. Whenever sunspots appear in pairs, each sunspot in the pair represents a pole of the magnetic field. The annual number of sunspots varies in an 11-year cycle.

Program Resources

- **Science Explorer Series** *Astronomy,* Chapter 2, solar wind
- ◆ **Teaching Resources** 1-2 Review and Reinforcement, p. 19; 1-2 Enrich, p. 20

Earth Leaves a Record Earth's magnetic field also acts on rocks that contain magnetic material, such as rock on the ocean floor. The ocean floor is produced from molten material that seeps up through a long crack in the ocean floor, known as the mid-ocean ridge. When the rock is molten, the iron it contains lines up in the direction of Earth's magnetic field. As the rock cools and hardens, the iron is locked in place. This creates a permanent record of the magnetic field.

As scientists studied such rock, they discovered that the direction and strength of Earth's magnetic field has changed over time. In fact, Earth's magnetic field has completely reversed direction every million years or so.

The yellow arrows in Figure 16 indicate the direction of Earth's magnetic field. Notice that the patterns of bands on either side of the ridge are mirror images. This is because the sea floor spreads apart from the mid-ocean ridge. So rocks farther from the ridge are older than rocks near the ridge. The magnetic record in the rock depends on when the rock was formed.

You might be wondering why Earth's magnetic field changes direction. If so, you're not alone. Scientists have asked the same question. Earth's magnetic field arises from the motion of molten metal in Earth's core. Changes in the flow of that metal result in changes in Earth's magnetic field. But the details of this theory have not been worked out, and so scientists cannot explain why the flow changes. Maybe someday you will be able to shed light on this area.

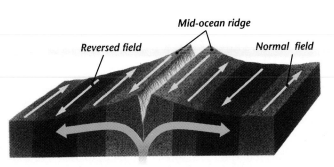

Figure 16 When volcanic lava on the ocean floor hardens into rock, the direction of Earth's magnetic field at that time is permanently recorded.

 Section 2 Review

1. How is Earth like a magnet?
2. Compare Earth's geographic poles with its magnetic poles.
3. How does a compass work?
4. What evidence of changes in Earth's magnetic field is found in rocks?
5. **Thinking Critically Developing Hypotheses** Some insects and birds have tiny particles of iron in parts of their body that are connected by nerves to their brain. What could be the function of the iron particles?

 **Science at Home**

Explore your home with a compass. Use the compass to discover objects that are magnetized. For example, test the top and bottom of the stove, refrigerator, or a metal filing cabinet. Try metal objects that have been in the same position over a long period of time. Explain why these objects attract or repel a compass needle.

Media and Technology

📀 **Interactive Student Tutorial CD-ROM** N-1

💿 **Exploring Physical Science Videodisc**
Unit 5, Side 1, "The Northern Lights"
Chapter 4

Answers to Self-Assessment

Caption Question

Figure 15 An aurora is caused by charged particles from the sun entering Earth's magnetic field and interacting with atoms in the atmosphere.

---

3 Assess

Section 2 Review Answers

1. Earth has a magnetic field and has a north magnetic pole and a south magnetic pole.
2. Earth's geographic poles mark the ends of Earth's axis and are fixed in place. The magnetic poles attract the needle of a compass and move with time.
3. A compass has a magnetic needle that can spin freely. The north pole of the compass always points towards Earth's north magnetic pole.
4. When rocks are in a molten state, the magnetic material is free to move. Because it is attracted to Earth's magnetic field, the domains align with Earth's magnetic field. When the rocks cool and harden, the magnetic material is locked in place. By examining the pattern of magnetic material, scientists can study the magnetic history of Earth.
5. The iron particles in their bodies might be used for navigation, like a compass.

 **Science at Home**

Materials *compass*
Prior to the activity, draw a refrigerator sitting on the surface of Earth in North America. Draw magnetic lines running through it from north to south to show the alignment of the domains with the magnetic field of Earth. Point out that the side of the refrigerator facing north should become N (north-seeking) because it is nearest the north magnetic pole.

Performance Assessment

Oral Presentation Have students create presentations on an aspect of Earth's magnetic properties. Encourage students to create visual aids such as diagrams and charts to accompany their presentations.

Objectives

After completing the lesson, students will be able to
- describe the relationship between electric current and a magnetic field;
- define and give examples of conductors and insulators;
- identify the characteristics of an electric circuit.

Key Terms electric charge, electric current, electric circuit, conductor, insulator, resistor, resistance, superconductor

1 Engage/Explore

Activating Prior Knowledge

Ask a volunteer to describe what he or she does when they want to use an electrical appliance such as a hairdryer. *(Plug it in, then switch it on.)* Tell students that when they do this, they are creating and closing an electrical circuit.

DISCOVER

Skills Focus inferring
Materials *2 wires (20 cm long with insulation stripped from ends), light bulb, bulb holder; 3 compasses, D cell (1.5 volt)*
Time 25 minutes
Tips Tell students that they are going to construct an electric circuit and that electricity will flow through the circuit when it is closed.
Expected Outcome The light bulb lights and some of the compass needles move when students touch the free end of the wire to the battery, thus closing the circuit.
Think It Over Students should infer that electricity in the wire creates a magnetic field.

SECTION
3 Electric Current and Magnetic Fields

DISCOVER ·ACTIVITY· · ·

Are Magnetic Fields Limited to Magnets?

1. Obtain two wires with the insulation removed from both ends. Each wire should be 20 to 30 cm long.
2. Connect one end of each wire to a socket containing a small light bulb.
3. Connect the other end of one of those wires to a D cell.
4. Place 3 compasses near the wire at any 3 positions. Note the direction in which the compasses are pointing.
5. Center the wire over the compasses. Make sure the compass needles are free to turn.
6. Touch the free end of the remaining wire to the battery. Observe the compasses as current flows through the wire. Move the wire away from the battery, and then touch it to the battery again. Watch the compasses.

Think It Over
Inferring What happened to the compasses? What can you infer about electricity and magnetism?

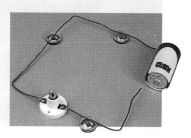

GUIDE FOR READING

- How is an electric current related to a magnetic field?
- How are conductors different from insulators?
- What are the characteristics of an electric circuit?

Reading Tip As you read, use the headings to make an outline.

30 ◆ N

In 1820, the Danish scientist Hans Christian Oersted (ur sted) was teaching a class at the University of Copenhagen. During his lecture, he allowed electricity to flow through a wire, just as electricity flows through wires to your electrical appliances. When electricity flowed, he noticed that the needle of a compass near the wire changed direction.

Oersted's observations surprised him. He could have assumed that something was wrong with his equipment. Instead, he investigated further. He set up several compasses around a wire. Oersted discovered that whenever he turned on the electricity, the compass needles lined up in a circle around the wire.

Oersted's discovery showed that magnetism and electricity are related. But just how are they related? To find out, you must learn about electric current.

Electric Current

You learned in Section 1 that all matter contains particles called electrons and protons. Electrons and protons have a property called **electric charge.** Electrons are negatively charged, and protons are positively charged.

◀ Oersted's demonstration

READING STRATEGIES

Reading Tip You may want to have students work with partners to outline the section as they read. Suggest students take turns reading aloud the information under a heading and paraphrasing it. Then have students work together to outline the information under the heading.

Study and Comprehension Before students read, have them prepare charts with the headings *What I Know, What I Want to Know, What I Learned.* Then have students fill in the first column with what they already know about electricity and magnets, conductors, and insulators, and the characteristics of an electric current. Next, have them list questions about these topics. Then have students write answers to the questions as they read.

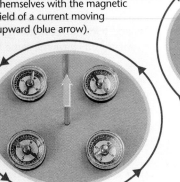

B. Compass needles align themselves with the magnetic field of a current moving upward (blue arrow).

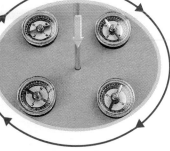

C. Compass needles reverse their directions to align with the magnetic field of a current moving downward.

Figure 17 Current in a wire affects a compass needle.
A. With no current flowing, the compass needles all point to magnetic north.

When electric charges flow through a wire or similar material, they create an electric current. **Electric current** is the flow of charge through a material. The amount of charge that passes through the wire in a unit of time is the rate at which electric current flows. The unit of current is the ampere (amp or A), named for André-Marie Ampère. You will often see the name of the unit shortened to "amp." The number of amps tells the amount of charge flowing past a given point each second.

What does all of this have to do with magnetism? **An electric current produces a magnetic field.** The lines of the magnetic field produced by a current in a straight wire are in the shape of circles with the wire at their center. You can see in Figure 17 that compasses placed around a wire line up with the magnetic field. The iron filings in Figure 18 map out the same field. The direction of the current determines the direction of the magnetic field. If the current is reversed, the magnetic field reverses as well. You can see this from the compasses in Figure 17C.

Moving Charge and Magnetism

Ampère carried out many experiments with electricity and magnetism. He hypothesized that all magnetism is a result of circulating charges. Atoms, for example, can become magnets because of the motion of the electrons. Based on modern knowledge of magnetism, Ampère's hypothesis is correct. All magnetism is caused by the movement of charges.

☑ *Checkpoint* What particles have electric charge?

Figure 18 Iron filings show the field lines around a wire that carries a current.
Observing What is the shape of the field lines?

2 Facilitate

Electric Current

Using the Visuals: Figure 17

Ask students to note the directions in which the compass needles are pointing in each photo in Figure 17. Point out that in the first photo, there is no current in the wire. Direct attention to the photo in the center. Ask: **How can you tell there is current in the wire?** (*The compass needles react to the magnetic field of the wire.*) Point out that the third photo shows what happens when the direction of the current is reversed and ask students to explain how they can tell. (*The compass needles are reversed.*)
learning modality: visual

Moving Charge and Magnetism

Addressing Naive Conceptions

Students may be confused by the idea that magnetism is caused by moving charges because permanent magnets such as bar magnets do not seem to have moving parts. Ask: **Why can't you see moving particles in a magnet?** (*Moving particles are too tiny to see. In a solid, vibrating particles stay in the same relative positions.*) **learning modality: verbal**

Program Resources

◆ **Teaching Resources** 1-3 Lesson Plan, p. 21; 1-3 Section Summary, p. 22

Media and Technology

🎧 **Audiotapes** English-Spanish Summary 1-3

Answers to Self-Assessment

Caption Question
Figure 18 The field lines are in the shape of circles.

☑ *Checkpoint*
Electrons and protons

Ongoing Assessment

Oral Presentation Call on students at random to state in their own words how magnetism and electricity are related according to Oersted's observations. Remind them to refer to compasses and electrical wire in their explanations.

Electric Circuits

Demonstration

Materials *3 wires (20 cm long with insulation stripped from ends), contact switch, light bulb, bulb holder, D cell (1.5 volt)*

Time *5 minutes*

This demonstration allows students to observe how a switch is used in an electric circuit. Make a circuit using the contact switch, bulb, battery, and wires. Ask: **How does the switch operate to light the bulb?** *(The switch is a conductor that, when closed, allows electricity to flow, lighting the bulb.)* **What happens when the switch is opened?** *(The switch breaks the circuit stopping the flow of electric current.)* Summarize the activity by suggesting that students draw a circuit incorporating all the components, including the switch, used in a circuit.

learning modality: visual

Conductors and Insulators

Real-Life Learning

Use a picture from a current magazine ad for an electric power tool to show how insulators are built into the product to protect the operator from harm. As an example, show a picture of a power drill that has a plastic handle and rubber tubing wrapped around the power cord. Have students work in groups of three or four. Suggest that each group first brainstorm a list of electric appliances and tools that are built with insulators such as rubber, glass, or plastic. Then have each group find pictures of products in daily newspaper advertisements, old magazines, and flyers. Have each group share its results with the class. You may wish to have the students prepare a class bulletin board that illustrates the uses of insulators in electric power tools and appliances.

cooperative learning

Electric Circuits

An electric current will not flow automatically through every wire. Current flows only through electric circuits. An **electric circuit** is a complete path through which electric charges can flow. All electrical devices, from toasters to radios to electric guitars and televisions, contain electric circuits.

All circuits have the same basic features. **First, a circuit has a source of electrical energy.** Energy is the ability to do work. **Second, circuits have devices that are run by electrical energy.** A radio, a computer, a light bulb, and a refrigerator are all devices that convert electrical energy into another form of energy. A light bulb, for example, converts electrical energy to electromagnetic energy (it gives off light) and thermal energy (it gives off heat).

Third, electric circuits are connected by conducting wires and a switch. In order to describe a circuit, you can draw a circuit diagram. *Exploring Electric Circuits* on the next page shows a circuit diagram along with the symbols that represent the parts of the circuit. As you read, identify the parts of a circuit and their symbols.

Conductors and Insulators

Electric current flows through metal wires. Will it also flow through plastic or paper? The answer is no. Electric current does not flow through every material.

Electric currents move freely through materials called **conductors.** Metals, such as copper, silver, iron, and aluminum, are good conductors. **In a conductor, some of the electrons are only loosely bound to their atoms.** These electrons, called conduction electrons, are able to move throughout the conductor. As these electrons flow through a conductor, they form an electric current.

Did you ever wonder why a light goes on the instant you flip the switch? How do the electrons get to your lamp from the electric company so fast? The answer is that electrons are not created and sent to you when you flip a switch. They are present all along in the conductors that make up the circuit. When you flip the switch, conduction electrons at one end of the wire are pulled while those at the other end are pushed. The result is a continuous flow of electrons as soon as the circuit is completed.

Insulators are a different kind of material in which charges are not able to move freely. **The electrons in an insulator are bound tightly to their atoms and do not flow easily.** Examples of insulators are rubber, glass, sand, plastic, and wood.

✓ Checkpoint *What moves freely in a conductor?*

Figure 19 Charges behave like the chairs on a ski lift. Charges in all parts of a conducting wire begin to flow at the same time.

EXPLORING Electric Circuits

Electric circuits are all around you. They are so common that you probably don't think about them. An electric circuit has several basic features.

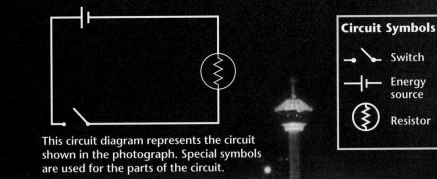

This circuit diagram represents the circuit shown in the photograph. Special symbols are used for the parts of the circuit.

Circuit Symbols

⌐•⌐ Switch

—|⊦— Energy source

Ⓩ Resistor

Battery
A source of electrical energy makes charges move around a circuit.

Resistor
A device such as a light bulb, appliance, or computer converts electrical energy to another form. Such a device is called a resistor.

Switch
A switch is used to open and close the circuit. When the switch is closed, the electric circuit is complete. When the switch is open, the circuit is broken. Charges cannot flow through a broken path.

Chapter 1 **N ♦ 33**

Media and Technology

🖵 **Transparencies** "Exploring Electric Circuits," Transparency 4

💿 **Exploring Physical Science Videodisc**
Unit 5, Side 1, "What Is Electricity?"

Chapter 1

Answers to Self-Assessment

✓ *Checkpoint*
In a conductor, electrons (or charges) move freely.

EXPLORING

Electric Circuits

Encourage students to compare the symbols used in circuit diagrams to the actual items represented. *(For example, the resistor symbol resembles the filament in a light bulb. The switch symbol resembles a knife switch.)* Ask students to describe how the symbols are useful for engineers. *(Sample: Using symbols allows engineers to describe only the parts of the circuit that are important. For example, light bulbs, toasters, and computers have resistors, so they are represented by the same symbol.)*

Extend Have students bring in circuit diagrams of small appliances to review the symbols. **learning modality: visual**

Ongoing Assessment

Oral Presentation Have students give one example of a conductor and one of an insulator and describe the difference between them.

N ♦ 33

Conductors and Insulators, continued

Sharpen your *Skills*

Classifying

Materials *3 10-cm wires with insulation stripped from ends; 2 alligator clips; light bulb; D cell; conductors and insulators to test such as keys, foam, erasers, pencil lead, foil, wax paper, paper clips*

Time 20 minutes

 **Tips** Remove the insulation from the wires. You may want to construct circuits yourself before the activity. Students can then work in groups to test the materials. Students should open the circuits when they are not testing materials to conserve batteries.

Expected Outcome Conductors—metal objects, graphite in pencil lead; insulators—paper, foam, wooden objects. Students will know which materials are conductors because the bulb will light as the circuit is completed. The bulb will not light when insulators are tested.

Extend Ask students to explain why it is important not to use an appliance that has a cord with broken or cracked insulation. *(The rubber around a cord acts as an insulator. If there is no insulation, students may receive electric shocks.)*

Electrical Resistance

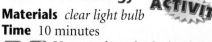
Integrating Technology

Materials *clear light bulb*
Time 10 minutes

Have students look closely at a light bulb and compare it to the one in Figure 20. Emphasize the only way the filament can light is if the bulb is part of a complete circuit so the electrical charge runs through it. Challenge students to identify the points inside and outside the light bulb where the circuit is connected. **learning modality: visual**

Figure 20 Electric current passes through the tungsten filament of a light bulb. As it resists the flow of charge, the filament heats up until it glows.

Sharpen your Skills

Classifying

Gather several objects such as keys, foam, pencil lead, aluminum foil, wax paper, and paper clips. Predict which items will be conductors.

1. Obtain three 10-cm wires with the insulation removed from both ends.

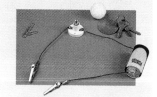

2. Construct a circuit like the one shown. Use the wires, a light bulb, a D cell, and two alligator clips.

3. Insert a test object between the two clips. Observe the light bulb. Repeat the test with each of the other objects.

Which objects are conductors? Which are insulators? How do you know?

Electrical Resistance

As charges flow through a circuit, they pass through resistors. A **resistor** uses electrical energy as it interferes with, or resists, the flow of charge. The opposition to the movement of charges flowing through a material is called **resistance.**

The resistance of a material depends on its atomic structure. Think about walking through a room with people in it. If the people are spread out, you can easily walk through the room without colliding with anyone. But if the people are crowded together, you will bump into people as you move through the room. In a similar way, an electron collides with particles in a material. During each collision, some of the electron's energy is converted to thermal energy (felt as heat) or electromagnetic energy (seen as light). The more collisions, the more electrical energy is converted.

The Light Bulb Thomas Edison used resistance when he was developing his electric light bulb. Edison experimented with many materials. He needed one that would conduct electric current, but would offer enough resistance to make the material heat up and glow. Edison tried cotton threads, copper wires, silk fibers, shredded corn husks, and even human hair, before he settled on charcoal made from bamboo slivers. Eventually, bamboo was replaced with wire made from tungsten. Tungsten is a metal that can get hot enough to glow without melting.

Background

History of Science In his effort to produce an electric light, Edison filled over 40,000 pages with notes. His goal was to produce an incandescent lamp by using electricity to heat material in a vacuum until it produced light. In October, 1879, Edison watched the first incandescent light bulb burn for 40 hours—the first commercially practical incandescent light bulb.

From 1876 to 1886, Edison devoted his life to invention. His major inventions include the phonograph, the motion-picture projector, celluloid film, the carbon telephone transmitter, a stock ticker, and the alkaline storage battery. When Edison died in 1931, he had patented 1,093 inventions.

Figure 21 The magnetic field of the superconductor repels the magnetic cube. Thus the cube floats above the superconductor, much like the maglev train in Section 1.

Superconductors Scientists have discovered that some materials become superconductors at very low temperatures. A **superconductor** is a material that has no electrical resistance. A superconductor is very different from an ordinary conductor. Without resistance, a current flows through a superconductor with no loss of energy. Using superconducting wires would reduce wasted electrical energy and make electrical devices more efficient. Superconductors strongly repel magnets, as you can see in Figure 21. But their use as magnets is limited. A strong magnetic field destroys the superconductivity of a substance, turning it back into an ordinary conductor!

The greatest problem with superconductors is that very low temperatures are required. However, new materials have been found that become superconducting at higher temperatures. At the present time, researchers are working to making superconductors practical.

Section 3 Review

1. Are electricity and magnetism related? Explain.
2. What is the difference between a conductor and an insulator? Give an example of each.
3. What is an electric circuit?
4. **Thinking Critically Relating Cause and Effect** Why does a compass needle move when placed near a wire carrying an electric current? What do you think happens to the compass needle when the circuit is shut off?

Check Your Progress
CHAPTER PROJECT 1

Construct an electric circuit for your fishing rod with a D cell and a piece of insulated wire about 12 meters long. Your fishing rod will need a switch. Making a switch is a matter of closing a circuit. One way to do this is to tape one end of your wire to one end of the battery and then to touch the other end of the wire to the other end of the battery. Think of a less awkward way of controlling the fishing rod.

Program Resources

- **Science Explorer Series** *Sound and Light,* Chapter 3, compares different sources of visible light, incandescent bulbs, fluorescent, neon, mercury, sodium, halogen, etc.
- **Teaching Resources** 1-3 Review and Reinforce, p. 23; 1-3 Enrich, p. 24

Media and Technology

Interactive Student Tutorial CD-ROM N-1

Including All Students

Students who need additional challenges may want to research applications of superconductors. Tell students that the special magnetic properties of superconductors allow them to be used in many scientific applications.
learning modality: verbal

3 Assess

Section 3 Review Answers

1. Yes; an electric current in a wire creates a magnetic field.
2. A conductor allows charge to flow through it. Examples are copper and other metals. An insulator does not allow charge to pass through easily. Examples are paper, wood, plastic.
3. An electric circuit is a complete path through which electric charges can flow.
4. The electric current sets up a magnetic field that is much stronger than Earth's magnetic field. When the circuit is shut off, the compass will point toward Earth's magnetic north pole.

Check Your Progress
CHAPTER PROJECT 1

Provide materials for students to experiment with different designs for switches. Encourage students to keep design logs with sketches of each switch they try and detailed notes of how well it works. Students should plan how their circuits will be attached to their fishing rods.

Performance Assessment

Skills Check Have students work in small groups to design electric circuits that light bulbs with power from a battery. Students should diagram their circuits and label the energy source, conductor, switch, and resistor.

Portfolio Students can save their designs in their portfolios.

How It Works

Build a Flashlight

Preparing for Inquiry

Key Concept In order for bulbs to light, they must be part of a complete current. The bulb must be connected so that the current travels through the filament.

Skills Objectives Students will be able to
◆ make model flashlights that include a complete electric circuit;
◆ predict the arrangement of circuit components that will function as the best flashlight circuit;
◆ design a better switch.

Time 40 minutes

Advance Planning Have students collect and bring in cardboard tubes from paper towels and/or bathroom tissue. Have several different types of commercial flashlights available for students to examine.

Alternative Materials Provide aluminum foil baking cups instead of having students make their own reflectors.

Guiding Inquiry

Invitation Ask students if they have ever had an experience when the flashlight they were using failed. Have volunteers describe what they did to make the flashlight work again. (*Samples: Unscrewed the cap and put it back on, took out the batteries and put them back in, removed the cap and cleaned the connections, replaced the bulb or batteries.*) Have a class discussion about how these repairs relate to the structure of an electric circuit.

Introducing the Procedure

Have students examine the photo of the students working on the flashlight. Make sure students can identify all the components needed to construct a complete circuit.

Troubleshooting the Experiment

◆ If the bulb does not light, check to see that connections are making firm contact. Test the bulb to be certain it is not burned out. Test the battery to make sure it can light the bulb.

BUILD A FLASHLIGHT

Imagine that you are camping in a forest. You hear noises outside your tent; something is rustling and bumping around nearby. At this moment, there is one device you might *really* appreciate having—a flashlight. Have you ever examined one to determine how it works?

Problem

How can you build a flashlight that works?

Skills Focus

making models, observing, inferring

Materials

one cardboard tube	one D cell
flashlight bulb	aluminum foil
paper cup	duct tape
scissors	

2 lengths of wire, about 10 cm, with the insulation stripped off about 2 cm at each end
1 length of wire, 15–20 cm, with the insulation stripped off each end

Procedure

1. Check that the D cell fits inside the cardboard tube. Make two holes in the side of the tube about 2–3 cm apart. The holes should be near the middle of the tube.
2. Use duct tape to connect a 10-cm wire to each terminal of the battery. Touch the other ends of the wires to a flashlight bulb in order to find where to connect them. (*Hint:* Most bulbs have a bottom contact and a side contact. If there is no obvious side contact, try touching the metal on the side of the base.)
3. Line a paper cup with aluminum foil. Use a pencil to poke a hole in the bottom of the paper cup. The hole should be slightly smaller than the bulb, but large enough to allow the base of the bulb through.
4. Insert the base of the light bulb through the hole. Be sure the bulb fits securely.
5. Pass the long wire through one of the holes in the tube. Tape it to the inside of the tube, leaving about 2 cm outside the tube. The other end should reach the end of the tube.
6. Place the battery in the tube. Pass the wire attached to the bottom of the battery through the other hole in the tube. (Make sure the two wires outside the tube can touch.)
7. Make a sling from duct tape to hold the battery inside the tube.

◆ Students may find it easier to construct the flashlight if they cut the tube open lengthwise on the side opposite the two wire holes. This will help them see the relative positioning of the various components. This may also help in fitting the battery in the tube.

Analyze and Conclude

1. The aluminum foil is the reflector for this flashlight. It reflects some of the light forward for better illumination.

2. No. The orientation of the battery affects only the direction of the current. The bulb will light if current is flowing in either direction.
3. The circuit must include the bulb filament, so the bulb must be connected at both contact points.
4. To make a brighter bulb, add more batteries or use a different type of bulb. To make the flashlight stronger, use a plastic or metal case, or wrap something around the cardboard for more strength.

8. Attach the wires from the end of the tube to the contact points on the bulb.
9. Tape the cup on top of the tube, keeping all connections tight.
10. Touch the two free ends of the wires together to see if the bulb lights. If it doesn't, check to be sure all connections are taped together securely.

Analyze and Conclude

1. What is the purpose of lining the cup with aluminum foil?
2. Does it matter which way the battery is placed in the tube? Explain.
3. Why does the bulb have to be connected at two points in order for it to light?
4. How could you make your flashlight brighter? How could you make it more rugged?

5. Compare your flashlight to a manufactured one. Explain the differences.
6. **Apply** Design a more convenient switch for your flashlight. You may want to use materials such as paper clips, brass fasteners, or aluminum foil. Have your teacher approve your switch design and then build and test the switch.

Getting Involved

People use different types of flashlights for different purposes. Some are narrow and flexible while others are wide and sturdy. Compare several different flashlights. Describe the flashlights. Note the type and number of batteries required, the type of switch used, and any other features that you observe. Suggest useful applications for each flashlight. Then design a new flashlight based on a need that you observe.

5. In the commercial flashlight, there is a permanent switch that is easy to operate; the case is plastic or metal; the bulb can be easily removed and replaced. Commercial flashlights must be durable and reliable, and operate in a variety of situations.
6. Students' designs should have a convenient way to make contact between the two free ends of the wires coming out of the tube. Make sure they do not close the circuit for more than a few seconds to avoid overheating.

Extending the Inquiry

Getting Involved Ask students to describe situations in which people rely on flashlights. *(Sample: Camping trips, power outages, emergencies)* Show them a variety of flashlights (disposable, common hand-held, camping lantern). Ask students to compare and contrast the flashlights by observing them closely and carefully. Encourage students to determine which flashlights would be best for each situation. Students should use what they learn in this discussion to design a flashlight for a specific purpose.

Program Resources

◆ **Teaching Resources** Chapter 1 Real-World Lab, pp. 32–33

Objective

After completing the lesson, students will be able to
- identify characteristics and cite uses of an electromagnet.

Key Terms solenoid, electromagnet

1 Engage/Explore

Activating Prior Knowledge

Remind students that magnetic fields occur around moving charges, such as those in a current-carrying wire. Ask students to brainstorm a list of machines or appliances that generate magnetic fields. (*Samples: junkyard cranes, televisions*) Challenge students to think of some ways that the relationship between electricity and magnetism could be useful.

Skills Focus forming operational definitions
Materials *1 m bell wire or magnet wire, iron nail, D cell, paper clips*
Time 20 minutes
Tips Use wire with very thin enamel insulation so that a large number of turns fit easily in a compact space around the nail. Caution students not to close the circuit for too long. If the wire becomes hot, it will magnetize the nail and attract paper clips when the current is turned off.
Expected Outcome The device will attract paper clips when the circuit is complete, but not when the circuit is open.
Think It Over Like a bar magnet—attracts paper clips; unlike a bar magnet—magnetism can be "switched off." Definition of electromagnet—magnet that can be turned on and off because an electric current is used to create the magnetic field.

DISCOVER · ACTIVITY

How Do You Turn a Magnet On and Off?

1. Wind one meter of wire tightly around an iron nail so that you have at least 25 turns. Leave about 15 centimeters of wire on each end.
2. Attach one end of the wire to one terminal of a D cell.
3. Briefly touch the other end of the wire to the other terminal of the D cell. **CAUTION:** *Do not leave the switch closed for more than two or three seconds at a time. The wire will heat up.*
4. With the circuit complete, bring a paper clip near the nail.
5. Add paper clips one at a time and repeat Steps 3 and 4.

Think It Over
Forming Operational Definitions The device you constructed is called an electromagnet. How does it compare with a bar magnet? Based on your observations, define "electromagnet."

GUIDE FOR READING

- What are the characteristics of an electromagnet?

Reading Tip Before you read, preview the illustrations. Write down any questions you have about the illustrations. Answer them as you read the section.

You learned in Section 3 that a current in a wire creates a magnetic field around the wire. By turning the current on and off, you can turn the magnetic field on and off. So by using an electric current to create a magnet, you produce a magnetic field that you can control.

Solenoids

The magnetic field around a current-carrying wire forms a cylinder around the wire. If the wire is twisted into a loop, the magnetic field lines become bunched up inside the loop. You can see this by looking at the iron filings in Figure 22. The strength of the

Figure 22 The magnetic field around a loop of wire bunches up in the center.

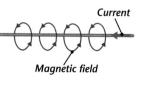

Current

Magnetic field

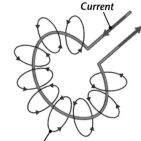

Current

Magnetic field

READING STRATEGIES

Reading Tip As students preview the illustrations, have them write descriptions of the pictures as if they were describing them to someone who had not seen them. After students read the section, have them rewrite the descriptions to add information they learned from their reading.

Study and Comprehension After students read the section, have them close their textbooks. Write the headings

Solenoids, Multiplying Magnetism, Increasing the Strength of an Electromagnet, and *Recording Information* on the board. Instruct students to copy the headings on a sheet of paper and write as much key information as they can recall under each heading. Then have students open their books and add any additional main ideas and important details. Students can use their papers as study guides.

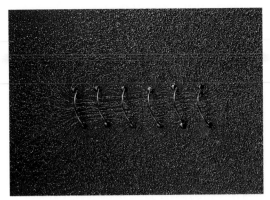

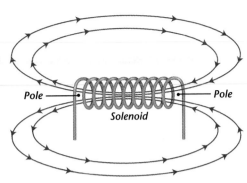

Pole — Solenoid — Pole

Figure 23 The magnetic field around a solenoid resembles that of a bar magnet. *Comparing and Contrasting How is a solenoid different from a bar magnet?*

magnetic field increases as the number of loops is increased. If the wire is bent into a second loop, the concentration of magnetic field lines within the loop is twice as great.

By winding a current-carrying wire into a coil you have strengthened the magnetic field in the center of the coil. The two ends of the coil act like poles. The iron filings around the loops of wire in Figure 23 line up much as they would around a bar magnet. A current-carrying coil of wire with many loops is called a **solenoid.** A solenoid creates a magnetic field that can be turned on and off by switching the current on and off. The north and south poles change with the direction of the current.

Multiplying Magnetism

If a ferromagnetic material such as iron is placed inside a solenoid, the magnetic field is increased. Recall how a ferromagnetic material acts. When iron is placed within the solenoid's magnetic field, it becomes a magnet as well. A solenoid with a ferromagnetic core is called an **electromagnet.** The temporary magnetic field of an electromagnet is produced by the current in the wire and the magnetized core. The overall magnetic field can be hundreds or thousands of times stronger than the magnetic field produced by the current alone. **An electromagnet is a strong magnet that can be turned on and off.**

An electromagnet is ideal for lifting heavy pieces of scrap metal. Have you ever seen stacks of junked cars? The flattened auto bodies are shredded into small metal fragments. The iron and steel fragments are picked up by a huge electromagnet on a crane. When the switch is turned on, current flows and the electromagnet lifts the metallic scrap and the crane moves it. When the switch is turned off, the pieces of scrap fall from the magnet.

☑ *Checkpoint* What is a solenoid?

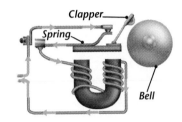

Clapper

Spring

Bell

Figure 24 A solenoid is used to ring an alarm bell. When current flows through the circuit, the coil acts as a magnet. The strip of iron on the spring is attracted to the electromagnet and the clapper strikes the bell. At the same time, the spring opens the circuit and stops the current. The spring returns the clapper to its resting position.

Answers to Self-Assessment

Caption Question

Figure 23 The magnetic field of a solenoid can be turned on and off.

☑ *Checkpoint*

A solenoid is a current-carrying coil of wire with many loops, which can be part of an electromagnet.

2 Facilitate

Solenoids

Building Inquiry Skills: Making Models

Materials *coiled spring toy, long thin rope*
Time 10 minutes

Have students place the rope inside the spring toy so the spring makes a cylinder around the cord, then tie the ends of the rope to the outermost links of the spring toy. Students can bend the cord into a loop and observe what happens to the spring toy. Ask: **How does this model the magnetic field around a current-carrying wire in an electromagnet?** (*The field lines in the electromagnet—coils in the spring toy—bunch up inside a loop in the wire—the current-carrying wire.*) **limited English proficiency**

Multiplying Magnetism

Inquiry Challenge

Materials *wooden dowel, insulated connecting wire, several identical iron nails, 1.5-V battery, iron objects*
Time 20 minutes

Have groups of students construct electromagnets and develop hypotheses on how the addition of iron nails might affect their strength. **cooperative learning**

Increasing the Strength of an Electromagnet

Building Inquiry Skills: Relating Cause and Effect

Ask: **What would happen if you increased the number of coils in a solenoid?** (*The magnetic field of the solenoid would be strengthened.*)
learning modality: logical/ mathematical

Ongoing Assessment

Drawing Have each student draw a diagram of an electromagnet and explain how it works.

N ◆ 39

Recording Information

Integrating Technology

ACTIVITY

Challenge students to work in small groups and make a flowchart showing how the sound of their voice is recorded on audio tape and played back. Once the flowchart is complete, groups can evaluate one another's work. **cooperative learning**

3 Assess

Section 4 Review Answers

1. Sample: An electromagnet is a coil of current-carrying wire that acts as a magnet when the current is turned on.
2. An electromagnet can be turned on and off; its strength can be increased by adding loops of coil, using more current, or using a different core.
3. Electromagnets are used in doorbells, video and audio recording equipment, and in scrap metal separators.
4. Yes. A strong magnet will alter the magnetic pattern in the metal powder on the tape.

Check Your Progress

CHAPTER PROJECT 1

Make sure students know how to connect the electromagnets to the circuits. To make testing easier, encourage students to create two or three different solenoid coils of 100, 175, and 250 turns, and test them all. Remind students to keep the switch open unless they are making direct observations. Students should make several trials with each electromagnet.

Performance Assessment

Writing Ask students to design an electromagnet for a specific purpose. Students should describe how the electromagnet works and name one way it can be strengthened.

Portfolio Students can save their designs in their portfolios.

Increasing the Strength of An Electromagnet

There are a number of ways you can increase the strength of an electromagnet's field. You can increase the current in the solenoid. You can add more loops of wire to the solenoid. You can wind the coils of the solenoid closer together. Also, you can increase the strength of an electromagnet by using a stronger ferromagnetic material for the core.

Recording Information

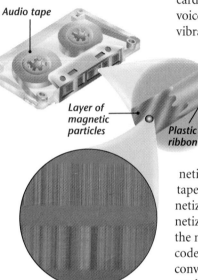

Figure 25 A micrograph shows a pattern of magnetic domains on a cassette tape.

Audio tape

Layer of magnetic particles

Plastic ribbon

Magnified photograph of tape

INTEGRATING TECHNOLOGY When you record information on audio tapes, videotapes, computer disks, or credit cards, you are using electromagnets. Think about recording your voice with a tape recorder. When you talk into a microphone, the vibrations of your voice are changed into an electric current that varies with your voice. That current is used in an electromagnet in the recording head of the tape recorder to produce a magnetic field. Since the current changes, the magnetic field of the electromagnet changes as well.

A recording tape consists of a plastic ribbon coated with a thin layer of metal powder. The metal particles of the powder are magnetized by the magnetic field of the electromagnet in the recording head. As the tape moves past the electromagnet, the metal particles are magnetized more or less by the electromagnet. The strength of magnetization of the particles changes with the changing strength of the magnetic field. The magnetic pattern in the tape becomes a code for your voice. When you play the tape back, the code is converted back into sound. In a similar way, electromagnets are used to record images and sounds on videotape and all sorts of information on computer disks.

Section 4 Review

1. Describe an electromagnet in your own words.
2. How is an electromagnet different from a permanent magnet?
3. What are some uses for electromagnets?
4. **Thinking Critically Predicting** Will bringing a strong magnet near a computer or video tape cause damage to the recording? Explain your answer.

Check Your Progress

CHAPTER PROJECT 1

Construct an electromagnet by wrapping a length of insulated wire around one or more iron nails. Attach the ends of the wire to the circuit containing your switch. Test your electromagnet by dipping it into a pile of paper clips to see how many it can pick up at one time. Experiment with the strength of your electromagnet by changing one variable at a time.

Background

Integrating Science Magnetic Resonance Imaging (MRI) uses powerful electromagnets. The magnetic fields needed for this procedure are so strong that people in the room cannot wear magnetic materials such as jewelry, pens, and watches. These materials would be attracted to the huge electromagnet and fly across the room at dangerous velocities.

Program Resources

◆ **Teaching Resources** 1-4 Review and Reinforce, p. 27; 1-4 Enrich, p. 28
◆ **Integrated Science Laboratory Manual** N-1, "Electromagnetism"

Media and Technology

Interactive Student Tutorial CD-ROM N-1

SECTION 1 The Nature of Magnetism

Key Ideas

◆ Unlike magnetic poles attract; like magnetic poles repel.
◆ A magnetic field is a region around a magnet in which magnetic attraction acts.
◆ Magnetic domains are regions in which the magnetic fields of atoms are aligned.
◆ For an object to be magnetic, most of its domains must line up in the same direction.

Key Terms

magnetism	nucleus
magnetic poles	protons
magnetic field	electrons
magnetic field lines	magnetic domain
atom	ferromagnetic material
element	permanent magnet

SECTION 2 Magnetic Earth

INTEGRATING EARTH SCIENCE

Key Ideas

◆ Earth has a north magnetic pole and a south magnetic pole.
◆ A compass can be used to find directions because its needle lines up with Earth's magnetic poles.
◆ Earth's magnetic poles are not at exactly the same locations as the geographic poles.
◆ The magnetosphere is the magnetic field of Earth as shaped by the solar wind.

Key Terms

compass	solar wind
magnetic declination	magnetosphere
Van Allen belts	aurora

SECTION 3 Electric Current and Magnetic Fields

Key Ideas

◆ Electric current is electric charge in motion.
◆ An electric current produces a magnetic field.
◆ An electric current flows through a continuous loop known as a circuit.
◆ Electric charges flow freely through materials called conductors. Charges do not flow freely through insulators.
◆ Resistance is the opposition to the movement of charges flowing through a material.

Key Terms

electric charge	insulators
electric current	resistor
electric circuit	resistance
conductors	superconductor

SECTION 4 Electromagnets

Key Ideas

◆ A solenoid creates a magnetic field by means of a current flowing through a coil of wire.
◆ An electromagnet is a solenoid with an iron core.
◆ The factors that determine the strength of an electromagnet are the amount of current, the number of turns of wire in the coil, how close together the turns of wire are, and the type of magnetic core.

Key Terms

solenoid	electromagnet

USING THE INTERNET ACTIVITY

www.science-explorer.phschool.com

Program Resources

◆ **Teaching Resources** Chapter 1 Project Scoring Rubric, p. 12; Chapter 1 Performance Assessment Teacher Notes, pp. 130–131; Chapter 1 Performance Assessment Student Worksheet, p. 132; Chapter 1 Test, pp. 133–136

Review Content:

Multiple Choice

1. c 2. d 3. c 4. d 5. b

True or False

6. true 7. magnetite, or lodestone
8. magnetic 9. electric charge, or current 10. true

Checking Concepts

11. In a magnetic material, the domains (which act as tiny magnets) are aligned. In the middle of the magnet, north and south poles balance each other, but the ends of a magnet are unpaired poles. Diagrams should show that a magnet broken in half will have a north and south pole.

12. A material becomes a magnet when the domains of the material are turned to point in the same direction.

13. Earth acts like a magnet because it produces a magnetic field and has magnetic poles.

14. An aurora is a region of bright colored light produced by the interaction of particles from the solar wind and particles in Earth's atmosphere. Most of the solar wind is deflected by Earth's magnetic field, but some particles penetrate the field and enter Earth's atmosphere near the poles, where the magnetic forces are strongest.

15. Charges, or current, flowing through a wire set up a magnetic field that is stronger than Earth's magnetic field.

16. Electric charges move easily through conductors. Insulators do not allow electric charges to pass through them easily. Graphite and most metals are good conductors. Wood, plastic, and rubber are good insulators.

17. Students' drawings should show an electric circuit with a source of electrical energy and a device that is run by electrical energy, connected by connecting wires and a switch.

18. Sample: Magnets in your clothes could be attracted to electromagnets in your laundry hamper, so your clothes would pick themselves up. Students should mention whether their device depends on like poles repelling or unlike poles attracting one another. When they use an electromagnet, they should

---

Reviewing Content

For more review of key concepts, see the Interactive Student Tutorial CD-ROM.

Multiple Choice

Choose the letter of the answer that best completes each statement.

1. The region in which magnetic forces act is called a
   a. line of force.
   b. pole.
   c. magnetic field.
   d. field of attraction.

2. An example of a ferromagnetic material is
   a. plastic.
   b. wood.
   c. copper.
   d. iron.

3. The person who first suggested that Earth behaves as a magnet was
   a. Ampère.
   b. Oersted.
   c. Gilbert.
   d. Columbus.

4. The region in which Earth's magnetic field is found is called the
   a. atmosphere.
   b. stratosphere.
   c. aurora.
   d. magnetosphere.

5. A coil of current-carrying wire with an iron core is called a(an)
   a. ferromagnet.
   b. electromagnet.
   c. compass.
   d. maglev.

True or False

If the statement is true, write true. If it is false, change the underlined word or words to make the statement true.

6. Like poles of magnets <u>repel</u> each other.

7. The type of magnetic mineral found in nature is called <u>platinum</u>.

8. A compass needle points in the direction of Earth's <u>geographic</u> north pole.

9. An electric circuit is a complete path through which <u>domains</u> can flow.

10. You can <u>increase</u> the strength of an electromagnet by adding more turns of a wire to it.

Checking Concepts

11. Explain why you are not left with one north pole and one south pole if you break a magnet in half. Draw a diagram to support your answer.

12. How does a material become a magnet?

13. How does Earth act like a magnet?

14. What is an aurora? How is it produced?

15. Why does a compass needle change direction when it is placed near a current-carrying wire?

16. How is a conductor different from an insulator? Give two examples of each.

17. Draw a simple electric circuit. Label and define the basic parts.

18. Writing to Learn Did you ever think of a chore that would be much easier if you only had some futuristic device? Here's your chance. Describe a task that you would like to make easier. Then think about how you could use an electromagnet to carry out the task. Be creative in describing your design.

Thinking Visually

19. Concept Map Copy the concept map about magnetism onto a separate sheet of paper. Then complete it and add a title. (For more on concept maps, see the Skills Handbook.)

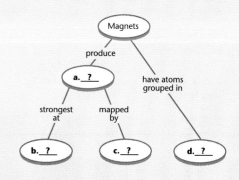

---

describe the source of electric current. Although it is important that the idea utilize the properties of magnets, devices do not have to be realistic.

Thinking Visually

19. Sample title: Magnetism; **a.** Magnetic fields **b.** The poles **c.** Magnetic field lines **d.** Domains

Applying Skills

20. B produces a stronger magnetic field than A because it has a core. B produces a stronger magnetic field than C because there are more turns of wire.

21. D is the strongest due to the number of turns and the core.

22. Experiments could involve changing the size of the core or adding a stronger battery.

Applying Skills

Use the illustration of four electromagnets to answer Questions 20–22.

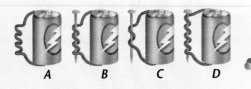

A   B   C   D

20. **Predicting** Will device A or B produce a stronger magnetic field? Will device B or C produce a stronger magnetic field? Explain your choices.
21. **Controling Variables** Can you tell which electromagnet is the strongest of the four? Explain why or why not.
22. **Designing Experiments** Without changing the number of turns of wire, how could you change the strength of each electromagnet?

Thinking Critically

23. **Problem Solving** Cassia borrowed her brother's magnet. When she returned it, it was barely magnetic. What might Cassia have done to the magnet?
24. **Comparing and Contrasting** What is the difference between a magnetized iron bar and an unmagnetized one?
25. **Drawing Conclusions** Why might an inexperienced explorer get lost using a compass?
26. **Relating Cause and Effect** Why does opening a switch in an electric circuit stop the flow of current?
27. **Applying Concepts** How are the uses of an electromagnet different from those of a permanent bar magnet?
28. **Inferring** A compass points north until a bar magnet is brought next to it. The compass needle is then attracted or repelled by the magnet. What inference can you make about the strengths of the magnetic fields of Earth and the bar magnet?

depends on the geographic location.
26. Only with a closed switch will a circuit have a complete path for current to flow.
27. Electromagnets can be turned on and off and can be very strong, so they are used for applications that require making patterns, such as data storage, or that require lifting and releasing.
28. Although Earth's magnetic field covers a larger area, its local effect is less than that of the bar magnet. So the bar magnet has a stronger field.

Performance Assessment

Present Your Project
Organize the class into groups and allow them to practice using their devices and work cooperatively to improve their designs before the final presentation. Set up plastic containers and allow each student or team to "fish"—lift paper clips out of one container and drop them into another—for one minute. If you wish, add iron nails to the first container. Before students fish, have them describe their designs to the class. Determine whether the success of the design will be measured by how many paper clips the electromagnet can pick up each time, or by how many paper clips are transferred over the entire minute.
Reflect and Record Students should compare their designs with those of other students and determine what combination of features would make the best design.

Performance Assessment

CHAPTER PROJECT 1

Present Your Project Test your final electromagnet. Cut the tops off two empty plastic milk containers. Practice moving paper clips from one container to the other until you are ready for a "fishing" competition. After your teacher gives you a one-minute opportunity to fish, compare the most successful designs in the class.

Reflect and Record In your journal, describe the features of other students' designs that worked well. Which switch designs were easiest to operate? What contributed to making the strongest magnets?

Getting Involved

In Your Neighborhood Describe how to get from your school to three different locations in your neighborhood. You might include such locations as a store, a park, a lake, a movie theater, or a gymnasium. Include locations that require several turns. Your instructions should include compass direction, distances, and landmarks. As you write instructions, explain how to use a compass. Give your map to another student to see if he or she can follow your directions.

Thinking Critically

23. Cassia could have dropped the magnet or exposed it to heat. Either action can jostle the domains out of alignment.
24. The domains in a magnetized iron bar are all arranged in the same direction. The domains in the unmagnetized iron bar are not aligned.
25. The explorer might not know about magnetic declination. If the explorer follows the compass direction exactly, he or she will wind up off course. The amount of declination

Program Resources

◆ **Inquiry Skills Handbook** Provides teaching and review of all inquiry skills

Getting Involved

In Your Neighborhood Conduct a class review on using the compass. Students should be able to specify direction using the angles with respect to magnetic north shown on the compass. Have students practice by giving them a short series of directions between two points in your classroom or school.

Sections	Time	Student Edition Activities	Other Activities	
CHAPTER PROJECT 2 **Cause for Alarm** p. 45	Ongoing (2–3 weeks)	Check Your Progress, pp. 61, 67 Wrap Up, p. 75	TE	Chapter 2 Project Notes, pp. 44–45
1 Electric Charge and Static Electricity pp. 46–55 ◆ Describe the interaction of like and unlike electric charges. ◆ Define and describe static electricity and state how it differs from electric current. ◆ Describe lightning and other forms of static discharge.	5 periods/ 2½ blocks	**Discover** Can You Move a Can Without Touching It?, p. 46 **Sharpen Your Skills** Drawing Conclusions, p. 48 **Try This** Sparks Are Flying, p. 50 **Skills Lab: Developing Hypotheses** The Versorium, pp. 54–55	TE TE TE TE	Demonstration, p. 47 Including All Students, p. 49 Real-Life Learning, p. 50 Building Inquiry Skills: Drawing Conclusions, p. 52
2 Circuit Measurements pp. 56–63 ◆ Explain what causes flow of electric current in terms of electrical potential, potential difference, and voltage. ◆ Describe the relationship between voltage and the flow of electric current. ◆ Define resistance and state how it affects the flow of current. ◆ Calculate resistance using Ohm's law.	4 periods/ 2 blocks	**Discover** How Can Current Be Measured?, p. 56 **Try This** Down the Tubes, p. 59 **Sharpen Your Skills** Calculating, p. 60 **Real-World Lab: How It Works** Constructing a Dimmer Switch, pp. 62–63	TE TE TE ISLM	Building Inquiry Skills: Making Models, p. 57 Inquiry Challenge, p. 58 Demonstration, p. 59 N-2, "Building Electric Circuits"
3 Series and Parallel Circuits pp. 64–67 ◆ Describe and construct a series circuit. ◆ Describe and construct a parallel circuit.	2 periods/ 1 block	**Discover** Do the Lights Keep Shining?, p. 64 **Sharpen Your Skills** Predicting, p. 66	TE TE	Inquiry Challenge, p. 65 Building Inquiry Skills: Inferring, p. 66
4 *INTEGRATING HEALTH* **Electrical Safety** pp. 68-72 ◆ Identify safety devices used to protect people from common electrical hazards. ◆ Describe how a lightning rod protects a building. ◆ Explain how the severity of an electrical shock is related to current, voltage, and resistance.	2½ periods/ 1–2 blocks	**Discover** How Can You Blow a Fuse?, p. 68	TE TE TE TE	Real-Life Learning, p. 69 Including All Students, p. 69 Demonstration, p. 70 Building Inquiry Skills: Comparing and Contrasting, p. 71
Study Guide/Chapter Review pp. 73–75	1 period/ ½ block		ISAB	Provides teaching and review of all inquiry skills

 For Standard or Block Schedule The Resource Pro® CD-ROM gives you maximum flexibility for planning your instruction for any type of schedule. Resource Pro® contains Planning Express®, an advanced scheduling program, as well as the entire contents of the Teaching Resources and the Computer Test Bank.

CHAPTER PLANNING GUIDE

Program Resources	Assessment Strategies	Media and Technology
TR Chapter 2 Project Teacher Notes, pp. 34–35 TR Chapter 2 Project Overview and Worksheets, pp. 36–39 TR Chapter 2 Project Scoring Rubric, p. 40	SE Performance Assessment: Chapter 2 Project Wrap Up, p. 75 TE Check Your Progress, pp. 61, 67 TE Performance Assessment: Chapter 2 Project Wrap Up, p. 75 TR Chapter 2 Project Scoring Rubric, p. 40	Science Explorer Internet Site
TR 2-1 Lesson Plan, p. 41 TR 2-1 Section Summary, p. 42 TR 2-1 Review and Reinforce, p. 43 TR 2-1 Enrich, p. 44 TR Chapter 2 Skills Lab, pp. 57–59	SE Section 1 Review, p. 53 SE Analyze and Conclude, p. 55 TE Ongoing Assessment, pp. 47, 49, 51 TE Performance Assessment, p. 53 TR 2-1 Review and Reinforce, p. 43	Audiotapes: English-Spanish Summary 2-1 Transparency 7, "Electric Fields" Transparency 8, "Exploring Static Electricity" Transparency 9, "Electroscope" Interactive Student Tutorial CD-ROM, N-2
TR 2-2 Lesson Plan, p. 45 TR 2-2 Section Summary, p. 46 TR 2-2 Review and Reinforce, p. 47 TR 2-2 Enrich, p. 48 TR Chapter 2 Real-World Lab, pp. 60–61	SE Section 2 Review, p. 61 SE Analyze and Conclude, p. 63 TE Ongoing Assessment, pp. 57, 59 TE Performance Assessment, p. 61 TR 2-2 Review and Reinforce, p. 47	Exploring Physical Science Videodisc, Unit 5 Side 1, "What Is Electricity?" Audiotapes: English-Spanish Summary 2-2 Interactive Student Tutorial CD-ROM, N-2
TR 2-3 Lesson Plan, p. 49 TR 2-3 Section Summary, p. 50 TR 2-3 Review and Reinforce, p. 51 TR 2-3 Enrich, p. 52	SE Section 3 Review, p. 67 TE Ongoing Assessment, p. 65 TE Performance Assessment, p. 67 TR 2-3 Review and Reinforce, p. 51	Audiotapes: English-Spanish Summary 2-3 Transparency 10, "Series and Parallel Circuits" Transparency 11, "Household Circuits" Interactive Student Tutorial CD-ROM, N-2
TR 2-4 Lesson Plan, p. 53 TR 2-4 Section Summary, p. 54 TR 2-4 Review and Reinforce, p. 55 TR 2-4 Enrich, p. 56 SES Book D, *Human Biology and Health,* Chapter 1	SE Section 4 Review, p. 72 TE Ongoing Assessment, pp. 69, 71 TE Performance Assessment, p. 72 TR 2-4 Review and Reinforce, p. 55	Exploring Physical Science Videodisc, Unit 5 Side 1, "Electric Bodies" Exploring Physical Science Videodisc, Unit 5 Side 1, "Lightning Strikes" Audiotapes: English-Spanish Summary 2-4 Interactive Student Tutorial CD-ROM, N-2
TR Chapter 2 Performance Assessment, pp. 137–139 TR Chapter 2 Test, pp. 140–143	SE Chapter Review, pp. 73–75 TR Chapter 2 Performance Assessment, pp. 137–139 TR Chapter 2 Test, pp. 140–143 CTB Test N-2	Computer Test Bank, Test N-2 Interactive Student Tutorial CD-ROM, N-2

Key: **SE** Student Edition   **TE** Teacher's Edition   **TR** Teaching Resources
CTB Computer Test Bank   **SES** Science Explorer Series Text   **ISLM** Integrated Science Laboratory Manual
ISAB Inquiry Skills Activity Book   **PTA** Product Testing Activities by *Consumer Reports*   **IES** Interdisciplinary Explorations Series

Meeting the National Science Education Standards and AAAS Benchmarks

National Science Education Standards	Benchmarks for Science Literacy	Unifying Themes

Physical Science (Content Standard B)

◆ **Transfer of energy** Static electricity can be transferred through friction, conduction, and induction. *(Section 1)* Electrical circuits conduct electric current when a potential difference allows current to flow. *(Sections 2, 3; Chapter Project; Real-World Lab)*

Life Science (Content Standard C)

◆ **Structure and function in living systems** Various structures, such as the heart and nervous system, rely on electrical charges to function; electric shock can damage these systems. *(Section 4)*

Science and Technology (Content Standard E)

◆ **Design a solution or a product** Students design an alarm circuit and a dimmer switch. *(Chapter Project; Real-World Lab)*

Science in Personal and Social Perspectives (Content Standard F)

◆ **Natural hazards** Lightning strikes are caused by a massive discharge of static electricity. To reduce the risk of being struck by lightning, avoid water and lie low if outside during a storm. *(Sections 1, 4)*

History and Nature of Science (Content Standard G)

◆ **History of Science** Benjamin Franklin contributed to our understanding of electricity in addition to his many other endeavors. *(Section 4)*

1B Scientific Inquiry Students control variables as they construct a versorium and design a dimmer switch. *(Skills Lab; Real-World Lab)*

2C Mathematical Inquiry Students use Ohm's law to determine the relationship among resistance, current, and voltage. *(Section 2)*

3B Design and Systems Students use their understanding of currents and electricity to create an alarm circuit and a dimmer switch. *(Chapter Project; Real-World Lab)*

4E Energy Transformation Electrical charges cannot be created or destroyed, but only transferred from one object to another. *(Section 1)* Electrical energy is the attraction of opposite charges and the repulsion of like charges. Electrons flow according to the potential difference between parts of a circuit. In a circuit, electrons flow from a voltage source through wire and resistors. *(Sections 1, 2, 3; Chapter Project; Skills Lab)*

8C Energy Sources and Use Electrical energy flows from a voltage source. *(Section 2)* Circuit breakers and fuses are used to protect circuits in which current becomes too high. *(Section 4)*

11A Systems Current increases when resistors are added to a parallel circuit and decreases when resistors are added to a series circuit. *(Section 3)*

◆ **Energy** Electricity is a form of energy caused by the flow of electrons. Interactions between electric fields can cause electrons to flow. Voltage, resistance, and current are measurements of electrical energy. In the human body, energy from a high current can disrupt normal electrical activity. *(Sections 1, 2, 4; Chapter Project; Skills Lab; Real-World Lab)*

◆ **Systems and Interactions** Electrons flow from an area of high potential energy to an area of lower potential energy. Electrons in a series circuit stop flowing when any part of the circuit is broken; electrons in a parallel circuit continue flowing through remaining paths when a single path is broken. *(Sections 1, 3; Chapter Project; Skills Lab, Real-World Lab)*

Media and Technology

Exploring Physical Science Videodisc

◆ **Section 2** "What Is Electricity?" introduces electricity and explains its atomic structure by modeling electrical charges.

◆ **Section 4** "Electric Bodies" describes how electricity plays an important role in the functioning of parts of the body.

◆ **Section 4** "Lighting Strikes" features Ben Franklin who introduces the viewer to lighting and explains its characteristics. Important safety tips are also included.

Interactive Student Tutorial CD-ROM

◆ **Chapter Review** Interactive questions help students to self-assess their mastery of key chapter concepts.

Student Edition Connection Strategies

◆ **Section 4 Integrating Health,** p. 68
Social Studies Connection, p. 70

USING THE INTERNET

www.science-explorer.phschool.com

Visit the Science Explorer Internet site to find an up-to-date activity for Chapter 2 of *Electricity and Magnetism.*

ACTIVITY	**Time** (minutes)	**Materials** Quantities for one work group	**Skills**
Section 1			
Discover, p. 46	10	**Consumable** balloon **Nonconsumable** empty aluminum can	Inferring
Sharpen Your Skills, p. 48	10	**Consumable** tissue paper **Nonconsumable** hole punch, plastic comb	Drawing Conclusions
Try This, p. 50	10	**Consumable** 2 foam plates, tape **Nonconsumable** scissors, aluminum pie plate	Inferring
Skills Lab, pp. 54–55	30	**Consumable** foam cup, aluminum foil, paper **Nonconsumable** plastic foam plate, pencil, wool fabric, scissors	Developing Hypotheses
Section 2			
Discover, p. 56	25	**Consumable** electrical tape **Nonconsumable** 1 meter bell wire, wire cutters and strippers, metric ruler, magnetic compass, two 1.5-volt bulbs and sockets, D cell and holder, modeling clay	Inferring
Try This, p. 59	15	**Consumable** water **Nonconsumable** two 200-mL beakers, funnel, ring stand, clear tubing of various lengths and widths, stopwatch	Making Models
Sharpen Your Skills, p. 60	15	**Consumable** No special materials are required.	Calculating
Real-World Lab, pp. 62–63	30	**Consumable** thick lead from mechanical pencil **Nonconsumable** flashlight bulb in socket; D cell; uninsulated copper wire, the same length as the pencil lead; rubber tubing, the same length as the pencil lead; 1 wire 10–15 cm long; 2 wires 20–30 cm long, with alligator clip attached to one end	Observing, Predicting, Designing Experiments
Section 3			
Discover, p. 64	15	**Nonconsumable** 4 light bulbs with sockets, 2 dry cells with holders, several lengths of insulated wire	Observing
Sharpen Your Skills, p. 66	20	**Nonconsumable** dry cell, 3 light bulbs, insulated wire, switch	Predicting
Section 4			
Discover, p. 68	15	**Nonconsumable** dry cell, light bulb, 2 alligator clips, very fine steel wool (00 or 000 grade)	Developing Hypotheses

A list of all materials required for the Student Edition activities can be found on pages T14–T15. You can order Materials Kits by calling 1-800-828-7777 or by accessing the Science Explorer Internet site at **www.science-explorer.phschool.com.**

Cause for Alarm

For students who have difficulty learning technical concepts, the chance to build an alarm will provide a fun and firsthand look at electric charges and parallel and series circuits.

Purpose In this project, students will have the opportunity to design and construct an alarm circuit that will be triggered by an outside event.

Skills Focus After completing the Chapter 2 Project, students will be able to
◆ apply concepts related to electric current;
◆ relate cause and effect to solve problems related to basic circuit design;
◆ design experiments in which they test their circuits;
◆ communicate their findings about circuitry to their classmates.

Project Time Line This project will take approximately two weeks to complete. Students will begin by brainstorming possible events to which their detector switches will respond. Then they will plan their detector switches and draw diagrams of their designs. Once you have approved their plans, they may construct their alarms. The students will then conduct several tests on their circuits, modifying them if necessary. At the conclusion of this project, students will demonstrate their alarms to the class, describing how their circuits work. Before beginning the project, see Chapter 2 Project Teacher Notes on pages 34–35 in Teaching Resources for more details on carrying out the project. Also distribute to students the Chapter 2 Project Overview, Worksheets, and Scoring Rubric on pages 36–40 in Teaching Resources.

Suggested Shortcuts Limit the number of choices students have for events to detect. Students could work in groups to reduce the amount of time required for presentations. Alternatively, you could use a few generic setups consisting of a light bulb or buzzer, one or two dry cells, and about 3 meters of wire. Have individual students connect their detector switches to the wire during the presentation part of the project.

CHAPTER 2 Electric Charges and Current

WHAT'S AHEAD

44 ◆ N

Possible Materials Provide a wide variety of materials from which students can choose, and encourage students to suggest and use other materials as well. Each student will need one or two 1.5-volt dry cells, about 3 meters of insulated wire, and a light bulb. Make sure to select bulbs that require only 1.5 volts for a single battery, or 3 volts for two batteries connected in series. Additionally, students may need aluminum foil, paper clips, screws, washers, nails, metal cans, electrical tape, basins or bowls, water, or salt.

Launching the Project Tape an uninsulated end of a piece of wire to a penny. Connect the other end of the wire to a light bulb. Use another piece of wire to connect the light bulb to a dry cell. Tape the other pole of the dry cell to an empty metal can. Ask the students what will happen if you drop the penny into the can. (*The light will go on.*) Tell them that this device is a Penny Detector; it shows one way that contact can be made between the ends of two wires.

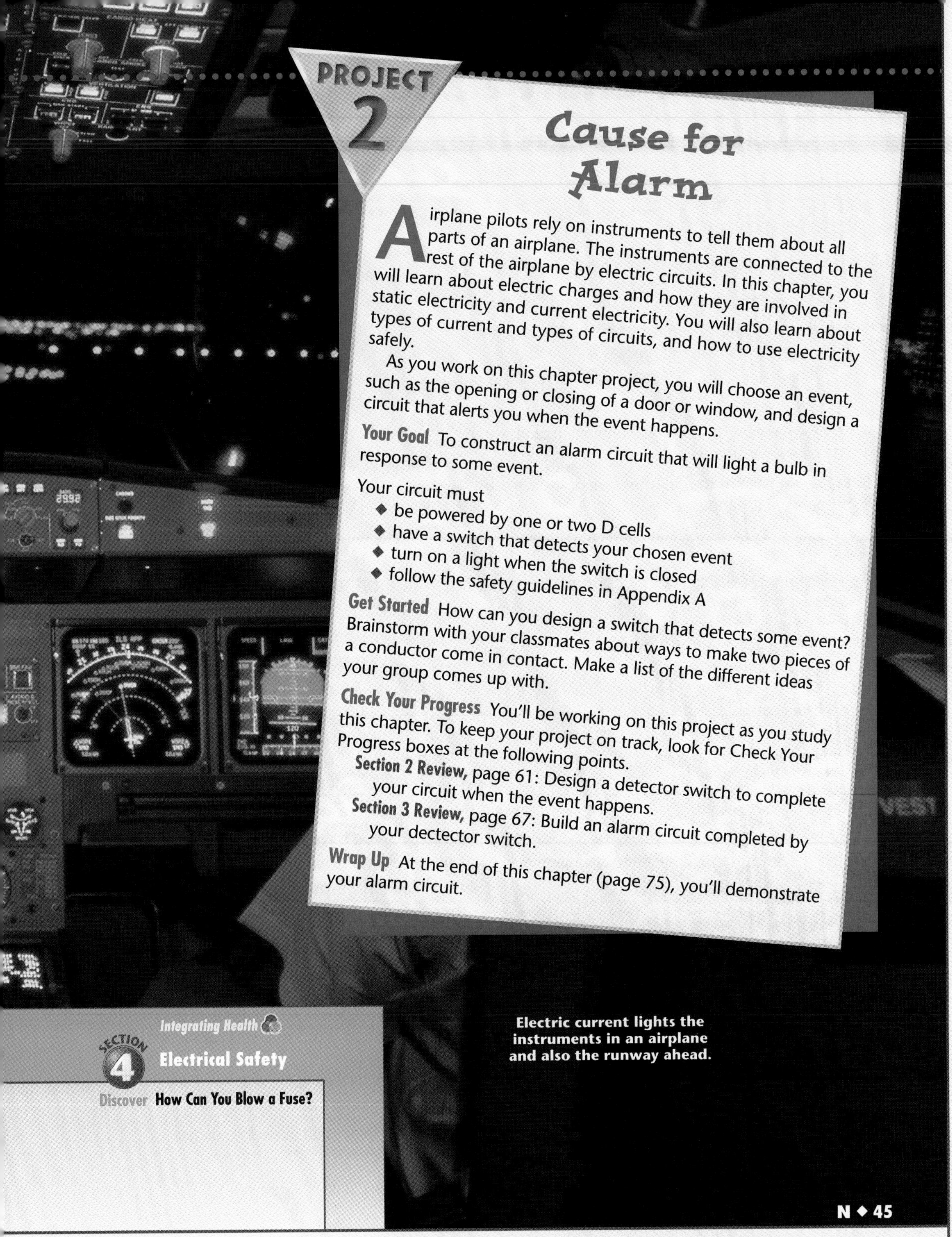

Cause for Alarm

Airplane pilots rely on instruments to tell them about all parts of an airplane. The instruments are connected to the rest of the airplane by electric circuits. In this chapter, you will learn about electric charges and how they are involved in static electricity and current electricity. You will also learn about types of current and types of circuits, and how to use electricity safely.

As you work on this chapter project, you will choose an event, such as the opening or closing of a door or window, and design a circuit that alerts you when the event happens.

Your Goal To construct an alarm circuit that will light a bulb in response to some event.

Your circuit must
- be powered by one or two D cells
- have a switch that detects your chosen event
- turn on a light when the switch is closed
- follow the safety guidelines in Appendix A

Get Started How can you design a switch that detects some event? Brainstorm with your classmates about ways to make two pieces of a conductor come in contact. Make a list of the different ideas your group comes up with.

Check Your Progress You'll be working on this project as you study this chapter. To keep your project on track, look for Check Your Progress boxes at the following points.

Section 2 Review, page 61: Design a detector switch to complete your circuit when the event happens.

Section 3 Review, page 67: Build an alarm circuit completed by your dectector switch.

Wrap Up At the end of this chapter (page 75), you'll demonstrate your alarm circuit.

SECTION

4 **Electrical Safety**

Integrating Health

Discover **How Can You Blow a Fuse?**

Electric current lights the instruments in an airplane and also the runway ahead.

Allow time for students to read the description of the project in their text and the Chapter Project Overview on pages 36–37 in Teaching Resources. Then encourage discussions on circuitry and events they can use to close their circuits. Answer any initial questions students may have.

Program Resources

- **Teaching Resources** Chapter 2 Project Teacher Notes, pp. 34–35; Chapter 2 Project Overview and Worksheets, pp. 36–39; Chapter 2 Project Scoring Rubric, p. 40

Performance Assessment

The Chapter 2 Project Scoring Rubric on page 40 of Teaching Resources will help you evaluate how well students complete the Chapter 2 Project. Students will be assessed on
- how well they apply concepts related to electric current and circuits;
- the clarity of the circuit diagram they draw of their device;
- how well they conduct experiments to test and revise their circuits;
- the thoroughness and organization of their presentations.

By sharing the Chapter 2 Scoring Rubric with students at the beginning of the project, you will make it clear to them what they are expected to do.

SECTION 1 Electric Charge and Static Electricity

Objectives

After completing the lesson, students will be able to

◆ describe the interaction of like and unlike electric charges;
◆ define and describe static electricity and state how it differs from electric current;
◆ describe lightning and other forms of static discharge.

Key Terms electric field, static electricity, friction, conduction, induction, conservation of charge, static discharge, electroscope

1 Engage/Explore

Activating Prior Knowledge

Before class, rub together a piece of polyester fabric and nylon sock so that they stick together. Show students the fabric and sock clinging to each other. Ask: **Would you expect to find glue or some other form of matter between these two fabrics?** *(no)* Then ask: **What holds the fabrics together?** *(Sample: Electricity; static cling)* Explain that students will learn more about the forces that hold two fabrics together as they explore electric charges.

Skills Focus inferring
Materials *empty aluminum can, balloon*
Time 10 minutes
Tips Make sure students rub the balloon vigorously. Avoid doing this activity on a damp or rainy day.
Expected Outcome The can follows the balloon in either direction.
Think It Over Students may suggest that an invisible force is attracting the can. If the balloon is charged, then opposite charges in the can are attracted to it.

SECTION 1 Electric Charge and Static Electricity

DISCOVER ····················· ACTIVITY····

Can You Move a Can Without Touching It?

1. Place an empty aluminum can on its side on the floor.
2. Blow up a balloon. Then rub the balloon back and forth on your hair several times.
3. Hold the balloon about 3 to 4 centimeters away from the can.
4. Slowly move the balloon farther away from the can. Observe what happens.
5. Move the balloon to the other side of the can and observe what happens.

Think It Over
Inferring What happens to the can? What can you infer from your observation?

GUIDE FOR READING

◆ How do electric charges interact?
◆ How does static electricity differ from electric current?
◆ How are electrons transferred in static discharge?

Reading Tip Before you read, preview the headings and record them in outline form. Fill in details as you read.

You're in a hurry to get dressed for school, but you can't find one of your socks. You quickly head for the pile of clean laundry. You've gone through everything, but where's the sock? The dryer couldn't have really destroyed it, could it? Oh no, there it is. Your sister has found the sock stuck to one of her shirts. What makes clothes stick together? The explanation has to do with tiny electric charges.

Types of Electric Charge

The charged parts of atoms are electrons and protons. As you have learned, protons and electrons are charged particles. When two protons come close, they push one another apart. In other words, they repel each other. But if a proton and an electron come close, they attract one another.

Why do protons repel protons but attract electrons? The reason is that they have different types of charge. Protons and electrons have opposite charges. The charge on the proton is

Figure 1 The interaction of electric charges is making this girl's hair stand on end.

READING STRATEGIES

Reading Tip Before students write the section headings in outline form, ask them how many major headings they will have in the outline. *(six)* Explain that subheadings such as *Electric Fields Around Single Charges* will appear as subheads of the outline, preceded by capital letters. Have students leave room for additional information under each heading. As students read, they can fill in the supporting information.

Study and Comprehension After students read the section, have them review their outlines. Then instruct them to use the outlines to write questions based on the information about electric charge and static electricity. Have students form pairs and take turns asking and answering each other's questions.

| No charge | Like charges repel | Like charges repel | Unlike charges attract |

Figure 2 Charged objects exert forces on each other. They can either attract or repel.
Interpreting Diagrams What is the rule for the interaction of electric charges?

called positive (+), and the charge on the electron is called negative (−). The names positive and negative were given to charges by Benjamin Franklin in the 1700s. They have been used by scientists ever since.

Interactions Between Charges

The two types of charge interact in specific ways. **Charges that are the same repel each other. Charges that are different attract each other.**

Does this sound familiar to you? This rule is the same as the rule for interactions between magnetic poles. Recall that magnetic poles that are alike repel each other and magnetic poles that are different attract each other.

There is one important thing about electric charges that is different from magnetic poles. Recall that magnetic poles do not exist alone. Whenever there is a south pole, there is always a north pole. Electric charges can exist alone. In other words, a negative charge can exist without a positive charge.

☑ *Checkpoint* How are the interactions between electric charges similar to the interactions between magnetic poles?

Electric Fields

Just as magnetic poles exert their forces over a distance, so do electric charges. An electric charge exerts a force through the **electric field** that surrounds the charge. An electric field extends outward from every charged particle.

When a charged particle is placed in the electric field of another charged particle, it is either pushed or pulled. It is pushed away if the two charges are the same. It is pulled toward the other charge if the two charges are different.

Answers to Self-Assessment

Caption Question

Figure 2 Charges that are the same repel; charges that are different attract each other.

☑ *Checkpoint*

Like electric charges, magnetic poles that are alike repel each other, and magnetic poles that are unlike attract each other.

2 Facilitate

Types of Electric Charge

Addressing Naive Conceptions

Some students may think that neutral objects cannot interact with charged objects because they do not have an overall net charge. Explain that neutral objects contain equal numbers of positive and negative charges and can be attracted to both negatively and positively charged objects. **learning modality: verbal**

Interactions Between Charges

Using the Visuals: Figure 2

As students examine the visual, have them point their index fingers downward to represent the suspended objects in the diagram. Ask them to show two neutrally charged objects, two objects with the same charge, and two objects with opposite charges. (*Students should hold their fingers still; move their fingers apart; move their fingers together.*) **learning modality: kinesthetic**

Electric Fields

Demonstration

Materials *inflated balloon, wool cloth, faucet*

Time 15 minutes

Allow students to observe how a charge exerts a force through an electric field. Vigorously rub the balloon with the wool cloth, then turn on the faucet so that water flows in a steady stream. Have students observe what happens as you bring the charged balloon near the stream of water. (*The water will bend towards the balloon.*) **learning modality: visual**

Ongoing Assessment

Writing Have students describe the types of electric charges and the kinds of interactions between them.

Electric Fields, continued

Using the Visuals: Figure 3

Direct students to place a finger on the negatively charged particle. Ask: **Why are the arrows facing toward your finger?** *(The arrows show the direction that a positive charge would move—toward a negative charge.)* Then have students place a finger on the center of the positively charged particle. Encourage them to trace a circle around the area of the strongest electric field. *(Students should trace the area nearest the particle.)* Finally, have students describe how the electric fields are altered in 3B. Ask: **How does the field between + and − differ from the field between + and +?** *(Attraction instead of repulsion)*
learning modality: visual

Drawing Conclusions

Materials *tissue paper, hole punch, plastic comb*
Time 10 minutes
Tips Avoid performing this activity on a damp or rainy day. The tissue paper should be attracted to the comb. Students should conclude that the comb and tissue paper are oppositely charged.
Extend Have students find out what happens if they run a comb through their hair several times and then hold it a short distance from their hair.

Static Charge

Language Arts Connection

Help students understand static electricity by explaining that the term *static* comes from the Greek word *statikos*, which means "standing still." Ask: **How does static electricity differ from electric currents?** *(Static electricity does not flow continuously. It can stay in one place, or stand still.)* **learning modality: verbal**

Drawing Conclusions

1. Tear tissue paper into small pieces, or cut circles out of it with a hole punch. **ACTIVITY**
2. Run a plastic comb through your hair several times.
3. Place the comb close to, but not touching, the tissue paper pieces. What do you observe?

What can you conclude about the electric charges on the comb and the tissue paper?

Figure 3 Electric charges can attract or repel one another. **A.** The arrows show that a positive charge repels another positive charge. A negative charge attracts a positive charge. **B.** When two charged particles come near each other, the electric fields of both particles are altered.

Electric Fields Around Single Charges You will recall using magnetic field lines to picture a magnetic field in an earlier chapter. In a similar way, you can use electric field lines to visualize the electric field. Electric field lines are drawn with arrows to show the direction of the force on a positive charge.

The electric fields in Figure 3A are strongest where the lines are closest together. You can see that the strength of the electric field is greatest near the charged particle. The field decreases as you move away from the charge.

Electric Fields Around Multiple Charges When there are two or more charges, the resulting electric field is altered. The electric fields due to the individual charges combine. Figure 3B shows the electric fields from two sets of charges.

☑ *Checkpoint* *Where is an electric field strongest?*

Static Charge

If matter consists of charged particles that produce electric fields, why aren't you attracted to or repelled by every object around you—your book, your desk, or your pen? The reason is that each atom has an equal number of protons and electrons. And the size, or magnitude, of the charge on an electron is the same as the size of the charge on a proton. So each positive charge is balanced by a negative charge. The charges cancel out and the object as a whole is neutral. As a result there is no overall electrical force.

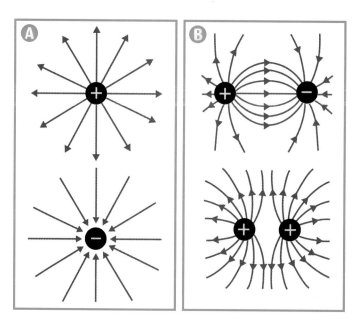

Background

History of Science The early study of electricity was hindered because generating and storing electricity was difficult. In 1745 and 1746, a German scientist, Ewald von Kleist, and a Dutch scientist, Pieter van Musschenbroek, developed the *Leyden jar.* The jar was named in honor of van Musschenbroek, who lived in the city of Leiden. The first Leyden jars consisted of a glass vial or jar that was partially filled with water. The jar was sealed with a cork, and the cork was pierced with a thick conducting wire or nail so that one end of the wire or nail was in the water. The jar was charged by bringing the end of the wire or nail into contact with a device that generated static electricity. Scientists could then use the stored static electricity at a later time in their experiments.

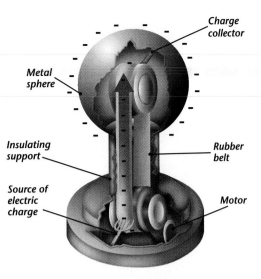

Figure 4 A Van de Graaff generator produces static electricity. Electrons are carried up a rubber belt and are transferred to the metal sphere. The charge built up on the sphere is enough to send a spark several meters through the air.

Labels on figure: Charge collector; Metal sphere; Insulating support; Source of electric charge; Rubber belt; Motor

Charged Objects Protons are bound tightly in the center of an atom, but electrons can sometimes leave their atoms. Whether or not an electron will move depends on the material. Atoms in insulators, such as wood, rubber, plastic, and glass, hold their electrons tightly. Atoms in conductors, such as gold, silver, copper, and aluminum, hold some of their electrons loosely. These electrons move freely from atom to atom within the material.

A neutral object can become charged by gaining or losing electrons. If an object loses electrons, it is left with more protons (positive charge) than electrons (negative charge). Thus the object is positively charged overall. If, instead, an object gains electrons, it has more electrons than protons. Thus it has an overall negative charge.

The buildup of charges on an object is called **static electricity.** Static electricity behaves quite differently from electric currents. In an electric current, charges move continuously. **In static electricity, charges build up, but they do not flow.**

Transferring Charge Exactly how do charges build up? Charges must be transferred from one object to another. There are three methods by which charges are transferred: friction, conduction, and induction. **Friction** is the transfer of electrons from one object to another by rubbing. **Conduction** is the transfer of electrons from a charged object to another object by direct contact.

Addressing Naive Conceptions

Some students may assume that a negatively charged object has fewer charges than its positively charged counterpart. Explain that neutral atoms lose electrons to become positive and gain electrons to become negative. **learning modality: verbal**

Including All Students

Materials *plastic jar, 6 red marbles, 3 blue marbles*

Time 10 minutes

Tips The following activity will help students who are having difficulty understanding how objects become charged. Explain that red marbles represent electrons and blue marbles represent protons. Place the three blue marbles in the jar. Then ask: **If this jar is an atom, how many electrons, or red marbles, must you add to give the atom a neutral charge?** *(three)* Once students have added the marbles, have them demonstrate how to make the atom positively charged and negatively charged. *(Take electrons out of the jar; add electrons to the jar.)* **limited English proficiency**

Building Inquiry Skills: Classifying

Challenge students to identify the method of transferring charge in each of the following examples: rubbing a glass rod with a wool cloth *(friction)*; touching the glass rod to a metal door knob *(conduction)*; holding a charged rod near a metal rod *(induction)*. **learning modality: logical/mathematical**

Media and Technology

Transparencies "Electric Fields," Transparency 7

Answers to Self-Assessment

✓ *Checkpoint*

An electric field is strongest where the lines are closest together.

Ongoing Assessment

Writing Have students describe the buildup of static electricity.

Static Charge, continued

Real-Life Learning

Materials *fabric softener* *sheets*

Time 30 minutes

Have students investigate how well the fabric softener sheets reduce static cling. Ask them to predict what will happen if they use one sheet, half of a sheet, or no sheet in the dryer. Encourage students to check their predictions by helping with the family laundry. Then have them briefly describe their conclusions.
learning modality: kinesthetic

Static Discharge

Skills Focus inferring
Materials *2 foam plates, scissors, tape, aluminum pie plate*
Time 10 minutes

Tips You may want to prepare the plates in advance. Perform this activity on a dry day, and, if possible, in the dark. Students should observe that each time they touch the pie plate, they see a spark. They should explain their observations by saying that when they put the pie plate on the foam, the electrons in the foam repel the electrons in the metal. When they touch the pie plate, the electrons leap to their hand, making a spark. After the electrons jump to their hand, the pie plate is short of electrons and it attracts electrons when they touch it again. This causes another spark. When they put the pie plate back on the foam, the process starts all over again.

Extend Have students experiment to see how changing the length of time they rub the foam plate on their hair affects the outcome of this activity. **learning modality: visual**

Sparks Are Flying

You can make your own lightning.

1. Cut a strip 3 cm wide from the middle of a foam plate. Fold the strip to form a T. Tape it to the center of an aluminum pie plate as a handle.

2. Rub a second foam plate on your hair. Put it upside down on a table.

3. Use the handle to pick up the pie plate. Hold the pie plate about 30 cm over the foam plate and drop it.

4. Now, very slowly, touch the tip of your finger to the pie plate. Be careful not to touch the foam plate. Then take your finger away.

5. Use the handle to pick up the pie plate again. Slowly touch the pie plate again.

Inferring What did you observe each time you touched the pie plate? How can you explain your observations?

Induction is the movement of electrons to one part of an object by the electric field of another object. The three methods of transferring charge are illustrated in *Exploring Static Electricity*.

Keep in mind that charges are not created or destroyed. If an object gives up electrons, another object gains those electrons. Electrons are only transferred from one location to another. This is known as the law of **conservation of charge.**

Static Cling Static electricity explains why clothes stick together in the clothes dryer. In a dryer, different fabrics rub together. Electrons from one fabric rub off onto another. In this way, the clothes become charged. A positively charged sock might then be attracted to a negatively charged shirt—the clothes stick together.

Your clothes are less likely to stick together if you use a fabric softener sheet. These sheets add a thin coating to your clothes as they bounce around in the dryer. The coating prevents electrons from rubbing off the clothing, so the clothes don't become charged.

Can you think of situations in which you might want to increase static electricity? Think about wrapping leftover food in plastic wrap. Plastic wrap picks up a charge when you unroll it. Since plastic is an insulator, the charge cannot move off it. So the wrap keeps its charge. When you place the plastic wrap on a container, it charges the edges of the container by induction. The force between the opposite charges on the wrap and the container causes the wrap to cling.

Static electricity allows you to make copies quickly. In a photocopier, a drum is given a negative static charge that is the image of the page to be copied. This charged image picks up positively charged particles of a very fine black powder. The drum then rolls against a negatively charged piece of paper, and the powder is transferred to the paper. Finally, the paper is heated to melt the powder, and the powder sticks to the paper.

☑ *Checkpoint* *What is the law of conservation of charge?*

Static Discharge

An object that gains a static charge doesn't hold the charge forever. Electrons tend to move, returning the object to its neutral condition. **When a negatively charged object and a positively charged object are brought together, electrons move until both objects have the same charge.** The loss of static electricity as electric charges move off an object is called **static discharge.**

Humidity If you rub a balloon on your clothing and then hold it next to a wall, it should stick. But the balloon may not always stick. Why is that? The answer could have to do with the weather.

Background

Facts and Figures When the textile industry began to produce synthetic materials such as nylon, polyester, and acrylic, consumers began to demand products to reduce static cling. Anti-static agents can be applied to textiles as they are being produced. Additionally, people can add liquid fabric softeners to their wash or put fabric softening sheets in their dryers.

The molecules of the active ingredient in both liquid and sheet fabric softeners are charged at one end and uncharged at the other. The charged end is attracted to the fabric surface. In this way, the softeners coat the surface of the clothing and reduce the electrical charge transferred due to the friction between clothes in the dryer.

EXPLORING Static Electricity

Static electricity involves the transfer of electrons from one object to another. Electrons are transferred by friction, conduction, or induction.

CHARGING BY FRICTION

When you rub two objects together, electrons move from one object to the other. This is known as charging by friction.

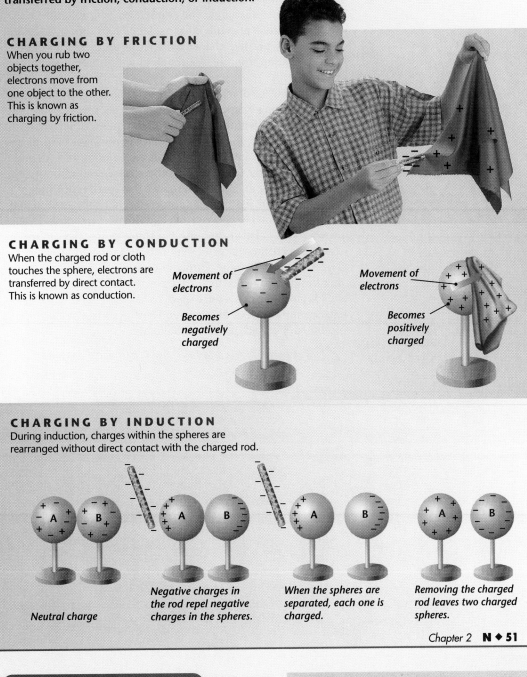

CHARGING BY CONDUCTION

When the charged rod or cloth touches the sphere, electrons are transferred by direct contact. This is known as conduction.

Movement of electrons

Becomes negatively charged

Movement of electrons

Becomes positively charged

CHARGING BY INDUCTION

During induction, charges within the spheres are rearranged without direct contact with the charged rod.

Neutral charge

Negative charges in the rod repel negative charges in the spheres.

When the spheres are separated, each one is charged.

Removing the charged rod leaves two charged spheres.

As students examine each method of electron transfer, have them trace the flow of electrons away from or toward the objects involved. For Charging by Friction, ask: **Which object gains electrons?** *(The rod)* **Which object loses electrons?** *(The cloth)* For Charging by Conduction, ask: **Which object gains electrons?** *(Left: the sphere; right: the cloth)* **Which object loses electrons?** *(Left: the rod; right: the sphere)* Then ask: **Which example shows movement of electrons without direct contact?** *(Charging by Induction)* **How do spheres A and B become charged without direct contact with the rod?** *(The rod repels negative charges on sphere A. Since the spheres are touching, electrons travel to sphere B. When the spheres are separated, there is a positive charge (deficit of electrons) on sphere A and a negative charge (surplus of electrons) on sphere B.)* **Extend** Have students demonstrate charge by friction by transferring charge to a thin strip of plastic wrap. If small pieces of tissue paper stick to the plastic wrap, then the transfer was successful.
learning modality: visual

Media and Technology

Transparencies "Exploring Static Electricity," Transparency 8

Answers to Self-Assessment

✓ *Checkpoint*

The law of conservation of charge states that electrons are only transferred from one location to another; they are never destroyed.

Ongoing Assessment

Skills Check Have students use a wool cloth and plastic comb to demonstrate how to place static charge on an object and how to cause static discharge.

Cultural Diversity

Many ancient cultures had myths about lightning. Some students will be familiar with the Greek god, Zeus, who hurled lightning bolts from the sky when he was angry. Norse mythology refers to the god Thor, who threw lightning bolts as weapons against demons. The Hindu religion has a god of lightning and thunder—Indra. The Bantu of Africa have a lightning-bird god called Umpundulo that threatens during storms. The Navajo people believed that lightning bolts held tremendous spiritual and healing powers. Ask students: **Why do you think so many ancient cultures explain lightning as a weapon of powerful gods?** (*Samples: It looks sharp; it can start fires; it comes with a loud noise.*) **learning modality: verbal**

Detecting Charge

Building Inquiry Skills: Drawing Conclusions

Materials *newspaper*
Time 15 minutes

Guide students in detecting charge. Have them tear two long strips from a sheet of newspaper. Tell students to hold the strips together at one end with one hand. Ask: **Do the strips contain an electric charge? How can you tell?** (*The strips do not appear to have a charge because they do not attract or repel each other.*) Using the thumb and forefinger of the other hand, students should lightly stroke downward on the strips for 1 minute. Ask: **What do you observe when you stop stroking the strips?** (*They repel each other.*) Finally, ask: **How are the strips similar to an electroscope?** (*They both indicate the presence of a charge.*)
learning modality: kinesthetic

On a humid day, the air is filled with water molecules. Extra electrons on an object are carried off by molecules of water in the air. Thus the charges do not have a chance to build up on objects such as the balloon.

Sparks and Lightning Have you ever felt a shock from touching a doorknob after walking across a carpet? That shock is the result of static discharge. For example, as you walk across the carpet, electrons may rub off the soles of your shoes. This gives you a slight positive charge. When you touch the doorknob, electrons jump from the doorknob to your finger, making you neutral again.

Lightning is a dramatic example of static discharge. Lightning is basically a huge spark. During thunderstorms, air swirls violently. Water droplets within the clouds become electrically charged. Notice in Figure 5 that electrons collect in the lower parts of the cloud. To restore a neutral condition, electrons move from areas of negative charge to areas of positive charge. As electrons jump, they produce an intense spark. You see that spark as lightning.

Much of the lightning in a storm occurs between different regions of a cloud or between different clouds. But some lightning reaches Earth. This is because the cloud causes the surface of Earth to become charged by induction, as shown in Figure 5. Negative charges on the bottom of a cloud repel electrons, leaving the surface of Earth with a positive charge. If the charge buildup is sufficient, a huge spark of lightning is produced. The spark jumps between the cloud and Earth's surface or tall objects on the surface, such as trees or buildings.

☑ *Checkpoint* *How can you get a shock from a doorknob?*

Figure 5 Lightning is a spectacular discharge of static electricity. Lightning can occur within a cloud, between two clouds, or between a cloud and Earth.

Background

Facts and Figures While scientists have a clear understanding of cloud-to-ground lightning strikes, they are still learning more about an unusual electrical phenomenon called ball lightning. Ball lightning appears as a colored, moving sphere of electricity several inches in diameter. Most frequent sightings have occurred near the ground and during thunderstorms that typically produce atmospheric lightning. The ball can look red, orange, or yellow. Sometimes a viewer hears a hissing sound when near the ball, and the ball can produce a distinct smell. The ball lightning only lasts a short time. Sometimes it explodes, other times it fizzles out quickly. Ball lightning can cause damage by burning or melting. Scientists do not know if, or how, ball lightning is related to normal lightning.

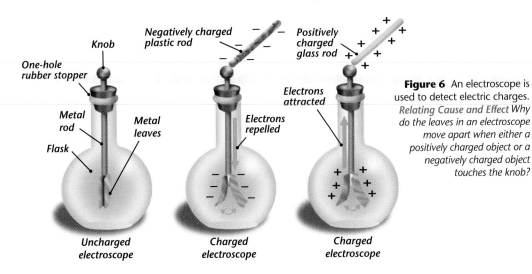

Knob

One-hole rubber stopper

Negatively charged plastic rod

Positively charged glass rod

Metal rod

Flask

Metal leaves

Electrons repelled

Electrons attracted

Uncharged electroscope

Charged electroscope

Charged electroscope

Figure 6 An electroscope is used to detect electric charges. *Relating Cause and Effect Why do the leaves in an electroscope move apart when either a positively charged object or a negatively charged object touches the knob?*

Detecting Charge

Electric charge is invisible, but it can be detected by a special instrument called an **electroscope.** A typical electroscope consists of a metal rod with a knob at the top. At the bottom of the rod are two sheets, or leaves, of very thin metal (aluminum, silver, or gold). When the electroscope is uncharged, the leaves hang straight down.

When a charged object touches the metal knob, electric charge travels along the rod and into or out of the leaves. The leaves then have a net charge. Since the charge on both leaves is the same, the leaves repel each other and spread apart.

The leaves of an electroscope move apart in response to either negative charge or positive charge, so you cannot use an electroscope to determine the type of charge. You can use an electroscope only to detect the presence of charge.

Section 1 Review

1. How do particles with the same charge interact? How do particles with opposite charges interact?
2. What is static electricity?
3. What are the three ways by which static charge is produced?
4. How is static electricity discharged?
5. How does an electroscope detect charge?
6. **Thinking Critically Comparing and Contrasting** How are electric charges similar to magnetic poles? How are they different?

Science at Home

Rub a balloon against your hair and bring the balloon near one of your arms. Then bring your other arm near the front of a television screen that is turned on. Ask a family member to explain why the hairs on your arms are attracted to the balloon and to the screen. Explain that this is evidence that there is a static charge on both the balloon and the screen.

Section 1 Review Answers

1. Particles with the same charge repel each other. Particles with opposite charges attract each other.
2. Static electricity is the buildup of charge.
3. Static charge can build up by friction, conduction, or induction.
4. During electric discharge, charges escape the charged object by jumping from one object to another or by attaching to water or dust particles.
5. When a charged object touches the knob of an electroscope, electrons travel from an area of high electron density to an area of low electron density—through the electroscope to the leaves. The leaves of the electroscope acquire the same charge and repel each other.
6. Electric charges and magnetic poles both act over a distance, set up a field, and exert attractive and repulsive forces. Electric charges exist separately, while magnetic poles cannot be isolated.

Science at Home

Materials *balloon, television set*

Students should avoid doing this activity on humid days. Students should readily feel the hairs of their arm attracted to the screen or observe that their hair is attracted. They may even feel very tiny sparks jump from the screen.

Program Resources

◆ **Teaching Resources** 2-1 Review and Reinforce, p. 43; 2-1 Enrich, p. 44

Media and Technology

Interactive Student Tutorial CD-ROM N-2

Transparencies "Electroscope," Transparency 9

Answers to Self-Assessment

Caption Question

Figure 6 Because both leaves contain the same charge, they repel each other.

☑ Checkpoint

A shock from a doorknob results from static charge. When you walk across carpet, electrons rub onto your shoes and give you a positive charge. When you touch the doorknob, electrons jump from the knob to your finger.

Performance Assessment

Writing Have students explain how an electroscope works. Students may include an illustration if they wish. Portfolio Students can save their explanations and illustrations in their portfolios.

N ◆ 53

Developing Hypotheses

The Versorium

Preparing for Inquiry

Key Concept A neutral object (the versorium) is attracted to a charged object.

Skills Objectives Students will be able to
◆ develop hypotheses to explain observed behavior of the foil versorium;
◆ predict the behavior of the paper versorium and design an experiment to test it.

Time 30 minutes

Advance Planning
◆ On the day of the lab, test the plastic foam plates and wool to be sure they develop adequate static charge. To save time, cut the 3-cm by 10-cm strips of aluminum foil and paper in advance. Buy wool fabric at fabric or craft stores.
◆ To prepare the meter stick and balloon for the Invitation, push a thumbtack into the center of the narrow edge of a meter stick at the 50-cm mark. Test it to see if it balances. If not, add bits of clay to make it balance.

Alternative Materials Any set of materials that develops a static charge will work. Examples: wool fabric and balloon, plastic bag and plastic foam plate, acetate transparency and plastic foam plate, fur and balloon.

Guiding Inquiry

Invitation Place the balanced meter stick on the thumbtack on a table in front of the class and rub a plastic balloon on a student's hair. Ask the students what the charge on the meter stick is. *(neutral)* Bring the balloon close to the meter stick. It will be attracted to the balloon. Ask students to explain what is happening. *(Most students probably will not know. The electric charge on the balloon is attracting the oppositely charged particles in the meter stick.)*

Introducing the Procedure
◆ Show students how to construct the versorium. Tell them to make sure the tent is balanced loosely on the top of the pencil so that the tent can turn freely.

THE VERSORIUM

You are going to build a device that was first described in 1600 by Sir William Gilbert. He called this device a *versorium*, which is a Latin word meaning "turnabout." As you construct a versorium, you will use the skill of developing hypotheses.

Problem

Why does a versorium turn?

Materials

foam cup · plastic foam plate · pencil
aluminum foil · wool fabric · paper
scissors

Procedure

1. Cut a piece of aluminum foil approximately 3 cm by 10 cm.
2. Make a tent out of the foil strip by gently folding it in half in both directions.
3. Push a pencil up through the bottom of an inverted cup. **CAUTION:** *Avoid pushing the sharpened pencil against your skin.* Balance the center point of the foil tent on the point of the pencil as shown.
4. Make a copy of the data table.
5. What will happen if you bring a foam plate near the foil tent? Record your prediction in the data table.
6. What will happen if you rub the foam plate with a piece of wool fabric and then bring it near the foil tent? Record your prediction.
7. What will happen if you bring the rubbed wool near the foil tent? Again record your prediction.
8. Test your predictions and record your observations in the data table.
9. Develop a hypothesis to explain your observations. Be sure to use an "If . . . then . . ." statement.

DATA TABLE			
	Unrubbed Foam Plate	Rubbed Foam Plate	Rubbed Wool Fabric
Aluminum tent: Prediction			
Aluminum tent: Observation			
Paper tent: Prediction			
Paper tent: Observation			

◆ Remind students to slowly bring the plastic foam plate or the wool fabric near—but not touching—the versorium tent.

Troubleshooting the Experiment
◆ Make sure the objects you choose develop sufficient static charge to attract the versorium tent.
◆ Humidity may affect the static charge.

Expected Outcome

Both the foil versorium and the paper versorium should be attracted to the rubbed foam plate and rubbed wool fabric. The foam plate that was not rubbed with wool fabric should cause no change.

Analyze and Conclude

1. Neutral. In its original state, the foil has not gained or lost any electrons.
2. The foam plate and the wool fabric acquired a static electric charge because electrons were transferred between them by rubbing.
3. The foil is attracted to the foam plate and

10. Use your hypothesis to predict how your observations would change if you used a piece of paper instead of the aluminum foil.

11. Design an experiment to test your hypothesis about the paper versorium. Record your predictions and observations.

Analyze and Conclude

1. At the beginning of the lab, is the foil negatively charged, positively charged, or neutral? Explain your answer.

2. What was the effect of rubbing the foam plate with the wool fabric?

3. Explain the behavior of the aluminum foil as the foam plate is brought near it. Explain the behavior as the wool fabric is brought near it.

4. After you bring the materials near it, is the foil negatively charged, positively charged, or neutral? Explain your answer.

5. How is the paper tent charged before and after you bring the objects near it? How do you know?

6. Explain the behavior of the paper versorium as the foam plate is brought near it, and as the wool fabric is brought near it.

7. Modify your hypothesis to account for the difference, if any, between the results for the foil versorium and the paper versorium.

8. Can you use a versorium to determine whether an object is positively or negatively charged? Explain.

9. Why should you avoid touching the foam plate or the wool fabric to your clothing or any other object while you are using it to test a versorium?

10. **Think About It** How useful was your hypothesis? Did your hypothesis lead to predictions of what you actually observed?

Design an Experiment

What other materials besides foam or wool might have an effect on the versorium? Think of other materials you could use to make the versorium tent. Make predictions, and test the materials to see if they respond in a fashion similar to the aluminum foil and paper tents.

the wool fabric. When the negatively charged plate is brought near, it repels the electrons, creating a positive end of the versorium that is attracted to the plate. When the positively charged wool is brought near, it attracts the electrons, creating a negative end of the versorium that is attracted to the wool.

Program Resources

◆ **Teaching Resources** Chapter 2 Skills Lab, pp. 57–59

Sample Data Table

	Unrubbed foam plate	Rubbed foam plate	Rubbed wool fabric
Aluminum tent: prediction	No effect	Attracted	Attracted
Aluminum tent: observation	No effect	Attracted	Attracted
Paper tent: prediction	No effect	Attracted	Attracted
Paper tent: observation	No effect	Attracted	Attracted

4. The tent remains neutral because the foil does not touch the plate or wool and no charges are transferred. Students may say that the foil is oppositely charged compared to the plate or wool. Tell them the electrons in the foil are repelled by the presence of a negatively charged object (plate), leaving the positive end of the foil near the plate. The positive end of the foil is attracted to the negatively charged plate. When the positively charged wool is brought near the foil, it attracts electrons, creating a negative end on the versorium that is attracted to the wool.

5. The paper tent remains neutral. This is evident because the versorium is attracted by both positively and negatively charged objects.

6. The paper versorium is attracted to the foam plate and the wool fabric. Electrons are not free to move in the paper, but the paper is attracted to a positively charged object (fabric) because the electrons cluster on one side of the molecules. A negatively charged object (plate) attracts the positively charged side of the molecules.

7. Answers will vary according to students' original hypotheses. There is no difference in results for the foil versorium and the paper versorium.

8. No. The versorium cannot detect the sign of the charge on an object since the tent is equally attracted to any charged object.

9. Touching the foam plate or wool fabric to clothing will redistribute the charges, allowing all or most of the charge to leak off. The plate would become neutral and lose its effect.

10. Students who hypothesized that the paper tent would not be affected by the plate or fabric could not have predicted the results. Students who hypothesized correctly probably predicted the actual results.

Extending the Inquiry

Design an Experiment Students may want to try materials such as inflated balloons, plastic rulers that have been rubbed with plastic sandwich bags, or objects charged with a Van de Graff generator, if available. Other materials for the versorium tent might be plastic, cardboard, wood, or other metal foils.

SECTION 2 Circuit Measurements

Objectives

After completing the lesson, students will be able to

♦ explain what causes the flow of electric current in terms of electrical potential, potential difference, and voltage;

♦ describe the relationship between voltage and the flow of electric current;

♦ define resistance and state how it affects the flow of current;

♦ calculate resistance using Ohm's law.

Key Terms electrical potential, potential difference, voltage, voltage source, voltmeter, ammeter, Ohm's law

1 Engage/Explore

Activating Prior Knowledge

Ask: **Is it easier to drink a milkshake through a narrow straw or a wide straw?** *(Wide straw)* Explain that the narrow straw is more resistant to the flow of milkshake; therefore, you have to suck harder to get the milkshake to flow through the straw. Tell students they will learn about analogous concepts of resistance, voltage, and electric current in this chapter.

DISCOVER

Skills Focus inferring
Materials *1 meter bell wire, wire cutters and strippers, metric ruler, magnetic compass, electrical tape, two 1.5-volt bulbs and sockets, D cell and holder, modeling clay*
Time 25 minutes

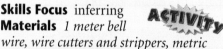 **Tips** Remove insulation from the ends of wire. Demonstrate how to connect the batteries and then how to rewire the circuit in Step 6 each time a bulb and socket are removed.
Expected Outcome The compass deflects more as bulbs and sockets are removed from the circuit.
Think It Over The most current flowed when no bulbs were in the circuit. Students may explain that removing bulbs increases current.

DISCOVER ·········· ACTIVITY

How Can Current Be Measured?

1. Obtain four pieces of wire with the insulation removed from both ends. Each piece should be about 25 cm long.

2. Wrap one of the wires four times around the compass as shown. You may use tape to keep the wire in place.

3. Build a circuit using the remaining wire, wrapped compass, two bulbs, and a D cell as shown. Adjust the compass so that the wire is directly over the compass needle.

4. Make sure the compass is level. If it is not, place it on a lump of modeling clay, so that the needle swings freely.

5. Observe the compass needle as you complete the circuit. Record the number of degrees the needle turns.

6. Repeat the activity using only one bulb, and again with no bulb. Record the number of degrees the needle turns.

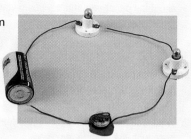

Think It Over

Inferring Based on your observations of the compass, when did the most current flow in your circuit? How can you explain your observations?

GUIDE FOR READING

♦ What causes electric current to flow?

♦ How does increasing voltage affect current?

♦ How does increasing resistance affect current?

Reading Tip Before you read, preview the boldfaced vocabulary terms. Write them down, leaving spaces between them for notes.

Y ou're on a visit to a botanical garden. After a walk through the plush greenery, you rest by an artificial waterfall constructed in the middle of the garden. The continuous flow of water over the falls is soothing. You might be wondering what a waterfall could possibly have to do with electricity. Although there is an electric pump that keeps the water flowing, it is not the pump that matters. The falling water itself, or any flowing liquid, is similar to the current in an electric circuit.

Electrical Potential

What happens to the water when it gets to the top of the waterfall? Naturally, the water falls down. When you lift something, you give it energy by doing work against the force of gravity. The type of energy that depends on position is called potential energy.

An object will move from a place of high potential energy to a place of low potential energy. The potential energy of the water is greater at the top of the waterfall than at the bottom. So water flows from the top to the bottom.

In a similar way, electrons in a circuit have potential energy. This potential energy, however, is related not to height but rather to the force exerted by electric fields. The potential energy per unit of electric charge is called **electrical potential.**

READING STRATEGIES

Reading Tip After students write down the boldfaced terms, discuss what they already know about each term's meaning. Have students speculate about the meanings of unfamiliar words or terms, based on word roots or affixes. With a term such as *potential difference*, have students speculate about its meaning based on definitions of each word in the term. Then have students read the section, making notes for each term.

Study and Comprehension Divide the class into five groups. Assign each group one of the five major headings. Suggest students summarize the information in the heading. Encourage students to prepare drawings or diagrams to accompany their summaries. Have each group rehearse, then give, its presentation. Have a question-and-answer session after each presentation, in which "audience" members ask questions based on the summaries.

Voltage

Just as water flows downhill, electrons flow from places of higher potential to places of lower potential. The difference in electrical potential between two places is called the **potential difference.** The unit of measure of potential difference is the volt (V). For this reason, potential difference is also called **voltage.** Electrons will flow as long as there is a potential difference, or voltage between two parts of a circuit.

Recall that the flow of electrons through a material is called electric current. Now you know what causes current to flow. **Voltage causes current to flow through an electric circuit.**

Figure 7 The diagram shows how a hidden pump feeds the waterfall in the photo. The movement of the water is similar to the current in an electric circuit.

Program Resources

◆ **Teaching Resources** 2-2 Lesson Plan, p. 45; 2-2 Section Summary, p. 46
◆ **Integrated Science Laboratory Manual,** N-2, "Building Electric Circuits"

Media and Technology

🎧 **Audiotapes** English-Spanish Summary 2-2

2 Facilitate

Electrical Potential

Including All Students

Students may have difficulty visualizing electrical potential. Refer students to Figure 7. Point out that the pump in the photo raises the water from the bottom of the waterfall to the top of the waterfall. Ask: **What happens when the water reaches the top of the waterfall?** (It flows to the bottom.) **Why?** (Because potential energy at the top of the waterfall is higher than at the bottom, and objects move from a place of high potential to a place of low potential.) Explain that electrons also flow from a place of high potential energy to low. Electrical potential, however, is related to force rather than height. **learning modality: verbal**

Voltage

Building Inquiry Skills: Making Models

Materials 2 plastic cups, water, cotton string, stack of books
Time 15 minutes

Have students set up a simple siphon to model voltage and current. They should fill a cup with water, stick one end of the string into the cup, and place the cup on the stack of books. Then, they should put the free end of the string into an empty cup that is positioned below the first cup. Have students observe the siphon after 15 minutes. Water should be visible in the second cup. Ask: **What part of the model is similar to voltage?** (Water in the first cup) Then ask: **What represents current?** (Water flowing from the first cup to the second) **learning modality: kinesthetic**

Ongoing Assessment

Writing Have students write two or three sentences explaining why voltage is needed for current to flow.

Using the Visuals: Figure 8

Direct students to examine the potential difference in each image. Using a ruler, have students compare the difference in height of the ends of each pipe. Ask: **Which image represents the voltage source with the lowest potential difference?** *(The first image)* **learning modality: visual**

Inquiry Challenge

Materials *plastic bottle with small hole in bottom and cap removed, water, flexible plastic tubing, modeling clay*
Time 20 minutes

Ask groups to design a model that represents what happens as voltage, or potential difference, increases. Assign students specific tasks, such as manipulating potential difference, evaluating the force of the flowing water, and comparing the water model with electric current. Check student plans and then allow them to test their models. *(Sample model: Students could place tubing in the bottom of the bottle, sealing it with modeling clay if necessary, and fill the bottle with water. When the end of the plastic tube is at the same height as the top of the water bottle, no water flows—equal voltage. As the bottle is raised (or the end of the tubing lowered), the water flows faster and faster—higher and higher voltage difference.)* **cooperative learning**

Students can save their design plans in their portfolios.

Resistance

Language Arts Connection

The term *resistance* has several meanings. Challenge students to find the meaning of resistance in the phrases: "Resistance is futile," and "He belonged to the French Resistance." They may research the phrases in an encyclopedia or dictionary. Ask: **How is the scientific meaning for *resistance* similar to its meaning in these other phrases?** *(In all cases it means "to work against or to act in opposition.")* **learning modality: verbal**

Figure 8 As the difference in height between the two ends of the pipe increases, the flow of water increases. *Making Models How is the water pipe a model for voltage and current?*

Voltage Sources

What happens to the water when it gets to the bottom of the waterfall in the botanical garden? If nothing brings the water back to the top, the water flow will quickly stop. But this waterfall has a pump that pushes the water back up to the top. Once the water returns to the top, it can flow back down again. Another way to describe this process is to say that the pump maintains the potential difference between the top and bottom of the falls. As long as this difference exists, the water can continue to flow.

An electric circuit also requires a device to maintain a potential difference, or voltage. A **voltage source** creates a potential difference in an electric circuit. Batteries and generators are examples of voltage sources.

You will learn more about voltage sources in the next chapter. For now, all you need to know is that a voltage source has two terminals. The potential difference, or voltage, between the terminals causes charges to move around the circuit.

Some voltage sources are stronger than others. You can compare voltage to the downward slant of the pipe near the top of the waterfall. If a pipe is nearly level, the water just trickles out as shown in Figure 8. But if one end is much higher than the other, the rate of water flow is greater. The greater the difference in height, the greater the flow of water. **Just as an increase in the difference in height causes a greater flow of water, an increase in voltage causes a greater flow of electric current.**

Resistance

The amount of water that flows through a pipe in the waterfall depends on more than just the angle of the pipe. It also depends on the pipe through which the water travels. A long pipe will resist

Background

History of Science From the mid-eighteenth through the early nineteenth century, scientists believed that electricity was a fluid, just like water. In 1733, one of the pioneers of electrical science, a French chemist named Charles DuFay, proposed that electricity was made up of two fluids—vitreous electricity and resinous electricity. DuFay based his theory on observations of an electrified glass rod and cork pieces.

When DuFay electrified a glass rod, it attracted the cork pieces. If he let the rod touch the cork pieces, the pieces were repelled from the rod and by each other. DuFay presumed that matter typically had a balanced amount of each type of electricity. However, when there was an excess of vitreous electricity, objects attracted each other. An excess of resinous electricity caused objects to repel each other.

Figure 9 Water flows more easily through a short, wide pipe than through a long, narrow pipe. Similarly, electrons flow more easily through wires that are short and thick.

the flow of water more than a short pipe. And a thin pipe will resist the flow of water more than a wide pipe. In addition, a clogged pipe will offer more resistance than a clean pipe.

Current Depends on Resistance In a similar way, the amount of current that flows in a circuit depends on more than just the voltage. Current also depends on the resistance offered by the material through which it travels. Recall that electrical resistance is the opposition to the flow of charge. **The greater the resistance, the less current there is for a given voltage.**

The resistance of a wire depends on the thickness and length of the wire. Long wires have more resistance than short wires. Thin wires have more resistance than thick wires. Resistance also depends on how well the material conducts current. Electrons are slowed down by interactions with atoms of the wire. Electrons flow freely through conductors, but not through insulators.

One more factor, temperature, affects electrical resistance. In Chapter 1 you learned that electrical resistance can decrease as temperature decreases. You can also say that as the temperature of most conductors increases, resistance increases as well.

Path of Least Resistance Perhaps you have heard it said that someone is taking the "path of least resistance." This means that the person is doing something the easiest way. In a similar way, if an electric current can travel through either of two paths, it will travel through the one with the lower resistance.

Have you ever seen a flock of birds perched comfortably on high-voltage power lines? The reason the birds don't get hurt is that current flows through the path of least resistance. Since a bird's body offers more resistance than the wire, current continues to flow directly through the wire without harming the bird.

☑ *Checkpoint* What two factors affect the flow of a current?

Down the Tubes
Use water to make a model of an electric current.

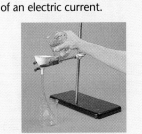

1. Set up a funnel, tubing, beaker, and ring stand as shown.
2. Have a partner start a stopwatch as you pour 200 mL of water into the funnel. Be careful not to let it overflow.
3. Stop the stopwatch when all of the water has flowed into the beaker.

Making Models How did your model represent electric current, voltage, and resistance?

Chapter 2 **N ◆ 59**

Skills Focus making models **ACTIVITY**

Materials *water, two 200-mL beakers, funnel, ring stand, clear tubing of various lengths and widths, stopwatch*

Time 15 minutes

Tips Have students work in pairs. Keep paper towels handy to clean up any spills.

Making Models The water represents current. The length and width of the tubing determine the resistance. The height of the tube represents voltage or potential difference.

Extend Challenge students to find out what happens when they increase or decrease resistance by using tubing of different lengths and widths. **learning modality: kinesthetic**

Demonstration

Materials *latex glove, water, push pin, scissors, sink or basin* **ACTIVITY**

Time 10 minutes

✂ To demonstrate for students the path of least resistance, fill the glove until the water is about 4–6 cm from the top of the wrist. Then tie the wrist. Hold the glove over the sink or basin with the fingers pointed upward, and put a single pinhole in one finger of the glove. Then snip the tip off a different finger. Ask students to predict what will happen if you turn the glove back over. Allow students to observe the water flowing out of the fingers of the glove. Ask: **Which path offered the least resistance? Why?** *(The path through the finger with the larger hole, because the water flowed out of it more quickly.)* **learning modality: visual**

Answers to Self-Assessment

Caption Question

Figure 8 An increase in the difference in height between the ends of the water pipe causes a greater flow of water, just as an increase in voltage causes a greater flow of electric current.

☑ *Checkpoint*
Voltage and resistance

Ongoing Assessment

Drawing Have students sketch two wires and explain why one creates more resistance in a circuit than the other. Students can save their sketches in their portfolios.

Ohm's Law

Addressing Naive Conceptions

If an ammeter indicates a greater flow rate, some students may incorrectly infer that the electrons are traveling through the circuit at greater speeds. Explain that the ammeter shows an increase in flow rate if more electrons are flowing past a point even if their speed does not change. Therefore, a change in current should never be described as faster or slower; rather, students should describe a change in current as "more" or "less."
learning modality: verbal

Including All Students

If students have difficulty applying Ohm's law, provide them with a memory device. Draw a circle on the board. Draw a horizontal line to divide the circle in half. In the top half, write the letter V. Divide the bottom half of the diagram with a vertical line. In the left side write the letter I and in the right, the letter R. Tell students to copy the diagram and to include the words *voltage, current,* and *resistance.* Tell students that to find any quantity if you know the other two, cover the unknown quantity with your finger. When the symbols are side by side, you multiply, and when they appear one over the other, you divide. Ask: **If you know voltage and resistance, how do you find current?** (*Cover the letter I (current). You get V over R; therefore, you divide voltage by resistance.*) **learning modality: visual**

Sharpen your Skills

Calculating

Materials *none*
Time 15 minutes
The missing values are: 5 ohms; 1.5 volts; 0.1 amps; 30 ohms; 20 ohms; 6 volts. As voltage increases and resistance stays the same, current increases.

Extend Have students measure the voltage and current of a battery-powered clock or radio, using either a multimeter or voltmeter and ammeter, and calculate the resistance in the circuit.

Figure 10 This multimeter can measure resistance, voltage, and small currents.

Sharpen your Skills

Calculating
Find the missing value in each row.

Voltage (V)	Current (A)	Resistance (Ω)
1.5	0.30	?
?	0.05	30
1.5	?	15
3.0	0.10	?
3.0	0.15	?
?	0.2	30

How are voltage, current, and resistance related?

Ohm's Law

In the 1820s, the German physicist Georg Ohm experimented with many substances to study electrical resistance. He analyzed various types of wire in order to determine the characteristics that affect a wire's resistance. As a result of Ohm's valuable experiments, the unit of resistance is named the ohm (Ω).

How can you measure the resistance of a wire? In order to measure resistance, Ohm set up a voltage between two points on a conductor. He then measured the current produced. Potential difference, or voltage, is measured with a device called a **voltmeter.** Current, which has units of amps, is measured with a device called an **ammeter.** Voltmeters and ammeters are often combined into a single device like the one in Figure 10.

Ohm found that the resistance for most conductors does not depend on the voltage across them. A conductor or any other device that has a constant resistance regardless of the voltage is said to obey **Ohm's law.** Most of the conductors that you will learn about do obey Ohm's law.

Ohm's law states that the resistance is equal to the voltage divided by the current.

$$\text{Resistance} = \frac{\text{Voltage}}{\text{Current}} \quad \text{or} \quad \text{Ohms} = \frac{\text{Volts}}{\text{Amps}}$$

The letter R can be used to represent resistance, I to represent current, and V to represent voltage. This formula is shorter.

$$R = \frac{V}{I}$$

You can rearrange the resistance formula as follows.

$$I = \frac{V}{R} \quad \text{or} \quad V = IR$$

If any two of the values in these formulas are known, you can solve for the third value.

You can use the formulas to see how changes in resistance, voltage, and current are related. For example, what happens to current if voltage is doubled without changing the resistance? For a constant resistance, if voltage is doubled, current is doubled as well. Thus the greater the voltage, the greater the current.

What happens if, instead, you double the resistance without changing the voltage? If resistance is doubled, the current will be cut in half. So for a greater resistance, the current is less.

It is sometimes important to increase the resistance in a circuit in order to prevent too much current from flowing. Specially constructed resistors, some no larger than a grain of rice, are

---

Background

Facts and Figures The symbol for the unit ohm is the capital Greek letter *omega* (Ω). Many Greek letters are used in math and science. The ancient Greeks had highly developed mathematics skills, particularly in geometry. Their early contributions led to a universal acceptance of the Greek alphabet to represent abstract ideas in math and science. The Greek letter *delta* (Δ) signifies a change

in a mathematical value. *Alpha* (α), *beta* (β), and *gamma* (γ) are the first three letters of the Greek alphabet; they are used to represent radioactive emissions. The letter *sigma* (Σ) is used in mathematics to describe the sum of quantities in complicated equations. Perhaps the best known Greek letter is the letter *pi* (π), which stands for the ratio of the circumference of a circle to its diameter.

Sample Problem

An automobile headlight is connected to a 12-volt battery. If the resulting current is 0.40 amps, what is the resistance of the headlight?

Analyze. You know the voltage and the current. You are looking for the resistance.

Write the formula. $R = \dfrac{V}{I}$

Substitute and solve. $R = \dfrac{12\ V}{0.40\ A} = 30\ \Omega$

Think about it. The answer makes sense because you are dividing the voltage by a decimal number. The answer should be greater than either number in the fraction, which it is.

Practice Problems

1. In a circuit, 0.5 A is flowing through the bulb. The voltage across the bulb is 4.0 V. What is the bulb's resistance?
2. In order for a waffle iron to operate efficiently, a current of 12 A must flow through its coils. If the resistance is 10 Ω, what must the voltage be?

added to circuits. Televisions, radios, and other similar devices contain dozens of such resistors.

Some resistors do not obey Ohm's law. For instance, the resistance of a light bulb increases when the bulb is turned on and the filament heats up. A filament has the lowest resistance before it heats up, and so a cold filament conducts the most current. That is why a bulb most often burns out the instant you switch it on.

Section 2 Review

1. What is voltage?
2. How is voltage related to electric current?
3. How is resistance related to electric current?
4. **Thinking Critically Calculating** You light a light bulb with a 1.5-volt battery. If the bulb has a resistance of 10 ohms, how much current is flowing?
5. **Thinking Critically Relating Cause and Effect** In order to increase the amount of current flowing in a circuit, should you increase the voltage or the resistance? Explain.

Check Your Progress CHAPTER PROJECT 2

Pick the event that will close your switch, for example, the closing of a door. To make your switch, you might tape one of the free wires to a door and the other wire to the frame of the door. The wires will touch when the door closes. Here are some other ideas to explore: an object falling, a slight vibration or breeze, or a container filling with water. Draw a circuit diagram that includes a battery, a switch, and a light bulb.

Program Resources

◆ **Teaching Resources** 2-2 Review and Reinforce, p. 47; 2-2 Enrich, p. 48

Media and Technology

Interactive Student Tutorial CD-ROM N-2

Sample Problem

Students may find it easier to interpret the equation if they can visualize the problem. Suggest they draw a battery, connecting wires, and a headlight. Have them label the battery "12 V" and the wire "0.4 A," then work through the steps of the problem. **learning modality: logical/mathematical**

Answers to Practice Problems

1. $R = \dfrac{4.0\ A}{0.5\ A} = 8\ \Omega$
2. $V = 10\ \Omega \times 12\ A = 120\ V$

3 Assess

Section 2 Review Answers

1. Voltage is the potential difference between two places in a circuit.
2. Voltage causes electrons to flow; in other words, voltage causes current. The greater the voltage for a given resistance, the greater the current.
3. The greater the resistance for a given voltage, the lower the current.
4. Current (I) = Volts (V)/Resistance (R): $I = \dfrac{1.5\ V}{10\ \Omega} = 0.15\ A$
5. To increase the amount of current, increase voltage or decrease resistance. Because $I = V \div R$, an increase in V or a decrease in R will cause an increase in I.

Check Your Progress CHAPTER PROJECT 2

Help students understand that a switch is simply a device that allows electricity to flow where it couldn't before. Be sure they realize that their choice will have a large influence on how their detector switch is designed.

Performance Assessment

Organizing Information Have students create concept maps using the terms *electrical potential*, *voltage*, *resistance*, *current*, *ohms*, *amperes*, and *volts*.

Portfolio Students can save their concept maps in their portfolios.

Constructing a Dimmer Switch

Preparing for Inquiry

Key Concept The brightness of a bulb is controlled by the amount of current flowing in the circuit, which in turn depends on the voltage and the resistance in the circuit.

Skills Objectives Students will be able to
♦ observe that the bulb gets dimmer as the amount of resistance in the circuit increases;
♦ predict what will happen if they increase or decrease the resistance in the circuit;
♦ adapt procedures to test their predictions.

Time 30 minutes

Advance Planning Cut the copper wire and rubber tubing to the same length as the pencil lead.

Alternative Materials Any non-conductor, such as wood or plastic, can be substituted for the rubber tubing.

Guiding Inquiry

Invitation Ask students to think about sitting in a movie theater just as the show is about to begin. Ask: **When people are arriving, are the lights on or off?** *(on)* **During the show are the lights on or off?** *(off)* **Do the lights all go off suddenly?** *(No. They gradually get dimmer.)*

Introducing the Procedure

♦ Explain that pencil lead is not made of lead at all, but graphite, a form of carbon. Inform students that the drawing part of a pencil is called lead because people used to draw on paper with the metal lead before pencils were invented.
♦ Refer students to the circuit in the photo.
♦ For a quantitative comparison, ask students to use small pieces of paper through which they view the bulb. They can compare the brightness by how many pieces of paper they can see the bulb through. This procedure will work best in a slightly darkened room.

Real-World Lab

Constructing a Dimmer Switch

Most light switches turn a light bulb on and off. There doesn't seem to be any setting in between. Suppose you wanted to find a way to dim lights slowly. Think about how you would design a switch that controls the brightness of a bulb.

Skills Focus

observing, predicting, designing experiments

Problem

What materials can be used to make a dimmer switch?

▲ Engineer at a sound mixing board

Materials

flashlight bulb in a socket
D cell
thick lead from mechanical pencil
uninsulated copper wire, the same length as the pencil lead
rubber tubing, the same length as the pencil lead
1 wire 10–15 cm long
2 wires 20–30 cm long, with alligator clip attached to one end

Procedure

1. Construct the circuit shown in the photo. To begin, attach wires to the ends of the D cell.
2. Connect the other end of one of the wires to the bulb in a socket. Attach a wire with an alligator clip to the other side of the bulb.
3. Attach an alligator clip to the other wire.
4. The pencil lead will serve as a resistor that can be varied—a variable resistor. Attach one alligator clip firmly to the tip of the pencil lead. Be sure the clip makes good contact with the lead. (*Note:* Pencil "lead" is actually graphite, a form of the element carbon.)
5. Will the brightness of the bulb increase or decrease if you slide the other alligator clip back and forth along the lead? Test your prediction.
6. What will happen to the brightness of the bulb if you replace the lead with a piece of uninsulated copper wire? Adapt your pencil-lead investigation to test the copper wire.

Troubleshooting the Experiment

♦ Poor contact between the alligator clip and the pencil lead can be improved by buffing the lead with sandpaper.

Expected Outcome

♦ As students include more pencil lead in the circuit, the total resistance increases and current decreases, so the bulb becomes dimmer. When they move the clips close together so the circuit contains less graphite, the total resistance decreases and the bulb becomes brighter.
♦ Students' results should show that the copper wire conducts well no matter its length. The rubber tubing doesn't conduct at all.

Analyze and Conclude

1. Resistance. The amount of resistance increases as the length of pencil lead in the circuit increases.
2. The bulb got dimmer as the length of lead in the circuit increased.

7. Predict what will happen to the brightness of the bulb if you replace the pencil lead with a piece of rubber tubing. Adapt your pencil-lead investigation to test the rubber tubing.

Analyze and Conclude

1. What variable did you manipulate by sliding the alligator clip along the pencil lead in Step 5?
2. What happened to the brightness of the bulb when you slid the alligator clip along the pencil lead?
3. Explain your reasoning in making predictions about the brightness of the bulb in Steps 6 and 7. Were your predictions supported by your observations?
4. Do you think that pencil lead has more or less resistance than copper? Do you think it has more or less resistance than rubber? Use your observations to explain your answers.

5. Which material tested in this lab would make the best dimmer switch? Explain your answer.
6. **Apply** If you wanted to sell your dimmer switch to the owner of a movie theater, how would you describe your device and explain how it works?

More to Explore

The volume controls on some car radios and television sets also contain variable resistors, called rheostats. The sliding volume controls on a sound mixing board are rheostats, as well. Older homes and theaters may use rheostats to adjust lighting. Where else in your house would variable resistors be useful? (*Hint:* Look for applications where the output is graduated rather than all or nothing.)

3. Copper wire is an excellent conductor and rubber is an excellent insulator. The predictions should have been supported by the students' observations.
4. The tests show that pencil lead is a better resistor than copper wire; rubber tubing is a better resistor than pencil lead.
5. Pencil lead. Copper wire would have to be very long to offer enough resistance, and rubber does not conduct electricity at all.
6. Students should explain that the device is a switch that uses variable resistance to allow for full light for patrons to find their seats and safely exit the theater, and dim light for viewing the movie.

Extending the Inquiry

More to Explore Samples: electric heater controls, electric dryer, ceiling fan, exercise treadmill, variable-speed tools

Safety

Caution students to be careful not to break the flashlight bulb. Review the safety guidelines in Appendix A.

Program Resources

◆ **Teaching Resources** Chapter 2 Real-World Lab, pp. 60–61

Objectives

After completing the lesson, students will be able to

◆ describe and construct a series circuit;

◆ describe and construct a parallel circuit.

Key Terms series circuit, parallel circuit

1 Engage/Explore

Activating Prior Knowledge

Ask students what happens to the flow of electricity in a lamp when they turn the lamp switch on. (*Electricity flows from the socket, through the wire, and to the light bulb.*) Then ask: **If the wire between the switch and the light bulb is cut, what happens when you flick on the switch? Why?** (*Nothing happens because the electricity cannot flow to the bulb.*)

········ **DISCOVER** ········

Skills Focus observing
Materials *4 light bulbs with sockets, 2 dry cells with holders, several lengths of insulated wire*
Time 15 minutes

Tips Remove insulation from ends of wire. Students may need help reading the circuit diagrams. Point out the symbols for bulb, wire, and battery. You may want to have students include a switch in their circuits.

Think It Over The remaining bulb in the series circuit goes out; the remaining bulb in the parallel circuit does not. Students might recognize that the parallel circuit has two paths, so the current continues to flow through the remaining path. The series circuit has only one path.

SECTION 3 Series and Parallel Circuits

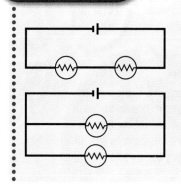

DISCOVER ·········· **ACTIVITY**

Do the Lights Keep Shining?

1. Construct both of the circuits shown using a battery, several insulated wires, and two light bulbs for each circuit.

2. Connect all wires and observe the light bulbs.

3. Now unscrew one bulb in each circuit. Observe the remaining bulbs.

Think It Over

Observing What happened to the remaining light bulbs when you unscrewed the first bulb? How can you account for your observations?

GUIDE FOR READING

◆ How many paths can current take in a series circuit?

◆ How does a parallel circuit differ from a series circuit?

Reading Tip As you read, create a table comparing series and parallel circuits.

It's a cool, clear night as you stroll by the harbor with your family. The night is dark, but the waterfront is bright thanks to the thousands of twinkling white lights that outline the tall ships. They make a striking view.

As you walk, you notice that a few of the lights are burned out. The rest of the lights, however, burn brightly. If one bulb is burned out, how can the rest of the lights continue to shine? The answer depends on how the electric circuit is designed. The parts of a circuit can be arranged in series or in parallel.

Figure 11 The lights that line the rigging of this ship are parts of a parallel circuit. If one goes out, the rest keep shining.

READING STRATEGIES

Reading Tip Help students create tables by writing a table such as the one shown on the board. Encourage students to copy the table and fill in the information as they read.

	Series Circuit	Parallel Circuit
Definition		
Paths		
Resistance		
Examples		

Study and Comprehension Have students preview the section by reading the headings and subheadings, and by looking at the photographs. Encourage students to suggest questions they have about series circuits, parallel circuits, and household circuits. Write the questions on the board. After students read the section, have them work as a class to answer the questions on the board. Encourage them to research answers not found in the section.

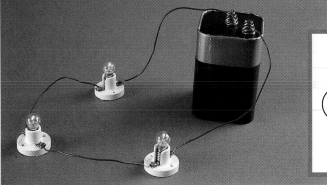

Series Circuits

If all the parts of an electric circuit are connected one after another, the circuit is a **series circuit**. Figure 12 illustrates a series circuit. **In a series circuit, there is only one path for the current to take.** For example, a switch and the device it controls are connected in series with each other.

One Path A series circuit is very simple to design and build, but it has some disadvantages. What happens if a bulb in a series circuit burns out? A burned-out bulb is a break in the circuit, and there is no other path for the charges to take. So if one light goes out, all the lights go out.

Added Resistors Another disadvantage of a series circuit is that the light bulbs in the circuit become dimmer as more bulbs are added. Why does that happen? Think about what happens to the overall resistance of a series circuit as you add more bulbs. The resistance increases. Remember that if resistance increases, current decreases. So as light bulbs are added to a series circuit, the current decreases. The result is that the bulbs burn less brightly.

Ammeters Different meters are wired into circuits in different ways. Recall from the previous section that an ammeter is used to measure current. If you want to measure the current through some device in a circuit, the ammeter should be connected in series with the device.

☑ *Checkpoint* *How does resistance change as you add bulbs to a series circuit?*

Parallel Circuits

Could the lights on the ships have been connected in series? No—if the lights were part of a series circuit, all of the lights would have gone off when one burned out. What you saw, however, was that a few lights were burned out and the rest were brightly lit.

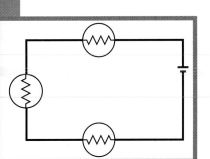

Figure 12 A series circuit provides only one path for the flow of electrons. *Applying Concepts What will happen to the other bulbs if one bulb burns out?*

Program Resources

◆ **Teaching Resources** 2-3 Lesson Plan, p. 49; 2-3 Section Summary, p. 50

Media and Technology

🎧 **Audiotapes** English-Spanish Summary 2-3

📽 **Transparencies** "Series and Parallel Circuits," Transparency 10

Answers to Self-Assessment

Caption Question

Figure 12 If one bulb burns out, the other two bulbs will not light.

☑ *Checkpoint*

The more bulbs you add to a series circuit, the greater the resistance.

---

2 Facilitate

Series Circuits

Using the Visuals: Figure 12

Direct students to use their index fingers to trace the path of electricity through the circuit. Ask: **What happens to the electrons when they reach the bulbs?** *(They move through the filaments and cause the bulbs to glow.)* Have students infer what would happen to the electrons if a wire was cut. *(The electrons would stop flowing and the bulbs would not light.)* **learning modality: visual**

Inquiry Challenge

Materials *several insulated wires, light bulbs, dry cell*

Time 25 minutes

🔒 ♻ Challenge student groups to design experiments that show how adding resistors (light bulbs) to a series circuit decreases the brightness of the bulbs. Assign students specific tasks such as assembling materials, designing the circuit, building the circuit, and evaluating the brightness of the bulbs. Have students compile a list of materials and prepare a circuit design for your approval. Ask: **What will you use as a control for your experiment?** *(Sample: A series circuit with one light bulb)* Encourage students to formulate a general statement about the effect of resistors on current in a series circuit. *(Sample: Adding resistors reduces the current in a series circuit.)* **cooperative learning**

Ongoing Assessment

Oral Presentation Have students name one advantage and one disadvantage of series circuits.

Parallel Circuits

Including All Students

Encourage students who have difficulty distinguishing between parallel and series circuits to draw circuit diagrams of each. Students can add captions that explain the effect on current and resistance when bulbs (resistors) are added to the circuit. **learning modality: visual**

 Students can save their diagrams in their portfolios.

Building Inquiry Skills: Inferring

Materials *strings of holiday lights*

Time 10 minutes

Challenge students to infer if a particular string of holiday lights is arranged in a series or a parallel circuit. Caution students to use care when plugging the lights into the wall. Ask: **How can you tell if the lights are arranged in a parallel circuit?** *(If you remove one light bulb and the rest of the string stays lit, then the bulbs are in a parallel circuit.)* To extend the activity, challenge students to create a circuit diagram for their string of lights. **learning modality: logical/ mathematical**

Sharpen your Skills

Predicting

Materials *dry cell, 3 light bulbs, insulated wire, switch*

Time 20 minutes

Tips Help students recognize that this circuit contains one bulb in series and two bulbs in parallel. Students should observe that the series bulb is brighter than the bulbs in parallel, and that the bulbs in parallel are of the same brightness. The series bulb is brighter than the two parallel bulbs because it receives the same amount of current that the two bulbs in parallel share.

Extend Have students predict what would happen if another bulb (resistor) were added to the parallel circuit. *(The total current in the circuit increases; the bulb in series becomes brighter, the bulbs in parallel become dimmer.)* **learning modality: visual**

Figure 13 A parallel circuit provides several paths for the flow of electrons. More current flows, and the bulbs are brighter than in the series circuit.

Sharpen your Skills

Predicting

1. Look at the circuit diagram below. Predict whether all three light bulbs will shine with the same brightness.

2. Construct the circuit using a dry cell and three identical light bulbs. Observe the brightness of the bulbs.

Does this circuit behave like either a parallel circuit or a series circuit? Explain.

The ships' lights were connected in parallel circuits. In a **parallel circuit,** the different parts of the circuit are on separate branches. Figure 13 shows a parallel circuit. **In a parallel circuit, there are several paths for current to take.** Notice that each bulb has its own path from one terminal of the battery to the other.

Several Paths What happens if a light burns out in a parallel circuit? If there is a break in one branch, current can still move through the other branches. So if one bulb goes out, the others remain lit. Switches can be placed along each branch so that individual bulbs can be turned on and off without affecting the others.

Added Branches What happens to the resistance of a parallel circuit when you add a branch? Although you might think that the overall resistance increases, it actually decreases. To understand this, consider the flow of water once again. Suppose water is being released from a reservoir held by a dam. If the water is allowed to flow through one pipe, a certain amount of water comes out. But if two pipes are used instead of one, twice as much water flows. The water will flow more easily because it has two paths to take. The same is true for a parallel circuit. As new paths, or branches, are added, the electric current has more paths to follow, and so total resistance decreases.

What does this tell you about current? If resistance decreases, the current must increase. The increased current travels along the new branch without affecting the original branches. So as you add branches to a parallel circuit, the brightness of the light bulbs does not change.

Voltmeters Recall from Section 2 that a voltmeter is used to measure voltage. When you measure the voltage across some device, the voltmeter and the device should be wired as parallel circuits.

Background

History of Science The first practical light bulb, or incandescent lamp, was developed in 1878 by the British chemist Sir Joseph Swan and in 1879 by the American inventor Thomas Edison. These bulbs had carbon filaments placed inside a glass that had been emptied using a vacuum. Edison went on to develop lighting systems using power lines to connect incandescent lamps. People did not immediately welcome electric lights. Before electricity, gas lighting was popular. As Edison and others developed electric appliances such as the light bulb, electric lamps began to replace gas lighting.

Figure 14 Parallel circuits are used in your home.
Interpreting Diagrams How many circuits does this house have?

Household Circuits

Would you want the circuits in your home to be series circuits? Of course you would not. With a series circuit, all the electrical devices in your home would go off every time a light bulb burned out or a switch was turned off. Instead, the circuits in your home are parallel circuits.

Electricity is fed into a home by heavy wires called lines. These lines have very low resistance. You can see in Figure 14 that parallel branches extend out from the lines to wall sockets, appliances, and lights in each room. The voltage in these household circuits is 120 volts. Switches are located in places where they can be used to control one branch of the circuit at a time.

Section 3 Review

1. What are the two types of electric circuits? You can draw a diagram of each to explain your answer.
2. What happens to the bulbs in a series circuit if one of the bulbs burns out? Explain.
3. What happens to the bulbs in a parallel circuit if one of the bulbs burns out? Explain.
4. **Thinking Critically Comparing and Contrasting** You are building a string of lights using several bulbs. How is the brightness of the lights related to whether you connect the bulbs in series or in parallel?

> **Check Your Progress** CHAPTER PROJECT 2
> Construct a circuit, either series or parallel, that lights a bulb when the switch is closed. Use the detector switch you designed earlier to close the circuit. Test the circuit to make sure that the switch closes when the event you are detecting occurs. Then make sure that the bulb lights when the switch is closed.

Program Resources

◆ **Teaching Resources** 2-3 Review and Reinforce, p. 51; 2-3 Enrich, p. 52

Media and Technology

Transparencies "Household Circuits," Transparency 11

Interactive Student Tutorial CD-ROM N-2

Answers to Self-Assessment
Caption Question
Figure 14 This house has four circuits.

Household Circuits

Real-Life Learning

Challenge students to design an electrical wiring plan for a room. They should include outlets and light fixtures in their drawings. Make sure the drawings show parallel circuits. **learning modality: visual**

3 Assess

Section 3 Review Answers

1. Series and parallel circuits. Diagrams should be labeled correctly.
2. The circuit is broken and all of the bulbs go out.
3. The bulbs in the other branches remain lit because the electricity can follow more than one complete path.
4. If the bulbs are connected in a series circuit, the bulbs will be dimmer than if each were used alone. If they are connected in a parallel circuit, adding bulbs will not change the brightness of the others.

> **Check Your Progress** CHAPTER PROJECT 2
> If students are having a hard time getting their switches to work properly, help them along by providing hints on how to get the two ends of the wires to make electrical contact. Most of the completed circuits will be in the form of parts and wires that are held together in primitive ways and that just lie loosely on a tabletop. Encourage students to improve the durability and appearance of their designs.

Performance Assessment

Drawing Have students draw two circuit diagrams—one that shows three bulbs in a series circuit and one that shows three bulbs in a parallel circuit.

Portfolio Students can save their circuit diagrams in their portfolios.

SECTION 4 Electrical Safety

Objectives

After completing the lesson, students will be able to
- identify the safety devices used to protect people from common electrical hazards;
- describe how a lightning rod protects a building;
- explain how the severity of an electric shock is related to current, voltage, and resistance.

Key Terms short circuit, third prong, grounded, lightning rod, fuse, circuit breaker

1 Engage/Explore

Activating Prior Knowledge

Show students the symbol for electrical hazard. Ask: **What does this symbol indicate?** *(There is a danger of shock.)* Ask students to name one or two ways that they can avoid electrical shock dangers. *(Sample: Keep electrical appliances away from water; do not overload outlets; do not touch or cut electrical wires.)*

DISCOVER

Skills Focus developing hypotheses
Materials *dry cell, light bulb, 2 alligator clips, very fine steel wool (00 or 000 grade)*
Time 15 minutes
Tips Use unrusted, unsoaped steel wool. If students cannot make a good contact between the steel wool fiber and the alligator clips, suggest they wrap a small piece of aluminum foil around the end of the fiber, crimp it, then clamp the alligator jaws on it.
Expected Outcome The steel wire will flash and burn; the bulb will go out.
Think It Over If the steel wool becomes so hot it melts or burns, then the circuit will be broken.

SECTION 4 Electrical Safety

DISCOVER •••••••••••••••••••••••••••••• ACTIVITY

How Can You Blow a Fuse?

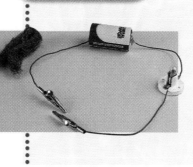

1. Begin by constructing the circuit shown using a D cell, a light bulb, and two alligator clips.
2. Pull a steel fiber out of a piece of steel wool. Wrap the ends of the steel fiber around the alligator clips.
3. Complete the circuit and observe the steel fiber and the bulb.

Think It Over
Developing Hypotheses Write a hypothesis to explain your observations.

GUIDE FOR READING

- How does a lightning rod protect a building?
- What safety devices are used in electric circuits?
- How is injury from an electric shock on the human body related to current?

Reading Tip As you read, make a list of ways that you can protect yourself from an electric shock.

The ice storm has ended, but it has left a great deal of destruction in its wake. Trees have been stripped of their branches, and a thick coating of ice covers the countryside. Perhaps the greatest danger is from the downed high-voltage lines left sparking in the streets. Residents are being warned to stay far away from them. What makes these power lines so dangerous?

Becoming Part of a Circuit

The sparks from those power lines should give you a clue as to what the danger is. One of the two parts of an electric company's circuit is a "live" wire carrying energy from the generating plant. The other part is a return or "ground" from the customer back to the generating plant. If a power line is damaged, the ground connection may be made through Earth itself. A person who touches a downed power line could create a short circuit to Earth through his or her body. A **short circuit** is a connection that allows current to take an unintended path. Rather than flowing through the return, or ground wire, the current would flow through the person.

The unintended path in a short circuit may offer less resistance than the intended path. So the current through a short circuit can be high. The result is a potentially fatal electric shock.

Exposed Wires Fallen high-voltage power lines are not the only potential source of electric shocks. Many people are hurt or killed by shocks from common household circuits. If you touch your hand to a 120-volt circuit, a potential difference, or voltage, is created between your hand and Earth. Since current flows when there is voltage, current will flow through your body.

READING STRATEGIES

Reading Tip Suggest students list ways to protect themselves from electric shock in a chart with the headings *Way to Prevent Shock* and *Why This Prevents Shock*. They can use their charts to remember the main ideas in the section.

Study and Comprehension After students read the section, have them work with partners to list main ideas and supporting details for the information under each heading of the section. Provide students with examples of graphic organizers that students can use to record the main ideas and details.

Figure 15 Power must be shut off while work crews repair damaged lines.

The wires to the electrical devices in your home are protected by insulation. Sometimes that insulation wears off, leaving the wire exposed. If you touch such a wire, you become part of the circuit. You will get a painful, possibly harmful shock.

In some cases, the exposed wire is inside an electrical device such as a toaster. If the wire comes in contact with the outside metal case of the toaster, the entire toaster will conduct electricity. Then you could receive a shock from simply touching the toaster.

Resisting Current Is there any way to protect yourself if you become part of a circuit? The soles of your shoes will normally provide a large resistance between your feet and the surface of Earth. As a result, the current would not be enough to cause serious injury. But what happens if you're barefoot, or are standing in the bathtub when you touch the circuit? In either case, your resistance will be smaller. Ordinary tap water is not a very good conductor of electricity, but it does decrease your resistance. This means that the voltage can still produce enough current to seriously injure you.

Grounding

Additional grounding wires protect people from shocks. If a short circuit occurs in a device, current will go directly into Earth through a low-resistance grounding wire. In this way a person who touches the device will be protected.

Third Prong Have you ever noticed that some plugs have a third prong on them, as shown in Figure 16? The two flat prongs connect the appliance to the household circuit. This **third prong,** which is round, connects the metal shell of an appliance to the ground wire of a building.

In order to protect people from shocks, electrical systems are grounded. A circuit is electrically **grounded** when charges are able to flow directly from the circuit into the ground connection.

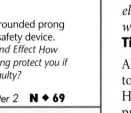

Figure 16 The rounded prong on this plug is a safety device. *Relating Cause and Effect How does the third prong protect you if the appliance is faulty?*

Program Resources

◆ **Teaching Resources** 2-4 Lesson Plan, p. 53; 2-4 Section Summary, p. 54

Media and Technology

 Audiotapes English-Spanish Summary 2-4

Answers to Self-Assessment

Caption Question

Figure 16 The third prong sends current directly into the ground if a short circuit occurs.

2 *Facilitate*

Becoming Part of a Circuit

Building Inquiry Skills: Applying Concepts

Have students draw a circuit diagram that a shows a circuit with an exposed wire. Ask: **Why does touching the exposed wire create a short circuit?** (*By touching the wire, the person creates a new path with less resistance for the current to follow.*) **learning modality: visual**

Real-Life Learning

Materials *appliances commonly used in the bathroom, such as hair dryers, curling irons, and electric shavers*
Time 15 minutes

Direct students to examine the labels on the appliances. Ask: **Why do the labels caution users against operating the appliances near water?** (*Tap water is a conductor that can decrease resistance to current. If you become part of the circuit while in contact with water, you can be seriously injured.*) **learning modality: verbal**

Grounding

Including All Students

Materials *two- and three-prong plugs, electrical outlet hardware (not wired to wall)*
Time 10 minutes

Allow students who are visually impaired to feel the difference between the plugs. Have students locate the grounding prong. Allow them to examine the electrical outlet to find out how the wires in the plugs fit into the circuit. **learning modality: kinesthetic**

Ongoing Assessment

Writing Have students write a definition of a short circuit and describe examples of three short circuits.

Building Inquiry Skills: Inferring

Ask students to infer why people playing golf during a thunderstorm are in danger. (*The golfer could act as a lightning rod. The golfer attracts the electrons in a lightning bolt just as lightning rods do.*) Ask: **What is the safest thing to do if you are caught in a storm while golfing?** (*Go indoors as quickly as possible or lie flat on the ground away from tall objects.*) **learning modality: logical/mathematical**

Social Studies CONNECTION

Have reference materials available for students to research Benjamin Franklin's life story. Encourage them to share one interesting fact or anecdote with the class.

In Your Journal Encourage students to create a headline and an illustration to accompany their articles. Compile students' articles in a Ben Franklin Portfolio to display in the classroom or school library. **learning modality: verbal**

Fuses and Circuit Breakers

Demonstration

Materials *dry cell, 4 light bulbs, insulating wire, ammeter, switch*

Time 15 minutes

Demonstrate how adding resistors increases current. Build a parallel circuit using the light bulbs; place an ammeter between the last light bulb and the dry cell. Have students check the ammeter reading. Ask them to predict what will happen if you add resistors (light bulbs). (*The current will increase.*) Then add two more branches to the parallel circuit by attaching two more light bulbs. Allow students to compare a second ammeter reading with the first to check their predictions. **learning modality: visual**

Figure 17 A lightning rod attracts charges from a lightning bolt and carries them to Earth.

Social Studies CONNECTION

Benjamin Franklin was not only a talented experimenter, but also an inventor, statesman, philosopher, printer, musician, and economist.

In Your Journal

Read about the life and work of Benjamin Franklin. Choose one event or aspect of his life and write a newspaper article describing his work to your readers. For example, you might write about how Franklin founded the first lending library so that people who couldn't afford to buy books could read them.

Lightning Rods With the idea of grounding, Benjamin Franklin was able to invent the lightning rod. A **lightning rod** is a metal rod mounted on the roof of a building in order to protect a building. Recall from Section 1 that charge is induced on Earth's surface during a thunderstorm. Lightning results from the transfer of charge from a charged cloud to an oppositely charged object on Earth. Franklin realized that charges are more crowded on pointed objects than on flat ones. So electrons in a lightning bolt are attracted to a pointed object such as a lightning rod.

A lightning rod is connected to a grounding wire. When lightning strikes the rod, charges flow through the rod, into the wire, and then into Earth. This protects the building.

If you think about how a lightning rod works, you will understand how to stay safe during a thunderstorm. It is not safe to stand under a tall conductor, such as a tall, wet tree. Even worse would be to hold a pointed metal object, such as an umbrella. If you are outside during a storm, the best way to protect yourself from lightning is to stay low and dry.

☑ *Checkpoint* Why does lightning strike a lightning rod?

Fuses and Circuit Breakers

A wire that carries more current than it is designed to carry will become hot. If it becomes too hot, it can melt the insulation on the wire. The hot wire can then come in contact with flammable materials in the walls of a building, causing a fire.

Electric current can become too high if a circuit is overloaded. Recall that as you add branches to a parallel circuit, the total resistance decreases and the current increases. If you use too many appliances at once, the current can become dangerously high. Overloading a circuit might result in a fire. **In order to prevent circuits from overheating, devices called fuses and circuit breakers are added to circuits.**

A **fuse** is a device that contains a thin strip of metal that will melt if too much current flows through it. When the strip of metal melts, or "blows," it breaks the circuit and stops the flow of current. If you have ever plugged in too many appliances at once, the electricity might have gone out because a fuse was blown. Once the overload is corrected, the fuse can be replaced and the electricity restored.

When a fuse burns out, it cannot be used again. To avoid the problem of having to replace fuses, circuits in new buildings are protected by devices called circuit breakers. A **circuit breaker** is a safety device that uses an electromagnet to shut off the circuit when the current gets too high. It's easy to reset the circuit breaker. All you have to do is pull back a switch—but only after turning off some of the appliances that are causing the high current in the circuit.

Electric Shocks

Why is it so important to protect the human body from electric shocks? The human body depends on electrical signals. Tiny electrical pulses, for example, control the beating of your heart. Similarly, electrical signals control your breathing and the movement of your muscles. If your body receives an electric current from a source outside it, the current will interfere with the normal processes within your body.

Current in the Body The shock you feel from static discharge after walking across a carpet on a dry day is not the same as the shock from touching a fallen power line. **The severity of an electric shock depends on the current.**

A current of less than 0.01 amp is almost unnoticeable. Between 0.1 amp and 0.2 amp, however, a current can be dangerous. Such a current might cause an irregular heartbeat and disrupt the flow of blood to your body. A current entering your hand can travel through your arm and across your heart. Currents greater than 0.2 amp cause burns and can stop your heart.

Resistance in the Body The current of an electric shock is related to voltage and resistance. The voltage is determined by the source of the shock. You can safely handle the 1.5-volt batteries for a radio, but you could be killed by touching power lines that carry thousands of volts.

The current that results from that voltage depends on the resistance of the human body. Resistance in the human body is affected by several factors. One factor is the conducting ability of body tissue. Living cells have a low resistance to electric current. This is

Figure 18 Both fuses and circuit breakers open a circuit when current gets too high.
Applying Concepts What is the maximum current that the yellow fuse can carry?

Program Resources

Science Explorer Series *Human Biology and Health,* Chapter 1

Media and Technology

Exploring Physical Science Videodisc
Unit 5, Side 1,
"Electric Bodies"
Chapter 9

Answers to Self-Assessment

Caption Question

Figure 18 The yellow fuse can carry a maximum current of 20 amps.

☑ *Checkpoint*

The charges on the pointed lightning rod are crowded, so electricity in a lightning bolt is extremely attracted to the lightning rod.

Building Inquiry Skills: Comparing and Contrasting

Materials *fresh fuse, burned-out fuse*
Time 15 minutes

ACTIVITY

Allow students to examine the fuses, then list the differences between the two. Ask: **How do the fuses look different?** (*The used fuse has darkened glass and the metal strip is missing (or melted). The fresh fuse has clear glass and the metal strip is intact.*) Then ask students to infer why the metal strip is enclosed in glass. (*When the metal heats and melts, it cannot touch anything that can catch on fire. The glass keeps the fuse from starting a fire.*) **learning modality: visual**

Electric Shock

Including All Students

Allow students who need an additional challenge to research how the heart carries electrical impulses. Ask students to draw a diagram showing how impulses cause the different parts of the heart to contract so that blood will flow continuously. Based on their research, ask students to make inferences about the effect of electric shock on the heart. (*The flow of current prevents the heart from relaxing after a contraction. This stops the beating motion of the muscle.*) **learning modality: verbal**

Ongoing Assessment

Writing Ask students to explain why wet skin and dry skin allow different amounts of current to pass through the body.

3 Assess

Section 4 Review Answers

1. Electrical charges from a lightning bolt are attracted to the electrical charges crowded on the lightning rod. Charge is transferred from the lightning bolt to the lightning rod, which then conducts the charge to the ground.
2. Fuses and circuit breakers are both designed to keep circuits from overloading and overheating. When current is too high, a fuse melts and the circuit opens, while a circuit breaker has a switch that opens and breaks the circuit. A fuse is used once and then thrown away, while a circuit breaker can be reset and reused.
3. No. The severity of the shock depends on the amount of current, where on the body it strikes, and how long it lasts.
4. The Empire State Building is hit often because it is tall and close to the clouds. Often, the path of least resistance for a lightning bolt is along the roof of the Empire State Building.

Science at Home

Caution students not to approach a fuse box or circuit breaker without an adult. Students who live in apartment buildings may need to look outside their units for circuit breakers. Encourage students to share their diagrams with family members.

Performance Assessment

Writing Have students describe how voltage, current, and resistance can contribute to electric shock in the human body.

---

because the fluid in human cells contains ions, which are charged particles that conduct electricity.

Another factor is whether your skin is wet or dry. If your skin is very dry, your resistance might be very high. When your skin is wet, however, your resistance might be hundreds of times lower. So you are more likely to suffer a serious electric shock if you are wet than if you are exposed to the same voltage when you are dry.

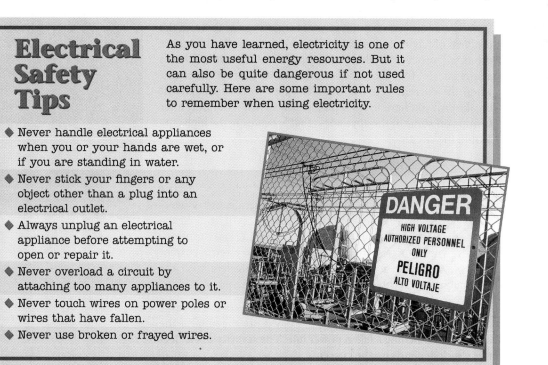

Electrical Safety Tips

As you have learned, electricity is one of the most useful energy resources. But it can also be quite dangerous if not used carefully. Here are some important rules to remember when using electricity.

- ◆ Never handle electrical appliances when you or your hands are wet, or if you are standing in water.
- ◆ Never stick your fingers or any object other than a plug into an electrical outlet.
- ◆ Always unplug an electrical appliance before attempting to open or repair it.
- ◆ Never overload a circuit by attaching too many appliances to it.
- ◆ Never touch wires on power poles or wires that have fallen.
- ◆ Never use broken or frayed wires.

DANGER
HIGH VOLTAGE
AUTHORIZED PERSONNEL
ONLY
PELIGRO
ALTO VOLTAJE

Section 4 Review

1. Describe how a bolt of lightning passes through a lightning rod to the ground.
2. How are fuses and circuit breakers alike? How are they different?
3. Are all electrical shocks to the body equally dangerous? Explain.
4. **Thinking Critically Applying Concepts** Why do you think the Empire State Building in New York City is often hit by lightning?

Science at Home

Along with members of your family, find out if the circuits in your home are protected by fuses or circuit breakers. **CAUTION:** *Be careful not to touch the wiring as you inspect it.* How many circuits are there in your home? Make a diagram showing the outlets and appliances on each circuit. Explain the role of fuses and circuit breakers. Ask your family members if they are aware of these devices in other circuits, such as in a car.

Program Resources

- ◆ **Teaching Resources** 2-4 Review and Reinforce, p. 55; 2-4 Enrich, p. 56

Media and Technology

 **Interactive Student Tutorial CD-ROM** N-2

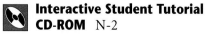 **Exploring Physical Science Videodisc**
Unit 5, Side 1,
"Lightning Strikes"

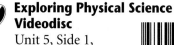

Chapter 2

SECTION 1 Electric Charge and Static Electricity

Key Ideas
◆ Like charges repel each other and unlike charges attract each other.
◆ An electric field is produced in the region around an electric charge. The field can be represented by electric field lines.
◆ Static electricity results when electrons move from one object to another, or from one location to another within an object.
◆ During an electric discharge, charges leave a charged object, making the object neutral.

Key Terms
electric field
static electricity
friction
conduction

induction
conservation of charge
static discharge
electroscope

SECTION 2 Circuit Measurements

Key Ideas
◆ Electric current flows when voltage is applied to a circuit.
◆ Voltage, which is measured in volts, is the potential difference between two places in a circuit.
◆ Resistance, which is measured in ohms, is the opposition to the flow of charge.
◆ If resistance is held constant, an increase in voltage produces an increase in current.
◆ If voltage is held constant, an increase in resistance produces a decrease in current.

Key Terms
electrical potential
potential difference
voltage
voltage source
voltmeter
ammeter
Ohm's law

SECTION 3 Series and Parallel Circuits

Key Ideas
◆ A series circuit is a circuit in which charges have only one path to flow through.
◆ A parallel circuit is a circuit that contains different branches through which charges can flow. Household circuits are parallel circuits.

Key Terms
series circuit

parallel circuit

SECTION 4 Electrical Safety

INTEGRATING HEALTH

Key Ideas
◆ Fuses, circuit breakers, and grounded plugs are all important safety devices found in electric circuits.
◆ A lightning rod provides a conducting path to Earth, so that electric charges from lightning can travel directly into Earth without damaging a structure.
◆ The human body can be seriously injured by shocks, even those of less than one ampere.

Key Terms
short circuit
third prong
grounded

lightning rod
fuse
circuit breaker

USING THE INTERNET

ACTIVITY

www.science-explorer.phschool.com

Chapter 2 **N ◆ 73**

Program Resources

◆ **Teaching Resources** Chapter 2 Project Scoring Rubric, p. 40; Chapter 2 Performance Assessment Teacher Notes, p. 137; Chapter 2 Performance Assessment Student Worksheet, p. 139; Chapter 2 Test, pp. 140–143

Reviewing Content:
Multiple Choice
1. d 2. b 3. a 4. b 5. c

True or False
6. true 7. gains 8. Induction 9. true
10. fuse

Checking Concepts
11. The electric field enables a charge to exert an electric force at a distance. The field surrounding a positive charge exerts a repulsive force on other positive charges and an attractive force on negative charges.
12. Static electricity is a buildup of charges.
13. An object is charged if it has more or less than its normal number of electrons. An object can become charged by friction, conduction, or induction. Friction: Electrons are rubbed off one object onto another object. Conduction: One charged object touches another and transfers charges. Induction: A charged object is near a neutral object, causing a rearrangement of charges in the neutral object.
14. Once static electricity builds up, objects can return to their neutral state by releasing electrons. Lightning is the sudden discharge of electrons.
15. Ohm's Law states that resistance equals the voltage divided by current. Ohm's Law relates current, resistance, and voltage.
16. Volts, amperes (amps), and ohms
17. Samples: Never handle electric appliances while in water, since some water contains ions which conduct electricity; never handle frayed wires; never overload a circuit; never touch power lines.
18. Both fuses and circuit breakers open a circuit when the current is too great. A fuse does so by melting, thereby breaking the path of electrons. A circuit breaker does so by opening a switch.
19. An ammeter measures current. A voltmeter measures voltage. Ammeters are wired in series. Voltmeters are wired in parallel.
20. Students' letters should describe the features of both types of circuits. They should point out that a parallel circuit

---

Reviewing Content

For more review of key concepts, see the Interactive Student Tutorial CD-ROM.

Multiple Choice
Choose the letter of the answer that best completes each statement.

1. A particle that carries a negative electric charge is called a(n)
   a. neutron.　　b. atom.
   c. proton.　　d. electron.
2. When you charge an electroscope by touching it with a charged balloon, the process is called
   a. friction.　　b. conduction.
   c. induction.　　d. grounding.
3. The potential difference that causes charges to move in a circuit is
   a. voltage.
   b. resistance.
   c. current.
   d. electric discharge.
4. An example of a voltage source is a
   a. voltmeter.
   b. battery.
   c. resistance.
   d. switch.
5. A circuit that is connected to Earth is said to be
   a. series.　　b. parallel.
   c. grounded.　　d. discharged.

True or False
If the statement is true, write true. If it is false, change the underlined word or words to make the statement true.

6. Your hair might be attracted to your comb as your hair and the comb become <u>oppositely</u> charged.
7. A neutral object becomes negatively charged when it <u>loses</u> electrons.
8. <u>Conduction</u> is the process of charging an object without touching it.
9. Electrical resistance is low in a good <u>conductor</u>.
10. A <u>circuit breaker</u> contains a thin strip of metal that melts if too much current passes through it.

Checking Concepts

11. Describe the electric field surrounding a charge.
12. What is static electricity?
13. What does it mean to say that an object is charged? Describe the three ways in which an object can become charged.
14. How is lightning related to static electricity?
15. State and describe Ohm's Law.
16. What units are used to measure voltage, current, and resistance?
17. Discuss three safety rules to follow while using electricity.
18. How do fuses and circuit breakers act as safety devices in a circuit?
19. What type of meter is used to measure current? To measure voltage? How should each meter be connected in a circuit?
20. **Writing to Learn** You are an electrician about to design the electrical wiring system for a new house. Your plans call for parallel circuits, but the owners insist that a series circuit will be simpler and cheaper. Write a letter to the owners explaining why you need to use parallel circuits. Include drawings with your letter.

Thinking Visually

21. **Venn Diagram** Copy the Venn diagram comparing series and parallel circuits. Then complete it and add a title. (For more information on Venn Diagrams, see the Skills Handbook.)

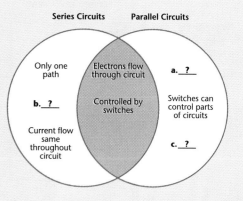

---

will enable them to switch off certain devices without shutting off all the others. Students should illustrate a parallel circuit as it might be designed for a home.

Thinking Visually

21. Sample title: Two Types of Circuits; **a:** Multiple paths; **b:** Switch controls entire circuit; **c:** Current flow can be different.

Applying Skills

22. Both. Bulbs 2 and 3 are parallel to each other, and in series with Bulb 1.
23. If Bulb 1 were removed, the others would go out because the circuit would be broken. If Bulb 2 were removed, the others would remain lit because the current has another route to follow.
24. None of the bulbs would be lit if the switch were open because the switch breaks the flow of current back to the battery.

Applying Skills

Use the illustration of an electric circuit to answer Questions 22–25.

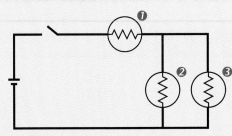

22. Classifying Is the circuit in the illustration series or parallel?

23. Controlling Variables Would the other bulbs continue to shine if you removed Bulb 1? Would they shine if you removed Bulb 2 instead? Explain your reasoning.

24. Predicting Will any of the bulbs be lit if you open the switch? Explain.

25. Making Models Redraw the circuit diagram to include a switch that controls only Bulb 3.

Thinking Critically

26. Comparing and Contrasting Compare the force a proton exerts on another proton with the force a proton exerts on an electron. Explain your answer.

27. Problem Solving A toaster is plugged into a 120-volt socket. If it has a resistance of 20 ohms, how much current will flow through the toaster coils? Show your work.

28. Classifying Identify each of the following statements as characteristic of series circuits, parallel circuits, or both:

a. $I = V \div R$

b. Total resistance increases as more light bulbs are added.

c. Total resistance decreases as more branches are added.

d. Current in each part of the circuit is the same.

e. A break in any part of the circuit will cause current to stop.

29. Applying Concepts Explain why the third prong of a grounded plug should not be removed.

29. The third prong is designed to send any stray current into the ground. A faulty device might have a casing at a high voltage. A person touching the device would then receive a shock.

Performance Assessment

Wrap Up

CHAPTER PROJECT 2

Present Your Project Prepare a description and circuit diagram for your display. If any parts of your alarm circuit are not visible, you should draw a second diagram showing how all the parts are assembled. Then present your alarm to your class and explain how it could be used.

Reflect and Record Describe the reliability of your switch. Does it work most of the time? All of the time? If your alarm circuit were to be used for a full year, would it still work? Draw sketches in your journal of parts of your alarm that would need to be redesigned so that it would last longer.

Getting Involved

In Your Community Create an electrical safety display for your school hallway or town library. Cut out pictures from magazines or newspapers, or draw some of your own. Show examples of situations in which safety precautions should be taken. Then describe the different safety precautions for those situations.

Performance Assessment

Wrap Up

CHAPTER PROJECT 2

Present Your Project Many students will need to make final connections and adjustments when they set up their projects. Have four students at a time set up their projects at separate stations. Then the class can move from station to station to see a demonstration of each project. If one student requires more time to set up than others, encourage students to visit the other three stations first. The presenter should ask other students if they can explain how the device works. Then the presenter can fill in the missing pieces of the explanation with remarks and diagrams. Following the demonstration, presenters should turn in one-page descriptions.

Reflect and Record The reliability of an alarm circuit will be affected by the performance of the switch and the effectiveness of the wiring. The batteries and light bulb may not last a year. This could be remedied by using a buzzer rather than a light bulb and using power from an electrical outlet rather than from batteries.

---

25. Students' drawings should show the switch either before or after Bulb 3.

Thinking Critically

26. Protons exert repulsive forces on other protons but attractive forces on electrons. Like charges repel each other; opposite charges attract each other.

27. $\frac{120 \text{ volts}}{20 \text{ ohms}} = 6$ amperes

28. a. both **b.** series **c.** parallel **d.** series **e.** series

Program Resources

◆ **Inquiry Skills Activity Book** Provides teaching and review of all inquiry skills

Getting Involved

In Your Community Samples: Not flying a kite near power lines; baby-proofing electrical outlets where there are small children; never handling electric appliances while in water; never handling frayed wires; never overloading a circuit.

Sections	Time	Student Edition Activities	Other Activities	
CHAPTER PROJECT 3 **Electrical Energy Audit** p. 77	Ongoing (2–3 weeks)	Check Your Progress, pp. 81, 91, 98 Wrap Up, p. 109	TE	Chapter 3 Project Notes, pp. 76–77
1 **Electricity, Magnetism, and Motion** pp. 78–83 ◆ Describe how electrical energy can be converted into mechanical energy. ◆ Explain how a galvanometer measures current and how an electric motor converts current to mechanical energy.	3 periods/ 1½ blocks	**Discover** How Does a Magnet Move a Wire?, p. 78 **Real-World Lab: How It Works** Building an Electric Motor, pp. 82–83	TE ISLM	Demonstration, p. 79 N-3, "Electricity From a Lemon"
2 **Generating Electric Current** pp. 84–91 ◆ Describe how an electric current can be induced. ◆ Explain how a generator induces electric current and compare it to a motor. ◆ Identify the main sources of energy for electric power generation.	4 periods/ 2 blocks	**Discover** Can You Produce Electric Current Without a Battery?, p. 84 **Try This** Keeping Current, p. 86 **Sharpen Your Skills** Classifying, p. 87	TE TE TE	Inquiry Challenge, p. 85 Demonstration, p. 86 Including All Students, p. 87
3 **Using Electric Power** pp. 92–98 ◆ Define and calculate power and usage of electrical energy. ◆ Describe how transformers change the voltage of electric current. ◆ Describe the transmission of electric current from power station to users.	3½ periods/ 1–2 blocks	**Discover** How Can You Make a Bulb Burn More Brightly?, p. 92 **Sharpen Your Skills** Observing, p. 95	TE IES IES	Real-Life Learning, p. 93 "Back to the Thirties," pp. 38–39 "Fate of the Rain Forest," pp. 16–19
4 *INTEGRATING CHEMISTRY* **Batteries** pp. 99–106 ◆ Describe how batteries use chemical reactions to produce electric current. ◆ Explain how electrochemical cells can be combined to make a battery.	4 periods/ 2 blocks	**Discover** Can You Make Electricity With Spare Change?, p. 99 **Skills Lab: Drawing Conclusions** Electricity Grows on Trees, pp. 104–105	TE TE TE	Inquiry Challenge, p. 101 Demonstration, p. 102 Real-Life Learning, p. 102
Study Guide/Chapter Review pp. 107–109	1 period/ ½ block		ISAB	Provides teaching and review of all inquiry skills

For Standard or Block Schedule The Resource Pro® CD-ROM gives you maximum flexibility for planning your instruction for any type of schedule. Resource Pro® contains Planning Express®, an advanced scheduling program, as well as the entire contents of the Teaching Resources and the Computer Test Bank.

CHAPTER PLANNING GUIDE

Program Resources	Assessment Strategies	Media and Technology
TR Chapter 3 Project Teacher Notes, pp. 62–63 **TR** Chapter 3 Project Overview and Worksheets, pp. 64–67 **TR** Chapter 3 Project Scoring Rubric, p. 68	**SE** Performance Assessment: Chapter 3 Project Wrap Up, p. 109 **TE** Check Your Progress, pp. 81, 91, 98 **TE** Performance Assessment: Chapter 3 Project Wrap Up, p. 109 **TR** Chapter 3 Project Scoring Rubric, p. 68	Science Explorer Internet Site
TR 3-1 Lesson Plan, p. 69 **TR** 3-1 Section Summary, p. 70 **TR** 3-1 Review and Reinforce, p. 71 **TR** 3-1 Enrich, p. 72 **TR** Chapter 3 Real-World Lab, pp. 85–87	**SE** Section 1 Review, p. 81 **SE** Analyze and Conclude, p. 83 **TE** Ongoing Assessment, p. 79 **TE** Performance Assessment, p. 81 **TR** 3-1 Review and Reinforce, p. 71	Audiotapes: English-Spanish Summary 3-1 Transparency 12, "Electric Motor" Interactive Student Tutorial CD-ROM, N-3
TR 3-2 Lesson Plan, p. 73 **TR** 3-2 Section Summary, p. 74 **TR** 3-2 Review and Reinforce, p. 75 **TR** 3-2 Enrich, p. 76 **SES** Book E, *Environmental Science,* Chapter 6	**SE** Section 2 Review, p. 91 **TE** Ongoing Assessment, pp. 85, 87, 89 **TE** Performance Assessment, p. 91 **TR** 3-2 Review and Reinforce, p. 75	Exploring Physical Science Videodisc, Unit 4 Side 2, "Wired to the Sun" Audiotapes: English-Spanish Summary 3-2 Transparency 13, "Induction of Electric Current" Transparency 14, "AC Generator" Interactive Student Tutorial CD-ROM, N-3
TR 3-3 Lesson Plan, p. 77 **TR** 3-3 Section Summary, p. 78 **TR** 3-3 Review and Reinforce, p. 79 **TR** 3-3 Enrich, p. 80	**SE** Section 3 Review, p. 98 **TE** Ongoing Assessment, pp. 93, 95, 97 **TE** Performance Assessment, p. 98 **TR** 3-3 Review and Reinforce, p. 79	Exploring Physical Science Videodisc, Unit 5 Side 1, "Generating Electricity" Audiotapes: English-Spanish Summary 3-3 Transparency 15, "Transmission of Electric Power" Interactive Student Tutorial CD-ROM, N-3
TR 3-4 Lesson Plan, p. 81 **TR** 3-4 Section Summary, p. 82 **TR** 3-4 Review and Reinforce, p. 83 **TR** 3-4 Enrich, p. 84 **TR** Chapter 3 Skills Lab, pp. 88–89 **SES** Book L, *Chemical Interactions,* Chapter 4	**SE** Section 4 Review, p. 103 **SE** Analyze and Conclude, p. 105 **TE** Ongoing Assessment, p. 101 **TE** Performance Assessment, p. 103 **TR** 3-4 Review and Reinforce, p. 83	Exploring Physical Science Videodisc, Unit 5 Side 1, "Batteries" Audiotapes: English-Spanish Summary 3-4 Transparency 16, "Dry Cell and Car Battery" Interactive Student Tutorial CD-ROM, N-3
TR Chapter 3 Performance Assessment, pp. 144–146 **TR** Chapter 3 Test, pp. 147–150	**SE** Chapter Review, pp. 107–109 **TR** Chapter 3 Performance Assessment: pp. 144–146 **TR** Chapter 3 Test, pp. 147–150 **CTB** Test N-3	Computer Test Bank, Test N-3 Interactive Student Tutorial CD-ROM, N-3

Key: **SE** Student Edition **TE** Teacher's Edition **TR** Teaching Resources
CTB Computer Test Bank **SES** Science Explorer Series Text **ISLM** Integrated Science Laboratory Manual
ISAB Inquiry Skills Activity Book **PTA** Product Testing Activities by *Consumer Reports* **IES** Interdisciplinary Explorations Series

Meeting the National Science Education Standards and AAAS Benchmarks

National Science Education Standards	Benchmarks for Science Literacy	Unifying Themes
Science as Inquiry (Content Standard A) ◆ **Think critically and logically to make the relationships between evidence and explanations** Students carry out a home electrical energy audit to determine electrical energy use. *(Chapter Project)* Students evaluate the safety of disposing of dead batteries. *(Science and Society)* ◆ **Recognize and analyze alternative explanations and predictions** The dispute between Edison and Tesla involved using AC or DC current. *(Section 3)* **Physical Science** (Content Standard B) ◆ **Properties and changes of properties in matter** In an electrochemical cell, one electrode loses electrons while the other gains electrons. *(Section 4; Skills Lab)* ◆ **Transfer of energy** Motors and generators convert between electrical and mechanical energy. *(Sections 1–3; Real-World Lab)* In a wet or dry cell, chemical energy is converted into electrical energy. *(Section 4; Skills Lab)* **Science and Technology** (Content Standard E) ◆ **Implement a proposed design** Students build a motor and a cell. *(Real-World Lab; Skills Lab)* **Science in Personal and Social Perspectives** (Content Standard F) ◆ **Populations, resources, and environments** Batteries contain toxic compounds. Using rechargeable batteries is one alternative. *(Science and Society)* Some electrical energy resources are renewable while others are nonrenewable. *(Section 2)*	**1A The Scientific World View** Edison believed the high voltages of AC current would harm people, while Tesla believed the efficiency of AC current outweighed its risks. Tesla's system prevailed. *(Section 3)* **2B Mathematical Inquiry** Students calculate power and the cost of electrical energy using equations. *(Section 2; Chapter Project)* **3B Design and Systems** Students learn how an electric motor works and build an electrochemical cell. *(Real-World Lab; Skills Lab)* **3C Issues in Technology** The inexpensive production of batteries has led to a disposal problem. *(Science and Society)* **4D The Structure of Matter** In electrochemical cells, current is generated as reactants are converted into products. In a rechargeable battery, this current reverses the reaction. *(Section 4; Skills Lab)* **4E Energy Transformation** Electrical energy can be induced by passing a conductor through a magnetic field. *(Section 1)* Electrical energy can be converted into mechanical energy. Mechanical energy can be converted into electrical energy. A galvanometer measures the amount of electrical energy flowing through a circuit. *(Sections 1, 2; Real-World Lab)* Transformers alter the voltage of electrical energy in an alternating current. *(Section 3)* **8C Energy Sources and Use** Electrical energy can be generated from a variety of renewable resources and nonrenewable resources. *(Section 2)* **12A Values and Attitudes** Students examine the controversy between Tesla and Edison. *(Section 3)*	◆ **Energy** Electricity can be converted into many forms of energy, including mechanical and thermal. Energy from a magnetic field can induce electric current. Electrical energy can be generated from many sources, including solar energy, falling water, geothermal energy, and nuclear energy. Transformers can increase or decrease the voltage of electrical energy. Electrochemical cells store energy chemically and convert it into electricity. *(Sections 1, 2, 3, 4; Skills Lab; Real-World Lab; Chapter Project)* ◆ **Unity and Diversity** Electric motors and electric generators both use electromagnets to convert one form of energy into another form. Electric motors convert electric energy into mechanical energy; electric generators convert mechanical energy into electric energy. *(Sections 1, 2; Real-World Lab)* ◆ **Systems and Interactions** When a loop of wire spins inside a magnetic field, current is generated. Electric current can be alternating or direct, depending on the type of generator that produces the current. Wet and dry cells pass electrons from a positive to a negative terminal; a cell is made up of two electrodes submerged in an electrolyte. *(Sections 1, 2, 3, 4; Skills Lab; Real-World Lab)* ◆ **Stability** A magnetic field always exists around a current-carrying wire. *(Section 1)*

Media and Technology

Exploring Physical Science Videodisc
◆ **Section 2** "Wired to the Sun" tours a solar-powered home and defines active and passive solar systems.
◆ **Section 4** "Batteries" explains how chemical energy is converted to electrical energy inside a battery and models how dry-cell and wet-cell batteries work.

Interactive Student Tutorial CD-ROM
◆ **Chapter Review** Interactive questions help students to self-assess their mastery of key chapter concepts.

Student Edition Connection Strategies

◆ **Section 1** Social Studies Connection, p. 80
◆ **Section 2** Integrating Environmental Science, p. 91
◆ **Section 3** Science and History, pp. 96–97
◆ **Section 4** Integrating Chemistry, p. 99

USING THE INTERNET ACTIVITY

www.science-explorer.phschool.com

Visit the Science Explorer Internet site to find an up-to-date activity for Chapter 3 of *Electricity and Magnetism*.

ACTIVITY	Time (minutes)	Materials — Quantities for one work group	Skills
Section 1			
Discover, p. 78	20	**Nonconsumable** books, ruler, copper wire, steel nail, horseshoe magnet, circuit wire, switch, battery	Inferring
Real-World Lab, pp. 82–83	45	**Consumable** 2 large paper clips, empty film canister, sandpaper **Nonconsumable** D cell; permanent bar magnet; 3 balls of clay; pliers; 2 insulated wires, approximately 15 cm each; enamel-coated wire, 22–24 gauge, approximately 1 meter	Making Models, Inferring
Section 2			
Discover, p. 84	10	**Nonconsumable** 1-m wire, galvanometer or multimeter, horseshoe magnet	Developing Hypotheses
Try This, p. 86	20	**Nonconsumable** 1-m wire, galvanometer or multimeter, bar magnet	Interpreting Data
Sharpen Your Skills, p. 87	10	**Nonconsumable** 2 identical hand generators	Classifying
Section 3			
Discover, p. 92	15	**Nonconsumable** light bulb in socket, hand generator, 1-m insulated copper wire	Posing Questions
Sharpen Your Skills, p. 95	10	**Nonconsumable** household appliances such as toasters, microwaves, mixers, and blenders	Observing
Section 4			
Discover, p. 99	15	**Consumable** paper towels, salt water **Nonconsumable** 1 penny, 1 dime, metal polish, scissors, stirring rod, mixing cup, 2 10-cm copper wires, bulb in socket, voltmeter	Observing
Skills Lab, pp. 104–105	30	**Consumable** 2 apples **Nonconsumable** 2 galvanized (zinc coated) nails about 10-cm long, 2 pieces of copper about the same size as the nails, 3 30-cm pieces of insulated wire with about 2 cm of insulation removed from each end, 2 marble-sized lumps of clay, 4 clothes pins (the "pinch" type with springs), calculator powered by one 1.5-volt dry cell	Drawing Conclusions

A list of all materials required for the Student Edition activities can be found beginning on page T14. You can order Materials Kits by calling 1-800-828-7777 or by accessing the Science Explorer Internet site at **www.science-explorer.phschool.com.**

Electrical Energy Audit

Students rely on electrical energy every day but often regard it as an invisible, inexhaustible quantity. This project gives them an opportunity to calculate the amount of energy that is used in their homes.

Purpose In this project, students have the opportunity to apply chapter concepts to their daily lives by analyzing energy use in their homes. By the end of the project, they should understand which appliances are heavy electrical energy users and cost the most to operate.

Skills Focus After completing the Chapter 3 Project, students will be able to

◆ observe and measure electrical energy use;

◆ analyze data to determine how much energy is used in an average week;

◆ communicate their findings about the consumption and cost of electricity to their classmates.

Project Time Line This project will take approximately two weeks to complete. Students begin by brainstorming a list of appliances in their homes and making data tables in which they can monitor the use of these items. After recording the amount of time each appliance was used during a one-week period, students calculate energy in kilowatt-hours for all items monitored. Students should then interpret their data, display their observations in a visual format such as a graph, and present their findings to the class. Before beginning the project, see Chapter 3 Project Teacher Notes on pages 62–63 in Teaching Resources for more details on carrying out the project. Also distribute to students the Chapter 3 Project Overview, Worksheets, and Scoring Rubric on pages 64–68 in Teaching Resources.

Possible Materials Students will need paper for their data tables, writing tools, and calculators. Students may want to use poster board, colored markers, or other materials to prepare their presentations.

Launching the Project Lead a class discussion in which students consider

WHAT'S AHEAD

SECTION 1 Electricity, Magnetism, and Motion
Discover **How Does a Magnet Move a Wire?**
Real-World Lab **Building an Electric Motor**

SECTION 2 Generating Electric Current
Discover **Can You Produce Electric Current Without a Battery?**
Try This **Keeping Current**
Sharpen Your Skills **Classifying**

SECTION 3 Using Electric Power
Discover **How Can You Make a Bulb Burn More Brightly?**
Sharpen Your Skills **Observing**

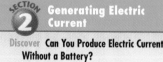

which appliances in their homes require the most power to operate and which appliances use the most energy every week.

Allow time for students to read the description of the project in their text and the Chapter Project Overview on pages 64–65 in Teaching Resources. Then encourage discussions on the appliances students will monitor. Answer any initial questions students may have and allow time for students to review the Chapter 3 Project Worksheets on pages 66–67 in Teaching Resources.

Electrical Energy Audit

Have you ever heard someone complain about high electric bills? Electricity can be expensive, but there are good reasons why. Generating electricity and delivering it to customers is a complicated business.

In this chapter, you will discover how electricity is generated and used. As you work through the chapter, you will study electrical energy consumption in your home.

Your Goal To analyze the ways you use electricity at home and to determine how much electricity you and your family use.

To complete the project you will
- prepare a list of appliances in your home, including lights, that use electricity
- record the length of time each appliance is used during an average week
- calculate how much electrical energy is used to operate each appliance
- follow the safety guidelines in Appendix A

Get Started Begin by preparing a data table you can use to keep track of your observations. You should include columns for the name of the appliance, whether it is plugged in or battery operated, the primary use of the appliance, and the number of hours it is used each day.

Check Your Progress You'll be working on this project as you study this chapter. To keep your project on track, look for Check Your Progress boxes at the following points.

Section 1 Review, page 81: List all of the electric appliances in your home.

Section 2 Review, page 91: Calculate the amount of time each appliance is used during a week.

Section 3 Review, page 98: Calculate the amount of energy consumed by each appliance.

Wrap Up At the end of the chapter (page 109), you will calculate the total amount of electrical energy consumed and determine which appliance in your home uses the most electrical energy.

High-voltage transmission lines glisten in the sunlight.

Integrating Chemistry

SECTION 4 Batteries

Discover **Can You Make Electricity With Spare Change?**
Skills Lab **Electricity Grows on Trees**

Program Resources

◆ **Teaching Resources** Chapter 3 Project Teacher Notes, pp. 62–63; Chapter 3 Project Overview and Worksheets, pp. 64–67; Chapter 3 Project Scoring Rubric, p. 68

Performance Assessment

The Chapter 3 Project Scoring Rubric on page 68 of Teaching Resources will help you evaluate how well students complete the Chapter 3 Project. Students will be assessed on
- the completeness of their data table entries, including total amount of time each appliance was used during the week and the number of kilowatt-hours each used;
- the graphical presentation of their data including style, neatness, labeling, and accuracy;
- the thoroughness and organization of their presentations and how well they demonstrate their understanding of the main ideas behind their data.

By sharing the Chapter 3 Scoring Rubric with students at the beginning of the project, you will make it clear to them what they are expected to do.

Electricity, Magnetism, and Motion

Objectives

After completing the lesson, students will be able to

♦ describe how electrical energy can be converted into mechanical energy;

♦ explain how a galvanometer measures current and how an electric motor converts current to mechanical energy.

Key Terms energy, electrical energy, mechanical energy, galvanometer, electric motor, commutator, brushes, armature

1 Engage/Explore

Activating Prior Knowledge

Ask students to list devices that use electricity. Then ask: **Which of these devices produce sound? Light? Movement?** *(Student answers will vary depending on the items.)* **What is the energy source?** *(electricity)*

⋯⋯⋯ DISCOVER ⋯⋯⋯

Skills Focus inferring
Materials *books, ruler,*

insulated or enameled copper wire, steel nail, horseshoe magnet, circuit wire, switch, battery
Time 20 minutes
Tips The nail should be parallel to the horseshoe magnet. Test the device in advance to be sure the magnet is strong enough to attract the electromagnet.
Think It Over The electromagnet swings when the switch is closed. It swings in the opposite direction when the battery connections are reversed. Electricity in a wire creates a magnetic field that interacts with the magnet. The force between them causes the wire to move.

Electricity, Magnetism, and Motion

DISCOVER ⋯⋯⋯⋯⋯⋯⋯⋯⋯⋯⋯⋯⋯⋯ ACTIVITY ⋯

How Does a Magnet Move a Wire?

1. Make an electromagnet by winding insulated copper wire around a steel nail.

2. Make a pile of books, and place a ruler between the top two books.

3. Hang the electromagnet over the ruler so that it hangs free.

4. Complete the circuit by connecting the electromagnet to a switch and a battery.

5. Set a horseshoe magnet near the electromagnet. Then close the switch briefly and observe what happens to the electromagnet.

6. Reverse the wires connected to the battery and repeat Step 5.

Think It Over

Inferring What happened to the electromagnet when you closed the switch? Was anything different when you reversed the wires? How can you use electricity to produce motion?

GUIDE FOR READING

♦ How can electrical energy be converted into mechanical energy?

♦ What do galvanometers and electric motors do?

Reading Tip Preview the figures and captions. Then read to find out how magnetic forces and electric current are related to motion.

What comes to mind when you think about electricity? You may think of the bright lights of a big city, or the music from the radio in your bedroom. If you are familar with electric motors like the one in a movie projector, then you already know about a very important application of electricity. Electricity can produce motion.

Electrical and Mechanical Energy

As you have learned, magnets can produce motion. They can move together or move apart, depending on how their poles are arranged. You have also learned that an electric current in a wire produces a magnetic field similar to that of a magnet. So you can understand that a magnet can move a wire, as it would move another magnet.

The wire at the top of Figure 1 is placed in a magnetic field. When current flows through the wire, the magnetic field pushes the wire down. If the current is reversed, the magnetic field pulls the wire up. The direction in which the wire moves depends on the direction of the current.

READING STRATEGIES

Reading Tip Have students preview the figures and captions with partners. Ask them to list unfamiliar terms, leaving space to define the terms as they read the section. Then have them do the same with questions they have about the relationship between magnetic forces and electric current. After students finish reading, have them read their questions aloud and challenge classmates to answer them.

Study and Comprehension After students read the section, have them imagine they are newspaper or television reporters. Ask them to write news stories on one of these topics: Galvanometers, How an Electric Motor Works, the Parts of a Motor. Encourage students to answer the questions What? Why? and How? in their stories. Suggest students use information from the Reading Tip activity in their stories. Invite volunteers to read their stories aloud.

The interaction between electricity and magnetism can cause something to move—in this case, a wire. The ability to move an object some distance is called **energy.** The energy associated with electric currents is called **electrical energy.** And the energy an object has due to its movement or position is called **mechanical energy.**

Energy can be changed from one form into another. **When a current-carrying wire is placed in a magnetic field, electrical energy is converted into mechanical energy.** This happens because the magnetic field of the current makes the wire move.

☑ *Checkpoint* *What is energy?*

Galvanometers

The straight wire in Figure 1 moves up or down in the magnetic field. What will happen if you bend a wire into a loop before placing it in a magnetic field? Look at the rectangular loop of wire in Figure 2. The current in the wire travels up one side of the loop and down the other. In other words, current travels in opposite directions on the two sides of the loop.

Since the direction the wire moves depends on the direction of the current, the two sides move in opposite directions. Once each side has moved as far up or down as it can go, it will stop moving. The result is that the loop rotates half a turn.

The rotation of a loop of wire in a magnetic field is the basis of a device called a **galvanometer,** which is used to measure small currents. In a galvanometer several loops of wire are suspended between the poles of a magnet. The loops of wire are also attached to a pointer and to a spring, as in Figure 2. When current flows through the wire, the current produces a magnetic field. This field interacts with the field of the magnet, causing the loops of wire and the pointer to rotate. **Electric current is used to turn the pointer of a galvanometer.** The force of the

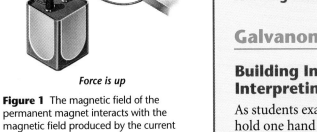

Force is down

Force is up

Figure 1 The magnetic field of the permanent magnet interacts with the magnetic field produced by the current in the wire. *Interpreting Diagrams How does the direction of the current affect the force on the wire?*

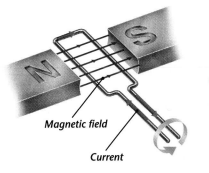

Magnetic field

Current

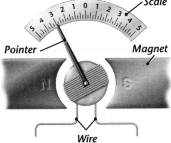

Scale

Pointer

Magnet

N   S

Wire

Figure 2 Since current travels in a different direction in each half of the wire loop (left), one side is pushed down while the other is pulled up. A galvanometer (right) uses loops of wire to move a pointer.

Program Resources

◆ **Teaching Resources** 3-1 Lesson Plan, p. 69; 3-1 Section Summary, p. 70
◆ **Integrated Science Laboratory Manual,** N-3, "Electricity from a Lemon"

Media and Technology

🎧 **Audiotapes** English-Spanish Summary 3-1

Answers to Self-Assessment

Caption Question

Figure 1 When the direction of the current changes, the direction of the force changes.

☑ *Checkpoint*

Energy is the ability to move an object some distance.

---

2 Facilitate

Electrical and Mechanical Energy

Using the Visuals: Figure 1

Ask: **What is different in the two diagrams?** (*The direction of the current*) Have students describe what is happening in each diagram. (*First: There is a downward force on the wire. Second: There is an upward force on the wire.*) **learning modality: visual**

Galvanometers

Building Inquiry Skills: Interpreting Diagrams

As students examine Figure 2, have them hold one hand flat to represent the loop of wire, then trace the path of current around their hand. Have students move their hands to show what happens when the loop of wire is placed in a magnetic field like the one in the diagram. (*Students should turn their hands sideways.*) **limited English proficiency**

Demonstration

Materials *compass, electrical tape, insulated wire (1.2 m), board (10 × 15 cm), 12-V battery, wire strippers*
Time 20 minutes

ACTIVITY

To build a galvanometer, affix the underside of the compass to the wood with a loop of tape, then wrap the wire around the board and the compass, with stripped ends of the wire protruding from opposite sides of the board. Attach the wires to the battery. Ask: **How can you tell when current is flowing through the wire?** (*The compass needle is deflected.*) **learning modality: visual**

Ongoing Assessment

Writing Have students describe how electrical energy can be converted into mechanical energy.

Social Studies CONNECTION

Remind students that until about 100 years ago, electrical appliances did not exist. Encourage students to imagine how they would perform everyday tasks, such as vacuuming, washing clothes, and ironing, without electricity. Invite volunteers who have visited museums dedicated to reproducing early American life to describe some of the tools or methods used by people before electricity.

In Your Journal Students' posters should describe the advantages of using the new electrical appliance. You may want to provide examples of advertisements for students to refer to. Students may be interested in comparing modern newspaper ads to ads from the turn of the century. **learning modality: visual**

Using the Visuals: Figure 3

Have students examine the figure. Ask: **How does the motor convert electrical energy into mechanical energy?** (*The wire loop rotates in continuous half-turns, flipping every time the current changes direction.*) **learning modality: visual**

Including All Students

Some students may have difficulty remembering the meanings of the terms *commutator* and *armature*. Have students look up the origins of the words. (Commutate—*Latin for "commute or exchange;"* armature—*Latin for "to arm"*) Challenge students to develop memory devices to help them recall the terms. (*Samples: Commute-mutator: the current commutes through the wire; the commutator mutates its direction of travel. An armature with many loops is heavily armed.*) **learning modality: verbal**

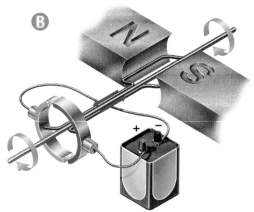

Figure 3 A loop of wire in a motor spins continuously. **A.** The magnetic field of the loop makes it rotate to a vertical position. **B.** As the loop of wire passes the vertical position, each half of the commutator makes contact with the opposite brush. The direction of current flow changes, and so does the direction of the magnetic force on the loop. The loop continues to spin the same direction.

Social Studies CONNECTION

The sewing machine was invented before electricity came into general use. Find out about the sewing machine, the refrigerator, or some other household device that was originally operated without an electric motor.

In Your Journal

Sketch an advertising poster that could have been used to introduce the new, electrically operated version of the device. Be sure to show how electricity has improved the machine and the lives of its users.

interaction of the fields acts against the spring. So the amount of rotation of the loops of wire and the pointer depends on the amount of current in the wire. A galvanometer has a scale that is marked to show how much the pointer turns for a known current. An unknown current can then be measured with a galvanometer.

☑ *Checkpoint* How does a galvanometer work?

Electric Motors

The wire in the magnetic field of a galvanometer cannot rotate more than half a turn. Suppose you could make a loop of wire rotate continuously. Instead of moving a pointer, the wire could turn a rod, or axle. The axle could then turn something else, such as the blades of a fan or blender. Such a device would be an electric motor. An **electric motor** is a device that uses an electric current to turn an axle.

An electric motor converts electrical energy into mechanical energy. An electric motor is different from a galvanometer because in a motor, a loop of current-carrying wire spins continuously.

How a Motor Works How can you make a loop of wire continue to spin? The direction of the force on the wire depends on the current and the magnetic field. In a motor, current is reversed just as the loop gets to the vertical position. This reverses the force on

---

Background

History of Science The first generator that could be readily used by consumers and industry was built in 1871 by a French inventor, Zénobe-Théophile Gramme (1826–1901). He demonstrated his device, called the Gramme dynamo, at an exhibition in Vienna in 1873. It had iron-cored electromagnets and an iron ring armature surrounded by a winding, and during the exhibition Gramme discovered the dynamo could run in reverse and function as a motor as well as a generator.

Gramme's dynamo was a direct current (DC) generator, and supplied a basis for the early supply of direct electric current.

each side of the loop. The side of the loop that was pushed up on the left is now pushed down on the right. The side of the loop that was pushed down on the right is now pushed up on the left. The current reverses after each half turn so that the loop spins continuously in the same direction.

Parts of a Motor A **commutator** is a device that reverses the flow of current through an electric motor. You can see in Figure 3 that a commutator consists of two parts of a ring. Each half of the commutator is attached to one end of the loop of wire. When the loop of wire rotates, the commutator rotates as well. As it moves, the commutator slides past two contact points called **brushes**. Each half of the commutator is connected to the current source by one of the brushes.

As the loop of wire gets to the vertical position, each half of the commutator makes contact with the other brush. Since the current runs through the brushes, changing brushes reverses the direction of the current in the loop. Changing the direction of the current causes the loop of wire to spin continuously.

Instead of a single loop of wire, practical electric motors have dozens or hundreds of loops of wire wrapped around an iron core. This arrangement of wires and iron core is called an **armature**. Using many loops increases the strength of the motor and allows it to rotate more smoothly. Large electric motors also use electromagnets in place of permanent magnets.

Figure 4 This armature contains hundreds of coils of wire. *Interpreting Photos Where is the axle of the motor?*

Section 1 Review

1. How can electricity be used to produce motion?
2. What energy conversion takes place in an electric motor and a galvanometer?
3. What measurement can be made with a galvanometer?
4. Describe how the commutator and brushes of an electric motor operate.
5. **Thinking Critically Relating Cause and Effect** Why is it important to change the direction of the current in a motor?

Check Your Progress

CHAPTER PROJECT 3

List the appliances in your home that use electricity. Check your home room by room. Throughout the course of one week, keep a record of the amount of time each appliance is used. Make a row in your data table for each appliance. Each row in the table will contain a space for the amount of time the appliance is used each day. You may want to leave a small note pad and pencil next to appliances used by others.

Program Resources

◆ **Teaching Resources** 3-1 Review and Reinforce, p. 71; 3-1 Enrich, p. 72

Media and Technology

Interactive Student Tutorial CD-ROM N-3

Transparencies "Electric Motor," Transparency 12

Answers to Self-Assessment

Caption Question

Figure 4 It runs through the center of the armature.

✓ Checkpoint

Current passes through loops of wire in a magnetic field. The magnetic field from the wire interacts with the other magnetic field, causing the loops of wire and a pointer attached to the loops to rotate.

Ask students to infer what would happen to a running motor if there were a gap between the brush and the commutator. (*The flow of electricity would be interrupted and the motor would stop turning.*) **learning modality: verbal**

3 Assess

Section 1 Review Answers

1. As current flows through an electromagnet in a magnetic field, a magnetic force will act on the electromagnet and cause it to move.
2. Electrical energy into mechanical energy
3. A galvanometer can measure small currents.
4. As the loop of wire rotates, the commutator rotates against the brushes, which are connected to the battery. The connection allows current to flow in the wire. When the wire reaches its vertical position, each side of the commutator contacts the opposite brush, causing the direction of the current to change.
5. When the wire in a motor turns halfway, it will stop moving. Since the direction of the magnetic field depends on the direction of current, reversing the current allows the loop to rotate a full circle.

Check Your Progress

CHAPTER PROJECT 3

Mention to students appliances they may not have thought about, such as an electric water heater or a furnace fan. Help students approximate electricity use for appliances that run discontinuously throughout the day. For example, a refrigerator uses about 2 kWh/day.

Performance Assessment

Drawing Have students draw a diagram of an electric motor and write captions to describe the relationship of the parts.

Building an Electric Motor

Preparing for Inquiry

Key Concept A motor is a device that converts electrical energy into mechanical energy.

Skills Objectives Students will be able to
- make a model of an electric motor;
- infer how the motor can be used to do useful work.

Time 45 minutes

Advance Planning Construct a motor yourself to make sure the materials you have available are appropriate and functional. Test the batteries to be certain they are strong enough to operate the motor.

Alternative Materials If film canisters are not available, use test tubes, glue sticks, thick markers, or any cylinder that is 1.5–3 cm in diameter as a guide for wrapping the coil.

Guiding Inquiry

Invitation Ask students to give examples of electric motors. (*Samples: Remote control model cars, motors in electric appliances such as refrigerators or vacuum cleaners, electric clocks*) Point out that most electric motors are very similar, even though they may perform very different functions.

Introducing the Procedure
- Show students how to wrap the magnet wire around the film canister.
- Demonstrate sanding the ends of the wire. For best results, hold the coil edgewise while sanding off the lower half of the insulation from one end of the wire.
- The ends of the coil wire are sharp; students must be careful not to poke themselves. If the coil is left on the paper clip supports for more than about 10 seconds, it may become very hot.

Troubleshooting the Experiment
If students have difficulty getting their motor to operate, try the following:
- Check both ends of the wire to see that

Building an Electric Motor

What does an electric trolley car have in common with a food blender, a computer disk drive, and a garage door opener? At first glance, these things may appear to be unrelated, but each one contains an electric motor. Electric motors are devices that convert electrical energy into motion. In this lab, you will build an operating electric motor.

Problem

How does an electric motor operate?

Skills Focus

making models, inferring

Materials

D cell
2 large paper clips
permanent circular magnet
3 balls of clay
empty film canister
pliers
sandpaper
2 insulated wires, approximately 15 cm each
enamel-coated wire, 22–24 gauge, approximately 1 meter

Procedure

1. Wrap about 1 meter of enamel-coated wire around a film canister. Leave approximately 5 cm free at each end.
2. Remove the film canister and wrap the two free ends three or four times around the wire coil to keep it from unwinding.
3. Use sandpaper to scrape off all the enamel from about 2 or 3 centimeters of one end of the coil of wire.

Bottom half of coating removed   *All coating removed*

4. Scrape off *half* of the enamel from about 2 or 3 centimeters of the other end of the wire. To do so, hold the coil edgewise and sand off the bottom half. See the illustration above.
5. Bend two paper clips as shown in the photo at the right. Hold them down with clay.
6. Place the free ends of the wire on the paper clips. Make sure the coil of wire is perfectly balanced. Adjust the paper clips and wire so that the coil can rotate freely.
7. Use clay to hold a permanent magnet in place directly below the coil of wire. The coil needs to be able to rotate without hitting the magnet.
8. Remove the insulation from the ends of two insulated wires. Use these wires to attach the paper clips to a D cell.
9. Give the coil a gentle push to start it turning. If it does not spin or stops spinning after a few seconds, check the following:
   - Are the paper clips in good contact with the D cell?
   - Will the coil spin in the opposite direction?
   - Will the coil work on someone else's apparatus?

---

one end has all the insulation sanded off and the other has half the insulation sanded off.
- Check the balance of the coil. If it has more weight on one side, it will not spin freely.
- Make sure the paper clips make firm contact with the D cell.
- Try the coil on another group's apparatus.
- Move the paper clips downward so the coil is closer to the permanent magnet.
- Lift the coil, reverse its connections, then set it back on the supports.
- Substitute a stronger permanent magnet.

Analyze and Conclude
1. Current flows when both uninsulated ends of the wire are in contact with the paper clips. Current does not flow when the unsanded half of the wire is in contact with the paper clip.
2. A complete circuit allows current to flow through the motor. A flowing current produces a magnetic field.
3. When the coil becomes magnetic, it is either pulled or pushed by the force of the permanent magnet.

Analyze and Conclude

1. How is the flow of current through the coil related to how you sanded the ends of the enamel-coated wire in Steps 3 and 4?
2. A magnetic field is produced when the motor is connected to the D cell. Explain why.
3. Why does the coil of wire rotate?
4. What was the purpose of removing all the insulation from one end of the wire but only half from the other end?

5. Why did the coil have to be balanced in Step 6?
6. What factors did you find that affected the motion of the coil?
7. **Apply** Your motor is capable of producing motion, but it is not capable of doing much useful work. What are some ways you could modify your motor to make it capable of doing useful work?

Design an Experiment

You have demonstrated the principles of a simple electric motor. List three factors that may affect the motion of the coil. Design experiments to test these factors. What will happen to the motor if the connections to the voltage source are reversed? Try it and find out.

4. When both uninsulated ends are in contact with the supports, the current flows and the coil rotates. If the current did not change, the coil would only be able to turn half way. The insulated part of the wire turns the current off, so the coil is allowed to continue turning. As it turns, the uninsulated parts again complete the circuit. This allows current to flow and the coil turns completely around.

5. If the wires are not balanced, the coil will move unsteadily. This causes one or both wires to lose their connection in the circuit.

6. The direction of the current determined which way the coil moved.

7. Students might suggest adding a foam or cork cylinder at the end of the coil wire and attaching a string so that as the motor turns, it lifts a paper clip or other light object. Other attachments would allow the machine to perform other tasks. Students might suggest that the amount of work the motor performs can be increased by making it more rugged, or larger. Other improvements might include using more cells.

Extending the Inquiry

Design an Experiment Students' plans should identify factors that may affect the rotation of the coil, such as the voltage, whether the coil is balanced, and whether the ends of the wire are insulated. Students should describe experiments to test these variables. Before students perform any work in the lab, check their plans for safety.

Safety

Caution students not to poke themselves with the sharp ends of the coil wire. If coil is left on the paper clip supports for more than about 10 seconds, it may become very hot. Review the safety guidelines in Appendix A.

Program Resources

◆ **Teaching Resources** Chapter 3 Real-World Lab, pp. 85–87

SECTION
2 Generating
Electric
Current

Objectives

After completing the lesson, students will be able to

◆ describe how an electric current can be induced;

◆ explain how a generator induces electric current and compare it to a motor;

◆ identify the main sources of energy for electric power generation.

Key Terms electromagnetic induction, alternating current, direct current, electric generator, slip rings, turbine, renewable resource, nonrenewable resource

1 Engage/Explore

Activating Prior Knowledge

Show students a hand-held calculator. Ask: **Where does this calculator get its energy?** *(Samples: A battery, the sun)* In this section, students learn more about ways to generate current in devices such as calculators.

Skills Focus developing hypotheses
Materials *1-m wire, galvanometer or multimeter, horseshoe magnet*
Time 10 minutes
Tips To save time, set up the wires and galvanometer before the activity. Wear goggles and use wire strippers to remove the insulation from the ends of the wires.
Expected Outcome A current is produced when the wire moves. The faster the wire moves, the greater the current.
Think It Over Steps 4 and 5; if a wire is moved between the poles of a magnet, then electric current can be generated.

DISCOVER

Can You Produce Electric Current Without a Battery?

1. Obtain one meter of wire with the insulation removed from both ends.

2. Connect the wire to the terminals of a galvanometer or a sensitive multimeter.

3. Hold the wire between the poles of a strong horseshoe magnet. Observe the meter.

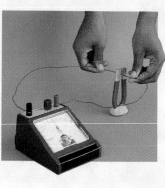

4. Move the wire up and down between the poles. Observe the meter.

5. Move the wire faster, and again observe the meter.

Think It Over

Developing Hypotheses In which steps does the meter indicate a current? Propose a hypothesis to explain how a current can exist without a battery. Be sure to use an "If . . . then . . ." statement.

GUIDE FOR READING

◆ What causes an electric current to be induced?

◆ How is a generator different from a motor?

◆ What are the main sources of energy for generating electricity?

Reading Tip Before you read, preview *Exploring Energy Resources* on pages 88 and 89. Write a list of any questions you have about generating electricity.

A n electric motor operates because electricity produces motion. Is the reverse true—can motion produce electricity? In 1831, scientists found out that motion in a magnetic field can cause an electric current to flow. That discovery has allowed electricity to be supplied to homes, schools, and businesses all over the world.

Induction of Electric Current

Before you can understand how electricity is supplied by your electric company, you need to know how electricity is produced. Figure 5 shows part of a wire coil placed in a magnetic field. The coil of wire is connected to a galvanometer.

Figure 5 When a coil of wire is moved up or down in a magnetic field, a current is induced in the wire.

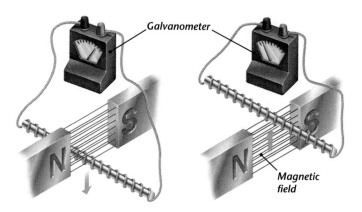

READING STRATEGIES

Reading Tip As students preview *Exploring Energy Resources,* have them choose one of the energy resources to learn more about. After students read the section and answer their questions about generating energy, have them research the energy resource. Suggest they write facts about the power resource on note cards. Invite volunteers to give brief presentations on their findings.

Study and Comprehension Have students use Venn diagrams to compare and contrast alternating and direct currents. Write the main headings from the section on note cards, one heading per card. Place the cards in a container. Have volunteers select a card, read aloud the heading, and summarize the information from the section that applies to the heading.

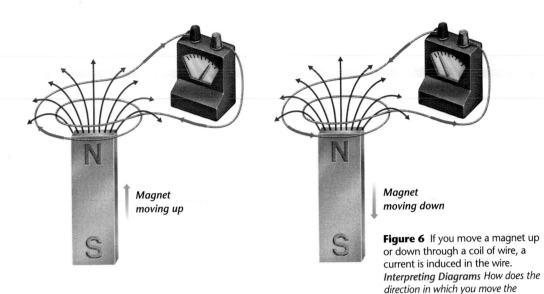

Magnet moving up

Magnet moving down

Figure 6 If you move a magnet up or down through a coil of wire, a current is induced in the wire. *Interpreting Diagrams How does the direction in which you move the magnet affect the current?*

If the wire is held still, the galvanometer does not register any current. But if the wire is moved up or down, the galvanometer indicates an electric current flowing in the wire. The current is produced without a battery or other voltage source! You saw this for yourself if you did the Discover activity.

Figure 6 shows a similar experiment in which a magnet is moved instead of a wire. The result is the same as before. An electric current is produced in the wire.

The key to using a magnet to produce a current in a conductor, such as the wire, is motion. **An electric current will be produced in a conductor when the conductor moves across the lines of a magnetic field.** Either the conductor can move through the field of a magnet or the magnet itself can move. A current flows in both cases.

Electromagnetic induction is the process of generating an electric current from the motion of a conductor through a magnetic field. The resulting current is an induced current.

☑️ *Checkpoint* *What are the two ways that a wire and a magnet can produce an induced current?*

Alternating and Direct Current

The direction of an induced current depends on the direction in which the wire or magnet moves. If, for example, the wire in Figure 5 is moved upward, the current travels in one direction. But if the wire is moved downward, the current travels in the opposite direction. **The flow of an induced current may be constant, or may change direction.**

Program Resources

◆ **Teaching Resources** 3-2 Lesson Plan, p. 73; 3-2 Section Summary, p. 74

Media and Technology

🎧 **Audiotapes** English-Spanish Summary 3-2

📽️ **Transparencies** "Induction of Electric Current," Transparency 13

Answers to Self-Assessment

Caption Question

Figure 6 The direction of current changes when the direction that the magnet moves changes.

☑️ *Checkpoint*

Electric current can be induced in a conductor when a coil of wire is moved in a magnetic field, or when a magnet is moved through a coil of wire.

2 Facilitate

Induction of Electric Current

Using the Visuals: Figures 5 and 6

Ask students to examine Figure 5. Ask: **How is the current produced?** *(The coil of wire is moved up and down between two magnets.)* As students examine Figure 6, ask: **In which diagram in the figure is the current moving clockwise? Counter-clockwise?** *(left; right)* Then ask: **What do the arrows above the magnet represent?** *(The magnetic field)* **learning modality: visual**

Inquiry Challenge

Materials *bar magnet, electromagnet (wire-wrapped nail), galvanometer*
Time 30 minutes

Have groups design experiments to demonstrate electromagnetic induction. Each student should perform a task, such as reading the galvanometer or moving the objects. *(Sample: Stroke the magnet along the nail while observing the meter.)* Ask: **What happens when the number of coils is doubled?** *(Current increases.)* **cooperative learning**

Alternating and Direct Current

Building Inquiry Skills: Communicating

Ask: **How can you change the direction of an induced current?** *(Change the direction in which the wire or magnet producing the current moves.)* **learning modality: verbal**

Ongoing Assessment

Oral Presentation Ask students to list materials they would need to generate an induced current.

Alternating and Direct Current, continued

Skills Focus interpreting data

Materials *1-m wire, galvanometer or multimeter, bar magnet*

Time 20 minutes

Tips Suggest students record their findings in data tables. Tell students they can increase the strength of the field by using more than one magnet.

Interpreting Data The results are affected by the number of loops, the strength of the field, the direction of the magnet, and how fast the magnet moves.

Extend Using the materials from the activity, challenge students to combine as many factors as they can in order to create the strongest current. **learning modality: kinesthetic**

Addressing Naive Conceptions

Students may believe that direct current is produced by a battery in the same way as a current is induced by a magnetic field. Explain that induced currents are produced when the energy of motion through a magnetic field is converted to electrical energy. Batteries do not involve motion or magnets; they convert chemical energy to electrical energy. **learning modality: verbal**

Generators

Demonstration

Materials *bicycle, bicycle dynamo*

Time 20 minutes

Have students compare the parts of the dynamo to the parts of the generator in Figure 7. Ask: **What causes the axle on the dynamo to turn?** (*The moving pedals of the bicycle*) Have students predict what happens when the pedals turn the axle. (*Sample: Electricity is generated.*) Rotate the pedals quickly so that the dynamo turns the bicycle light on. **learning modality: visual**

TRY THIS

Keeping Current

What factors affect an induced current?

1. Obtain a wire about one meter long with the insulation removed from both ends.
2. Coil the wire into about 15 loops.
3. Connect the ends of the wire to a galvanometer or multimeter.
4. Move the end of a bar magnet halfway into the coil. Observe the meter.
5. One at a time, change the following and observe the galvanometer: the number of loops, the strength of the magnet, the direction of the magnet, and how far and how fast you move the magnet into the coil.

Interpreting Data Which variables affect your results the most? The least? Explain your observations.

What would happen if a wire in a magnetic field were moved up and down repeatedly? The induced current in the wire would reverse direction repeatedly as well. This kind of current is called **alternating current,** or AC. A current consisting of charges that move back and forth in a circuit is an alternating current. The electric current in the circuits in your home is alternating current.

A current consisting of charges that flow in one direction only is called **direct current,** or DC. A battery produces direct current. When a battery is placed in a circuit, electrons move away from one end of the battery, around the circuit, and into the other end of the battery.

Generators

An **electric generator** converts mechanical energy into electrical energy. An electric generator is the opposite of an electric motor. **An electric motor uses an electric current to produce motion. A generator uses motion to produce an electric current.**

AC Generators A simple AC generator is shown in Figure 7. As the axle is turned, the loop of wire rotates in the magnetic field. One side of the loop moves up, and the other side moves down. This motion induces a current in the wire. The current travels up one side of the loop and down the other.

After the loop turns halfway, each side of the loop reverses direction in the magnetic field. The side that moved up now moves down, and vice versa. As a result, the current in the wire changes direction as well. In this way the generator produces an alternating current.

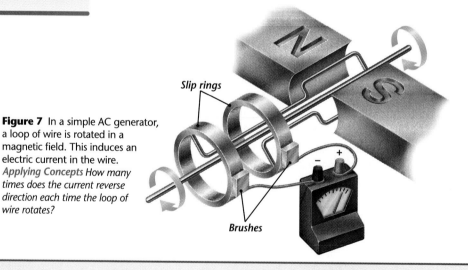

Figure 7 In a simple AC generator, a loop of wire is rotated in a magnetic field. This induces an electric current in the wire. *Applying Concepts How many times does the current reverse direction each time the loop of wire rotates?*

Slip rings

Brushes

Background

Facts and Figures Piezoelectricity is another way to change mechanical energy into electrical energy. Piezoelectricity is caused by the attraction of positive and negative charges on opposite sides of a crystal that is not a good electrical conductor, such as a thin slab of quartz. The crystal must be placed under pressure for the opposite charges to appear. When the piezoelectric effect occurs, the crystal undergoes a physical change, deforming slightly in shape due to the attraction of the opposite charges. By alternating the electric field, the crystal's deformation is also altered. Alternating electric fields cause mechanical vibrations of the same frequency. These vibrations can convert an electric signal into sound waves. Piezoelectricity has been used in phonograph pickups, and is used in electronic equipment, clocks, and watches.

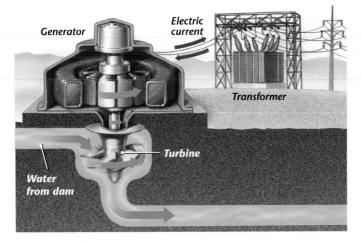

Generator

Electric current

Transformer

Turbine

Water from dam

Figure 8 In most generators, a source of mechanical energy turns huge turbines such as this one. The turbine is attached to the armature of a generator, which then produces electric current.

How does the current travel to the rest of the circuit as the axle turns? **Slip rings** are attached to the ends of the wire loop in a generator. As the loop turns, the slip rings turn with it. The slip rings make contact with the brushes. The brushes are connected to the rest of the circuit, just as they are in an electric motor. The slip rings and brushes allow the loop to turn freely, yet still allow current to travel from the loop to the rest of the circuit. Large generators use armatures similar to those in a motor. They contain hundreds of loops of wire wrapped around an iron core.

DC Generators A DC generator is like an AC generator, except that it contains a commutator instead of slip rings. Replacing the slip rings in the generator in Figure 7 will make it look just like the DC motor in Section 1. In fact, a DC generator and a DC motor are the same thing. If you run electricity through a DC motor, it will spin. But if you spin the motor, you will produce electricity. The motor becomes a DC generator.

☑ *Checkpoint* *What is an electric generator?*

Turbines

A generator converts mechanical energy into electrical energy. When an electric company generates electricity, this mechanical energy usually involves huge turbines that turn. A **turbine** is a circular device made up of many blades. The turbine shown in Figure 8 is just like a propeller turned by water.

Not all turbines are turned by water. **Flowing water from a dam, wind, steam from the burning of fuels, and even the ocean's tides can be used to turn turbines.** Several sources of energy are shown in *Exploring Energy Resources* on the next two pages.

Sharpen your Skills

Classifying ACTIVITY

1. Connect the wires from two hand generators to each other.

2. Have a partner hold one generator as you turn the crank on the other.

3. Now hold your generator as your partner turns the crank on the other one. Do not crank both generators at the same time.

Which hand generator acts like a motor and which acts like a generator? How do you know?

Classifying

Materials *2 identical hand generators*
Time 10 minutes
Tips Place the generators at one station and allow partners to take turns cranking. If the second generator does not crank, make sure the wire connections are tight.
Expected Outcome As one generator is cranked, the other crank also turns. As one is reversed, the other is also reversed.
Classifying The hand generator being cranked acts as a generator; it converts mechanical energy to electrical energy. The hand generator that is turned by the current acts as a motor; it converts electrical energy to mechanical energy.
Extend Ask: **How could you determine whether all the energy is converted to mechanical energy by the motor?** (*Turn the first crank 20 times and count the number of times the second crank turns.*)

Turbines

Including All Students

Materials *pinwheel*
Time 5 minutes

To help students understand how moving air can create enough power to spin a turbine, have students blow gently on pinwheels. (*The pinwheel spins slowly.*) Then ask: **What will happen if you blow harder?** (*The pinwheel will spin faster.*) Finally, have students infer what would happen if the pinwheel were connected to the armature of a generator. (*The faster the pinwheel spins, the more electricity will be generated.*) **limited English proficiency**

Media and Technology

🖳 **Transparencies** "AC Generator," Transparency 14

Answers to Self-Assessment

Caption Question

Figure 7 Twice

☑ *Checkpoint*

An electric generator is a device that uses motion to produce electric current.

Ongoing Assessment

Drawing Ask students to draw and label the parts of a motor.

Energy Resources

As students read about each energy source, have them identify the kind of energy that is used to provide electrical energy. Point out that chemical reactions often release energy that can be used to power turbines. For example, ask students

♦ **How does tidal energy turn a turbine?** *(When the tide moves large amounts of water, the water pushes the turbine.)* **What kind of energy is this?** *(Mechanical energy)*

♦ **What energy conversions take place when the sun's rays bounce off the reflective material and heat the water?** *(Light energy is converted into heat. The steam from the boiling water provides mechanical energy to turn the turbine and produce electrical energy.)*

Have students describe how fossil fuel energy can be converted into electrical energy. Ask: **What are the energy conversions that change fossil fuel energy into electrical energy?** *(Fossil fuel energy is chemical energy that is converted to heat; heat is converted to mechanical energy; mechanical energy is converted to electrical energy.)*

Extend Challenge groups of students to make flowcharts that show the energy conversions carried out by each energy resource. **learning modality: visual**

 Students can save their flowcharts in their portfolios.

EXPLORING *Energy Resources*

Electric power can be produced in several ways. Each kind of generating plant converts a particular kind of energy into electrical energy.

Solar Energy
The sun's rays can be focused on a tower by large mirrors to boil water. The resulting steam then turns a turbine. Solar cells can also collect the sun's energy and convert it directly into electrical energy.

Nuclear Energy
A tremendous amount of energy is stored in the nucleus of an atom. When the nucleus is split, the energy that is released is used to heat water. The water turns into steam, which expands and turns a turbine.

Energy From Falling Water
Hydroelectric plants near the bases of dams or waterfalls use water to turn turbines.

Background

History of Science The oldest dam known was built along the Nile River in Egypt about 5,000 years ago to supply water for the city of Memphis. When the Romans conquered parts of Spain, they left dams behind. Two of these, built with stone faces and filled with earth, still function. Few technological advances in dam construction appeared until the Industrial Revolution. By the mid-nineteenth century, scientists began to apply an understanding of structural engineering and the geological properties of soils and rocks to build taller, longer-lasting dams. As the physical structure of dams became more resistant to the forces of flood waters and shifting soils, new designs were developed; but the principal materials for building dams has remained the same. Most modern dams are still constructed out of stone masonry, concrete, and soil.

Geothermal Energy
In a few locations on Earth, underground water heated by molten rock turns to steam. This steam, which can be obtained through steam vents or drilling, is then used to turn a turbine.

Energy From Fossil Fuels
Coal, natural gas, and oil can be burned in generating plants to produce steam. The steam pushes against the blades of a turbine, causing it to turn.

Energy From Wind
A windmill is essentially a turbine. As the wind blows, it turns the blades of the windmill, which then turn a generator.

Tidal Energy
As tides move in and out in a basin behind a dam, the moving water can be used to turn a turbine.

Program Resources

🌑 **Science Explorer Series**
Environmental Science, Chapter 6

Media and Technology

💿 **Exploring Physical Science Videodisc**
Unit 4, Side 2,
"Wired to the Sun"

Chapter 7

Social Studies Connection

Challenge students to find out how electrical energy is generated in your area. Suggest students find out by calling the local power company or your city services department. Place a local map in the classroom, and have students place colored pins or flags where the power plants are located. Ask students to infer why your community chose a particular type of power plant for generating electricity. *(Samples: A large river or dam is available to generate hydroelectric power; plentiful fossil fuels are available for a fossil-fuel plant; steam vents are abundant to generate power geothermally.)* **learning modality: verbal**

Including All Students

Ask students to name different electrical devices they used this morning. Prompt them by asking questions such as: **Did you use an alarm clock to wake up? Did you use a hairdryer?** Suggest they also think about household appliances and toys. Then encourage students to discuss how their routines would change if the local power plant announced a severe power shortage due to lack of a nonrenewable resource. On the board, create lists of high-priority and low-priority uses for electricity in homes, as well as for the whole community. **learning modality: verbal**

Ongoing Assessment

Oral Presentation Ask each student to describe two ways to produce electric power.

Generating Electricity

Using the Visuals: Figure 9

Have students examine the circle graph and Figure 10 below it. Ask: **According to the graph, which energy source is used the most?** *(coal)* Based on the pros and cons listed in Figure 10, have students infer why this is the most common energy source. *(Coal is inexpensive and abundant.)* Have students determine which sources on the graph are used the least. *(Natural gas, hydroelectric, and other)* Ask: **What types of energy sources fall in the "other" category on the graph?** *(Wind, sun, geothermal, and tides)* Next have students identify the sources that can be used with the least damage to the environment. *(Tides, sun, wind)* Ask students to infer why these energy sources are not commonly used. *(Sample: They are costly to set up or impractical in some areas.)* **learning modality: logical/ mathematical**

 ## Integrating Environmental Science

Ask students: **Which of the energy sources in Figure 9 are renewable? Nonrenewable?** *(Renewable: hydroelectricity, wind, sun, geothermal power, tides; nonrenewable: coal, oil, natural gas, nuclear power)* **learning modality: verbal**

Building Inquiry Skills: Classifying

Encourage students to identify the ultimate source of the stored chemical energy in fossil fuels. *(The sun)* Then use student input to draw a flowchart on the board that shows the flow of energy from the sun to natural processors *(Plant and animal life)*, to fossil fuels *(Coal, natural gas, and oil)*, to man-made processors *(Electricity generating stations and oil refineries)*, and finally to principal users *(Industrial power, heating, cooling, lighting, transportation, etc.)*. **learning modality: verbal**

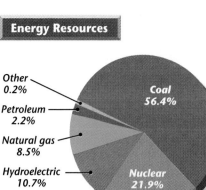

Energy Resources

Coal 56.4%

Other 0.2%

Petroleum 2.2%

Natural gas 8.5%

Hydroelectric 10.7%

Nuclear 21.9%

Figure 9 This circle graph shows which energy resources are used most commonly to generate electricity in the United States.

Generating Electricity

The leading resources for generating electricity in the United States are shown in the graph in Figure 9. Energy resources are limited by their availability on Earth. So not all energy resources are used as readily as others. Some resources have very small roles in generating electricity. Unless you live in certain parts of the United States, you may never have seen an array of windmills, solar mirrors, or even a dam. One thing to remember about the graph is that it shows only resources used to generate electricity. The gasoline that is burned in cars, and the natural gas that heats houses, are not shown here.

Cost is a very important factor in the generation of electricity. But the cost in dollars and cents is not the only thing to consider. Figure 10 summarizes some of the major positive and negative features of these energy resources.

Figure 10 No energy resource is ideal. All have positive and negative features. *Interpreting Tables What are the cons of hydroelectric energy?*

Pros and Cons of Energy Resources		
Resource	**Pros**	**Cons**
Coal	Moderate cost, large supply	Large deposits are localized. Mining damages land and water and is hazardous to miners. Burning coal produces air pollution.
Oil	Moderate cost, adequate supply	Large deposits are localized, and prices are variable. Oil spills damage land and water.
Natural gas	Moderate cost, adequate supply	Large deposits are localized.
Nuclear power	No air pollution	Construction of reactors is expensive. Waste disposal is an unsolved problem. There is a threat of nuclear accidents.
Hydroelectricity	Low cost, no wastes	Unused sites for dams are rare. Dams flood large areas and disturb wildlife in rivers.
Wind	Moderate cost, no wastes, inexhaustible supply	Winds are variable. Wind farms require large areas of land.
Sun	No wastes, inexhaustible supply	Solar generating plants are expensive. Sunlight varies with weather and time of day. Generating plants require large areas of land.
Geothermal power	Moderate cost, low operating costs	Geothermal sites are uncommon. Air pollution may be produced along with steam.
Tides	No wastes	Tidal sites are very uncommon. Power varies with tides. Construction is expensive.

Background

Integrating Science Burning fossil fuels release gases and particles into the air. In large quantities, these substances can endanger human health as well as the health of nearby ecosystems. Fossil-fuel combustion waste products, such as carbon monoxide, react in the presence of sunlight to form a brownish haze called smog. In Mexico City, smog and air pollution can reach levels in which simply breathing the outside air can be damaging. Climatic conditions can also increase air pollution problems. For example, during temperature inversions, Denver, Colorado, experiences a persistent cloud of smog that stalls over the city because the Rocky Mountains block the air from circulating. Using low-pollutant fuels, cleaning industrial smokestacks to remove particle pollutants, and moving to renewable energy resources for generating electricity will help to clean up air pollution.

One factor that does not appear in the table is carbon dioxide. Burning any fossil fuel releases carbon dioxide into the atmosphere. Scientists believe that the release of carbon dioxide may cause climates all over the world to become warmer. This climate change is called global warming. Reducing the use of fossil fuels would reduce the risk of climate change.

 INTEGRATING ENVIRONMENTAL SCIENCE Some sources of energy in Figure 10 are said to be renewable. A **renewable resource** is one that can be replaced in nature at a rate close to the rate at which it is used. In other words, the supply of a renewable resource is not fixed. Water is a renewable resource because the water supply is continually replaced by rain. Wind energy, tidal energy, geothermal energy, and solar energy are renewable resources as well.

Other sources of energy are said to be nonrenewable. A **nonrenewable resource** is one that exists in a fixed amount. The supply of a nonrenewable resource is limited. The supply cannot be replaced once it is used up. Fossil fuels, such as coal, oil, and petroleum, are nonrenewable resources. As you can see in Figure 9, coal leads all other sources in importance.

It is unlikely that the world's nonrenewable energy supplies will run out in your lifetime. Deposits of coal, in particular, are quite large. The United States has about one fifth of the world's coal. But fossil fuels cannot be replaced. Eventually even the largest deposits will be used up. For this reason, and to reduce the risk of global warming, the world's energy sources will probably shift away from fossil fuels.

Figure 11 A house like this one does not need to be connected to an electrical generating plant. Solar cells produce all of its electricity.

Section 2 Review

1. What is induction of electric current?
2. Compare and contrast a motor and a generator.
3. How is alternating current different from direct current?
4. Describe the different ways of spinning turbines to generate electricity.
5. **Thinking Critically Comparing and Contrasting** What is the difference between a renewable and a nonrenewable energy source? Give an example of each.

> **Check Your Progress** CHAPTER PROJECT 3
> After one week, add the numbers in the row indicating the daily use for each appliance. This will tell you the number of hours the appliance was used in a week. (*Hint:* Convert minutes to decimal portions of hours. For example, 6 minutes = 0.1 hour.)

Program Resources

◆ **Teaching Resources** 3-2 Review and Reinforce, p. 75; 3-2 Enrich, p. 76

Media and Technology

Interactive Student Tutorial CD-ROM N-3

Answers to Self-Assessment

Caption Question

Figure 10 The cons of hydroelectricity are that power sites are rare, and dams flood large areas and disturb wildlife in rivers.

Section 2 Review Answers

1. Induction is the process of producing a current from the motion of a loop of wire in a magnetic field.

2. A motor and a generator both have a magnet, a rotating armature, a complete electrical circuit, and a commutator. A motor uses electrical energy to produce motion, while a generator uses motion to produce electricity.

3. Alternating current changes direction repeatedly. Direct current moves in only one direction.

4. A turbine can be spun by water falling, wind power, the motion of the tides, steam produced from burning fossil fuels, geothermal energy, solar energy, or nuclear energy.

5. A renewable resource, such as water, can be replaced in nature at a rate close to the rate at which it is used. A nonrenewable resource, such as fossil fuel, exists in a fixed amount.

Check Your Progress CHAPTER PROJECT 3

Make sure students make daily entries into their data tables. As they begin to total the amount of time each appliance was in use, help them convert minutes to decimal hours so they can compare results more easily. For example:
6 min = 6 min × (60 min/h) = 0.1 h

Performance Assessment

Drawing Have groups of students design simple electrical power plants that use one energy resource. They should label the energy source, the turbine, and the generator.

Portfolio Students can save their designs in their portfolios.

Objectives

After completing the lesson, students will be able to

♦ define and calculate power and energy use;

♦ describe how transformers change the voltage of electric current;

♦ describe the transmission of electric current from power stations to users.

Key Terms power, transformer, step-up transformer, step-down transformer

1 Engage/Explore

Activating Prior Knowledge

Have students brainstorm simple ways that people can save money on their electric bills. (*Samples: Turn down the thermostat in winter; turn off lights when you leave the room.*) Then ask: **Why will doing these things save you money?** (*Because you have to pay for the electricity you use, using less electricity will save you money.*)

········ **DISCOVER** ········

Skills Focus posing questions

Materials *light bulb in socket, hand generator, 1-m insulated copper wire*

Time 15 minutes

Tips Test the bulb in advance to determine how rapidly students can crank the generator without burning the bulb out; caution students not to exceed that amount. Prepare the wire by removing the insulation from the ends. This activity can be set up in stations that students visit in turn.

Think It Over The faster you crank the generator, the brighter the bulb shines. Sample question: Is there a speed below which no light is produced?

DISCOVER ··············· **ACTIVITY**

How Can You Make a Bulb Burn More Brightly?

1. Attach a light bulb in its socket to a hand generator as shown.

2. Slowly crank the generator. Observe the brightness of the bulb.

3. Crank the generator a little faster and again observe the bulb.

4. Crank the generator quickly and observe the bulb once more.

Think It Over

Posing Questions How does the speed at which you crank the generator affect the brightness of the bulb? What questions do you need to ask to explain how the rate of generating electrical energy is related to the brightness of the bulb?

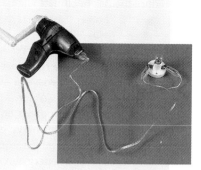

GUIDE FOR READING

♦ How can you calculate power and energy use?

♦ What is the function of a transformer?

♦ What makes alternating current suitable for long-distance transmission of energy?

Reading Tip As you read, use the headings in the section as an outline. Take notes in order to add details to your outline.

When you turn on an electrical appliance such as a toaster, stove, or microwave oven, you are using electrical energy. Each of these appliances converts electrical energy into heat. You can feel the heat given off as the appliance and its contents warm up. When you want heat, you usually want to convert a large amount of electrical energy in a short time. This is the same as saying you want a high rate of energy conversion.

Figure 12 Arc welding produces a white-hot glow as electrical energy is converted into heat.

READING STRATEGIES

Reading Tip After students use the headings in the section to make their outlines, have them rewrite the headings as questions. After students read the section, have them quiz partners, using the questions they generated.

Study and Comprehension Before students read the section, have them create charts with three columns, with the headings *What I Know, What I Want to Know,* and *What I Learned.* Have students fill in the first two columns with information and questions about electric power. As students read the section, have them fill in the third column. Invite volunteers to share any naive conceptions they had about electric power before they read the section, and how these were addressed as they read.

Electric Power

The rate at which energy is converted from one form into another is known as **power.** The unit of power is the watt (W), named for inventor James Watt. Watt made important improvements to the steam engine in the 1700s.

Power Ratings You are already familiar with different amounts of electric power. The power rating of a bright light bulb, for example, might be 100 W. The power rating of a dimmer bulb might be 60 W. The bright light bulb converts (or consumes) electrical energy at a faster rate than a dimmer bulb.

Calculating Power The power used by a bulb or appliance depends on two factors: voltage and current. **You can calculate power by multiplying voltage by current.**

$$Power = Voltage \times Current$$

or

$$Watts = Volts \times Amps$$

Using the symbols P for power, V for voltage, and I for current, this equation can be rewritten.

$$P = V \times I$$

You can rearrange this equation to solve for current.

$$I = \frac{P}{V}$$

Current is equal to power divided by voltage. As long as you have any two of the values in the equation, you can solve for the third.

Power Ratings for Common Appliances

Appliance	Power (W)
Stove	6,000
Clothes dryer	5,400
Water heater	4,500
Washing machine	1,200
Dishwasher	1,200
Hair dryer	1,200
Iron	1,100
Microwave oven	1,000
Coffee maker	1,000
Toaster	850
Food processor	500
Fan	240
Color television	100
Clock radio	12

Figure 13 Electrical appliances use energy at different rates.
Problem Solving How much energy would you use if you ran a washing machine for two hours?

Sample Problem

A household light bulb has approximately 0.5 amps of current flowing through it. Since the standard household voltage is 120 volts, what is the power rating for this bulb?

Analyze. You know the current and the voltage. You need to find the power.

Write the formula. $P = V \times I$

Substitute and solve. $P = V \times I = 120\ volts \times 0.5\ amps = 60\ watts$

Think about it. The answer is reasonable, because 60 watts is a common rating for household light bulbs.

Practice Problems
1. A flashlight bulb uses two 1.5-volt batteries in series to create a current of 0.5 amps. What is the power rating of the bulb?
2. A hair dryer has a power rating of 1,200 watts and uses a standard voltage of 120 volts. What is the current through the hair dryer?

Answers to Self-Assessment
Caption Question
Figure 13 2.4 kilowatt-hours

---

2 Facilitate

Electric Power

Real-Life Learning

Materials *2 light bulbs of different wattages, lamp*

Time 10 minutes

 Some light bulb manufacturers produce bulbs with power ratings slightly lower than standard wattages. Have students compare the brightness of a bulb of standard wattage and one of slightly lower wattage, which uses less energy and costs less to operate. Ask: **Is the reduction in power noticeable?** (*Not usually*) Then ask: **Are the low-wattage bulbs a good buy?** (*Yes; the difference is minimal and the bulbs cost less to operate.*) **learning modality: visual**

Sample Problem

Write $P = V \times I$ on the board. Have a volunteer translate the symbols into words. (*Power equals voltage times current.*) Ask: **How would you change the equation to find the value for current?** ($I = P \div V$) Then ask: **What equation would you use to solve the first practice problem?** ($P = V \times I$) **What should you substitute for the V?** ($1.5\ V + 1.5\ V = 3\ V$) Then ask: **What should you substitute for the I?** (*0.5 amps*)

Practice Problems
1. 3 volts $\times$ 0.5 amps = 1.5 watts
2. 1,200 watts $\div$ 120 volts = 10 amps

learning modality: logical/ mathematical

Ongoing Assessment

Skills Check Have students calculate the power rating for a battery-powered radio that uses six 1.5-V batteries and creates a current of 0.5 amps. (9 V $\times$ 0.5 amps = 4.5 watts)

Paying for Energy

Real-Life Learning

Show students a copy of an electric bill or obtain a sample bill from the power company. Have students use the equation to find the amount of energy used and the cost of each kilowatt-hour, and then compare their results to the total on the bill. In some communities, the rate charged for electric power varies depending on the time of day when it is used. Allow interested students to use several months' bills to determine the average use or to compare how the seasons affect electrical use. **limited English proficiency**

Including All Students

Students who need additional challenges may enjoy calculating how much it costs to a operate a clothes dryer for 2 hours if the electric company charges 4¢ per kWh. Students can refer to the table in Figure 13 to determine how many watts are used per hour by a dryer. *(5,400 watts × 2 h = 10,800 watts × h; 10,800 watts × h = 10.8 kWh; 10.8 kWh × 4¢/kWh = 43.2¢)* **learning modality: logical/mathematical**

Transformers

Building Inquiry Skills: Applying Concepts

Have students describe the high-voltage power lines that deliver electric current to their homes. Ask: **Is the voltage of these lines the same as the voltage in the wires in your house?** *(Students should realize that the voltage in outside lines is much higher.)* Encourage students to talk about the dangers presented by the high-voltage lines. *(Students may discuss the danger of being electrocuted by touching the wires or by being near wires that fall down during storms or by accident.)* **learning modality: verbal**

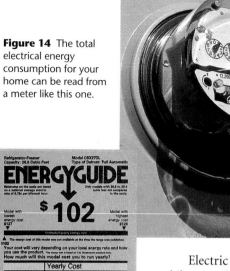

Figure 14 The total electrical energy consumption for your home can be read from a meter like this one.

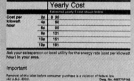

Figure 15 Most large electrical appliances have labels showing the amount of energy they consume in a year. A typical refrigerator uses more than 700 kWh per year, or about 2 kWh per day.

Paying for Energy

The electric bill that comes to your home charges for energy, not power. Energy use depends on both power and time. Some appliances convert electrical energy at a faster rate than others. And you use some appliances more often than others. **The total amount of energy used by an appliance is the power consumption multiplied by the time the appliance is in use.**

$$Energy = Power \times Time$$

$$E = P \times T$$

Electric power is usually measured in thousands of watts, or kilowatts (kW). And time is measured in hours. So the unit of electrical energy is the kilowatt-hour (kWh).

$$Kilowatt\text{-}hours = Kilowatts \times Hours$$

Ten 100-watt light bulbs turned on for one hour use 1,000 watt-hours, or 1 kilowatt-hour, of energy.

The electrical energy that flows into your home is measured by a meter. As more lights and appliances are turned on, you can observe the meter turning more rapidly. The electric company uses the meter to keep track of the number of kilowatt-hours used. You pay a few cents for each kilowatt-hour.

Transformers

Generating electricity costs money, and so your electric company is very interested in efficient ways of transmitting current. The most efficient way to transmit current over long distances is to maintain very high voltages—from about 11,000 volts to 765,000 volts. But electricity is used at much lower voltages (about 120 volts in the United States). How is this problem solved?

Voltage must be increased before it is sent out over the wires from a generating plant. Then it must be reduced again before it is distributed to customers. **A device that increases or decreases voltage is called a transformer.** A **transformer** consists of two separate coils of wire wrapped around an iron core. One coil, called the primary coil, is connected to a circuit in which an alternating current flows. The other coil, called the secondary coil, is connected to a separate circuit that does not contain a voltage source.

Background

Integrating Science One application of step-up transformers is electron microscopes. A scanning electron microscope is designed to scan the surface of extremely tiny objects, such as single-celled organisms. To form the image, a 5–25 kilovolt beam of electrons is aimed at the object. The electrons that bounce off the object are then converted to light, and the light is converted to an electric signal that forms a highly magnified image, up to 10,000 times larger than the actual object.

Ordinary transmission electron microscopes send out a beam of electrons with a voltage of 200–300 kilovolts. These electrons pass through the specimen and are collected on a photographic plate, yielding a magnification of up to 250,000 times.

When a current flows in the primary coil, it produces a magnetic field. The magnetic field changes as the current alternates. This changing magnetic field is like a moving magnetic field. It induces a current in the secondary coil.

Can a transformer work with direct current? The answer is no. A transformer works only if the current in the primary coil is changing. If the current does not change, the magnetic field does not change. No current will be induced in the secondary coil.

✓ *Checkpoint* *What are the parts of a transformer?*

Changing Voltage

How does a transformer change voltage? The answer has to do with the number of loops in the coils. If the number of loops in the primary and secondary coils are the same, the induced voltage is the same as the original voltage. However, if there are more loops in the secondary coil than in the primary coil, the voltage in the secondary coil will be greater. A transformer that increases voltage is called a **step-up transformer.**

Suppose there are fewer loops in the secondary coil than in the primary coil. The voltage in the secondary coil will be less than in the primary coil. A transformer that decreases voltage is called a **step-down transformer.**

Step-down Transformer

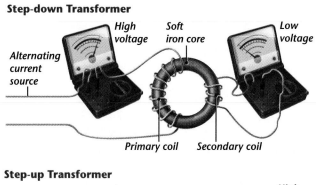

Step-up Transformer

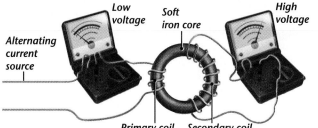

Figure 16 A step-up transformer increases voltage. A step-down transformer decreases voltage. *Comparing and Contrasting Compare the two transformers. Which transformer has a greater number of loops in the primary coil? In the secondary coil?*

Answers to Self-Assessment

Caption Question

Figure 16 The secondary coil has the greater number of loops in a step-up transformer. The primary coil has the greater number of loops in a step-down transformer.

✓ *Checkpoint*

A transformer consists of two separate coils of wire wrapped around an iron core.

Changing Voltage

Building Inquiry Skills: Interpreting Illustrations

After students study Figure 16, have them describe how the current in the primary loop creates current in the secondary loop. (*As the current in the primary loop alternates, the magnetic field around the wire changes. This changing field induces a current in the secondary coil.*) Ask: **Could a transformer be made that uses DC instead of AC?** (*No, current must change to induce current.*)
learning modality: visual

Changing Voltage, continued

Building Inquiry Skills: Applying Concepts

Ask students: **What kind of appliances need to have step-up transformers?** (*Devices that produce high-voltage outputs*) Then ask: **What kinds of devices need to have step-down transformers?** (*Devices that require less than the input voltage*) Have students brainstorm devices that they think might contain step-up or step-down transformers. Students can read the input/output voltages on the device labels to check their predictions. **learning modality: verbal**

Have students discuss how each development built on the previous ones. Encourage students to think about how experimentation contributed to these discoveries. Ask students to calculate how many years it took from the discovery of electromagnetism to the development of the household current we use today. (*68 years*)

Extend Have students find out what voltage and frequency are used in different parts of the world, such as Germany (*230 V, 50 Hz*), Japan (*100 V, 50/60 Hz*), Israel (*230 V, 50 Hz*), and Argentina (*220 V, 50 Hz*).

In Your Journal Provide materials for students to learn more about the scientists. Encourage students to be imaginative and include details in their letters. Students may want to describe the scientists' personalities as well as their work. **learning modality: verbal**

Some electrical devices contain tranformers of their own. For example, fluorescent lights, televisions, and X-ray machines require higher voltages than house current. So they contain step-up transformers. Other devices such as doorbells, electronic games, and answering machines, require lower voltages. They contain step-down transformers.

The War of the Currents

Modern electric companies use alternating current and transformers to distribute electric power. But about 100 years ago, there was a great deal of controversy over AC and DC.

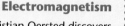

SCIENCE & History

The History of Electric Power

Several scientists were responsible for bringing electricity from the laboratory into everyday use.

1820
Electromagnetism

Hans Christian Oersted discovers that an electric current creates a magnetic field. The relationship between electricity and magnetism is called electromagnetism.

| 1800 | 1820 | 1840 |

1830–1831
Electric Induction

Michael Faraday and Joseph Henry each discover that an electric current can be induced by a changing magnetic field. Understanding induction makes possible the development of motors and generators.

Thomas Edison set up one of the first electric companies, the Edison Electric Light Company, in New York City. It supplied direct current at about 120 volts. Current traveling through long wires at that voltage would lose much of its energy in warming the wires. So Edison expected power generating plants to be small and quite close together.

A young immigrant from Croatia, Nikola Tesla, worked for Edison as an engineer for a short time. Tesla felt strongly that distribution of electricity to homes could be done safely and far more efficiently using alternating current. Generating plants could be located far apart. Step-up and step-down transformers

In Your Journal

Find out more about the work of Michael Faraday, Joseph Henry, or Hans Christian Oersted. Write a letter to a friend in which you describe your work as a research assistant for the scientist you choose. Include descriptions of his experimental procedures and the equipment he uses. Tell how his work has led to surprising discoveries.

1893
World's Columbian Exposition

Nikola Tesla's system of alternating current is used to light the world's fair in Chicago.

| 1860 | 1880 | 1900 |

1882
Direct Current

Thomas Edison opens his generating plant in New York City. The Pearl Street Station consists of six DC generators, serving an area of about 2.6 square kilometers.

1888
Alternating Current

Nikola Tesla receives patents for a system of distributing alternating current.

Chapter 3 **N ◆ 97**

Program Resources

◆ **Interdisciplinary Exploration Series** "Fate of the Rain Forest," pp. 16–19

Media and Technology

Exploring Physical Science Videodisc
Unit 5, Side 1, "Generating Electricity"

Chapter 5

The War of the Currents

Building Inquiry Skills: Posing Questions

Invite students to imagine that they could interview both Tesla and Edison. Have them write ten interview questions to ask each inventor. Encourage students to ask science and technology questions rather than questions of a personal nature. Then pair students and invite them to pretend that they are either Edison or Tesla. Students should try to answer each other's interview questions based on the work of the inventor. Encourage students to find the answers to any questions they have after the activity. **cooperative learning**

Real-Life Learning

Take students outside and have them locate the power line that connects your school to the city electrical supply. Challenge students to identify the transformer on the power line closest to your school. **CAUTION:** *Make sure students do not go near the power lines or transformer.* Have students infer whether the transformer is a step-up transformer or a step-down transformer and explain their inferences. (*Sample: This is a step-down transformer, because it must change the electricity from the high voltage that is carried through power line to the lower voltage that is used in the building.*) **learning modality: verbal**

Ongoing Assessment

Skills Check Have students create compare/contrast tables showing the advantages and drawbacks associated with using DC or AC to transmit electricity from a power plant to their homes.

3 Assess

Section 3 Review Answers

1. Electric power is the rate at which electrical energy is converted to another form of energy. It is calculated by multiplying voltage by current.

2. The electric company calculates energy by multiplying the power of an appliance by the time it is used. Electric meters measure energy in kilowatt-hours.

3. A transformer increases or decreases the voltage of an induced current. A transformer consists of two coils of wire wrapped around an iron core. An alternating current through one coil induces a current in the second coil.

4. Step-up transformers are used to increase voltage generated at a power plant, so that the voltage will be transmitted with minimal energy loss. Step-down transformers are used to reduce voltage from power lines to buildings; the lower voltage is safer for people to use.

5. 0.5 kWh = 500 watt-hours. 500 watt-hours ÷ 15 watts = 33.3 hours

Check Your Progress CHAPTER PROJECT 3
Appliances such as refrigerators, electric clothes dryers, furnaces, and air conditioners may have inaccessible appliance plates. Suggest students compile a class list of such appliances and contact the manufacturer or a local repair shop to find out the voltages and wattages.

Performance Assessment

Organizing Information Have students make flowcharts to show how electric current is altered as it moves from a generator to a low-voltage appliance, such as an answering machine.

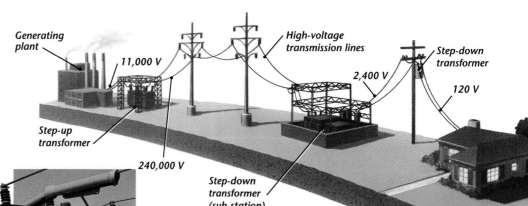

Generating plant

11,000 V

High-voltage transmission lines

Step-down transformer

2,400 V

120 V

Step-up transformer

240,000 V

Step-down transformer (sub-station)

Figure 17 Voltage is increased and decreased as alternating current is transmitted from its source to your home. This photo shows a transformer like the ones you might see in your neighborhood.

then would allow safe transmission with high voltages. **Using alternating current with transformers would reduce energy losses in the long transmission wires.** Tesla invented, among other devices, the first alternating current motor.

Edison thought that high voltages were dangerous. He also wanted to protect his investments in DC generating equipment.

For about 15 years, disagreement raged over which form of current was best. Tesla and the industrialist George Westinghouse eventually won the battle. In 1893 Tesla and Westinghouse were invited to light the World's Columbian Exposition in Chicago using alternating current. The lighting was spectacular! Tesla and Westinghouse were then given a contract for an alternating current system to harness the energy of Niagara Falls. Alternating current was so successful that eventually Edison's own company converted to alternating current as well. Alternating current has been used ever since.

Section 3 Review

1. What is electric power and how is it calculated?
2. How do electric companies calculate electrical energy?
3. How does a transformer work?
4. Explain why transformers are used in the transmission of electricity.
5. **Thinking Critically Problem Solving** One jelly-filled donut contains an amount of energy equal to about 0.5 kilowatt-hours. If that energy could be converted into electrical energy, how long would it keep a 15-watt night light lit?

Check Your Progress CHAPTER PROJECT 3
Determine the power ratings, in kilowatts, of the devices you listed. If power is not indicated on the device, you can calculate it from current and voltage. Find the amount of energy used by multiplying the power by the number of hours the device was used in a week. **CAUTION:** Get permission and adult help before looking for this information, especially on large appliances.

Program Resources

◆ **Teaching Resources** 3-3 Review and Reinforce, p. 79; 3-3 Enrich, p. 80

Media and Technology

Interactive Student Tutorial CD-ROM N-3

Transparencies "Transmission of Electric Power," Transparency 15

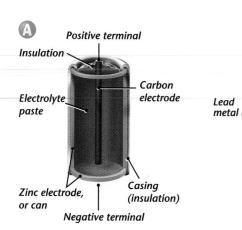

Left margin (teacher notes, partially cut off)

ochemical Cells,
ed

stration

flashlight that
o dry cells,
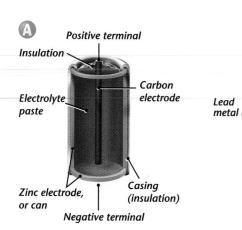

minutes

ents the flashlight. Ask: **What**
en if the flashlight only has
ll? *(The flashlight will not*
the switch on the flashlight to
ts' predictions. Then ask: **Why**
flashlight turn on?** *(The*
ds the second battery to be
learning modality:
ic

e Learning

at least three
atteries,
wered device
minutes planning and setup,
ys for observation

l groups of students design
out experiments to determine
nd of battery lasts the longest.
udents design their
ts, ask: **What variables must**
ol? *(Use batteries of the same*
d test them in the same device
same conditions.) Suggest
st the batteries in devices such
-powered radios or flashlights.
udents not to continuously
e that produces heat, since
present a fire hazard. Students
l the results of their experi-
ata tables. **limited English**
cy

Center-left column (Figure 21)

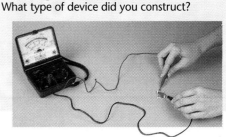

A — Positive terminal, Insulation, Electrolyte paste, Carbon electrode, Zinc electrode, or can, Casing (insulation), Negative terminal

B — Lead metal (−), Sulfuric acid, Lead oxide (+)

Figure 21 Electrochemical cells can be dry or wet. **A.** This diagram shows the parts of a typical dry cell. The electrolyte of a dry cell is a paste. **B.** A car battery is made up of several wet cells. A wet cell uses a liquid electrolyte.

Combining Electrochemical Cells Several electrochemical cells can be stacked together to form a battery. A **battery** is a combination of two or more electrochemical cells in a series. Today, single cells are often referred to as batteries. So the "batteries" you use in your flashlight are technically cells rather than batteries.

In a battery, two or more electrochemical cells are connected in series. The positive terminal of one cell is connected to the negative terminal of the next. The voltage of the battery is the sum of the voltages of the cells. You connect two cells in this way when you insert them into a flashlight. The total voltage of a battery is found by adding the voltages of the individual cells. If you use two 1.5-volt cells in your flashlight, the total voltage is 3 volts.

Wet Cells and Dry Cells There are two kinds of electrochemical cells: dry cells and wet cells. An electrochemical cell in which the electrolyte is a liquid is **wet cell**. Volta's battery consisted of wet cells because the electrolyte was salt water. The six-volt automobile battery in Figure 21B consists of three wet cells. In this case, the electrolyte is sulfuric acid. Twelve-volt batteries, which are more common, consist of six wet cells.

For many devices, it would not be convenient to have cells full of liquid that can spill or leak. Flashlights and many other devices use dry cells instead. A **dry cell** is an electrochemical cell in which the electrolyte is not really dry, but a paste. The dry cell in Figure 21A consists of a zinc can with a carbon rod down the center. The can is filled with a thick electrolyte paste. Metal caps are attached at each end for terminals and the cell is wrapped in a plastic coating.

102 ◆ N

Center-right column

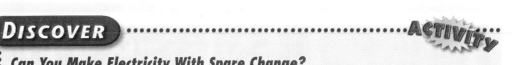

INTEGRATING CHEMISTRY

SECTION 4 Batteries

DISCOVER ACTIVITY

Can You Make Electricity With Spare Change?

1. Clean a penny with vinegar. Wash your hands.

2. Cut a 2-cm × 2-cm square from a paper towel and a similar square from aluminum foil.

3. Stir salt into a glass of warm water until the salt begins to sink to the bottom. Then soak the paper square in the salt water.

4. Put the penny on your desktop. Place the wet paper square on top of it. Then place the piece of aluminum foil on top of the paper.

5. Set a voltmeter to read DC volts. Touch the red lead to the penny and the black lead to the foil. Observe the reading on the voltmeter.

Think It Over
Observing What happened to the voltmeter? What type of device did you construct?

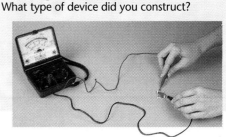

lectric generators are excellent sources of electrical energy. But what do you do if you need electrical energy on the go? Researchers have put a tracking device on the moose in Figure 18. The moose will carry the device deep into the wilderness. Fortunately, the tracking device contains a battery. Batteries are useful in many devices, such as portable radios, flashlights, toys, and calculators, to name just a few. In this section, you'll find out how a battery produces electrical energy.

GUIDE FOR READING
◆ How can chemical reactions generate electricity?
◆ How does a battery differ from an electrochemical cell?

Reading Tip As you read, write a phrase or sentence defining each boldfaced term, using your own words.

Figure 18 A battery-powered transmitter will allow researchers to study the movements of this brown-eyed, handsome moose.

Chapter 3 **N** ◆ 99

Right margin column

INTEGRATING CHEMISTRY

SECTION 4 Batteries

Objectives
After completing the lesson, students will be able to
◆ describe how batteries use chemical reactions to produce electric current;
◆ explain how electrochemical cells can be combined to make a battery.

Key Terms chemical energy, chemical reaction, electrochemical cell, electrode, electrolyte, terminal, battery, wet cell, dry cell, rechargeable battery

1 Engage/Explore

Activating Prior Knowledge
Ask students to name the different sizes of batteries that they can buy. *(Samples: D, A, AA, AAA)* Then ask: **What do you think the sizes indicate?** *(All of the samples listed here are 1.5 V; the size indicates length of battery life.)* Students learn more about batteries in this section.

· · · · · DISCOVER · · · · ·

Skills Focus observing ACTIVITY
Materials *penny, dime, metal polish, paper towels, scissors, salt, water, stirring rod, mixing cup, voltmeter*
Time 15 minutes
Tips Make sure students mix the salt thoroughly with the water. The paper towel squares should be thoroughly soaked.
Expected Outcome The voltmeter will show a reading of about 3 volts when connected to the circuit.
Think It Over The voltmeter needle moved. Students should recognize that the device they constructed is an energy source for a circuit. Some students may recognize this energy source is a battery.

Bottom Background box

Background

History of Science Although we remember Volta for his invention of the first electrochemical cell, a lesser-known French inventor developed the first truly portable battery—the dry cell. In 1866, Georges Leclanché (1839–1882) was working in Paris as an engineer. He coupled an electrolytic solution of ammonium chloride with a negative zinc terminal and a positive manganese dioxide terminal. The materials Leclanché used were inexpensive, and producing large numbers of the dry cells was relatively easy. As a result, Leclanché's battery became a commercial success. The least expensive dry cells available today are made using the same materials as Leclanché's battery.

Bottom Reading Strategies / Program Resources box

READING STRATEGIES

Reading Tip Before students begin reading, provide them with note cards. Instruct them to write boldfaced terms on one side of the card and definitions on the other side. When students have finished reading, partners can use the cards to quiz each other on the terms.

Program Resources
◆ **Teaching Resources** 3-4 Lesson Plan, p. 81; 3-4 Section Summary, p. 82

Media and Technology
 Audiotapes English-Spanish Summary 3-4

N ◆ 99

2 Facilitate

The First Battery

Health Connection

Tell students that doctors and physical therapists often manipulate muscles with electric current. Electric current is now used to treat people paralyzed by injuries or illnesses. A microcomputer is programmed to stimulate muscles in the same way that the nerve impulses normally do. Then in the treatment, microcomputers send electrical impulses into specific muscles. This allows patients to move their limbs to perform tasks such as sitting, standing, and walking. This new treatment is still in the experimental phase, but doctors are hopeful that it will allow patients to be restored to a full range of movement. **learning modality: verbal**

Building Inquiry Skills: Developing a Hypothesis

Ask students to write down Galvani's and Volta's hypotheses as "If . . . then . . ." statements. *(Galvani—If there is electricity present in living tissue, then it will conduct electricity to metals. Volta—If a chemical reaction occurs between two different metals and the salty solution in the frog's leg, then an electrical effect will occur.)* Ask: **What is the major difference between the hypotheses?** *(Galvani believed that the frog itself produced the electrical effect. Volta believed that a chemical reaction takes place between the metals and the frog.)* **learning modality: logical/mathematical**

The First Battery

A generator converts energy from one form into another, and so does a battery. Instead of mechanical energy, however, batteries start with chemical energy. **Chemical energy** is energy stored in chemical compounds.

Luigi Galvani The research that led to the development of the battery came about by accident. In the late 1700s, an Italian physician named Luigi Galvani was studying the anatomy of a frog. He was using a brass hook to hold a leg muscle in place. As he touched the hook to an iron railing, he noticed that the leg twitched. Galvani hypothesized that there was some kind of "animal electricity" present only in living tissue. This hypothesis was later proven to be incorrect.

Alessandro Volta An Italian scientist named Alessandro Volta argued that the electrical effect Galvani observed was actually a result of a chemical reaction. A **chemical reaction** is a process in which substances change into new substances with different properties. In this case, Volta believed that a chemical reaction occurred between the two different metals (the iron railing and the brass hook) and the salty fluids in the frog's leg muscle.

To prove his hypothesis, Volta placed a piece of silver on top of a piece of zinc. He separated the two metals with a piece of paper that had been soaked in salt water. Volta found that if he connected wires to the metals, current flowed. When he added more layers of iron, paper, and zinc, more current flowed. If you did the Discover activity, you constructed a stack similar to Volta's.

Figure 19 Alessandro Volta stacked metal plates and paper, making the first battery. Volta is shown demonstrating his battery to Napoleon in 1801.

Silver
Zinc
Moist paper

Volta had designed and built the first electric battery. In the year 1800, Volta made his discovery public. Although his battery was much weaker than those made today, it produced a current for a relatively long period of time. It was the basis of more powerful modern batteries.

☑ *Checkpoint* What metals were used in Volta's experiments on electricity?

Electrochemical Cells

In Volta's setup, each pair of metal pieces separated by paper soaked in salt water acted as an electrochemical cell. An **electrochemical cell** is a device that converts chemical energy into electrical energy. An electrochemical cell consists of two different metals called **electrodes.** The electrodes are partially immersed in a substance called an electrolyte. An **electrolyte** is a substance that conducts electric current. Volta used silver and zinc as electrodes and salt solution as his electrolyte.

A Simple Cell Look at the electrochemical cell in Figure 20. In this particular cell, the electrolyte is dilute sulfuric acid. Dilute means that the sulfuric acid has been mixed with water.

One of the electrodes in this cell is made of copper and the other is made of zinc. The part of an electrode above the surface of the electrolyte is called a **terminal.** The terminals are used to connect the cell to a circuit.

Chemical reactions occur between the electrolyte and the electrodes in an electrochemical cell. These reactions cause one electrode to become negatively charged and the other electrode to become positively charged. In this case, the zinc electrode becomes negatively charged and the copper electrode becomes positively charged. Because the electrodes have opposite charges, there is a voltage between them. Recall that voltage causes charges to flow. If the terminals are connected by a wire, electrons will flow from one terminal to the other. In other words, the electrochemical cell produces an electric current in the wire. Charges flow back through the electrolyte to make a complete circuit.

How do you know which metal will become the positive terminal and which will become the negative terminal? The answer depends on the metal strips used. Some metals, such as zinc and aluminum, are more likely to release electrons into the wire than other metals, such as copper and silver.

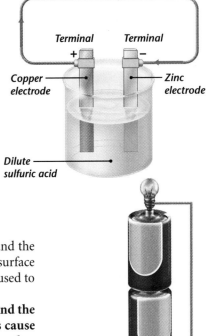

Terminal + | Terminal −
Copper electrode | Zinc electrode
Dilute sulfuric acid

Figure 20 An electrochemical cell consists of two electrodes made of different metals, and an electrolyte. *Predicting What would you expect the voltage to be if you connected two cells together as in a flashlight?*

🔧 🔲 Challenge students t electrochemical cell students to speculat the lemon might be Then have students will use the other m **didn't** circuit. (*A copper bar a electrodes; they will comple and tested with a bu* **kines** After students gathe allow them to assem the electrochemical current by connecti galvanometer or a s ask: **How can you a understanding abo cells to test wheth solution would be a** (*Place the electrodes see if they produce en the bulb or register o* experi **you co** voltage *under* studen as batt Cautio run a c that m can re ments **profi**

Elect
conti

Dem

Materi
require batteri
Time

Show s electrochemical cell **will ha** **one dr** *light.)* I test stu will use the other m cell. (*A copper bar a electrodes; they will comple and tested with a bu* **kinest**

Real-

Materi
brands battery
Time several

Have s and ca which To help experi **you co** voltage *under* studen as batt Cautio run a c that m can re ments **profi**

Writing Have stud parts of an electroch describe what each p (*Electrodes and an e are two different met partially immersed i The electrolyte is a s conducts electric cur*

Background

Facts and Figures Cars powered by batteries were developed in the late 1880s. Up until the 1920s, battery-powered cars were popular because they were easy to maintain and quiet to operate. When Henry Ford introduced the concept of mass production of automobiles, gasoline-powered cars became relatively inexpensive and electric cars became scarce. In the 1960s, the limited supply of fossil fuels spurred engineers to reinvent the electric car. Some modern electric cars use batteries or a battery coupled with a small internal combustion engine. A special motor controller regulates the flow of energy from the battery to the motor, so that the cars can accelerate and slow down. Most cars can drive between 40 and 120 miles before recharging their batteries. Electric cars can operate on a variety of batteries including lead-acid, nickel-metal hybrid, and lithium-ion.

Program Resources

🔵 **Science Explorer Series** *Chemical Interactions,* Chapter 4

Answers to Self-Assessment

Caption Question

Figure 20 The voltage would be equal to the sum of the voltages of the cells.

☑ *Checkpoint*

Volta used silver and zinc in his experiment.

Ongoing A

Dead and Rechargeable Batteries

An electrochemical cell will continue to produce a current until the electrodes and electrolyte are used up. During the reaction in an electrochemical cell, the original substances, known as the reactants, are changed into different substances. The new substances are known as products. A battery in which the reactants have run out is a dead battery.

Can you turn the products back into reactants in order to keep a battery going? In some cells, you can. In these cells the useless products can be converted back into the valuable reactants. Such a cell is said to be rechargeable. A battery made of these cells is a **rechargeable battery.** Not every substance can be recharged. The electrodes must be carefully chosen so that the reverse reaction is possible.

A reverse chemical reaction in which products change into reactants does not happen on its own. Electrical energy, however, can cause the reaction. A rechargeable battery uses electric current to convert the products of its chemical reaction back into reactants.

Have you ever seen someone turn on a laptop computer without plugging it in? The battery on a laptop computer is rechargeable. Once the battery has run down, the computer can be plugged into a wall socket. Electrical energy from the wall socket causes a reverse reaction in the battery. When this reverse reaction is complete, the battery is fully charged.

In one type of rechargeable battery, the reactants are nickel and cadmium. Nickel-cadmium, or NiCad, batteries are popular in cordless and cellular telephones, radios, compact disc players, and other devices that require extended use.

Figure 22 Unlike other batteries that must be discarded after they become dead, rechargeable batteries can be used over and over.

Section 4 Review

1. Describe the components of an electrochemical cell and explain how they produce voltage.
2. Explain how cells are arranged to make a battery.
3. How does a wet cell differ from a dry cell?
4. What is a rechargeable battery?
5. **Thinking Critically Applying Concepts** What would you tell an engineer who has suggested a design for a new battery using silver for both electrodes?

Science at Home

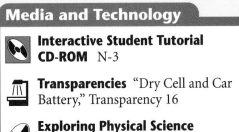

Can you revive a dead battery? Try the following with two old D cells and a flashlight. Test the flashlight with the old D cells and observe its brightness. Then ask a family member to remove the D cells and place them in direct sunlight to warm up. After an hour or more, use the cells to test the flashlight. How does the brightness of the bulb compare in the two tests? Explain to your family how a cell works. Then discuss what your observations indicate about the chemical reactions in the battery.

Dead and Rechargeable Batteries

Building Inquiry Skills: Inferring

Ask students: **Is recharging a battery a chemical reaction? Explain.** (*Yes. The electricity used to recharge the battery converts the products of the chemical reaction back to the reactants.*) **learning modality: verbal**

3 Assess

Section 4 Review Answers

1. An electrochemical cell consists of strips of two unlike metals placed in an electrolyte. Chemical reactions occur between the electrolyte and the electrodes. One electrode becomes negatively charged, and the other becomes positively charged.
2. The positive terminal of one cell touches the negative terminal of the next. The voltages combine.
3. A wet cell uses a liquid electrolyte. A dry cell uses a paste-like electrolyte.
4. A rechargeable battery has cells with products that can be converted back into reactants.
5. A battery must have two different metals to function.

Science at Home

Materials *2 D cells, flashlight*

After warming, the battery will light the bulb brightly, but the bulb may quickly dim again. Chemical reactions occur faster at higher temperatures, so the warm D cell produces more current, quickly depleting the energy of the D cell as the chemical reactions occur.

Program Resources

◆ **Teaching Resources** 3-4 Review and Reinforce, p. 83; 3-4 Enrich, p. 84

Media and Technology

Interactive Student Tutorial CD-ROM N-3

Transparencies "Dry Cell and Car Battery," Transparency 16

Exploring Physical Science Videodisc Unit 5, Side 1, "Batteries"

Chapter 3

Performance Assessment

Writing Have students explain how chemical reactions can produce electrical energy.

Portfolio Students can save their explanations in their portfolios.

Electricity Grows on Trees

Preparing for Inquiry

Key Concept Electrochemical cells use chemical reactions to produce electrical energy.

Skills Objectives Students will be able to
- solve problems by applying the concepts learned in this chapter;
- draw conclusions about the operation of the wet cell circuit.

Time 30 minutes

Advance Planning To save time, remove the insulation from the ends of the wire ahead of time.

Alternative Materials

- If calculators powered solely by a 1.5-volt dry cell are not available, use a dual-powered calculator (solar and dry cell) and cover the solar cells with a piece of black electrical tape.
- A wooden dowel the same length and diameter as a 1.5-volt dry cell can be fitted directly into the battery compartment after attaching a wire to each end with a small, flat-headed screw. The other ends of these wires would then be connected to the free nail and copper wire in the apples.
- The clothespins can be eliminated by using wires fitted with alligator clips.

Guiding Inquiry

Invitation Remove the dry cell from the calculator and have the students examine the empty compartment. Ask them to give examples of design features the calculator has for making good electrical contact with both ends of the dry cell. *(Springy metal terminals, snug fit for the dry cell)* Ask students if they believe that they will be able to run the calculator by plugging it into an apple instead of a battery.

Introducing the Procedure

For clarity, the electrodes in the photos are shown far apart. Tell students, however, that the nail and the copper piece in each piece of fruit should be as close as possible to each other without

actually touching. This is done in order to reduce internal resistance. The nail and copper wire should be stuck into the fruit as far as possible in order to maximize the current. Emphasize the need for tight connections everywhere in the circuit.

Troubleshooting the Experiment

- Rinse the nails and copper wires with clean water to prevent corrosion after they have been used. If clay is used to make

---

Skills Lab

Drawing Conclusions

ELECTRICITY GROWS ON TREES

An electrochemical cell changes chemical energy into electrical energy. In this lab, you will practice the skill of drawing conclusions as you make a simple electrochemical cell starting with an apple.

Problem

How can you make a simple wet cell out of common household materials?

Materials

2 galvanized (zinc coated) nails about 10 cm long
2 pieces of copper about the same size as the nails
3 30-cm pieces of insulated wire with about 2 cm of insulation removed from each end
2 marble-sized lumps of clay
4 clothes pins (the "pinch" type with springs)
2 apples
calculator powered by one 1.5-volt dry cell

Procedure

Part 1 Single Apple Power

1. Use the calculator to do some calculations to be sure it works.
2. Remove the dry cell from the calculator.
3. Stick a galvanized nail into an apple so that about three or four centimeters of the nail are showing. Stick a piece of stiff copper wire into the apple as well. **CAUTION:** *Take care handling sharp nails.*
4. Connect a piece of wire to the free end of the nail. Connect another piece of wire to the free end of the copper wire. Use clothespins to keep the connections tight.
5. Connect the free ends of the two wires to the open terminals of the calculator. Secure the connections with clothespins or pieces of clay.
6. Try using the calculator. If it doesn't work, be sure the connections are tight.
7. Reverse the connections. Again, be sure the connections are tight.

connections, care should be taken that it does not clog the terminals.

- You may need to help students connect the apples in series. Connect the wire from the nail on one apple to the copper on the other apple. Then the free nail and the free copper piece should be connected to the terminals of the calculator.
- Warn students to use care handling sharp nails.

8. If you get the calculator to work, try using it to do some calculations. If not, continue on.

Part 2 Double Apple Power

9. Make another apple cell by repeating Steps 3 and 4 with a second apple, nail, piece of copper, and two pieces of wire.

10. Experiment with different ways of connecting the second cell until the calculator works.

11. Do you think the apple cell will work if you use two galvanized nails in each apple instead of using copper? Design an experiment to find out.

Analyze and Conclude

1. Draw circuit diagrams for the arrangements from Parts I and II.

2. Relate the parts of the apple cell to a typical electrochemical cell.

3. How does the calculator perform when powered by one apple? By two apples? How can you account for any differences?

4. Does the calculator work as well with the apple as it does with a dry cell?

5. Did the apple cell work with two nails? Explain why or why not.

6. What parts of the apple battery correspond to the positive end and the negative end of a dry cell? How do you know?

7. **Think About It** What was the result of reversing the connections? Why do you think this happened?

More to Explore

Are apples the only fruit that can be used to make enough electricity to power a calculator? Try oranges, lemons, tomatoes, or other fruits. Are there other instruments or appliances that can be powered with apple wet cells? Try small toys, electronic games, or electronic clocks. (*Hint:* The apple cells generate a low voltage.)

Analyze and Conclude

1. Circuit diagrams should show the Part I diagram with one cell, and the Part II diagram with two.
2. The nail and the copper are the electrodes. The liquid in the apple is the electrolyte. Because the electrolyte is liquid, the apple cell is a wet cell.
3. If one apple is used, the calculator does not operate. The calculator requires 1.4 volts; one apple must provide less voltage than that. The calculators work when two apples are used.
4. yes
5. No. The electrodes must be different metals.
6. The nail electrode is the negative electrode and it corresponds to the flat end of the dry cell. The copper wire electrode is the positive electrode, and it corresponds to the protruding end of the dry cell. If the wires are connected in the opposite orientation, the calculator will not operate. It requires a direct current that flows in one specific direction.
7. Reversing the connections caused the electrons to flow in the opposite direction. The calculator will work with the electrons flowing in one direction but not in the opposite direction.

Extending the Inquiry

More to Explore Tomatoes, potatoes, lemons, oranges, and other moist edibles can be used in place of the apples. Explain that the acid in fruit acts as the electrolyte of the cell. If citrus fruits are used, squeeze them first to loosen up the juice. The juice in citrus fruits is confined to small capsules separated one from another. Squeezing the fruit breaks the capsules.

Safety

Caution students not to eat the apples. Warn them to use care handling sharp nails. Review the safety guidelines in Appendix A.

Program Resources

◆ **Teaching Resources** Chapter 3 Skills Lab, pp. 88–89

Disposing of Batteries—Safely

Purpose

To provide students with an understanding of the problems associated with the disposal of common household batteries.

Debate

Time one class period for research and preparation; 30 minutes to conduct the debate

◆ Tell students they will debate the proposition "Household batteries should not be thrown away because they can cause environmental damage." Inform them that in a debate, two groups discuss a proposition by presenting reasons that support their positions.

◆ Organize the class into two groups: one to support the proposition, the other to oppose it. Have groups investigate the issue from their points of view.

◆ Groups should critically and constructively support their viewpoints. The group that supports throwing away batteries can explore ideas such as using nontoxic types of batteries. Encourage students in the other group to offer alternatives for those affected by a trash ban.

◆ Remind students to pay attention to the tone of the debate. Arguments should be clear without using harsh language.

Extend Have students contact a local landfill supervisor or environmental expert to obtain relevant background information. Encourage them to prepare questions in advance.

You Decide

Have groups of students complete the first two steps before the debate to prepare their arguments. After the debate, direct students to write their speeches using the points they raised during the debate.

Disposing of Batteries—Safely

Americans use more than 2 billion batteries each year, for everything from flashlights and toys to cameras and computers. When batteries wear out, people throw most of them into the trash. The dead batteries end up buried in landfills or burned in incinerators.

The trouble with throwing away batteries is that they contain poisonous metals, such as mercury and cadmium. Mercury harms the nervous system, and cadmium can cause cancer. As batteries break down in landfills, they can release these metals into the soil. Eventually the metals can enter the water supply. Burning batteries in incinerators isn't any better, because the metals are released into the air as the batteries are burned. So what's the safest way to dispose of batteries?

The Issues

What Type of Battery Is Best? Alkaline batteries are used in toys, flashlights, radios, and watches. These batteries contain mercury. Even though there are some rechargeable alkaline batteries, most are thrown away once they are dead.

Nickel-cadmium (Ni-Cad) batteries are often used in hand-held video games and cordless telephones. These batteries contain cadmium. Ni-Cad batteries are rechargeable. One Ni-Cad battery can last as long as 12 single-use alkaline batteries. Yet they still don't last forever. Eventually they wear out and must be disposed of.

Where Should People Dispose of Batteries? Health experts say that batteries should be collected separately from ordinary trash and disposed of in secure, hazardous-waste landfills. These sites have clay or other materials underneath the waste to stop poisons from leaking into soil and water.

Some cities collect batteries at collection centers. Some stores also provide for special disposal or recycling. However, even when battery collection is offered, many people throw batteries into the trash simply because it's easier.

What Can People Do? Some government officials want laws that require manufacturers to reduce the amount of poisonous metals in batteries. At present, most states do not have such a law. In the last 20 years, manufacturers have lowered the amount of mercury used in alkaline batteries by 70 percent.

Local governments could fine people who don't follow the rules for disposal of batteries. But enforcing battery disposal rules would be expensive. It also would involve checking everyone's trash—a violation of people's privacy. A few states do require battery manufacturers to collect and recycle batteries. But this process is costly for companies and results in higher prices for batteries.

While people search for solutions, batteries continue to pile up.

You Decide

1. Identify the Problem
In your own words, explain the problem of safe battery disposal.

2. Analyze the Options
Examine the pros and cons of changing disposal regulations and changing the materials used to make batteries. In each case, who would the change affect?

3. Find a Solution
Your community is debating the problem of battery disposal. Take a position and write a speech supporting your opinion.

Background

Facts and Figures The toxic effect of leaking chemicals from household batteries has prompted new areas of research. One less damaging alternative to traditional batteries is the lithium battery. It has a much longer life span than conventional batteries and produces more voltage. It eventually discharges, and the breakdown of its components can harm ground water systems near landfills. However, fewer of these batteries will end up in landfills.

The most ecologically promising new batteries are portable solar-powered batteries that rely only on a light source to produce voltage. Solar batteries are now used in laptop computers. They are expensive, but as more economical solar batteries are produced, the need for the traditional nickel-cadmium battery may eventually be eliminated altogether.

SECTION 1 Electricity, Magnetism, and Motion

Key Ideas
◆ A magnetic field exerts a force on a wire carrying current, causing the wire to move.
◆ A galvanometer uses the magnetic force on a current-carrying wire to turn a pointer on a scale. The scale can then be used to measure current.
◆ An electric motor converts electrical energy into mechanical energy.

Key Terms
energy   electric motor
electrical energy   commutator
mechanical energy   brushes
galvanometer   armature

SECTION 2 Generating Electric Current

Key Ideas
◆ A current is induced in a wire in a moving or changing magnetic field.
◆ Current that moves in one direction only is called direct current. Current that reverses direction is called alternating current.
◆ A generator converts mechanical energy into electric energy.
◆ Mechanical energy is required to move a turbine. That energy can be supplied by falling water, the burning of fossil fuels, the wind, the sun, the tides, or steam from within Earth.

Key Terms
electromagnetic   slip rings
  induction   turbine
alternating current   renewable resource
direct current   nonrenewable
electric generator   resource

SECTION 3 Using Electric Power

Key Ideas
◆ Power is the rate at which energy is converted from one form into another. Power is calculated by multiplying voltage by current.
◆ A transformer increases or decreases voltage.
◆ Alternating current allows efficient power transmission because its voltage can be stepped up and stepped down.

Key Terms
power
transformer
step-up transformer
step-down transformer

SECTION 4 Batteries

INTEGRATING CHEMISTRY

Key Ideas
◆ An electrochemical cell consists of two different metals, called electrodes, and a substance through which charges can flow, called an electrolyte.
◆ A chemical reaction causes the electrodes to become oppositely charged. This causes current to flow in a circuit connected to the exposed part of the electrodes, or terminals.
◆ In a battery, two or more electrochemical cells are connected in series to increase the voltage.

Key Terms
chemical energy   terminal
chemical reaction   battery
electrochemical cell   wet cell
electrode   dry cell
electrolyte   rechargeable battery

USING THE INTERNET **ACTIVITY**
www.science-explorer.phschool.com

Program Resources

◆ **Teaching Resources** Chapter 3 Project Scoring Rubric, p. 68; Chapter 3 Performance Assessment Teacher Notes, pp. 144–145; Chapter 3 Performance Assessment Student Worksheet, p. 146; Chapter 3 Test, pp. 147–150

Reviewing Content:
Multiple Choice

1. a **2.** c **3.** a **4.** b **5.** b

True or False

6. true **7.** true **8.** electrochemical cell or battery **9.** true **10.** power

Checking Concepts

11. Similar: both convert electrical energy to mechanical energy. Different: the loop in a galvanometer can only turn half way, the loop in a motor can turn full circle. A motor uses commutators and brushes to reverse the direction of current in the loop.

12. A commutator-brush arrangement changes the direction of current in a DC motor. A commutator consists of two halves of a ring, each of which rubs past two stationary brushes. As the loop of wire in the motor rotates, the halves of the commutator switch from one brush to the other, changing the direction of current through the circuit.

13. In an AC generator, a loop (or many loops) of wire is turned in a magnetic field by mechanical means. As the loop turns, a current is induced in the wire. The direction of the current changes with each half revolution of the loop.

14. Both consist of moving electric charges. Alternating current changes direction. Direct current moves in one direction only.

15. A turbine is turned by a source of mechanical energy; the turbine is attached to the armature of a generator, which produces current.

16. Coal: pros—moderate cost, large supply; cons—mining and burning coal damage the environment. Wind power: pros—moderate cost, no wastes; cons—winds are variable, requires large area of land. Nuclear: pros—no air pollution; cons—reactors are expensive to build, there are no satisfactory methods of waste disposal.

17. The voltage is increased by a step-up transformer as it leaves the utility company. It is decreased by a step-down transformer before reaching its destination.

18. In chemical reaction, new substances are produced. Batteries contain electro-

Reviewing Content

For more review of key concepts, see the Interactive Student Tutorial CD-ROM.

Multiple Choice

Choose the letter of the answer that best completes each statement.

1. Electrical energy is converted into mechanical energy in a
  a. motor.   **b.** generator.
  c. transformer.   **d.** battery.

2. Mechanical energy is converted into electrical energy in a
  a. motor.   **b.** galvanometer.
  c. generator.   **d.** commutator.

3. A device that changes the voltage of alternating current is a
  a. transformer.
  b. motor.
  c. generator.
  d. galvanometer.

4. Power is equal to
  a. energy × time.
  b. voltage × current.
  c. energy × current.
  d. current ÷ voltage.

5. The metal plates in an electrochemical cell are called
  a. electrolytes.   **b.** electrodes.
  c. armatures.   **d.** brushes.

True or False

If the statement is true, write true. If it is false, change the underlined word or words to make the statement true.

6. The production of an electric current by a changing magnetic field is known as <u>induction</u>.

7. Several loops of wire wrapped around an iron core form the <u>armature</u> of an electric motor.

8. A <u>generator</u> converts stored chemical energy into electrical energy.

9. Large generators often get their mechanical energy from <u>steam</u>.

10. The rate at which energy is converted from one form into another is called <u>kilowatt-hours</u>.

Checking Concepts

11. How is a galvanometer similar to a motor? How is it different?

12. What is the role of the commutator and brushes in an electric motor?

13. Describe the operation of an AC generator.

14. Compare and contrast alternating and direct current.

15. What is the purpose of a turbine in generating electricity?

16. What are the pros and cons of coal, wind power, and nuclear power?

17. Explain how transformers are used to carry electricity from the utility company to your home.

18. What is a chemical reaction? How are chemical reactions related to batteries?

19. Writing to Learn Sometimes you may think that everything that could possibly be invented already exists. Many people thought the same thing during the 1800s. Write an article for a modern newspaper describing new uses for generators and motors.

Thinking Visually

20. Concept Map Copy the concept map about electromagnetism onto a separate sheet of paper. Then complete the concept map and add a title. (For more about concept maps, see the Skills Handbook.)

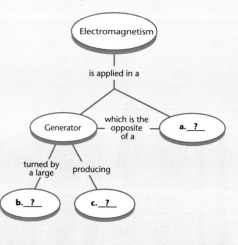

Applying Skills

21. Step-up; the primary coil has fewer loops than the secondary coil.

22. The primary coil is on the right, and the secondary coil is on the left.

23. At the moment the switch is closed, the galvanometer will show a current. At the moment the switch is opened, the galvanometer will show a current in the opposite direction. Opening and closing the switch produce changing current.

chemical cells that use chemical reactions between the electrodes and electrolyte to produce electric current.

19. Students should be creative in imagining life before electricity. They should note that motors can be used to do tasks previously done by people or animals. Generators can be used to provide electricity.

Thinking Visually

20. a. Motor **b.** Turbine **c.** Current or Electrical Energy

Applying Skills

Use the illustration to answer Questions 21–23.

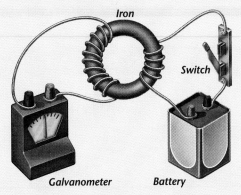

Iron

Switch

Galvanometer

Battery

21. **Classifying** What type of transformer is shown in the illustration? How do you know?

22. **Inferring** Which coil is the primary coil and which is the secondary coil?

23. **Predicting** What will the galvanometer show when the switch is closed? When the switch is opened? Explain why.

Thinking Critically

24. **Applying Concepts** How could you modify a battery to produce a higher voltage?

25. **Problem Solving** The voltage of a car battery is 12 volts. When the car is started, the battery produces a 40-amp current. How much power does it take to start the car?

26. **Comparing and Contrasting** Compare the cost of using the following two bulbs. Assume that each one is used for 5 hours a day for 360 days per year. The cost of electricity is 8 cents/kWh.
   a. A 100-watt light bulb that costs $1.00
   b. A fluorescent bulb that costs $9 but provides equal brightness with only 20 watts

27. **Making Diagrams** Make a diagram of a wire loop in a magnetic field. Show how the direction of a current in the wire is related to the direction of rotation of the loop.

Performance Assessment

CHAPTER PROJECT 3

Wrap Up

Present Your Project Present the results of your energy audit to the class in a visual format. You might make a bar, circle, or line graph showing the appliances and the energy they used. What appliance uses the most electrical energy in a week? Compare the appliances that are rated at 800 watts and higher. What do they have in common? How might this conclusion be helpful to a consumer who is interested in paying the least for electricity?

Record and Reflect In your journal, write about how you calculated energy use. What problems did you have? What information couldn't you collect?

Getting Involved

In Your Community Prepare an interview for a representative from your local utility company. Write down at least ten questions about how electricity is generated and transmitted. With the rest of your class, select the best questions. Get your teacher's permission to contact the utility company, and conduct a class interview. Ask for a brochure. Gather all of the information and prepare a poster displaying what you've learned.

Performance Assessment

CHAPTER PROJECT 3

Wrap Up

Present Your Project
Help students make visual displays of their data. Provide samples for them to refer to; power companies may have consumer information that includes graphical displays. Encourage them to prepare bar graphs of weekly electricity use in kilowatt-hours per appliance. They should present their graphs to the class as they describe the appliances in their home that use the most electricity.

Reflect and Record Students should analyze the project and should identify problems such as not being able to accurately record the time some appliances, such as furnaces, heat pumps, and refrigerators, are using electrical energy. Students' journal entries should describe how accurate students think their results are based on the problems they identified.

Getting Involved

In Your Community Rather than having numerous students contact the utility, have the class work together to make a list of questions and select one student or group to conduct an interview. Have students find out where the power company is located and how large an area it serves. Have groups of students prepare posters to share the information.

Thinking Critically

24. You could add more cells in series.
25. 12 V × 40 A = 480 watts
26. **a.** Find time in hours: 5 hours/day × 360 days = 1,800 hours. Then convert the given power to kilowatts: 0.1 kW. Next find energy by $E = Pt$: $E = 0.1$ kW × 1,800 h = 180 kWh. Multiply the energy by the price: Cost = 180 kWh × $0.08/kWh = $14.40. Finally, add in the cost of the bulb: $14.40 + $1.00 = $15.40
b. Power = 0.02 kW, so $E = 0.02$ kW × 1,800 h = 36 kWh; 36 kWh × $0.08/kWh = $2.88.

Program Resources

◆ **Inquiry Skills Activity Book** Provides teaching and review of all inquiry skills

Add the cost of the bulb: $2.88 + $9 = $11.88.
27. Diagrams should show that the direction of rotation changes with the direction of current.

Sections	Time	Student Edition Activities		Other Activities
CHAPTER PROJECT 4 **Bits and Bytes** p. 111	Ongoing (2–3 weeks)	Check Your Progress, pp. 118, 135 Wrap Up, p. 145	TE	Chapter 4 Project Notes, pp. 110–111
1 **Electronic Signals and Semiconductors** pp. 112–119 ◆ Describe the relationship between electronics and electricity. ◆ Define and compare analog and digital signals. ◆ Describe solid-state devices and identify the components of these devices.	4 periods/ 2 blocks	**Discover** Can You Send Information With a Flashlight?, p. 112 **Sharpen Your Skills** Communicating, p. 117 **Real-World Lab: Careers in Science** Design a Battery Sensor, p. 119	TE TE TE TE ISLM	Real-Life Learning, p. 114 Demonstration, pp. 115, 116 Building Inquiry Skills: Observing, p. 117 Including All Students, p. 118 N-4, "Constructing a Simple Computer Circuit"
2 **Electronic Communication** pp. 120–127 ◆ Define electromagnetic waves and state how they are used to transmit information. ◆ Describe how common devices such as telephones, televisions, and radios transmit and receive signals.	4 periods/ 2 blocks	**Discover** Are You Seeing Spots?, p. 120	TE TE TE TE	Building Inquiry Skills: Applying Concepts, p. 122; Making Models, pp. 122, 126 Inquiry Challenge, p. 123 Including All Students, p. 124 Real-Life Learning, p. 125
3 **Computers** pp. 128–137 ◆ Explain how a computer stores and processes information. ◆ Identify and describe the components of computer hardware and tell how computer software is related.	5 periods/ $2\frac{1}{2}$ blocks	**Discover** How Fast Are You?, p. 128 **Sharpen Your Skills** Calculating, p. 130 **Skills Lab: Making Models** The Penny Computer, pp. 136–137	TE TE TE	Building Inquiry Skills: Modeling, p. 129 Demonstration, p. 131 Building Inquiry Skills: Making Models, p. 134
4 **INTEGRATING TECHNOLOGY** **The Information Superhighway** pp. 138–142 ◆ Describe how a computer network works and state some advantages. ◆ Explain how the Internet is a type of computer network. ◆ Identify aspects of responsible computer usage.	$2\frac{1}{2}$ periods/ 1–2 blocks	**Discover** How Important Are Computers?, p. 138 **Try This** What a Web You Weave, p. 140	TE IES	Demonstration, p. 141 "The Glory of Ancient Rome," pp. 33, 39
Study Guide/Chapter Review pp. 143–145	1 period/ $\frac{1}{2}$ block		ISAB	Provides teaching and review of all inquiry skills

For Standard or Block Schedule The Resource Pro® CD-ROM gives you maximum flexibility for planning your instruction for any type of schedule. Resource Pro® contains Planning Express®, an advanced scheduling program, as well as the entire contents of the Teaching Resources and the Computer Test Bank.

CHAPTER PLANNING GUIDE

Program Resources	Assessment Strategies	Media and Technology
TR Chapter 4 Project Teacher Notes, pp. 90–91 **TR** Chapter 4 Project Overview and Worksheets, pp. 92–95 **TR** Chapter 4 Project Scoring Rubric, p. 96	**SE** Performance Assessment: Chapter 4 Project Wrap Up, p. 145 **TE** Check Your Progress, pp. 118, 135 **TE** Performance Assessment: Chapter 4 Project Wrap Up, p. 145 **TR** Chapter 4 Project Scoring Rubric, p. 96	🌐 Science Explorer Internet Site
TR 4-1 Lesson Plan, p. 97 **TR** 4-1 Section Summary, p. 98 **TR** 4-1 Review and Reinforce, p. 99 **TR** 4-1 Enrich, p. 100 **TR** Chapter 4 Real-World Lab, pp. 113–114	**SE** Section 1 Review, p. 118 **SE** Analyze and Conclude, p. 119 **TE** Ongoing Assessment, pp. 113, 115, 117 **TE** Performance Assessment, p. 118 **TR** 4-1 Review and Reinforce, p. 99	🎧 Audiotapes: English-Spanish Summary 4-1 💿 Interactive Student Tutorial CD-ROM, N-4
TR 4-2 Lesson Plan, p. 101 **TR** 4-2 Section Summary, p. 102 **TR** 4-2 Review and Reinforce, p. 103 **TR** 4-2 Enrich, p. 104	**SE** Section 2 Review, p. 127 **TE** Ongoing Assessment, pp. 121, 123, 125 **TE** Performance Assessment, p. 127 **TR** 4-2 Review and Reinforce, p. 103	📀 Exploring Physical Science Videodisc, Unit 5 Side 1, "The Telephone" 🎧 Audiotapes: English-Spanish Summary 4-2 📽 Transparencies 17, "Telephone"; 18, "Transmitting and Receiving Radio"; 19, "Television Reception" 💿 Interactive Student Tutorial CD-ROM, N-4
TR 4-3 Lesson Plan, p. 105 **TR** 4-3 Section Summary, p. 106 **TR** 4-3 Review and Reinforce, p. 107 **TR** 4-3 Enrich, p. 108 **TR** Chapter 4 Skills Lab, pp. 115–117	**SE** Section 3 Review, p. 135 **SE** Analyze and Conclude, p. 137 **TE** Ongoing Assessment, pp. 129, 131, 133 **TE** Performance Assessment, p. 135 **TR** 4-3 Review and Reinforce, p. 107	📀 Exploring Physical Science Videodisc, Unit 5 Side 1, "Then and Now," "The Cray Computer" 🎧 Audiotapes: English-Spanish Summary 4-3 📽 Transparency 20, "Exploring Computer Hardware" 💿 Interactive Student Tutorial CD-ROM, N-4
TR 4-4 Lesson Plan, p. 109 **TR** 4-4 Section Summary, p. 110 **TR** 4-4 Review and Reinforce, p. 111 **TR** 4-4 Enrich, p. 112	**SE** Section 4 Review, p. 141 **TE** Ongoing Assessment, p. 139 **TE** Performance Assessment, p. 141 **TR** 4-4 Review and Reinforce, p. 111	🎧 Audiotapes: English-Spanish Summary 4-4 💿 Interactive Student Tutorial CD-ROM, N-4
TR Chapter 4 Performance Assessment, pp. 151–153 **TR** Chapter 4 Test, pp. 154–157	**SE** Chapter Review, pp. 143–145 **TR** Chapter 4 Performance Assessment, pp. 151–153 **TR** Chapter 4 Test, pp. 154–157 **CTB** Test N-4	💾 Computer Test Bank, Test N-4 💿 Interactive Student Tutorial CD-ROM, N-4

Key: **SE** Student Edition **TE** Teacher's Edition **TR** Teaching Resources
CTB Computer Test Bank **SES** Science Explorer Series Text **ISLM** Integrated Science Laboratory Manual
ISAB Inquiry Skills Activity Book **PTA** Product Testing Activities by *Consumer Reports* **IES** Interdisciplinary Explorations Series

Meeting the National Science Education Standards and AAAS Benchmarks

National Science Education Standards	Benchmarks for Science Literacy	Unifying Themes
Science as Inquiry (Content Standard A) ◆ **Use mathematics in all aspects of scientific inquiry** Students learn binary number systems and model computers. *(Section 3; Skills Lab, The Penny Computer)* **Physical Science** (Content Standard B) ◆ **Transfer of energy** Electrical energy can flow as analog or digital signals through wires or as electromagnetic waves. Semiconductors are used to form solid-state devices in circuits. *(Sections 1, 2; Skills Lab, Designing a Battery Sensor)* **Science and Technology** (Content Standard E) ◆ **Evaluate completed technological designs and products** Students investigate various computer applications and make recommendations about new applications. *(Chapter Project)* ◆ **Understandings about science and technology** Computers are comprised of hardware and software that run information-processing applications. Computers operate on digital signals that use the binary system. *(Sections 3, 4; Skills Lab, The Penny Computer)* **Science in Personal and Social Perspectives** (Content Standard F) ◆ **Science and technology in society** Electronics, especially computers, have revolutionized how people store, process, and retrieve information. *(Sections 3, 4)* Students consider dangers of digitized pictures that can be altered to produce false images. *(Science and Society)*	**1C The Scientific Enterprise** Computers and computer networks quickly and efficiently process, store, and retrieve data. *(Sections 3, 4)* **3A Technology and Science** Electronics enable devices to operate; these help people to manipulate information at great speeds. *(Sections 1, 2, 3, 4; Chapter Project)* **3B Design and Systems** Computers use the binary system to sense, process, and alter information. Integrated circuits serve as the microprocessors in electronic devices. *(Sections 1, 2, 3, 4; Skills Lab, The Penny Computer)* **3C Issues in Technology** Students analyze the ethical problems with digitized photographs. *(Science and Society)* **4E Energy Transformation** Electronic impulses can be carried in digital pulses or as a continuous stream of information in analog signals. *(Section 1; Skills Lab, Designing a Battery Sensor)* Electromagnetic waves can carry information by altering the frequency or amplitude of waves. *(Section 2)* **7A Cultural Effects on Behavior** The rapid transfer of information via computers and computer networks have made information instantly available to people all over the world. *(Sections 3, 4)* **8D Communication** Information can be carried by many electronic devices that send signals via electricity and electromagnetic waves. Electromagnetic waves can carry information almost instantly. *(Section 2)*	◆ **Energy** Electronics use electrical energy to carry information. Semiconductors are substances that transfer energy better than insulators but not as well as conductors. *(Section 1; Skills Lab, Designing a Battery Sensor)* ◆ **Systems and Interactions** Analog and digital signals can be transferred by conduction or carried by electromagnetic waves to operate telephones, fax machines, radios, and televisions. *(Section 2)* Computers are electronic devices that process information and can be used to run a wide variety of applications. *(Section 3; Chapter Project; Science and Society)* Computer systems can be connected in Wide Area Networks so that information can travel great distances. *(Section 4)* ◆ **Unity and Diversity** There are many different types of solid state electronic devices, from the simplest diodes and transistors, to complex integrated circuits with millions of separate transistors and other elements. However, all depend on the same basic principles of solid state electronics. *(Section 1)* ◆ **Modeling** Students model how a computer uses binary numbers to count and add. *(Skills Lab, The Penny Computer)*

Media and Technology

Exploring Physical Science Videodisc
◆ **Section 2** "The Telephone" lets viewers review what they know about waves and sound as they learn about the history of the telephone.
◆ **Section 3** "Then and Now" traces the development of computers and discusses how they have changed our lives.
◆ **Section 3** "The Cray Computer" features the Cray computer and explains its functions in the running of the space shuttle, in the operation of submarines, and in the designing of aerospace vehicles.

Interactive Student Tutorial CD-ROM
◆ **Chapter Review** Interactive questions help students to self-assess their mastery of key chapter concepts.

Student Edition Connection Strategies

◆ **Section 1** Music Connection, p. 114
◆ **Section 3** Integrating Mathematics, p. 128
  Science and History, pp. 132–133
◆ **Section 4** Integrating Technology, p. 138

USING THE INTERNET ACTIVITY

www.science-explorer.phschool.com

Visit the Science Explorer Internet site to find an up-to-date activity for Chapter 4 of *Electricity and Magnetism.*

ACTIVITY	Time (minutes)	Materials Quantities for one work group	Skills
Section 1			
Discover, p. 112	15	**Nonconsumable** flashlight	Inferring
Sharpen Your Skills, p. 117	15	**Nonconsumable** dictionary	Communicating
Real-World Lab, p. 119	25	**Nonconsumable** 2 1.5-volt cells, bicolor LED (optional), LED, flashlight that uses 2 D cells, flashlight bulb and socket, two insulated wires (alligator clips on each end of each wire are optional)	Making Models, Designing Experiments
Section 2			
Discover, p. 120	10	**Nonconsumable** hand lens, color television	Classifying
Section 3			
Discover, p. 128	10	**Nonconsumable** calculators	Inferring
Sharpen Your Skills, p. 130	10	**Consumable** No special materials are required.	Calculating
Skills Lab, pp. 136–137	40	**Consumable** paper **Nonconsumable** 15 pennies, ruler, binary number table (Figure 22)	Making Models
Section 4			
Discover, p. 138	20	**Consumable** newspapers	Inferring
Try This, p. 140	30	**Consumable** poster board, glue **Nonconsumable** markers, colored pencils, scissors	Communicating

A list of all materials required for the Student Edition activities can be found on pages T14–T15. You can order Materials Kits by calling 1-800-828-7777 or by accessing the Science Explorer Internet site at **www.science-explorer.phschool.com.**

Bits and Bytes

In today's world, computers are used in every aspect of life, even those in remote wildlife habitats. This chapter gives students an opportunity to relate the structure and operation of computers to their applications.

Purpose In this project, students learn how common and useful computers are in everyday life. They also invent a new device that accomplishes a task they have chosen.

Skills Focus After completing the Chapter 4 Project, students will be able to
◆ observe how computers work;
◆ classify different functions of computer applications and identify types of data input and output information;
◆ communicate their findings about their research to their classmates.

Project Time Line This project will take a total of 18 days. On days 1 and 2, students discuss and list all the existing computer applications they know. From this list, they select an application that interests them, have it approved, and then start the project by listing what they already know about the application. On days 3 through 10, students conduct individual research. This can be done at the library, on the Internet, or by contacting a computer expert or a manufacturer's technical support line. On days 11 through 18, students create the concept for a new computer application. They will need time to consider the required inputs to the device and the resulting outputs. During this time, they work on posters, oral presentations, and other visual information for their projects. Before beginning the project, see Chapter 4 Project Teacher Notes on pages 90–91 in Teaching Resources for more details on carrying out the project. Also distribute to students the Chapter 4 Project Overview, Worksheets, and Scoring Rubric on pages 92–96 in Teaching Resources.

Possible Materials Students use paper and pencils for recording information during the research component, and

CHAPTER

4 Electronics

WHAT'S AHEAD

SECTION 1 Electronic Signals and Semiconductors
Discover **Can You Send Information With a Flashlight?**
Sharpen Your Skills **Communicating**
Real-World Lab **Design a Battery Sensor**

SECTION 2 Electronic Communication
Discover **Are You Seeing Spots?**

SECTION 3 Computers
Discover **How Fast Are You?**
Sharpen Your Skills **Calculating**
Skills Lab **The Penny Computer**

materials such as poster board, markers, and rulers for making their final presentations to the class.

Launching the Project To introduce the project and to stimulate student interest, ask: **What kinds of computer applications have you used?** (*Samples: Word processing programs, electronic mail programs*)

Allow time for students to read the description of the project in their text and the Chapter Project Overview on pages 92–93 in Teaching Resources. Then encourage

discussions on computers, their applications, and possible materials for the project. Answer any initial questions students may have.

If at all possible, give students Internet access for researching their computer applications. If your school has limited Internet resources, most local libraries have at least one computer connected to the Internet which is available to the public. You may wish to set up a session with the school's computer specialist or computer-class instructor to allow students to practice using Internet search engines.

Bits and Bytes

This red wolf wears a collar that sends radio tracking signals to naturalists.

Red wolves are very intelligent animals, but their survival is threatened. They may benefit from the work of scientists who track their movements with electronic equipment.

In a similar way, you benefit from electronics every day. Both a comfortable air-conditioned building and an airmail letter from thousands of miles away are made possible by electronics.

In this chapter you will learn about the devices that make computers possible, how computers work, and how they are used. As you complete the chapter, you will identify a new computer use, or application.

Your Goal To study an existing computer application and then propose and detail a new application.

Your project must
- ◆ show what the existing computer application does and explain its benefits
- ◆ explain how data are received and transformed by the computer
- ◆ describe each step that occurs as your new application runs

Get Started Brainstorm with your classmates about existing computer applications. Make a list of devices that use programmed information, such as clock radios, automated bank teller machines, and grocery store bar-code scanners.

Check Your Progress You'll be working on this project as you study this chapter. To keep your project on track, look for Check Your Progress boxes at the following points.

Section 1 Review, page 118: Research a computer application.
Section 3 Review, page 135: Develop a new computer application.

Wrap Up At the end of this chapter (page 145), you will present both the existing application and your new one to the class.

Integrating Technology 🌐
The Information Superhighway

Discover How Important Are Computers?
Try This What a Web You Weave

N ◆ 111

Have students work in small groups as a cooperative learning task. To ensure that every student will have ample opportunity to participate in evaluating a familiar application, each group should consist of no more than four students.

Program Resources

◆ **Teaching Resources** Chapter 4 Project Teacher Notes, pp. 90–91; Chapter 4 Project Overview and Worksheets, pp. 92–95; Chapter 4 Project Scoring Rubric, p. 96

Performance Assessment

The Chapter 4 Project Scoring Rubric on page 96 of Teaching Resources will help you evaluate how well students complete the Chapter 4 Project. Students will be assessed on
- ◆ the thoroughness and organization of their research into the origin and operation of their chosen computer applications;
- ◆ how well they apply chapter concepts to the development and description of new computer applications;
- ◆ the organization of their written descriptions and visual presentations of both computing devices;
- ◆ their ability to work cooperatively, if they work in groups.

By sharing the Chapter 4 Scoring Rubric with students at the beginning of the project, you will make it clear to them what they are expected to do.

Objectives

After completing the lesson, students will be able to

♦ describe the relationship between electronics and electricity;
♦ define and compare analog and digital signals;
♦ describe solid-state devices and identify the components of these devices.

Key Terms electronics, electronic signal, analog signal, digital signal, semiconductor, solid-state component, diode, transistor, integrated circuit, vacuum tube

1 Engage/Explore

Activating Prior Knowledge

Ask students to name several appliances that use electricity. Then ask: **Which of these gives you information?** (Sample: Clock, radio, television, answering machine) In this section, students learn what distinguishes electrical devices that carry information from other electrical devices.

DISCOVER

Skills Focus inferring
Materials flashlight
Time 15 minutes
Tips To save time, have students transmit a single word rather than an entire sentence.
Think It Over Students should have been able to transmit and decode messages using Morse code. A message read aloud would be composed of sounds. The light message uses patterns of flashing light to transmit information.

DISCOVER ··· ACTIVITY

Can You Send Information With a Flashlight?

1. Write a short sentence on a sheet of paper.
2. Morse code is a language that uses dots and dashes to convey information. Convert your sentence to dots and dashes using the International Morse Code chart at the right.
3. Turn a flashlight on and off quickly to represent dots. Leave the flashlight on a little longer to represent dashes. Practice using the flashlight for several different letters.
4. Use the flashlight to transmit your sentence to a partner. Ask your partner to translate your message and write down your sentence.

International Morse Code	A ·—	B —···	C —·—·	D —··	E ·
	F ··—·	G ——·	H ····	I ··	J ·———	K —·—	L ·—··
	M ——	N —·	O ———	P ·——·	Q ——·—	R ·—·	S ···
	T —	U ··—	V ···—	W ·——	X —··—	Y —·——	Z ——··

Think It Over

Inferring Were you able to transmit information using light? How does your light message differ from the same message read aloud?

GUIDE FOR READING

♦ How is electronics related to electricity?
♦ What are analog and digital signals?
♦ How are semiconductors used in solid-state devices?

Reading Tip As you read, write a phrase describing each boldfaced term in your own words.

N o matter where you live, you can't go far without seeing an electronic device. Your radio and television are electronic, and so are video cameras and telephones. Making popcorn in a microwave oven requires electronics. Even an automobile engine won't run without electronics.

Most of these devices are plugged into a source of electric current. You might wonder, then, why they aren't just called electrical devices. The difference between electrical and electronic devices is in the way that they use electric current.

Electricity Versus Electronics

So far in this book, you have been learning about electricity. In electrical devices, a continuous flow of electric current is required. A light bulb is an example of an electrical device because it relies on a continuous supply of electric current.

Electronics is the use of electricity to control, communicate, and process information. **Electronics treats electric currents as a means of carrying information.** If you did the Discover activity, you turned a beam of light on and off to send a message. You controlled the current by turning a flashlight on and off. You used the flashlight as an electronic device.

READING STRATEGIES

Reading Tip Before students begin reading, write the boldfaced terms on the board. Challenge students to define each term and tell what they know about it. Write students' responses on the board. Then have students complete the Reading Tip activity for the section. After students read the section, have them revise or add to the information on the board.

Study and Comprehension After students read the section, have them work in small groups to create drawings in which they present information from the section about one of these topics: analog and digital signals, semiconductors, solid-state devices, and vacuum tubes. Encourage students to include sketches and captions or labels.

Figure 1 Electronic controls can be found in many electrical appliances.

Electronic Signals

Electronics is based on electronic signals. An **electronic signal** is a varying electric current that represents information. Anything that can be measured or numbered, whether it is electrical or not, can be converted to a signal.

There are two basic kinds of electronic signals: analog signals and digital signals. Thermometers are a good example to show the difference between digital and analog.

Analog and Digital Devices You may have noticed that there are two different kinds of thermometers. One kind shows temperature as the height of a liquid in a tube. The height of the liquid rises and falls smoothly with the temperature. This is an analog thermometer. The other kind of thermometer is the kind you might see in front of a bank. It is called a digital thermometer. It shows a number that represents the temperature.

The number on this type of outdoor digital thermometer is constant for a few minutes, or perhaps several hours. Then the number changes suddenly by a whole degree. You probably know that the temperature doesn't really change so suddenly. But the thermometer can only show the temperature to the nearest degree, and so the temperature seems to jump.

Analog and Digital Signals The terms analog and digital are usually applied to the transmission of information using electric current. Just as there are two ways of representing temperature, there are two kinds of electronic signals. In **analog signals,** a current is varied smoothly to represent information. **An analog signal is created when a current is smoothly changed or varied.**

Figure 2 These two thermometers are examples of analog and digital devices. *Applying Concepts What do digital and analog clocks look like?*

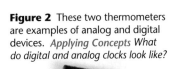

Electricity Versus Electronics

Language Arts Connection

Students still mastering English may have difficulty distinguishing between *electricity, electrical,* and *electronics.* Have students examine the suffix of the three terms. Ask them to think of other words that end in *-al, -ity,* and *-ics. (Samples: individual, conductivity, phonics)* Ask students to find out what the word endings mean, and to apply those meanings to their own definitions of the terms. *(-al means "related to," so electrical means related to electricity; -ity means "a state or quality," so electricity means the quality of transmitting electrons or sparks; -ics means "the science or art of," so electronics is the science of using electrons to transmit information.)* Have students write sentences using the words.
learning modality: verbal

Electronic Signals

Building Inquiry Skills: Classifying

Challenge students to think of other examples of digital and analog signals. To help them, ask: **When you change channels on the television, do you use a digital or an analog device? Explain.** *(Digital; you jump from channel to channel and do not scan the parts of the spectrum between channels.)* As students list devices, write them on the board under the appropriate headings.
learning modality: verbal

Program Resources

◆ **Teaching Resources** 4-1 Lesson Plan, p. 97; 4-1 Section Summary, p. 98
◆ **Integrated Science Laboratory Manual,** N-4, "Constructing a Simple Computer Circuit"

Media and Technology

🎧 **Audiotapes** English-Spanish Summary 4-1

Answers to Self-Assessment

Caption Question

Figure 2 A digital clock displays a number that represents time. An analog clock has an hour hand, a minute hand, and a face.

Ongoing Assessment

Writing Have students describe the difference between electricity and electronics.

Electronic Signals, continued

Real-Life Learning

Materials *analog oral thermometer, digital thermometer, alcohol*

Time 10 minutes

Instruct student groups to investigate whether analog or digital thermometers give the same reading. Each student should carry out a specific activity, such as having his or her temperature taken, reading the analog thermometer, or reading the digital thermometer. Students should swab the thermometers with alcohol and carefully rinse them under running water before and after each use. Demonstrate how to shake down and read an analog thermometer. Have students compare the readings. Ask: **What advantages does each thermometer have?** *(Sample: A digital thermometer reads temperature more quickly; an analog thermometer is cheaper to buy.)* **cooperative learning**

Music
CONNECTION

Tell students that electronic musical instruments were developed as far back as the early 1900s. Some of the earliest were electronic organs, followed by synthesizers that allowed the musician to stop at any point and listen to what had just been played. One interesting device is the theremin, a box in which radio tubes produce waves at two different ultrasonic frequencies. The interference between the waves produces audible sound.

In Your Journal If possible, choose recordings of different styles, including electronic music that uses electronic instruments to produce traditional music, and some that represents more abstract electronic or computer music. Students should describe the music and explain what they like or dislike. **learning modality: verbal**

Music
CONNECTION

With an acoustic instrument, sounds are created when part of the instrument vibrates. For instance, a drum is an instrument in which sound is created by a vibrating skin, or head. In the case of electronic music, the sounds are created as electronic signals.

In Your Journal

Listen to recordings of electronic and acoustic instruments. If possible, have someone play both types of instruments for you. Describe the sound of each type of instrument. How are they alike? How are they different? Which do you prefer?

In **digital signals,** pulses of current are used to represent information. **A digital signal consists of a current that changes in steps.** Rather than changing smoothly to represent information, a digital signal carries information in pulses. If you did the Discover activity, you used pulses of light to represent letters.

Sound Recordings The photos in Figure 3 show an analog sound recording. When you play an old plastic record, a needle runs along a spiral groove. As the needle moves back and forth in the groove, it creates a small electric current. This current matches the wavy pattern of the groove in the record.

The current produced by the needle forms an analog signal. The signal continuously changes as it copies the information on the record. The analog signal is fed into an amplifier and then into a speaker, which changes the signal back into sound.

As you can see in Figure 4, a CD, or compact disc, is very different. It contains microscopic holes, called pits. The level areas between the pits are called flats. These pits and flats are arranged in a spiral, like the groove on a record. Although you can't tell from the photograph, the spiral on a compact disc is divided into pieces of equal length. The arrangement of pits and flats within each piece of the spiral is a code. Each piece of this code represents the volume of sound at one instant.

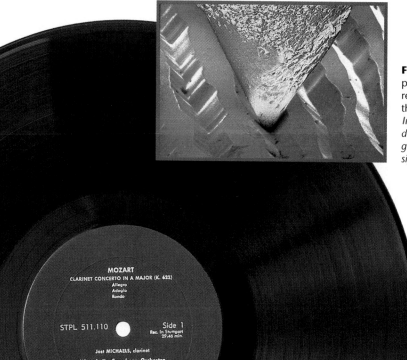

Figure 3 The magnified photo shows the needle of a record player moving along the groove of a record. *Interpreting Photos Why does the smooth shape of the groove represent an analog signal?*

Background

Facts and Figures Audiocassette tapes have unique features that CDs and analog records lack. They can be easily recorded on, then erased and reused. The narrow plastic ribbon in an audiocassette is coated with a layer of iron oxide or another substance that can be magnetized. When sounds are recorded, an electronic signal is passed through a device called a recording head. The tape moves over the recording head, and the electronic signal magnetizes parts of the tape. This creates a pattern of magnetism that can be run back through the tape player. During playback, the tape moves through the playback head, and the pattern of magnetized symbols is translated back into electronic signals. These signals are sent through an amplifier that transmits whatever sounds were first recorded on the tape.

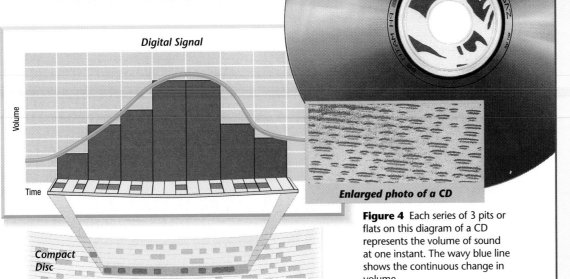

Digital Signal

Volume

Time

Compact Disc

Enlarged photo of a CD

Figure 4 Each series of 3 pits or flats on this diagram of a CD represents the volume of sound at one instant. The wavy blue line shows the continuous change in volume.

When the CD is played, it spins around, and a beam of light scans the pits and flats. Like the bar code scanner used in a supermarket, this beam produces tiny flashes of light. The light flashes are then converted to pulses of electric current, or a digital signal. The digital signal is fed into an amplifier and then a speaker, where it is changed back into sound.

☑ *Checkpoint* *What are the two types of electronic signals?*

Semiconductors

How can you control a voltage in order to transmit analog or digital signals? After all, you have learned that current flows continuously through a conductor, but does not flow at all through an insulator. Yet to transmit an electronic signal you need to be able to vary the current through a circuit. When you vary current, you use a semiconductor.

A **semiconductor** is a material that conducts current better than insulators but not as well as conductors. A semiconductor conducts electricity only under certain conditions.

How can a material conduct electricity only under certain conditions? Silicon and other semiconductors are elements that have extremely high resistance in their pure forms. However, if atoms of other elements are added to semiconductors, they conduct current much more easily. By controlling the number and type of atoms added, scientists produce two types of semiconductors. They combine these two types of semiconductors in layers. This structure allows the delicate control of current needed for electronic devices. Such control is impossible with true conductors.

Figure 5 The electrical resistance of pure silicon, shown here, is reduced by adding atoms of other elements to it.

Demonstration

ACTIVITY

Materials *flour, sieve or colander, paper towel, mixing bowl, scissors*
Time 10 minutes

Model how a semiconductor works by lining a sieve or colander with a paper towel. Fill the sieve with flour and hold it over the mixing bowl. Ask: **Does this container "conduct" or move flour well?** *(No, the flour is contained inside it and is not moving.)* Using the scissors, cut a hole in the center of the paper towel, then repeat the procedure. Students should observe that some of the flour begins to pass through the sieve. Ask: **How is this like a semiconductor?** *(A semiconductor conducts electricity only under specific conditions; the sieve passes flour through it only under specific conditions.)* Conclude by asking students how you might model a good conductor. *(Remove the paper towel so the flour passes through easily.)* **limited English proficiency**

Answers to Self-Assessment

Caption Question

Figure 3 Analog signals vary smoothly along a continuum, just as the needle in the groove of a record produces sound as the record moves.

☑ *Checkpoint*

Analog and digital

Ongoing Assessment

Writing Ask students to explain why semiconductors are used in devices that produce signals. *(Signals are transmitted by changes in current. Because semiconductors only conduct electricity under certain conditions, they can be used to produce these changes.)*

Solid-State Components

Using the Visuals: Figure 6

As students look at the figure, ask: **How does the symbol in the box illustrate the function of a diode in a circuit?** *(The symbol shows an arrow that points to a straight line; this symbolizes that current can only travel in one direction. A diode in a circuit allows current to flow in one direction.)* **learning modality: visual**

Demonstration

Materials *overhead projector*

Time 10 minutes

Some students may need extra help to understand how converters work. Draw a circuit diagram showing what happens when a battery-operated device with a converter is then connected to an electrical outlet. Display the diagram on the overhead projector. Then ask: **At what point in the diagram does alternating current flow?** *(Between the outlet and the converter)* Then ask: **At what point does direct current flow?** *(From the converter through the electrical device)* Point out that some converters contain transformers as well as diodes, so the DC voltage may be different than the AC voltage. **learning modality: visual**

Addressing Naive Conceptions

Students who have heard of transistor radios may think that the transistor is a device that allows radios to be small, or that the radio itself is a transistor. Explain that a transistor is the device inside the radio that amplifies the signal. Although transistors did replace much larger amplifiers and electric switches, the small size of the transistor radio also depends on its power source. The transistor radio, which was first made in the 1960s, was portable because it only needed small, lightweight batteries to operate. **learning modality: verbal**

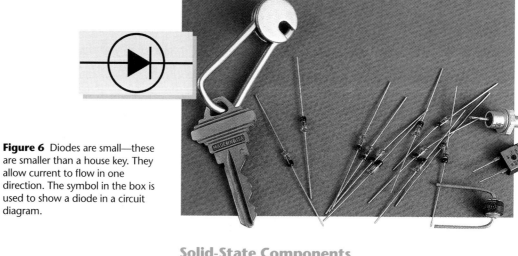

Figure 6 Diodes are small—these are smaller than a house key. They allow current to flow in one direction. The symbol in the box is used to show a diode in a circuit diagram.

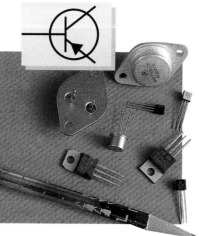

Figure 7 Transistors come in a variety of shapes and sizes. The symbol for a transistor is shown in the box. *Applying Concepts What is a transistor?*

Solid-State Components

A **solid-state component** is part of a circuit in which a signal is controlled by a solid material, such as a semiconductor. **The two types of semiconductors can be combined in different ways to produce different solid-state components. These components include diodes and transistors.** Since the 1950s, solid-state components have become dominant in electronic devices.

Diodes A solid-state component that consists of layers of the two types of semiconductors joined together is a **diode.** A diode allows current to flow in one direction only. If you connect a diode in a circuit in one direction, current will flow. But if you turn the diode around, current will not flow.

Recall that there are two types of current: alternating current and direct current. Your home uses alternating current. A battery-operated game uses direct current. Electronic devices are designed to run on only one type of current. However, you can plug some direct-current devices into an alternating-current outlet if you have a converter. A converter does not change the way the device operates. Instead, a converter changes, or converts, the current.

An alternating current reverses direction over and over again. When a diode is placed in a circuit with alternating current, the diode allows current to flow only when it is moving in one direction. So a converter allows only part of the alternating current to flow—the part flowing in one direction. Alternating current goes into the converter, but direct current comes out.

Transistors When a layer of either type of semiconductor is sandwiched between two layers of the other type of semiconductor, a transistor is formed. A **transistor** carries out one of two

Background

Integrating Science The semiconductors silicon and germanium belong to the carbon group, or Group IVa in the periodic table. This group lies between the metals and nonmetals. Most elements in the group, which includes carbon, silicon, lead, and tin, are familiar and abundant.

In the late 1880s, scientists predicted the existence of certain elements based on gaps

in the periodic table, including a gap in this group. In 1886, Clemens Winkler, a German chemist, discovered germanium, the element that fills in this gap. Germanium is widely used as a semiconductor in computers, but it can also be used in infrared detectors, as a coating for lenses, and to detect gamma radiation.

functions: it either amplifies an electronic signal or switches current on and off.

When electronic signals are sent, they gradually grow weak. When they are received, signals must be amplified, or made stronger, so that we can use them. Transistors revolutionized the electronics industry by making amplifiers much cheaper and more reliable.

When a transistor acts as a switch, it either lets current through or cuts it off. Millions of transistors that act as switches are what make computers work.

Integrated Circuits Single transistors have low cost and long lives. These advantages were multiplied by the invention of the integrated circuit. An **integrated circuit** is a circuit that has been manufactured on a tiny slice of semiconductor known as a chip. A chip smaller than 0.5 centimeters on each side can contain hundreds of thousands of components, such as diodes, transistors, and resistors. Electronic signals flow through integrated circuits at tremendous speeds because the various components are so close together. On some chips, the space between two components can be one-fiftieth as thick as a human hair. The high speed of signals and small size of integrated circuits make possible devices from video games to spacecraft.

☑ *Checkpoint* *What is a solid-state component?*

Figure 8 An integrated circuit chip is smaller than a fingernail. Yet the integrated circuit contains hundreds of thousands of diodes, transistors, and resistors.

Sharpen your Skills

Communicating

How do you make someone understand how tiny a chip is or how fast an electronic signal travels? An analogy can help communicate what a measurement means. An analogy uses a similarity between two things that are otherwise unlike each other. For example, "a chip is as small as a baby's fingernail" is an analogy. So is "an electronic signal moves as fast as a bolt of lightning." Write your own analogies to describe how many diodes there are in one integrated circuit chip.

Building Inquiry Skills: Observing

Materials *diode, multimeter*
Time 10 minutes

Have students work in pairs to measure the resistance both ways across a diode. They should position one multimeter probe securely on each diode terminal until a measurement is obtained, then reverse the probes to measure the resistance in the other direction. Ask: **Is the resistance the same in both directions?** *(No; the resistance is much higher in one direction than the other.)* Then ask: **How does this explain current flow through a diode?** *(Current flows through the diode in the direction of finite resistance, but does not flow through the diode in the direction of infinite resistance.)* **learning modality: visual**

Sharpen your Skills

Communicating

Materials *dictionary*
Time 15 minutes
Tips You may wish to pair students still mastering English with native speakers for this activity. Students should brainstorm a list of possible analogies and write a sentence for each.
Communicating Students' analogies will vary, but should rely on the idea that there are thousands of diodes in one integrated circuit chip. Sample analogies: *There are more diodes in one integrated circuit chip than there are potato chips in a 5-lb bag. There are as many diodes in an integrated circuit chip as there are grains of sand on a beach.*
Extend Have students write analogies for other terms used in the section.

Answers to Self-Assessment

Caption Question

Figure 7 A transistor is a device that amplifies an electronic signal or switches a current on and off.

☑ *Checkpoint*

Part of a circuit in which a signal is controlled by a solid material such as a semiconductor

Ongoing Assessment

Skills Check Ask students to list three solid-state components and describe how they control current.

Past and Future Electronics

Including All Students

Materials *small, nonworking electronic device such as transistor radio*

Time 20 minutes

Encourage students who need additional challenges to take apart the device and identify as many components as they can. In particular, have them look for solid-state components. **learning modality: kinesthetic**

3 Assess

Section 1 Review Answers

1. Electronics is the use of electric currents to control, communicate, and process information. An electronic signal is a varying electric current, electricity is a continuous flow of electric current.
2. Analog—current varies smoothly; digital—current changes in steps.
3. Integrated circuits, diodes, transistors
4. Diodes conduct current in one direction; they can convert AC into DC. Transistors amplify electronic signals or turn signals on and off.
5. Small integrated circuits have replaced large solid-state or vacuum tube components. Since the circuits became smaller, so did the devices.

Check Your Progress
CHAPTER PROJECT 4

Before they begin their research, encourage students to make some assumptions about how their chosen applications might work. Provide a collection of library books on computer applications to help them begin.

Performance Assessment

Organizing Information Have students make concept maps that link the key words in this section.

Portfolio Students can save their concept maps in their portfolios.

Figure 9 Although they made the first electronic devices possible, vacuum tubes like this one were large and heavy, and burned out frequently.

Past and Future Electronics

Electronic devices were not always small and convenient. In the 1940s, for example, some radios were as large as a chest of drawers, and a computer filled an entire room. Before solid-state devices were developed, electronics relied on bulky vacuum tubes to control electric current.

A **vacuum tube** is a sealed glass tube from which most of the air has been removed. A metal filament and plate are located inside the vacuum tube. When the filament is heated under certain conditions, electrons flow from the filament to the plate. Since the electrons can only flow in one direction, a vacuum tube acts as a diode. Adding a third piece between the filament and the plate produces a triode vacuum tube. This kind of tube is able to amplify a signal. Triode tubes were first used before 1910.

Once solid-state components became available, most vacuum tubes were quickly replaced. Solid-state components are much smaller and lighter than vacuum tubes. They give off less heat, use less electrical energy, are more dependable, and last longer. They are also less expensive.

In the years since the invention of the transistor, electronic devices have shrunk rapidly. The change is equivalent to shrinking a ship the size of the *Titanic* down to the size of a mouse.

Even solid-state components might someday be replaced in devices requiring extreme speed. Researchers are developing new electronic components based on superconducting materials and other new types of materials. Recall that when certain materials are cooled to very low temperatures, their resistance to the flow of electrons disappears entirely. This makes them superconductors. Superconducting components are faster and smaller than the smallest semiconductors.

Section 1 Review

1. What is electronics? How are electronic signals different from ordinary electricity?
2. How is an analog signal different from a digital signal?
3. What solid-state devices can be made from semiconductors?
4. What do diodes and transistors do in electronic devices?
5. Thinking Critically Applying Concepts How are integrated circuits related to the reduction in size of electronic devices?

Check Your Progress
CHAPTER PROJECT 4

Select an existing computer application that interests you. List what you know about it. Then find out how it was developed, how it works, and who uses it. Why is it useful? What signal is put into the computer? What signal comes out? In addition to doing research at the library, see if you can locate someone in your community who uses this application.

Program Resources

◆ **Teaching Resources** 4-1 Review and Reinforce, p. 99; 4-1 Enrich, p. 100

Media and Technology

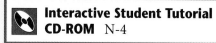 **Interactive Student Tutorial CD-ROM** N-4

Careers in Science

Design a Battery Sensor

In this lab, you will work in the role of an electrical engineer. First you will discover the properties of an electronic component called a light-emitting diode (LED). Then you will design a way to use the LED.

Problem

How can an LED be used to tell if a battery is installed correctly?

Skills Focus

making models, designing experiments

Materials

2 D cells   bicolor LED (optional)
LED   flashlight using 2 D cells
flashlight bulb and socket
two insulated wires with alligator clips

Procedure

Part 1
LED Properties

1. Attach one wire to each terminal of the LED.
2. Tape the two cells together, positive terminal to negative terminal, to make a 3-volt battery.
3. Attach the other ends of the wires to the terminals of the battery and observe the LED.
4. Switch the wires connected to the battery terminals and observe the LED again.
5. Repeat Steps 1–4, but substitute a flashlight bulb in its socket for the LED.

Part 2 Sensor Design

6. Many electrical devices that run on batteries will not run if the batteries are installed backwards (positive where negative should be). Design a device that uses an LED to indicate if batteries are installed backwards.
7. Draw your design. Show how the LED, the device, and the battery are connected. (*Hint:* The LED can be connected either in series or in parallel with the battery and the device.)
8. Make a model of your sensor to see if it works with a flashlight.

Analyze and Conclude

1. What did you observe in Part 1 when you connected the LED to the battery the first time? The second time?
2. Based on your observations, is the LED a diode? That is, does it allow current to flow in only one direction? How do you know?
3. Compare and contrast your results with the LED and with the flashlight bulb.
4. **Apply** Did you have any trouble designing and building your sensor in Part 2? If so, how did you revise your design? Describe how you could use your sensor with other electronic devices.

More to Explore

A bicolor LED contains two LEDs. The LED glows red when current travels through it in one direction. It glows green when current travels in the other direction. How do you think the LEDs within a bicolor LED are arranged? Think of at least one application for this component.

---

the LED is connected to allow current to flow only when the battery is in correctly.

Extending the Inquiry

More to Explore One LED allows current to travel in one direction, the other allows current to travel in the opposite direction. Students' applications should describe devices in which current flows in more than one direction. Sample: to indicate whether the diode in a converter has eliminated the AC.

Program Resources

◆ **Teaching Resources** Chapter 4 Real-World Lab, pp. 113–114

Design a Battery Sensor

Preparing for Inquiry

Key Concept LEDs emit light only when current is traveling in one direction.
Skills Objectives Students will be able to
◆ make model circuits that allow them to observe the properties of an LED;
◆ design experiments to discover the conditions under which an LED will emit light.
Time 25 minutes
Advance Planning Obtain enough large LEDs for the class; an electronics supply store is a good source.
Alternative Materials
◆ Many LEDs will work only with a battery of voltage greater than 2.5 V. Students can arrange two 1.5-V D cells in series.
◆ Tape LEDs to paper plates with terminals bent upward so students can make connections easily.

Guiding Inquiry

Invitation Show students one LED connected so that it is not lit (long wire on LED connected to negative terminal of D cell) and one connected so that it is lit (long wire connected to positive terminal.). Tell them they will discover how the LEDs are connected in this lab.

Expected Outcome
The LED will light only when the D cells are connected in one orientation. The flashlight will light with any orientation.

Analyze and Conclude
1. Answers will vary depending on which connection students tried first. The LED will light in one orientation and not in the opposite orientation.
2. Yes; it lights up when it conducts current in one direction. It does not conduct current in the opposite direction.
3. They both give off light; A light bulb allows current to travel in either direction, an LED only works when the current is moving in one direction.
4. The device should be designed so that

Objectives

After completing the lesson, students will be able to

◆ define electromagnetic waves and state how they are used to transmit information;

◆ describe how common devices such as telephones, televisions, and radios transmit and receive signals.

Key Terms electromagnetic wave, amplitude, frequency, amplitude modulation (AM), frequency modulation (FM), cathode ray tube (CRT)

1 Engage/Explore

Activating Prior Knowledge

Ask students how they think voices are transmitted over phone lines. (*Answers will vary.*) Ask: **Do you think the telephone is an electronic device? Explain.** (*Yes, because it transmits information.*)

DISCOVER

Skills Focus classifying
Materials *hand lens, color television*
Time 10 minutes

🔧 **Tips** If a color television is not available, use a VCR monitor or an RGB computer monitor. Encourage students who need practice seeing through hand lenses to spend extra time using the lenses to observe objects around the room.

Think It Over The three colors are red, green, and blue. Some students may realize that dots of these colors combine to form all the other colors on the screen.

SECTION 2 Electronic Communication

DISCOVER ··· ACTIVITY···

Are You Seeing Spots?

1. Turn on a color television. Hold a hand lens at arm's length up to the television screen.

2. Move the lens closer to and farther from the screen until you can see a clear image through it. What do you see within the image?

Think It Over

Classifying What three colors make up the images on the television screen? How do you think these colors make up the wide range of colors you see on television?

GUIDE FOR READING

◆ How is sound transmitted by a telephone?

◆ How are electromagnetic waves involved in the transmission of information?

◆ How do radio and television stations transmit signals?

Reading Tip Before you read, rewrite the headings in the section as *how, why,* or *what* questions. As you read, look for answers to these questions.

Have you ever thought about the amazing technology that enables you to see and hear an event as it happens half way around the globe? Since the first telegraph message was sent in 1844, people have become accustomed to long distance communication by telephone, radio, and television. Each improvement in the speed, clarity, and reliability of communication has come from advancements in the field of electronics.

Telephones

In a telephone, an electronic signal is transmitted at one end and received at the other. The first telephone was invented by Alexander Graham Bell in 1876. Even though the modern telephone hardly resembles Bell's version, the basic operation has not changed much over the decades. A telephone has three main parts: a transmitter, a receiver, and a dialing mechanism.

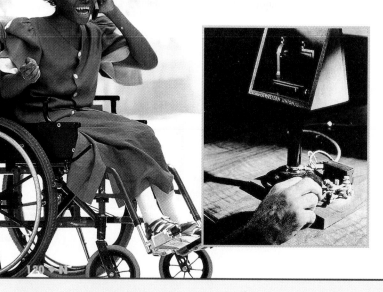

Figure 10 The clicking of a telegraph key (right) was an early form of electronic communication. Now we are accustomed to hearing the voices of people in other cities, or even on other continents.

READING STRATEGIES

Reading Tip Instruct students to rewrite the subheadings as well as the headings as *How, Why,* or *What* questions. Have students write answers to the questions or their guesses about answers on a separate sheet of paper. As students read the section, have them confirm or correct their answers. Then have them write the correct answers under the original questions.

Vocabulary As students read, have them write the boldfaced vocabulary terms in their science journals or on a sheet of notepaper. Instruct them to define the terms in their own words.

Study and Comprehension After students read, have them create flowcharts that show how sound is transmitted by telephone or how sound and images are transmitted by television.

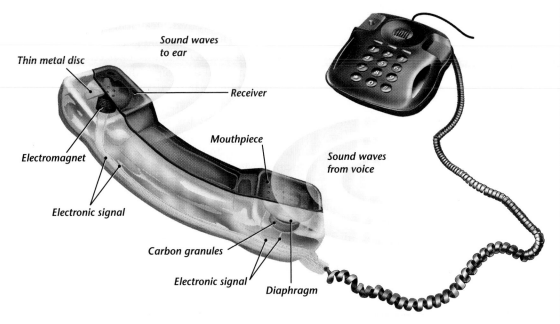

Thin metal disc

Sound waves
to ear

Receiver

Mouthpiece

Electromagnet

Sound waves
from voice

Electronic signal

Carbon granules

Electronic signal

Diaphragm

Figure 11 In telephone transmission, sounds are converted into electronic signals in the transmitter. *Interpreting Diagrams Where are the signals converted back into sounds?*

Transmitter Sound is converted into an electronic signal in the transmitter of a telephone. Converting sound into an electronic signal is possible because sound travels as waves of vibrating matter. For example, when you speak, your vocal cords vibrate back and forth. As they move, they cause the air particles around them to vibrate as well. By passing along the vibration, sound is able to travel through matter.

The transmitter of a telephone is located in the mouthpiece. When you speak into the mouthpiece, the sound waves of your voice cause a thin metal disk to vibrate. In early telephones, the disk pushed against a small chamber of carbon granules, or grains. When the disk vibrated in one direction, it pushed the grains together. When the disk vibrated in the opposite direction, it pulled the grains apart.

A current was passed through the carbon grains. The grains conduct current better when they are close together than when they are apart. So the strength of the current depended on the vibration of the disk, which matched the vibration of the voice.

In most of today's telephones, carbon grains have been replaced by semiconductors, and transistors are used to amplify the signal. Modern telephone equipment can also convert the electronic signals to a pattern of light that travels through optical fibers. In either case, the electronic signal is then sent through a series of switches and wires to the receiving telephone.

2 Facilitate

Telephones

Using the Visuals: Figure 11
Direct students to trace the path of energy from the transmitter to the receiver. Students should begin by placing an index finger on the mouthpiece of the telephone. Have them identify each part of the telephone and explain how the energy is transferred through each component when a person speaks into the phone. *(Sound waves enter the mouthpiece; sound energy is converted into electronic signals in the transmitter; electronic signals pass through the wires.)* Then ask: **What happens when sound is received from the person on the other end of the line?** *(At the receiver, electronic signals are turned back into vibrating sound waves.)* **learning modality: visual**

Building Inquiry Skills: Inferring
Ask: **How is sound converted into electronic signals in the mouthpiece of a telephone?** *(The vibrations caused by the sound cause the current to vary. The current in the circuit is a signal because it corresponds to the sound of the voice.)* Ask students to infer why cordless and mobile phones require batteries. *(To provide a source of current.)* **learning modality: logical/mathematical**

Program Resources
◆ **Teaching Resources** 4-2 Lesson Plan, p. 101; 4-2 Section Summary, p. 102

Media and Technology
 **Audiotapes** English-Spanish Summary 4-2

Transparencies "Telephone," Transparency 17

Answers to Self-Assessment
Caption Question
Figure 11 At the receiver

Ongoing Assessment
Oral Presentation Have students describe how speech is converted into electronic signals in a telephone transmitter.

Building Inquiry Skills: Applying Concepts

Materials *telephone with a screw-off mouthpiece and earpiece*

ACTIVITY

Time 10 minutes

CAUTION: *The telephones should not be plugged in.* Instruct students to carefully take apart the mouthpiece and earpiece and locate the thin metal disc and wires. Ask: **What do you predict would happen if the thin metal disc were removed from the earpiece?** *(The earpiece would stop working because it would not be able to produce sound.)* Ask: **What causes the metal disk to vibrate?** *(The electronic signals are transmitted as a changing current, which causes an electromagnet to push and pull on the metal disk.)*
learning modality: kinesthetic

Building Inquiry Skills: Making Models

Materials *sheet of white paper, markers, scissors, tape*

ACTIVITY

Time 15 minutes

To model the transmission of a fax, instruct students to color a large, dark letter on the paper. Then have them cut the paper into ten narrow strips. Next direct students to pass their strips, one at a time, to a partner. The partner should tape the strips together to form a complete sheet. Ask: **What do the strips of paper represent?** *(The strips of images transmitted by a fax machine)* Then ask: **How does a fax transmit images?** *(As electronic impulses)* **learning modality: logical/mathematical**

Figure 12 A fax machine uses some of the principles of a telephone to transmit images as electronic signals.

Figure 13 The microwaves used in radar are electromagnetic waves with a wavelength of a few centimeters.

Receiver **The telephone receiver, located in the earpiece, contains a small speaker. The speaker changes the electric current back into sound.** The receiver contains an electromagnet that attracts another thin metal disk. Since the amount of electric current changes according to the signal, the strength of the magnetic field around the electromagnet changes as well. This causes the disk to vibrate in a pattern that matches the electronic signal. The vibrating disk creates sound waves, which you hear when you listen to the telephone. Many modern receivers now use semiconductors instead of electromagnets.

Dialing Mechanism The third part of the telephone is the dial or push-button device. When you dial a telephone number, you are telling the switching system where you want the call to go. A dial telephone sends a series of pulses or clicks to the switching network. A push-button device sends different tones. These act as signals that can be interpreted by electronic circuits in the switching network.

Fax Machines A fax machine can send pictures or printed text by means of an electronic signal. To convert a page to a signal, a beam of light scans a page in very narrow strips. The pattern of dark and light in each strip is converted to a signal, and the signal is transmitted through a telephone line.

When another fax machine receives the signal, it prints out the strips, one after another. If you have ever looked closely at a faxed page, you can see that some of the edges of the image are irregular. This shows where the page has been printed in strips.

☑ *Checkpoint* What does a telephone transmitter do?

Electromagnetic Waves

You learned in the last section that electronic signals are transmitted through solid-state components within electronic devices. But, in the case of radio and television, the electronic

Background

History of Science Fax technology first appeared just seven years after the invention of the telegraph. In 1843, a Scottish mechanic took out a patent on a transmitter that could scan a raised surface, such as an etched or embossed piece of metal. The first demonstration of fax transmission took place at the 1851 World's Fair in London, England. Frederick Blakewell's device used a transmitter shaped like a cylinder; the image to be sent was written with a nonconducting substance on a piece of tinfoil. The foil was wrapped around the cylinder and scanned by a stylus that conducted electricity. At the other end, a similar apparatus was set up to transmit electrical impulses to a stylus that marked chemically treated paper with electric current.

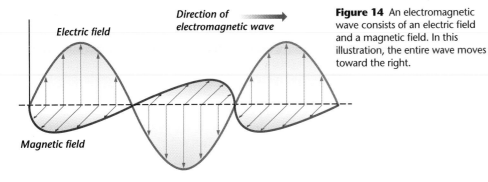

Electric field

Direction of electromagnetic wave

Magnetic field

Figure 14 An electromagnetic wave consists of an electric field and a magnetic field. In this illustration, the entire wave moves toward the right.

signal first has to travel over a long distance from a radio or television station. **Electronic signals can be carried over long distances by electromagnetic waves.**

Electric and Magnetic Fields You are already familiar with some types of waves, such as water waves or sound waves. Electromagnetic waves share some characteristics with these waves. However, electromagnetic waves do not need to travel through matter. An **electromagnetic wave** is a wave that consists of changing electric and magnetic fields.

A wave made out of electric and magnetic fields may sound a little strange at first. But you have already learned that electricity and magnetism are related. You know that a changing magnetic field produces an electric field. The reverse is also true—a changing electric field produces a magnetic field.

If a magnetic field is changing, like the up-and-down movements of a water wave, a changing electric field will form. The changing electric field that is formed then produces a changing magnetic field. The electric and magnetic fields will keep producing each other over and over again, as shown in Figure 14. The result is an electromagnetic wave.

You are already more familiar with electromagnetic waves than you may realize. The light that you see, the microwaves that heat food in a microwave oven, and the X-rays that a dentist or doctor uses are all types of electromagnetic waves.

Figure 15 Light from a rainbow consists of electromagnetic waves with wavelengths that are a tiny fraction of a centimeter. Wavelengths of X-rays are shorter still.

Using the Visuals: Figure 14

Make sure students understand that the figure represents two fields that are perpendicular to each other. Have students describe the direction of the electric field in relation to the page. *(The electric field is flat on the page, or in the same plane as the page.)* Then ask: **What is the direction of the magnetic field in relation to the page?** *(The magnetic field is perpendicular to the page. If the book was lying open on the desk, the field would be pointing to the ceiling and the floor.)*
learning modality: visual

Inquiry Challenge

Materials *stopwatch that measures to 0.001 second, flashlight, open area*
Time 20 minutes

Invite student groups to design experiments that demonstrate that the speed of an electromagnetic wave is faster than the speed of a sound wave. Each group should complete an experimental design plan that specifies what individual students will do. Some possible tasks include calculating the time it takes for a flashlight to be seen across a football field, calculating the time it takes for a clap to be heard across a football field, and creating the waves. Have students draw conclusions about the speed of wave transmission. *(The light, which is carried by electromagnetic waves, seems to travel instantly. The sound, which is carried by sound waves, travels slower.)* **cooperative learning**

Answers to Self-Assessment

☑ *Checkpoint*
A telephone transmitter converts sound into electronic signals.

Ongoing Assessment

Writing Ask students to name the parts of a telephone and explain how each part makes conversation possible.

Electromagnetic Waves, continued

Including All Students

Materials *overhead projector, blank transparency, marker*
Time 5 minutes

Students who need additional help with the concepts of frequency and amplitude may benefit from seeing diagrams of each. Draw two lines on the transparency about 4 cm apart to mark the top and bottom of the waves. As you slowly draw a wave, ask: **How should I change the wave to change the amplitude?** (*Make the waves shorter or taller.*) Then ask: **How should I change the wave to change the frequency?** (*Make the waves closer together or further apart.*)
learning modality: visual

Using the Visuals: Figure 16

Make sure students understand that the wave in 16A represents a simple electromagnetic wave. Ask: **Why is this considered a simple wave?** (*The amplitude and frequency are constant.*) Point out that the wave in 16B is not an electromagnetic wave; it represents the strength of an electric current. Ask: **How does this wave show that the current is carrying information?** (*It shows that the current is changing strength according to the information it carries.*) Have students compare the signal wave to the waves in 16C and 16D. Ask: **How can you tell that the wave in 16C carries the same information as the electronic signal?** (*It has the same shape as the wave.*) It may be more difficult for students to understand how the frequency-modulated wave in 16D represents the signal. Encourage students to compare the frequency pattern to the places where the signal wave moves up and down. Ask: **What part of the signal wave is represented when the waves in 16D are close together?** (*The crests*) **Far apart?** (*The troughs*) **learning modality: logical/mathematical**

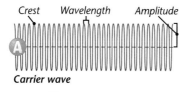
Figure 16 Amplitude or frequency of a carrier wave can be modulated.

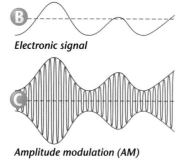

Carrier wave

Electronic signal

Amplitude modulation (AM)

Frequency modulation (FM)

Amplitude and Frequency Modulation All waves have certain basic characteristics. Figure 16A shows a simple wave moving from left to right. The high points are called crests and the low points are called troughs. Waves are described in terms of two quantities, amplitude and frequency. The **amplitude** is the height from the center line to a crest or trough. The **frequency** of a wave is the number of waves passing a given point each second.

The amplitude and frequency of an electromagnetic wave can be changed, or modulated, to carry an electronic signal. The wave that is modulated, shown in Figure 16A, is called the carrier wave. Figure 16B shows an electronic signal. In this case, the signal is an analog signal in which the strength, or amplitude, of an electric current changes.

The carrier wave can be modulated to match the electronic signal in two different ways, as shown in Figures 16C and 16D. One way is to change the amplitude of the carrier wave to match that of the signal. This process is known as **amplitude modulation (AM)**. The other way is to change the frequency of the carrier wave to match the amplitude of the signal. Then the space between the waves varies with the strength of the signal. This process is known as **frequency modulation (FM)**.

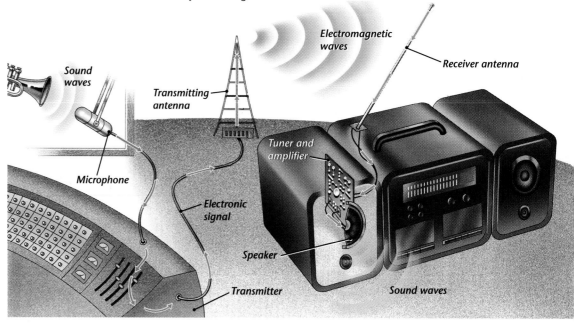
Figure 17 In radio transmission, sounds are converted to electronic signals that are carried by electromagnetic waves.

Radio

Voices or music on an AM or FM radio station are electronic signals carried by an electromagnetic wave. But where do the sounds you hear come from?

Transmission The process begins at a radio station, where sounds are converted into an electronic signal. If a musician plays into a microphone at a radio station, the sound waves produce a varying electric current. This current is an analog signal that represents the sound waves. It is sometimes called an audio signal.

The electronic audio signal is then sent to a transmitter. The transmitter amplifies the signal and combines it with an electronic carrier signal. The signal is then sent to an antenna, which sends out electromagnetic waves in all directions.

Reception Your radio has its own antenna that receives the electromagnetic waves from the radio station. The carrier wave has a specific frequency. You tune in to the wave by selecting that frequency on your radio. Your radio amplifies the signal and separates it from the carrier wave. The signal is then sent to the radio's speaker, which is the reverse of a microphone. The speaker converts the electronic signal back into sound.

Checkpoint What is an audio signal?

Television

Electromagnetic waves can be used to carry images as well as sound. The transmission of the images and sounds on television is very similar to that of radio sounds.

Transmission Television signals are usually sent from transmitting antennas on the ground. Sometimes, however, the signal is blocked by the landscape of an area or by nearby buildings. Or sometimes a transmitter cannot reach homes that are too far away. To solve these problems, local cable television networks have been developed. These networks distribute television signals through cables from a central receiver to individual homes.

Communications satellites are also used to relay television signals. A communications satellite orbits Earth, always staying above the same point on the ground. These satellites receive signals from one part of the planet and transmit them to another almost instantly. This enables you to watch events from around the world as they occur.

Figure 18 A communications satellite orbits Earth at the same rate at which Earth spins. Therefore it stays above the same point on Earth. *Applying Concepts How are communications satellites involved in the transmission of video signals?*

Real-Life Learning

Materials *radio with a tuning dial*
Time 10 minutes

Invite students to slowly turn the dial of the radio across the full range of frequencies. Ask: **What do the different numbers on the dial represent?** *(Different frequencies)* **What is another name for the broadcast frequency of a radio station?** *(The carrier frequency)* Then ask: **When the tuner passes a frequency that is not used for broadcasting, what do you hear?** *(static)* Finally, have students speculate why adjusting the dial makes the sound clearer. *(Adjusting the dial allows the tuner to pick up radio waves of a specific broadcast frequency.)* **learning modality: kinesthetic**

Television

Building Inquiry Skills: Inferring

Asks students to infer why television and radio stations rarely interfere with each other. *(They transmit at different frequencies.)* Provide a local newspaper or media guide and challenge students to find out what frequencies local television networks use to broadcast. Ask: **Are they higher or lower than radio frequencies?** *(Most will be higher.)* **learning modality: verbal**

Media and Technology

📺 **Transparencies** "Transmitting and Receiving Radio," Transparency 18

Answers to Self-Assessment

Caption Question

Figure 18 Satellites receive signals from one part of the planet and transmit them immediately to another part.

Checkpoint

An audio signal is an analog signal that represents sound waves.

Performance Assessment

Skills Check Direct students to make compare/contrast tables that show the characteristics of satellite, cable, and ground transmission television signals.

Television, continued

Building Inquiry Skills: Making Models

Materials *3 flashlights; red, green, and blue filters; rubber bands; string*
Time 15 minutes

Challenge students to use different combinations of filters to produce orange, purple, and yellow light. Students can fasten the filters onto the flashlights using the rubber bands. Ask: **What do you predict would happen if your television set suddenly could not produce any blue dots?** *(The colors on the screen would be limited to black and colors that can be made using red and green.)* Finally, have students tie the three flashlights together and aim the colored light beams at a white surface. Ask: **What device in a television set is similar to the three flashlights? Why?** *(A cathode-ray tube, because it contains each of the primary colors of light.)* **learning modality: visual**

Real-Life Learning

Explain to students that HDTV requires special televisions and special broadcast procedures. The signals for HDTV are digital instead of analog, and they contain much more information than regular television broadcasts. The new televisions have more lines per screen, so the signal has to contain more information. Old televisions cannot receive the new digital signals without a converter. Even with the converter, they cannot display the additional information. Another new type of television has an LCD (Liquid Crystal Display) screen similar to that of a calculator. The LCD screen is very thin and requires very little electricity to run. It has special properties that cause it to change when an electric current is applied. Allow interested students to research new television technologies and present their findings to the class. **learning modality: verbal**

Figure 19 To create a video signal, a television camera scans an image line by line. The camera works like a fax machine, but much faster.

At a television station, cameras turn the light and sound of live action into picture, or video, and audio electronic signals. Both signals are carried by electromagnetic waves.

Reception No matter how video and audio signals are sent, they are accepted by a receiver at your home. As in the case of radio, the carrier wave for each television station is at a specific frequency, which you tune in by selecting a channel on your television. Your television amplifies the signal and separates it from the carrier wave. The audio signal is converted back into sound by the television's speakers.

Cathode-Ray Tubes The video signal is sent to a very specialized type of vacuum tube known as a cathode-ray tube. A **cathode-ray tube (CRT),** or picture tube, is an electronic device that uses electrons to produce images on a screen. A CRT converts video signals into a pattern of light.

At one end of a CRT are three electron guns, one for each of the primary colors of light—red, blue, and green. The other end of a CRT is the screen that you see. The inside of the screen is coated with fluorescent materials, called phosphors, that glow when they are hit by an electron beam. The phosphors are arranged in clusters of three dots—one for each color. Each cluster is surrounded by dark space. You have seen the phosphors and dark spaces if you completed the Discover activity. The video signal is fed to the electron guns, causing each one to aim at the matching phosphor at the appropriate time. Your eyes combine the three colors to form all of the colors in the images you see.

A black and white television uses a single electron gun. The intensity of the beam is varied to produce a different brightness at each point on the screen. The result is different shades of black, white, and gray.

In order to produce the image, the electron beams must sweep across the entire screen in a zigzag pattern. The beams

---

Background

Facts and Figures Important dates in television history:

◆ 1884 German scientist Paul Nipkow patents a mechanical television system.
◆ 1925 Scottish engineer John Logie Baird demonstrates televising moving objects at Royal Institution, London.
◆ 1927 First public TV broadcasting begins in England (1930 in United States).

◆ 1928 Baird demonstrates first color TV.
◆ 1932 Radio Corporation of America (RCA) demonstrates first all-electronic TV using a cathode-ray tube in the receiver.
◆ 1939 First *regular* public TV broadcasting begins in the United States.
◆ 1951 First color TV broadcasting system begins in New York.

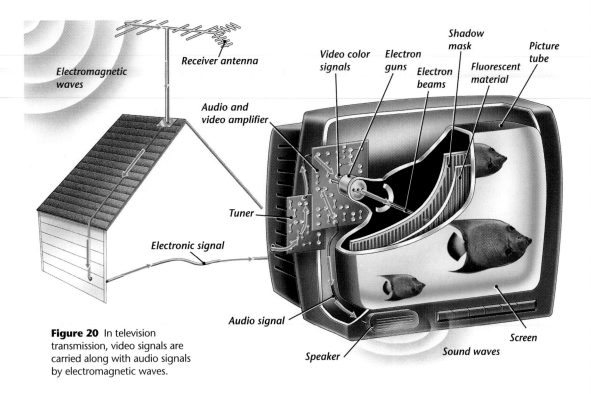

Electromagnetic waves

Receiver antenna

Video color signals

Electron guns

Electron beams

Shadow mask

Picture tube

Fluorescent material

Audio and video amplifier

Tuner

Electronic signal

Audio signal

Speaker

Sound waves

Screen

Figure 20 In television transmission, video signals are carried along with audio signals by electromagnetic waves.

scan across the screen in 525 horizontal lines before returning to the top of the screen. This pattern repeats 30 times each second!

Improved televisions allow broadcasters to transmit twice as many lines per screen. The images can be larger and sharper. These televisions are known as high-definition televisions (HDTV).

Section 2 Review

1. How does a telephone work?
2. What are electromagnetic waves? How can they carry electronic signals?
3. Describe how information is transmitted in radios and televisions.
4. What is a cathode-ray tube? How does it work to create a color television image?
5. **Thinking Critically Making Generalizations** How do you think solid-state devices have affected radios and televisions?

Science at Home

A remote-control device uses electromagnetic waves to program an electronic device—for instance, a television, VCR, radio, or toy—from a distance. Find a device with a remote control. Ask your family members to help you locate the receiver for the remote control on the device. Find out how far away from the device you can stand and still control the device. Find out what objects the waves will travel through. Will they bounce off mirrors? Off walls? Off your hand?

Chapter 4 **N ◆ 127**

Section 2 Review Answers

1. The transmitter changes sound waves into electronic signals. The receiver changes the electronic signals back into sound waves.
2. Electromagnetic waves are made up of changing electric and magnetic fields. Electronic signals can be carried by changing the amplitude or frequency of the waves.
3. Electronic signals in radios and televisions are transmitted through solid-state devices. The electronic signal is first sent from the broadcasting station using an electromagnetic wave.
4. A color cathode ray tube is a vacuum tube that contains three electron guns, one for each color of light. The electron beams are directed at a screen coated with a material that glows when electrons strike it. The electronic signal directs the electron beams to hit the appropriate color-producing phosphors, to reproduce the transmitted image.
5. Solid-state devices have allowed smaller, lighter, more efficient, and less expensive radios and televisions to be produced.

Science at Home

Materials *remote-control device, remote control*

The receiver will be a small round "window" on the device. The effective distance of the remote control will vary depending on the type of sensor. The waves will travel through clear plastic film, but not glass or students' hands. They bounce off mirrors and walls.

Program Resources

◆ **Teaching Resources** 4-2 Review and Reinforce, p. 103; 4-2 Enrich, p. 104

Media and Technology

Interactive Student Tutorial CD-ROM N-4

Transparencies "Television Reception," Transparency 19

Performance Assessment

Writing Have students write two short paragraphs describing how sound is transmitted over a telephone and a radio.

Portfolio Students can save their paragraphs in their portfolios.

N ◆ 127

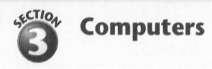
Objectives

After completing the lesson, students will be able to
- explain how a computer stores and processes information;
- identify and describe the components of computer hardware and tell how computer software is related.

Key Terms computer, binary system, bit, byte, computer hardware, central processing unit, input device, output device, random-access memory (RAM), read-only memory (ROM), disk drive, hard disk, diskette, optical disc, computer programmer, computer software

1 Engage/Explore

Activating Prior Knowledge

Virtually all students will have heard the term *computer* and have some notion of what a computer is. Many students will have access to a computer and may even use a computer at home or school. Allow students to discuss computers and how they are used. Make note of any misconceptions to be addressed.

DISCOVER

Skills Focus inferring
Materials calculator
Time 10 minutes
Tips Make sure students include a variety of different addition and subtraction problems involving numbers up to and including 99.
Expected Outcome Most students will be able to work faster and more accurately with the calculator than doing the problems by hand.
Think It Over Calculators provide a significant increase in accuracy and speed, especially when dealing with problems more complex than addition.

SECTION 3 Computers

DISCOVER .... **ACTIVITY**

How Fast Are You?

1. Write out ten math problems involving the addition or subtraction of two two-digit numbers.
2. Switch lists with a friend.
3. Take turns timing how long it takes each of you to solve the ten problems by hand.
4. Then time how long it takes each of you to solve the ten problems using a calculator. What is the time difference? Is there a difference in accuracy?

Think It Over
Inferring What are the advantages of using an electronic device to complete calculations?

GUIDE FOR READING

- How is information stored and processed in a computer?
- How is computer hardware different from computer software?

Reading Tip As you read, use the headings to make an outline about how computers work.

Figure 21 You may never have seen an abacus, but these devices can be used to perform complex calculations.

Over two thousand years ago, the first calculator was invented. But it was not what you may think. This calculating device is called an abacus. People use an abacus to count by sliding beads along strings.

In the United States, mechanical adding machines and abacuses have generally been replaced by electronic calculators and computers. Although the development of computers has occurred in less than a century, computers have become commonplace.

What Is a Computer?

A **computer** is an electronic device that stores, processes, and retrieves information. One of the reasons that computers can process and store so much information is that they do not store information in the same form that you see it—numbers, letters, and pictures. **Computer information is represented in the binary system.** The **binary system** uses combinations of just two digits, 0 and 1. Although computers can use analog signals, almost all modern computers are digital.

INTEGRATING MATHEMATICS You may be wondering how large numbers can be represented using only series of 1's and 0's. Begin by thinking about the numbers with which you are more familiar. You are used to using the base-10 number system. Each place value in a number represents the number 10 raised to some power. The digits 1 through 9 are then multiplied by the place value in each position. For example, the number 327 means 3×100 plus 2×10 plus 7×1.

READING STRATEGIES

Reading Tip Guide students by working as a class to outline the first topic in the section, as shown in this partial outline:
I. Computers Store, Process, and Retrieve Information.
   A. Most computers are digital.
   B. Computer information is represented in the binary system.
      1. The binary system uses 1's and 0's.

Study and Comprehension As students read, have them write answers to the questions: What is a computer? What is the binary system? What is computer hardware? How do computers store information? What is computer software? What do computer programmers do? Students can gather more information on their topic from classroom and school library resources. Encourage question-and-answer sessions after students read the section.

Binary System

Place Values 8 4 2 1	Expanded Value		Base-10 Number
1 =	(1 × 1) =	1 =	1
1 0 =	(1 × 2) + (0 × 1) =	2 + 0 =	2
1 1 =	(1 × 2) + (1 × 1) =	2 + 1 =	3
1 0 0 =	(1 × 4) + (0 × 2) + (0 × 1) =	4 + 0 + 0 =	4
1 0 1 =	(1 × 4) + (0 × 2) + (1 × 1) =	4 + 0 + 1 =	5
1 0 1 0 =	(1 × 8) + (0 × 4) + (1 × 2) + (0 × 1) =	8 + 0 + 2 + 0 =	10
1 0 1 1 =	(1 × 8) + (0 × 4) + (1 × 2) + (1 × 1) =	8 + 0 + 2 + 1 =	11
1 1 1 1 =	(1 × 8) + (1 × 4) + (1 × 2) + (1 × 1) =	8 + 4 + 2 + 1 =	15

The binary system is similar to the base-10 number system, except that the base number is 2. Notice in Figure 22 that the place values begin with 1, 2, 4, and 8 instead of 1, 10, 100, and 1,000. In the binary system, only the numbers 0 and 1 are multiplied by each place value.

Each 1 or 0 in the binary system is called a **bit,** short for **bi**nary digit. Arrangements of eight bits are called **bytes.** Computer memories are rated in kilobytes (one thousand bytes), megabytes (one million bytes), or even gigabytes (one billion bytes).

☑ *Checkpoint* What two digits are used in the binary system?

Computer Memory

There are many ways to record 0's and 1's. The pits and flats on a CD can represent 0's and 1's. CDs can store not just music, but any kind of data. Computers can also use magnetic tapes to store information. Magnetic tapes, such as video and audio tapes, record information by changing the arrangement of magnetic domains. The magnetic domains can be oriented in one direction to represent 1's, and in the opposite direction to represent 0's.

Computers also use integrated circuits, or chips. Chips contain thousands of tiny circuits with transistors that act as switches. A switch in the off position represents a 0 and a switch in the on position represents a 1. One chip may consist of as many as 16 million switches or bits.

Figure 22 Each place value in the binary system is double the value to its right. In this table, you see the binary numbers representing the base-10 numbers 1, 2, 3, 4, 5, 10, 11, and 15. *Interpreting Charts What is your age in the binary system?*

Figure 23 Electronic switches are shown in this enlarged view. They are part of a chip that can store over 500,000 bits of information.

N ◆ 129

Program Resources

◆ **Teaching Resources** 4-3 Lesson Plan, p. 105; 4-3 Section Summary, p. 106

Media and Technology

 Audiotapes English-Spanish Summary 4-3

Answers to Self-Assessment

Caption Question

Figure 22 Answers will vary, depending on students' ages. Sample: An 11-year-old student has a binary age of 1011. A 14-year-old student has a binary age of 1110.

☑ *Checkpoint*

0's and 1's

What is a Computer?

Integrating Mathematics

Have students write the numbers 10, 10 × 10, 10 × 10 × 10, and 10 × 10 × 10 × 10. Now write the binary equivalents of 2, 2 × 2, 2 × 2 × 2, and 2 × 2 × 2 × 2. Ask students if they recognize the pattern. *(10, 100, 1000, and 10000 in both cases)* **learning modality: verbal**

Using the Visuals

Have students examine Figure 22. Make sure they understand that each place in the binary system represents a power of 2 instead of a power of 10. Use several examples to show how any number can be represented by 0's and 1's. For example, decimal 3 becomes binary 11, 4 becomes 100, and so on. **learning modality: logical/mathematical**

Computer Memory

Building Inquiry Skills: Modeling

Materials *modeling clay, wooden matches or toothpicks*

Have pairs of students shape a piece of modeling clay into a strip about 8 cm × 1 cm × 1 cm. They can use a matchstick or toothpick to make eight evenly spaced holes in the strip of clay. Then let a stick in the hole represent 1 and no stick represent 0. Students should take turns arranging sticks in the holes to represent various binary numbers, challenging their partner to figure out the decimal equivalent. **cooperative learning**

Ongoing Assessment

Skills Check Have students write the binary equivalents of 8, 9, 16, and 17 and the decimal equivalents of 101 and 1001.

N ◆ 129

Computer Hardware

Addressing Naive Conceptions

People often say that any device that uses a microprocessor is a computer. A microprocessor-controlled washing machine or microwave oven is not the same as a desktop computer. Ask students to discuss the characteristics of a computer. Then list several common appliances and devices on the board and ask students to decide if they carry out all the functions of a desktop computer. **learning modality: verbal**

Sharpen your Skills

Calculating

Materials none
Time 10 minutes

Tips You may need to "walk" students through the calculations. Students should first calculate the number of pages (25 × 400 = 10,000), then the number of words (10,000 × 1,200 = 12,000,000), and finally the number of letters (12,000,000 × 6 = 72,000,000). Remind students that a gigabyte is 1,000,000,000 bytes. Students should realize that the encyclopedias would fit on the single gigabyte chip many times over.
Extend Challenge students to explain how they could estimate how many gigabyte chips it would take to hold the information from all the books in your school library. *(Sample: Repeat the above calculation for an "average" library book, then multiply by the number of books in the library.)* **learning modality: logical/mathematical**

Computer Hardware

Have students read and examine the visual essay. After students read the descriptions of each of the components of a computer system, ask: **Why is it important to have an input device?** *(To get information into the computer.)* **How is information obtained from the computer?** *(Through the output device.)* **learning modality: logical/ mathematical**

EXPLORING Computer Hardware

A computer system has several basic physical parts that are used to enter data into the computer, process the data, and retrieve information out of the computer.

Input Devices
The computer gathers data by means of input devices such as a keyboard, mouse, scanner, joystick, microphone, light pen, scanner, or touch-sensitive screen.

Modem
A modem, which connects a computer to a telephone line, can serve as both an input and an output device.

Monitor
Keyboard
Microphone
Scanner
Modem
Light pen
Mouse

Sharpen your Skills

Calculating

A set of encyclopedias contains 25 volumes with an average of 400 pages per book. Each page contains 1,200 words and the average word is 6 letters long. Suppose each letter requires 1 byte. Could the entire set fit on a single gigabyte chip?

Computer Hardware

The physical parts that allow a computer to receive, store, and present information make up the computer's hardware. **Computer hardware** refers to the permanent components of the computer. **Computer hardware includes a central processing unit, input devices, output devices, and memory storage devices.** Identify the different devices as you read *Exploring Computer Hardware*.

The central processing unit serves as the brain of a computer. The **central processing unit,** or CPU, directs the operation of the computer, performs logical operations and calculations, and stores information.

Data are fed to a CPU by an **input device.** There are several different types of input devices. The one most familiar to you is probably the keyboard. Other input devices are shown in *Exploring Computer Hardware*.

Background

Facts and Figures When computers are made using radically new technology, they are often called "new generation" computers. A generation is classified by the important step in technology that makes new applications possible. For example, the first commercial computer in the United States—the UNIVAC I, developed in 1951 for the U.S. Bureau of the Census—was a first-generation computer because it was the first digital computer that could process both names and numbers. The second generation of computers began in 1958, when the Control Data Corporation introduced smaller and faster computers for commercial purposes that used transistors. The third generation is defined by the use of semiconductor chips with integrated circuits. These were developed during the 1960s and 1970s.

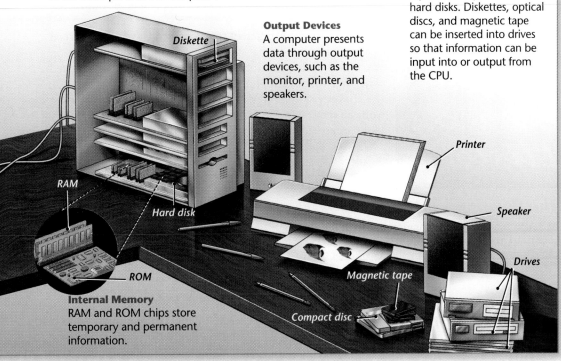

Central Processing Unit (CPU)
The CPU is the control center of the computer. The CPU processes and stores information, and coordinates the functions of the other parts of the computer.

Diskette

Output Devices
A computer presents data through output devices, such as the monitor, printer, and speakers.

External Memory
Information can be stored on hard disks, diskettes, optical discs, and magnetic tape. All computers use hard disks. Diskettes, optical discs, and magnetic tape can be inserted into drives so that information can be input into or output from the CPU.

RAM

Printer

Hard disk

Speaker

ROM

Drives

Internal Memory
RAM and ROM chips store temporary and permanent information.

Magnetic tape

Compact disc

Data from a computer are presented on an **output device.** A computer monitor, on which you view information, is the most familiar output device. Other output devices are shown in *Exploring Computer Hardware.*

Memory Devices

Computers store information in their memory. There are two general types of computer memory, internal and external. Chips on the main circuit board within the CPU are referred to as internal memory. **Random Access Memory** (RAM) is the temporary storage area for data while the computer is operating. Information stored in RAM is lost when the computer is turned off.

Information the computer needs to operate properly is stored in **Read Only Memory** (ROM). The CPU can read these data but cannot change them. Information in ROM is permanently stored and is not lost when the computer is turned off.

Media and Technology

Transparencies "Exploring Computer Hardware," Transparency 20

Exploring Physical Science Videodisc
Unit 5, Side 1, "Then and Now"
Chapter 7

Memory Devices

Demonstration

Materials *audio tape, tape player, strong magnet*
Time 15 minutes

Before class, record something on an audio tape, such as a portion of a popular song or a student reading a passage from the textbook. In class, play the tape. Ask students to describe how the information is stored on the tape. *(Most will know it has something to do with magnetism.)* Ask students to predict what will happen if the magnet is brought near the tape. *(Many students will predict the tape will be damaged.)* Pass the magnet back and forth over both sides of the audio tape and then play it again. Ask students to describe what happened. *(The information was lost.)* Explain that hard disk drives and other external memory devices also store the information magnetically. **learning modality: verbal**

Including All Students

Computer terminology has many acronyms and much technical language. It is easy for students to get lost in the jumble of words and letters. Ask: **What does CPU stand for?** *(Central Processing Unit)* **What does** *random-access memory* **mean?** *(The computer can easily retrieve any individual piece of information.)* **Why is it important for a computer to have read-only memory?** *(The computer needs basic instructions on how to turn itself on and find input and output devices.)* **learning modality: verbal**

Ongoing Assessment

Writing Have students choose one input device and one output device from pages 130–131 and describe how those devices function as part of a computer system.

Invite volunteers to read aloud the items on the time line. Guide students through the sequence of the technological developments shown. Ask: **What advantages do computers provide?** *(They allow people to get more done and work more accurately.)* **Are there any disadvantages to using computers?** *(They sometimes produce more information than people really need. Sometimes people can lose their jobs.)* **How have computers changed our lives?** *(Student responses will vary, but they might mention the Internet, word processing, electronic encyclopedias, electronic games, or increased productivity.)*

In Your Journal Students can find out more about the form of computer they have chosen in books about the history of computers or technology. They will also need to find out what other technologies were available and what needs the early computer could meet. General history books may also be valuable in giving students a sense of what was going on in the world at the time and how this technology could be useful to the world. **learning modality: visual**

Neither RAM nor ROM allow you to save information when you turn your computer off. For that reason, devices outside the main CPU circuit are used to store information. They are called external memory. The most widely used form of external storage is the disk. Information is read from a disk or entered onto a disk by a **disk drive.**

There are several different types of disks. **Hard disks** are rigid magnetic metal disks that stay inside the computer. Information on a hard disk remains in the computer and can be accessed whenever you use the computer.

Diskettes, or floppy disks, are thin, round plastic disks that you can remove from the computer and carry with you. Floppy disks are coated with magnetic material laid in circles. If you have

SCIENCE & History

The Development of Computers

Although some modern computers can fit in the palm of your hand, this wasn't always the case. Computers have come a long way in a relatively short period of time.

1823

The Difference Engine

British mathematician Charles Babbage designed the first computer, called the Difference Engine. It was a mechanical computing device that had more than 50,000 moving parts. For a later computer of Babbage's, Ada Lovelace wrote what is considered the first computer program.

1800	1850

1890

Census Counting Machine

Herman Hollerith constructed a machine that processed information by allowing electric current to pass through holes in punch cards. With Hollerith's machine, the United States census of 1890 was completed in one fourth the time needed for the 1880 census.

Background

History of Science In many ways, the logic that runs computers in the form of software is linked to the development of the hardware. As devices are invented that allow computers to control current in new ways, new methods of coding information are required.

The binary system used by digital computers is one example of the relationship between computer engineering and mathematics. The binary system is based on the system of logic called Boolean algebra which was developed in 1847 by a British mathematician, George Boole. In this system, statements are classified as either true or false. This logic could not be applied to computers until the study of electronics allowed engineers such as Atanasoff and Berry to manipulate electric current to produce electronic signals.

used such a diskette, you may be confused by the term *floppy*. This is because the floppy disk is encased in a hard, square plastic case for protection. If you slide the metal portion of the case to the side, you can see the floppy disk inside.

Another type of memory is an optical disc, also called a compact disc. An **optical disc** is a disc on which information is written and read by lasers. Optical discs can hold much greater amounts of information than diskettes. They are commonly used for video games. They also hold reference materials such as encyclopedias, magazines, and videos. Such optical discs are called CD-ROMs (Compact Disc—Read-Only Memory).

☑ *Checkpoint* What is read-only memory (ROM)?

In Your Journal

In 1953, there were only about 100 computers in the entire world. Today, there are hundreds of millions of computers in businesses, homes, government offices, schools, and stores. Select one of the early forms of the computer. Write a newspaper article introducing it and its applications to the public.

1946

ENIAC

The first American-built computer was developed by the United States Army. The Electronic Numerical Integrator and Calculator, or ENIAC, consisted of thousands of vacuum tubes and filled an entire warehouse. To change the program, programmers had to rewire the entire machine.

1900	1950	2000

1939

Binary System

American physicists John V. Atanasoff and Clifford Berry produced a working model of a computer based on the binary system. They recognized that the digits 1 and 0 could be easily represented by electronic components.

1974

Personal Computers

The first personal computer (PC) went on the market. Today's personal computer is 400 times faster than ENIAC, 3,000 times lighter, and several million dollars cheaper.

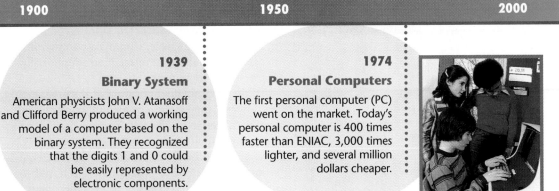

Chapter 4 **N ◆ 133**

Answers to Self-Assessment

☑ *Checkpoint*

Read-only memory (ROM) is permanently stored in the computer and is not lost when the computer is turned off. It contains information the computer needs to operate properly.

Real-Life Learning

Have students create analogies to describe the remarkable advances in the development of computers in the last 60 years. The analogies should be in the form: "If ___ had changed as much as computers, we would have ___ ." For example, they might say "If cars had changed as much as computers, we would have cars that would only cost $100, safely go 5,000 miles an hour, and get at least 1,000 miles per gallon."
learning modality: verbal

Building Inquiry Skills: Hypothesizing

Computers have roughly doubled in power every year since the first computer was developed. Have students form small groups and discuss whether this trend can continue indefinitely. After discussion, allow the groups to present their arguments to the whole class.
learning modality: verbal

Computer Software

Including All Students

Computer terms can be confusing to students, especially students with a limited grasp of English. Have students read the definition of computer software. Ask: **Why is it called *software*?** *(To distinguish the set of instructions, or program, from hardware.)* **limited English proficiency**

Computer Programming

Building Inquiry Skills: Making Models

Materials *none*
Time 15 minutes

Perform this activity in a large open area. Make sure that there are no obstacles. Organize the class into groups of four. Have two students in each group write "software" to direct the other two students to perform some simple operation such as picking up a pencil or sitting down. The other pair of students in each group should execute the "code" by doing exactly what it says and nothing more. Then the pairs can switch roles.
learning modality: kinesthetic

Computer Software

A computer needs a set of instructions that tell it what to do. **A program is a detailed set of instructions that directs the computer hardware to perform operations on stored information.** Computer programs are called **computer software.** Whenever you use a word processor, solve mathematical problems, or play a computer game, a computer program is instructing the computer to perform in a certain way.

One category of computer software is called the operating system of the computer. An operating system is a set of basic instructions that keep a computer running. Perhaps you have heard of the operating software known as DOS, or disk operating system. Unix is another example of operating software.

A second category of software is usually called applications software. Applications are particular tasks that a computer may carry out. These programs are grouped by their function, such as word processing, graphics, games, or simulations.

✓ *Checkpoint* What is a computer program?

Computer Programming

People who program computers are called computer programmers. **Computer programmers** use computer languages that convert input information into instructions that the CPU can understand. You may have heard the names of some computer languages, such as Fortran, Basic, C, and COBOL. Each language is designed for a specific purpose. Fortran, for example, allows users to complete complex calculations. It is not, however, practical for word processing.

Programmers create software by using a step-by-step development process. First, they outline exactly what the program will do. Second, they develop a flowchart. A flowchart is a diagram showing the order of computer actions and data flow. Third, they write the instructions for the computer in a particular language. Complicated programs may contain millions of instructions. And finally, they test the program.

If the program does not work as the programmers intend, they *debug* it by identifying any problems with their logic. The term *bug* was applied to a mysterious malfunction in an early computer. Programmers discovered a moth in a vital electrical switch. Thereafter the programmers referred to problems as bugs and fixing problems as debugging.

Figure 24 Computer programmers develop software with all sorts of applications, from typing simple sentences to training these oil rig operators.

Background

Facts and Figures Chess players must consider many possibilities at once, recognize patterns, and break complicated moves down into smaller moves. Because of this, people have long considered chess as a test of how well a machine performs complex tasks. Before the late nineteenth century, chess-playing "machines" with names like *The Turk* were displayed at carnivals. These machines actually contained a human chess player who played all the moves. Now chess-playing computers compete with human chess players. In 1996, a computer called Deep Blue played a six-game match against Gary Kasparov, a world champion. Deep Blue won the first game, but Kasparov won the match 4-2. However, in a 1997 rematch, Deep Blue, which had been upgraded to play at twice its original speed, beat Kasparov by one game.

Figure 25 Computers do not always take the form of desktop computers. Computer technology is used in devices as common as cameras and watches.

Computers at Work

Computer hardware and software are not always obvious. Just because you don't see an entire computer setup, you shouldn't assume a computer isn't involved. Do you wear a digital watch? If so, you are wearing a computer. Computer chips are used to control the timing of alarms and displays in digital watches.

Has a photographer ever taken your school picture? Computers and electronic sensors are used to monitor exposures in cameras. At the grocery store, computers are used to enter inventory bar codes into the cash register and add up your purchases. Computer chips are used to regulate engines in cars, monitor heating and cooling systems in buildings, and even to operate the locks on some doors. Look around. Computers are everywhere.

Section 3 Review

1. What is a computer? How does a computer store information?
2. How are computer hardware and software involved in the operation of a computer?
3. How do switches within a computer count to ten using binary code?
4. **Thinking Critically Classifying** Identify each of the following as an input device, output device, or both: keyboard, printer, diskette, scanner, touch-activated screen.

Check Your Progress

CHAPTER PROJECT 4

Choose a task that you would like to have done by a computer. Consider an activity such as mowing the lawn or watering the crops on a farm. Try to make your computer application original. Develop a series of steps that the computer would follow to complete the task. What input information is required? What is the resulting output from the computer? A flowchart diagram will help other students understand your new invention.

Program Resources

◆ **Teaching Resources** 4-3 Review and Reinforce, p. 107; 4-3 Enrich, p. 108

Media and Technology

Interactive Student Tutorial CD-ROM N-4

Answers to Self-Assessment

☑ *Checkpoint*

A computer program is a detailed set of instructions that directs the computer hardware to perform operations on stored information.

Computers at Work

Real-Life Learning

Many automobiles now include computerized engine monitors. Ask students to describe information such an engine monitor might process (*Sample: Engine temperature, engine load*), how that information gets into the computer (*Engine sensors*), and what the output device is (*Dashboard display or ignition controls*). **learning modality: verbal**

3 Assess

Section 3 Review Answers

1. A computer is a device that retrieves, processes, and stores information. Computers process information as patterns of 0's and 1's.
2. Hardware consists of the structures of the computer, such as input devices, output devices, the central processing unit, and memory-storage devices. Software refers to the sets of instructions that tell the computer what to do.
3. Students' answers should include a list of binary numbers from 0 to 1010.
4. Keyboard: input; printer: output; diskette: input or output; scanner: input; touch-activated screen: input or output

Check Your Progress

CHAPTER PROJECT 4

Encourage students to be creative in developing their own computing devices. Suggest they think of things that will make their lives easier, safer, or more pleasant or consider things that will benefit their community or the whole world.

Performance Assessment

Writing Have students write paragraphs describing the essential characteristics of a computer including at least one application that illustrates each essential characteristic.

The Penny Computer

Preparing for Inquiry

Key Concept The binary number system is used to transmit digital signals in the operation of computers.

Skills Objective Students will be able to
◆ model the operation of a computer using pennies to represent electronic switches.

Time 40 minutes

Advance Planning Make sure to have enough pennies on hand for each group to have 15 pennies.

Alternative Materials Checkers or other flat game pieces can be used instead of pennies. Make sure that one side is distinguishable from the other.

Guiding Inquiry

Invitation Write a series of 0's and 1's on the board, and ask students to tell you what number it represents. If necessary, review binary number systems with the students until they can read binary numbers as base-10 numbers.

Introducing the Procedure Have students review the procedure. Then toss a coin in the air and have volunteers call the toss. Say: **Who calls 1? Who calls 0?** When the coin lands, show students the result and ask them to tell you which way it landed. *(For this lab, heads-up represents 1, tails-up represents 0.)*

Troubleshooting the Experiment

Students will automatically think of the binary numbers in terms of decimal equivalents. For example, they may want to call 101 "one hundred and one" when, in fact, it has a value of 5. Remind students to record their binary numbers in tables as shown in Figures 1 and 3 and to refer to the top of the column to determine the value of the number in that place.

The Penny Computer

Computers can only count to 1! Computers use a binary number system that has only two digits, 0 and 1, to represent numbers. In a computer, a 0 is represented by a switch that is turned off, and a 1 by a switch that is turned on. You will make a model of a computer using pennies instead of switches.

Problem

How can pennies be used to model counting and adding in a computer?

Materials

15 pennies   paper   ruler
binary number table (Figure 22)

Procedure

Part 1   Binary Numbers

1. Review binary numbers. (See Figure 22 in this chapter.)
2. Before you use the computer, you need to learn the rules for counting with the penny code:
   ◆ A heads-up penny represents the digit 1.
   ◆ A tails-up penny represents the digit 0.

16	8	4	2	1
			🪙	🪙

Figure 1

3. Examine Figure 1. The row of pennies represents a binary number. In your notebook, write the binary number represented by the row of pennies.
4. Convert this binary number to a base-10 number. Write the result in your notebook. Remember that the binary number 101 is equivalent to 5:
   $(1 \times 4) + (0 \times 2) + (1 \times 1) =$
   $\quad 4 \quad + \quad 0 \quad + \quad 1 \quad = 5$
5. In your notebook, write the binary numbers 110, 111, 1000, 1001, and 10001.
6. Use pennies to represent these five binary numbers. Then convert the five binary numbers to their base-10 equivalents, and record.

Part 2   Adding with Binary Numbers

7. Learn the following rules for binary addition.

0	1	1
+0	+0	+1
0	1	10

The third rule may look odd, but remember that 10 in the binary system is equivalent to the number 2 in the base-10 system. The third rule shows you how to carry a 1 when adding binary numbers.

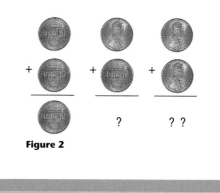

Figure 2

Analyze and Conclude

1. When students checked their work by converting to base 10, they should have found the same values. For example, in number 16, the binary number 11 represents the base-10 number 3. The binary number 110 represents the base-10 number 6. In binary, 11 + 11 = 110. In base 10, 3 + 3 = 6.

2. The largest number is 31. If all the pennies were heads up, the sum would be 16 + 8 + 4 + 2 + 1 = 31.

3. In order to express larger numbers, more pennies would have to be used. 32 would require 6 pennies, 64 would require 7 pennies.

4. Each byte would require 8 pennies. A 3-gigabyte computer would require (8 pennies/byte) (3,000,000,000 bytes) = 24,000,000,000 pennies. That's $240,000,000!

8. Using a heads-up penny for the digit 1, and a tails-up penny for the digit 0, the addition rules in Step 7 can be represented as shown in Figure 2. The first rule is complete. Use pennies to work out the other two. Copy the results in your notebook.

9. Look at Figure 3. It shows an addition problem done with the computer. Check that the arithmetic is done according to the rules you have learned. (Remember that you may have to carry a 1.)

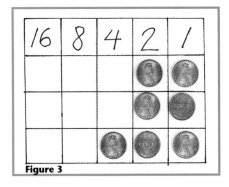

Figure 3

Part 3 Building a Binary Computer

10. Make a blank chart like the one in Figure 3. Be sure that each of the spaces in the three blank rows is large enough for a penny. This chart is your computer.

11. Put three pennies in the first blank row to represent the binary number 110.

12. Put three more pennies in the second row to represent the binary number 101.

13. Add together the two binary numbers. Use pennies to represent the sum.

14. Convert the three rows of pennies to base-10 numbers.

15. Use the base-10 numbers to check that you have done the problem correctly.

16. Next, use your computer to add the binary numbers 11 and 11. You will have to carry a 1 in two places. If you get the result 110, you have carried correctly.

17. Make up three other addition problems for your partner to solve. At least one of the binary numbers in each pair should have more than three digits. You will need to repeat Steps 10–15 each time. Write the problems in your notebook.

Analyze and Conclude

1. For the calculations you performed in Part 3, did you find the same results with the binary and base-10 systems?

2. What is the largest number that can be represented using 5 pennies? Explain.

3. How could you change your computer so you could represent larger numbers than your answer to Question 2? How could you represent 32 or 64 in the binary system? Use pennies to illustrate your answer.

4. **Think About It** In a computer, each on-off switch is called a bit. A byte is made up of 8 bits. How many pennies would be needed to model each byte? A typical personal computer may have a hard disk capacity of 3 gigabytes (3 billion bytes). How many pennies would be needed to model the number of bytes in the hard disk?

More to Explore

Find the rule that describes how your model can be used to double binary numbers. (*Hint:* You know that if you double the base-10 number 9, the answer is 18. What is 9 in binary? What is 18 in binary? Try other examples, and look for a pattern.) What is the relationship between a binary number and twice that number?

Extending the Inquiry

More to Explore The rule is that when a number is doubled, the entire number moves one place to the left, and the number on the far right becomes 0. It may help students to realize that the "one's place" in binary is always 0 for a doubled number, because doubled numbers are even. The "one's place" contains a 0 for even numbers and a 1 for odd. If students have trouble with this, ask them to compare this to what happens when a number is multiplied by 10 in the base-ten system. All the digits move to the left and the last (furthest right) digit becomes 0.

Program Resources

◆ **Teaching Resources** Chapter 4 Skills Lab, pp. 115–117

SECTION 4 The Information Superhighway

Objectives

After completing the lesson, students will be able to

♦ describe how a computer network works and state some advantages;

♦ explain how the Internet is a type of computer network;

♦ identify aspects of responsible computer usage.

Key Terms computer network, local area network, wide area network, Internet, World Wide Web, encryption, computer virus, chat room, intellectual property, freeware, shareware

1 Engage/Explore

Activating Prior Knowledge

Have students describe the Internet. Ask questions such as: **Could you send an electronic mail message to a computer company in another country? Could you play a game with someone in Japan? How?** (*Yes, the Internet connects computers all over the world.*)

········ DISCOVER ········

Skills Focus inferring
Materials *newspapers*
Time 20 minutes
Tips Bring in newspapers with relevant articles for students to look through. You may wish to limit the activity to a single page or section.
Think It Over Students should realize that all sorts of information is available through the computer and that computers have become important to every type of individual, business, and industry.

SECTION 4 The Information Superhighway

◖ DISCOVER ◗ ·· *ACTIVITY*

How Important Are Computers?

1. Obtain a local or national newspaper.
2. Look through the newspaper for articles that refer to computers, the Internet, the World Wide Web, or the information superhighway.
3. Write down the topics of the articles. For example, was the article about politics, cooking, money, or computers?
4. Create a data table to show your results.

Think It Over

Inferring What can you infer about the kinds of information available through the computer? How much do you think people use information that they obtain through computers?

◖ GUIDE FOR READING ◗

♦ What are the advantages of a computer network?

♦ What is the Internet?

♦ How can you use computers safely?

Reading Tip Before you read, list five things that you know about the Internet. Add to your list after you read the section.

Because of the Internet, the world is at your fingertips! You can send an e-mail message to someone on the other side of the planet. Through the World Wide Web, information is yours for the searching as you prepare a school report. The news, sport scores, travel information, and weather reports are all available at any time. How is this possible? The answer is through the use of a computer connected to a network.

Computer Networks

You have traveled on a network of roads and highways that connects cities and towns. A **computer network** is a group of computers connected by cables or telephone lines. **A computer network allows people in different locations to share information and software.**

Figure 26 This is an artist's view of the information superhighway. *Forming Operational Definitions How would you define this term?*

◖ READING STRATEGIES ◗

Reading Tip Before they read, have students create three columns on a sheet of paper, with the headings *What I Know, What I Want to Know,* and *What I Learned.* Have students fill in the first two columns with the five things they know about the Internet and five things they want to know. After students read, have them fill in the third column.

Concept Mapping Have students organize information about the Internet and the World Wide Web on two concept maps.

Study and Comprehension After students read the section, instruct them to paraphrase the information from the section. Remind students that paraphrasing means to restate a sentence or paragraph in your own words.

Figure 27 Cables connect computers in a local area network. People all over the world are connected by wide area networks such as the Internet.

There are two types of networks. A set of computers connected in one classroom or office building is known as a **local area network.** Computers connected across larger distances form a **wide area network.** In wide area networks, very powerful computers serve as a support connection for hundreds of less powerful computers.

The Internet

The most significant wide area network is the Internet. The **Internet** is a global network that links millions of computers in businesses, schools, and research organizations. **The Internet is a network of host computers that extends around the world.** You might say that the Internet is a network of networks. The Internet, along with other smaller networks, sometimes is called the information superhighway.

The Internet began in 1969 as a military communications system. Its purpose was to link computers used in military work. The links were designed so that communication would continue even if many computers were destroyed. In order for scientists to exchange data through their computers, colleges and universities were later added to the Internet.

Beginning in 1993, businesses were allowed to sell Internet connections to individuals. These businesses are known as Internet service providers. With easy access available, the Internet has grown at an incredible rate. Now the use of the Internet for entertainment, shopping, and everyday information gathering completely overshadows its original purpose.

2 *Facilitate*

Computer Networks

Real-Life Learning

Have students use the text and Figure 27 to compare how computers are connected in local area networks and wide area networks. If you have a local area network in your school, students may not realize that the computers are connected by cables. Explain that the cables are usually run through the walls and ceilings just like electrical wiring. If possible, show students how the computers are connected or arrange for the school's computer technician to give the class an overview of the systems in your school. **learning modality: verbal**

The Internet

Building Inquiry Skills: Communicating

Ask students who are familiar with the Internet to describe some signs that the Internet has grown beyond its original purpose. *(Samples: Many people have e-mail accounts, businesses advertise on the Internet, the connections are slow when a lot of people are online.)* Ask: **What are some ways that the Internet still allows private communication between people in the government or at universities?** *(Sample: Some parts of the Internet require passwords.)* **learning modality: verbal**

Program Resources

◆ **Teaching Resources** 4-4 Lesson Plan, p. 109; 4-4 Section Summary, p. 110
◆ **Interdisciplinary Exploration Series** "The Glory of Ancient Rome," pp. 38–39

Media and Technology

🎧 **Audiotapes** English-Spanish Summary 4-4

Answers to Self-Assessment

Caption Question

Figure 26 Sample: The information superhighway is a network of computers around the world that allows people to communicate over long distances almost instantly.

Ongoing Assessment

Oral Presentation Ask students to identify different types of networks and give an example of each.

World Wide Web

Materials *poster board, markers, colored pencils, scissors, glue*
Time 30 minutes
Tips Encourage students to design home pages that include several photos and links. Tell them to use colored pens to write words that serve as buttons to more information.
Extend Have students work together to design a web page for the class, using web page design software if possible.
learning modality: visual

Addressing Naive Conceptions

Students may think that the World Wide Web is the same as the Internet. Explain that the World Wide Web is only a part of the Internet. For example, a network of newsgroups, called Usenet, exists independent of the World Wide Web, although access to most groups is possible through web pages. Electronic mail also travels across the Internet, and there are many computers that serve as FTP (File Transfer Protocol) sites where people can store and download files.
learning modality: verbal

Using Computers Safely

Building Inquiry Skills: Applying Concepts

Students may have heard about viruses that can damage a computer's hard drive when a certain electronic mail message is opened, or about viruses that can be transmitted by using certain applications. Explain that viruses can only be transmitted when files and software are loaded onto a computer from a disk or from another computer over a network. Opening a web page or looking at a file that resides on another computer cannot allow a virus to enter your computer. **learning modality: verbal**

What a Web You Weave ACTIVITY

Many businesses and individuals have home pages on the World Wide Web. Such pages usually describe the characteristics of the business or person.

Communicating Design your own home page that describes your interests, hobbies, and achievements. A home page usually allows a user to click on certain words to find out more information about a particular topic. Be sure to include text, photographs, and art in your design.

Figure 28 Most networks require authorized users to have passwords. Never give your password to anyone you do not know well.

World Wide Web

You have probably seen advertisements for information available on the World Wide Web (WWW). The World Wide Web was developed in 1989. The **World Wide Web** is a system that allows you to display and view files, called pages, on the Internet. A Web page can include text, pictures, video, or sound. Prior to the development of the World Wide Web, Internet users could only view information in the form of words and numbers. Through the World Wide Web, users can look at images similar to those you might see on television or videos. Software programs called search engines allow people to search through the Web for information.

✓ *Checkpoint* *How has the World Wide Web changed the Internet?*

Using Computers Safely

Like any tool, computer networks have their pros and cons. For instance, information is so easy to transfer that it can get into the wrong hands. Networks are designed to protect credit card numbers, medical data, business records, and other information. Networks usually require authorization for you to enter, and have software designed to keep out unwanted users. You may have used a password to enter a local area network.

Another way to protect information is to code, or encrypt it. **Encryption** is a mathematical process of coding information so that only the intended user can read it.

Computer viruses, which are a form of computer vandalism, are another danger of the Internet. **Computer viruses** are programs that interfere with the normal operation of a computer. Much like a living virus, a computer virus enters a computer and reproduces itself. A virus can destroy information or even disable the computer.

Facts and Figures A technology called Motion Picture Experts Group 1 layer 3 (MP3) is changing the way people bring music into their homes. MP3 makes it possible to download music from the Internet and store it on a home computer. Downloading an album takes about 2 hours. Once downloaded, the album can be played on a battery-powered device that carries about 1 hour of CD-quality music on a computer chip. MP3 technology raises intellectual property issues because the files are not encrypted. Although artists can pass their work directly to consumers, so can others, simply by putting the music files on their Websites. People in the recording industry are concerned that MP3 will hurt both the industry and artists because royalties will not be paid.

Software is available that will detect viruses before they can infect a computer. **When you load a file from a network, you should always run virus-checking software.** Store downloaded programs on a diskette, to protect your hard drive.

One important kind of computer safety is your personal safety. Computer users are not screened. For this reason, be very careful about using chat rooms. **Chat rooms** are a feature of networks that allow two or more users to exchange messages. **You do not know who may be using a chat room, so you should never give out your name, address, or telephone number. Do not respond to offensive messages, and do not accept files from strangers.**

Intellectual Property

A computer program is a piece of intellectual property. **Intellectual property** is an idea, or artistic creation, such as a poem or book. Governments protect intellectual property by granting copyrights to authors and patents to inventors.

When you buy a computer program you are actually buying a license only for yourself to use that program. If a friend copies your program onto another computer, the author receives no payment. If the authors are not paid, it will not be worthwhile for them to improve their programs or to write new ones.

Besides the software that you have to buy, there are thousands of programs known as freeware or shareware which are available through the Internet. **Freeware** is software that the author has decided to let people use at no charge. **Shareware** is software that the author allows people to try out and use for a very low fee. The user pays the fee and registers the software with the author. Then the author usually continues to improve the pro-

Figure 29 The software that a school buys is licensed only for use on computers in the school.

Section 4 Review

1. What is a computer network? Why are networks used?
2. What is the Internet? What are some reasons for using the Internet?
3. What is a chat room?
4. **Thinking Critically Calculating** You receive a free disk with a game on it. There is a computer virus on the disk that doubles in size every time you play the game. How much larger has the virus grown by the time you have played the game ten times?

Science at Home

Although computers are commonplace today, this was not always the case. Interview a family member who grew up before computers were common. Prepare a list of questions for the interview. Find out whether that person has used a computer, what he or she thinks about computers, and how computers might have changed his or her life. Ask if the large number of applications for computers has come as a surprise.

Demonstration

Materials *computer with Internet access and virus-checking software, computer disk*
Time 15 minutes

ACTIVITY

Caution students that not all freeware and shareware Websites distribute legal copies of software. Use the Internet to find Websites with files that can be downloaded and legally used for free. Consult the Science Explorer Website for current references. Show students how to safely download freeware or shareware onto the disk and run a virus check before placing it on the computer's hard drive. **limited English proficiency**
www.science-explorer.phschool.com

3 Assess

Section 4 Review Answers

1. A computer network is several computers linked together by cables or telephone lines. Networks allow access to a tremendous store of information.
2. The Internet is a wide area network, or a network of networks that provides global access to people and resources.
3. A chat room is a feature of networks that allows users to exchange messages.
4. The virus has made 1,024 copies.

Science at Home

Students whose family members are unfamiliar with computers can brainstorm everyday applications that rely on computers and research how people performed those tasks before computers were common. They can present their results to the class.

Program Resources

◆ **Teaching Resources** 4-4 Review and Reinforce, p. 111; 4-4 Enrich, p. 112

Media and Technology

Interactive Student Tutorial CD-ROM N-4

Answers to Self-Assessment

Checkpoint

Users of the World Wide Web can now view information in the form of images instead of just words and numbers. Also, users can search for information with search engines.

Performance Assessment

Writing Have students write short stories describing computer applications they imagine will be possible in the future.

When Seeing ISN'T Believing

Purpose

To provide students with an understanding of the potential problems associated with digital manipulation of photographs.

Debate

Time one class period for research and preparation, 30 minutes to conduct the debate

- Explain to students that they will be debating the proposition that "Some digitally manipulated photographs can be misleading and cause a great deal of harm. Consequently, all altered photographs must be labeled." Inform them that a debate is not an argument. In a debate, two groups discuss a proposition by presenting reasons that support their positions.
- Separate the class into two groups: one to support the proposition, the other to oppose it. Have groups review and investigate the issue from their respective points of view.
- Both groups should critically and constructively support their viewpoints. Encourage students in the group that supports labeling to explore ideas such as avoiding courtroom errors and preventing incorrect information from being disseminated. Encourage students in the other group to think about the implications of First Amendment restrictions.
- Remind students to pay attention to the tone of the debate. Arguments should be clear and succinct without using harsh language.

Extend If there is time, have students contact a local graphic or computer artist. See if you can arrange a classroom viewing of some digitally altered images. Encourage students to prepare questions in advance. Alternatively, challenge students to search the Internet for other ways in which this issue affects society.

SCIENCE AND SOCIETY

When Seeing ISN'T Believing

The combination of computers and photography can make magic. A computer can turn the bits of light, dark, and color in a photo into a code. By using the computer to change the code, a technician can change any part of a photo.

This way of working with photos is called digital manipulation. Fuzzy pictures can be made clearer and sharper. Colors can be brightened or completely changed. Tiny or hidden details can be made easier to see and understand. Old or stained photos can be made to look like new. Objects or people in a photo can even be added, removed, or moved around.

But some people worry that digital manipulation could be used to cheat or harm people. Are there ways to be informed and entertained by digital manipulation without being fooled by it?

The Issues

What Are the Dangers of Manipulated Photos? It's nearly impossible to tell the difference between a digitally changed photo and an unchanged one. Suppose, for example, a photographer has one photo of the mayor hugging her husband and another photo of a well-known criminal. With digital "magic," an unethical person could create a photo of the mayor hugging the criminal. Not only could newspapers, magazines, and TV stations mislead the public, but witnesses might try to use faked photographs in court cases.

How Can People Protect Themselves? Governments could pass laws against changing photographs. Such laws would be hard to enforce, however, because digital manipulation is so hard to detect. Laws might also make it difficult to use digital manipulation for useful purposes. And such laws might violate the right of free speech. Our courts consider photos a kind of speech, or expression.

Another option is for photographers or organizations to police themselves. They could write codes of conduct. The United States armed forces already have a code for photos (for instance, photos taken from military airplanes). Under this code, it is all right to make photos clearer digitally. But it is not all right to add, take away, or move around parts of a photo. Some photographers who work for newspapers have suggested a similar code for themselves.

Should Manipulated Photos Be Marked? One safeguard might be to put a symbol on any digitally manipulated photo. That way viewers would be warned. But opponents point out that nearly every photo seen in newspapers and magazines is changed a little, usually just to make the colors more clear. If every photo had the symbol, people wouldn't be able to see the difference between a photo whose image had been made clearer and one in which something had been faked. People might stop trusting any photo.

You Decide

1. Identify the Problem
In your own words, describe the problems created by digital manipulation of photos.

2. Analyze the Options
List reasons for and against
a. passing a law against changing any photo digitally,
b. letting photographers make their own code of conduct, and
c. marking all digitally manipulated photos with a special symbol.

3. Find a Solution
You run a TV station. Your assistants want to use two digitally changed photos, one in a commercial and one in a news story. Will you let them use one, or both, or neither? Explain.

Background

Facts and Figures Photographs have not always been accepted as evidence in court because they are a representation of a thing, but not the thing itself.

Traditional photography produces a negative, a piece of film that shows what the photograph originally looked like. Digital photographs have no negatives, and the original file can be deleted once changes have been made. New legislation is being developed to determine under what circumstances digital photography can be used as evidence. For example, traditional photographs are accepted as evidence in federal courts as long as it can be proved they are direct copies of the original negative. Eventually, the differences between digital and traditional photography will require the law to change its definition of evidence.

SECTION 1 Electronic Signals and Semiconductors

Key Ideas
◆ Electronics uses electric currents to carry information. An electronic signal, analog or digital, is the basis of electronics.
◆ Semiconductors are used to make solid-state devices such as diodes, transistors, and integrated circuits.

Key Terms
electronics
electronic signal
analog signal
digital signal
semiconductor

solid-state component
diode
transistor
integrated circuit
vacuum tube

SECTION 2 Electronic Communication

Key Ideas
◆ Sounds are converted into electronic signals in radios, televisions, and telephones. The electronic signal is then transmitted to a receiver that converts the electronic signals back into sound.
◆ Electromagnetic waves consist of changing electric and magnetic fields. Such waves can be used to carry electronic signals.
◆ Televisions receive video information in addition to audio information. The video signal causes electron beams to be focused on a screen coated with a fluorescent material.

Key Terms
electromagnetic wave
amplitude
frequency
amplitude modulation (AM)
frequency modulation (FM)
cathode ray tube

SECTION 3 Computers

Key Ideas
◆ Computer information is represented in the binary system.
◆ Computer hardware includes the central processing unit, input devices, output devices, and memory storage devices.
◆ Computer programs are called software. Software consists of detailed instructions that tell the computer what to do.

Key Terms
computer
binary system
bit
byte
computer hardware
central processing unit
input device
output device
random-access memory (RAM)

read-only memory (ROM)
disk drive
hard disk
diskette
optical disc
computer programmer
computer software

SECTION 4 The Information Superhighway

INTEGRATING TECHNOLOGY

Key Ideas
◆ Computers are connected by computer networks. The Internet is a network of host computers that extends around the world.
◆ Safe use of computer networks includes checking for viruses, and using chat rooms with caution.

Key Terms
computer network
local area network
wide area network
Internet
World Wide Web
encryption

computer virus
chat rooms
intellectual property
freeware
shareware

USING THE INTERNET
ACTIVITY
www.science-explorer.phschool.com

You Decide
Have groups of students complete the first two steps before the debate to prepare their arguments. After the debate, direct students to write their explanations using the points they raised during the debate.

Program Resources

◆ **Teaching Resources** Chapter 4 Project Scoring Rubric, p. 96; Chapter 4 Performance Assessment Teacher Notes, pp. 151–152; Chapter 4 Performance Assessment Student Worksheet, p. 153; Chapter 4 Test, pp. 154–157

Reviewing Content:
Multiple Choice
1. c 2. b 3. d 4. a 5. d

True or False
6. converter 7. true 8. cathode-ray tube
9. Input 10. true

Checking Concepts
11. An analog signal involves continuous change. In electronics, this might mean changing the strength of a signal to match changes in the strength of a sound. A digital signal involves pulses of current. Digital information is recorded in a binary system with two digits, either 1 or 0.

12. Diode—device that allows current to flow in one direction only; transistor—device that amplifies a signal or switches current on and off; integrated circuit—device that places thousands of electronic components on a slice of silicon smaller than 1 cm^2.

13. Students' illustrations should show that electromagnetic waves are composed of changing electric and magnetic fields. Examples: X-rays, visible light, infrared

14. Sounds are converted into electronic signals at the radio station. The signals are broadcast as an electromagnetic wave. The signals are changed back into sounds in the speakers of a radio.

15. A cathode-ray tube produces a stream of electrons directed at a screen. The inside of the screen is coated with phosphors which glow when hit by electrons.

16. The World Wide Web is a part of the Internet that makes the transmission of photos and other images possible. The Internet is the entire worldwide network of computers.

17. Paragraphs should describe how the magazine can be researched, marketed, or even published on the Internet.

Thinking Visually
18. **a.** A transmitter converts sound waves to an electronic signal.
b. The receiver converts the electronic signal to sound waves.

C H A P T E R 4 R E V I E W

Reviewing Content

For more review of key concepts, see the Interactive Student Tutorial CD-ROM.

Multiple Choice
Choose the letter of the best answer.

1. A sandwich of 3 layers of semiconductor that is used to amplify an electric signal is known as a (an)
   a. diode.
   b. modem.
   c. transistor.
   d. integrated circuit.

2. A radio speaker
   a. converts sound to an electronic signal.
   b. converts an electronic signal to sound.
   c. places an electronic signal on an electromagnetic wave.
   d. controls the function of an electron gun.

3. If you wanted to transfer information from one computer to another you might use a
   a. hard disk.   b. RAM chip.
   c. ROM chip.   d. diskette.

4. An example of a computer output device is a
   a. printer.   b. keyboard.
   c. program.   d. CPU.

5. A group of computers connected by cables or telephone lines is a
   a. microprocessor. b. CPU.
   c. modem.   d. network.

True or False
If the statement is true, write true. If it is false, change the underlined word or words to make the statement true.

6. A <u>transistor</u> changes alternating current into direct current.

7. Before semiconductors, electronic devices used <u>vacuum tubes</u> to control electric current.

8. A <u>microphone</u> is the part of a television that produces the image.

9. <u>Output</u> devices feed data into a computer.

10. The <u>Internet</u> can be described as a network of computer networks.

Checking Concepts
11. Compare an analog signal with a digital signal.
12. Define each of the following in your own words: diode, transistor, and integrated circuit.
13. Draw an illustration of an electromagnetic wave. Give three examples of electromagnetic waves.
14. Explain how a radio show is broadcast and received.
15. How does a cathode-ray tube create a picture?
16. How is the World Wide Web different from the Internet?
17. **Writing to Learn** Imagine that you have started your own small magazine. Choose a topic for your magazine, such as sports, fashion, science, or cooking. Then write three to four paragraphs describing how a computer and access to the Internet might help you.

Thinking Visually
18. **Flowchart** Copy the flowchart about telephone communication onto a sheet of paper. Complete the flowchart by filling in the missing steps. (For more on flowcharts, see the Skills Handbook.)

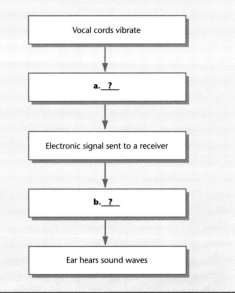

Vocal cords vibrate

↓

a. ?

↓

Electronic signal sent to a receiver

↓

b. ?

↓

Ear hears sound waves

Applying Skills
19. Students should sketch an electromagnetic wave with an amplitude pattern that matches the shape of the wave in A.
20. This is a carrier electromagnetic wave, which is made up of an electric and a magnetic field.
21. C is AM, or amplitude modulated; D is FM, or frequency modulated.

Thinking Critically
22. Solid-state devices are lighter, smaller, use

less energy, give off less heat, are more reliable, and are less expensive.
23. 54,000 images
24. Students' programs should describe each step involved in the activity. The steps should be broken down into simple parts and should be listed in order.
25. Both systems are used to perform calculations with numbers. The decimal system has ten digits, the binary system has only two digits, 0 or 1. Each digit in a decimal or binary number is located in a particular place in the

Applying Skills

Use the illustration below to answer Questions 19–21.

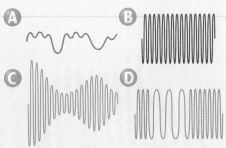

Ⓐ   Ⓑ

Ⓒ   Ⓓ

19. **Predicting** What would the audio signal in part A look like if it were converted to an AM radio signal? Draw a sketch to illustrate your answer.

20. **Communicating** What is represented in part B? Describe its basic characteristics.

21. **Classifying** Two radio transmitters send out electronic signals shown as part C and part D. How are the two forms alike and how are they different?

Thinking Critically

22. **Comparing and Contrasting** What are some advantages of solid-state devices over vacuum tubes?

23. **Problem Solving** Each image on a television screen lasts for 1/30th of a second. How many images appear on the screen during a 30-minute program?

24. **Applying Concepts** A computer program is a list of instructions that tells a computer how to perform a task. Write a program that describes the steps involved in some task, such as walking your dog, taking out the trash, setting the table, or playing a game.

25. **Calculating** How do base-10 numbers and binary numbers differ? Explain how you read and write numbers in each system. Give examples.

26. **Making Judgments** Why does a government protect a computer program as the intellectual property of the author?

Performance Assessment

Wrap Up

Present Your Project Present both the existing computer application and the new one you invented to the class. Provide diagrams of each and describe their operation. You might want to pretend you are trying to sell your new invention to the class. Prepare a poster describing the task that your new application will be doing. Show yourself enjoying the benefits!

Reflect and Record In your journal, discuss what you've learned about computer applications. Think about the new computer application you developed. Is there a way to make it even better or more useful than you already have?

Getting Involved

In Your Community Select a business or office in your town, such as a school, library, or grocery store. Then select one electronic device: a telephone, television, radio, or computer. With permission, conduct an interview with the manager or other employee. Find out how the device is involved in their operations. Prepare a poster showing how the device is used, and what information it transmits.

---

number. Students should give examples of each system.

26. Computer programs are protected by copyright laws, just as books or other intellectual products are. This allows the author of the program to profit from his or her work.

Program Resources

◆ **Inquiry Skills Activity Book** Provides teaching and review of all inquiry skills

---

Performance Assessment

Wrap Up

Present Your Project As students give their reports, their classmates can take brief notes, writing down the major characteristics of each application. Encourage students to present their new applications as if they are trying to sell them to the class. Students should describe how the application works and should explain why it is useful.

Reflect and Record Students can use ideas that were presented by other students in discussion to improve their programs. Students should describe how their research led them to a new understanding of computers and their applications.

Getting Involved

In Your Community Have students research the organization they are interested in to find out what kinds of electronic devices it uses now. Students should compile a list of questions before they conduct their interviews. You may want to have students work together to perform their research as a class activity. Students' posters should show how their device allows the business to connect to other services it uses.

Edison: Genius of Invention

This interdisciplinary feature presents the central theme of Thomas Edison by connecting four different disciplines: science, language arts, mathematics, and social studies. The four explorations are designed to capture students' interest and help them see how the content they are studying in science relates to other school subjects and to real-world events. The unit is particularly suitable for team teaching.

1 Engage/Explore

Activating Prior Knowledge

Help students recall what they learned in Chapter 2, Electric Charges and Current, by asking questions such as: **How do you make electric charge flow in a circuit?** *(Apply a voltage)* **How do series and parallel circuits differ?** *(In a series circuit, there is only one path for the charges to follow. In a parallel circuit, there are several paths.)* **What is resistance?** *(Something that slows down the flow of charge)*

Introducing the Unit

Ask: **Have you ever been without electricity? What was it like?** *(Lead students to discuss what alternatives to electric appliances they had and what they had to do without.)* **Have you ever had to make do using only gas, oil, or candles? How is electricity better?** *(Answers will vary. Samples: oil and gas are hot in summer and can be dangerous; candles do not provide much light.)* Clarify that Edison received little school education. Instead, he was home schooled. If students are interested, share with them the Background information on pages 147 and 148.

E·D·I·S·O·N—
Genius of Invention

WHAT INVENTOR GAVE US

- *sound recording?*
- *motion pictures?*
- *electric lighting?*

Edison at his workbench

This scene shows New York City in 1881. An electric light high above Madison Square outshines the gas light in the foreground.

In 1881, the electric light in the picture at the left was a novelty. Streets and some homes were lit with gas, while other homes used oil lamps or candles. Thomas Edison was still developing his system of indoor electric lighting.

Electric lights brought with them a system of power distribution which made other uses of electricity possible. If you try to imagine living without any electrical appliances, you will understand the changes in everyday life that Edison started.

Thomas Edison (1847–1931) had almost no schooling. Yet his mind always bubbled with ideas. In addition to his lighting system, Edison invented the phonograph and the movie camera. He also made improvements to the the telegraph and telephone. At the time of his death, Edison held 1,093 patents. A patent is a government license protecting an inventor's right to make and sell a product. One of Edison's most important ideas was never patented. He created the first laboratory for industrial research.

Program Resources

◆ **Teaching Resources** Interdisciplinary Explorations, Science, pp. 118–120; Language Arts, pp. 121–123; Mathematics, pp. 124–126; Social Studies, pp. 127–129.

The Wizard of Menlo Park

Edison's research laboratory in Menlo Park

Before 1900 most inventors worked alone. Edison, in contrast, depended on a strong team of research co-workers to carry out his ideas. Edison had an unusual ability to inspire those who worked for him. A very hard worker himself, he demanded that everyone on his team also work long hours.

In 1870, he set up a workshop in Newark, New Jersey, to test new ideas and designs. Some of Edison's original team stayed with him for years. They included a Swiss clockmaker, an English engineer, and an American mechanic.

By 1876 Edison had enough money to set up an "invention factory." He chose the small town of Menlo Park, New Jersey. Menlo Park became the world's first industrial research laboratory. Soon a mathematician and a glass blower joined the team.

Edison's team often made improvements on other people's inventions. The light bulb is an example. Other scientists had invented electric lamps, but their light bulbs burned rapidly. The problem was to find a material for the filament that would not overheat or burn out quickly.

The Menlo Park team spent months testing hundreds of materials. First they rolled up each material into a long thin strand. Then they carbonized it, which meant baking it until it turned to charcoal. Then they tested it in a vacuum, or absence of air. Most materials failed in only a few minutes or a few hours. Edison tried platinum, a metallic element, with some success, but then went back to carbonized fibers. The team improved the vacuum inside the bulb. The glass blower tried differently shaped bulbs.

The breakthrough came in 1879. The successful filament was a length of ordinary cotton thread, carefully carbonized. In December, the newspapers carried the headlines: "Success in a Cotton Thread" and "It Makes a Light, Without Gas or Flame."

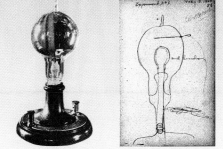
A light bulb is made of a wire, or filament, inside a glass bulb. Most of the air is removed from the bulb, making a vacuum. Electricity flowing through the wire makes it white hot, so that it glows. Edison's drawing of a light bulb is at the right.

Science Activity

Work together as a team to invent a new electrical device.

♦ What is the problem? What might make your life easier?

♦ What are the solutions? Brainstorm for possible products that use an electrical circuit. Write down all possible ideas.

♦ Evaluate each solution. List the supplies you will need. Note any new skills you should learn. Agree on the best solution.

♦ Plan your design and make a labeled drawing.

Write down the materials you will need and the steps you will use to build your device.

Background

History After having scarlet fever as a child, Edison began to lose his hearing. Eventually he was completely deaf in one ear and had only slight hearing in the other. Edison felt this was a benefit because he could not hear what he called "foolish small talk" and had more time to think. Despite ear surgeries, Edison's hearing continued to decline.

Possibly because of his hearing loss, Edison did poorly in school. The teacher was very strict and punished students for asking questions. Because Edison liked to ask questions, he was punished. The teacher declared that Edison was too confused to be able to learn. Edison's mother met with the teacher and became very angry. She then decided to teach Edison at home.

---

2 Facilitate

♦ Explain that Edison screened his employees very carefully. A social studies worksheet gives a sample general knowledge test that Edison gave job applicants.

♦ Ask: **How did having people with so many different backgrounds help Edison?** (*Different people brought diverse ideas and knowledge to problems.*) Point out that Edison was years ahead of his time in recognizing the importance of valuing diversity of background.

♦ Ask: **Why do you think people worked so hard for Edison?** (*Accept all reasonable answers.*)

♦ Clarify that many of Edison's patents were improvements on devices that already existed.

♦ Explain that most living material is made of molecules that contain carbon.

Science Activity

Suggest that students think of electrical devices they feel do not work effectively. Have students think of ways these devices could be improved.

To extend the science activity, students could work with older students or adults and try to build their device. Students may also wish to investigate whether their device should be patented and how they could apply for a patent.

Teaching Resources The following worksheets correlate with this page: Resistors in a Current, page 118; Serendipity in Science, page 119; and Make an Invention Timeline, page 120.

3 Assess

Activity Assessment

Students should clearly state the problem, describe how their invention solves the problem, and lists the supplies they will need. Students should include a labeled drawing.

2 Facilitate

- Ask: **Why was it shrewd to build the generating station downtown?** (*The major companies downtown would help Edison spread the word about the advantages of electric lighting.*)
- Ask: **What is a financier?** (*A banker who arranges large-scale financing*)
- Ask: **What does the reporter mean by "grateful to the eye"?** (*Answers may vary. Samples: gentle, kind, didn't tire out his eyes*) **Have you ever tried to read by candlelight? Was it hard?** (*Flickering candlelight is hard to read by and soon hurts the eyes.*)

Language Arts Activity

Suggest that small groups of students brainstorm about the advantages of electric power. If students have ever been without power for several days, have them recall the inconveniences.

To extend this activity, have students imagine that electricity is just being introduced into homes and businesses for the first time. People are as suspicious of electricity as they sometimes are of other new technologies. Ask students to imagine the fears and protests that people might have had about having electricity in their homes.

Teaching Resources The following worksheets correlate with this page: What is Morse Code?, page 121; Write a Tall Tale, page 122; and Write a Persuasive Letter, page 123.

3 Assess

Activity Assessment

Check that students' advertisements or articles are persuasive and incorporate as many advantages as possible.

Lighting Manhattan

Edison recognized the value of publicity. Besides being a productive inventor, he knew how to promote himself. He made glowing predictions about his new electric system. Electricity would soon be so cheap, he said, that "only the rich would be able to afford candles."

Edison demonstrated his electric lights in spectacular displays at expositions in Paris and London. These displays led to his setting up companies in France, England, the Netherlands, and other parts of Europe.

When he built his first neighborhood generating station, Edison made a shrewd choice of location. The Pearl Street power station brought light and power to about 2.6 square kilometers of downtown Manhattan. It supplied businesses and factories as well as private homes. The circuits could light 400 light bulbs. Some of those lights were in the offices of J. P. Morgan, the leading banker and financier of the time. Others lights were located in the offices of *The New York Times*. Here's what the *Times* reporter wrote on September 5, 1882.

New York City—Broadway in the 1880s

THE NEW YORK TIMES, September 5, 1882

"Yesterday for the first time The Times Building was illuminated by electricity. Mr. Edison had at last perfected his incandescent light, had put his machinery in order, and had started up his engines, and last evening his company lighted up about one-third of the lower City district in which The Times Building stands. . . .

It was not until about seven o'clock, when it began to grow dark, that the electric light really made itself known and showed how bright and steady it is. . . . It was a light that a man could sit down under and write for hours without the consciousness of having any artificial light about him. There was a very slight amount of heat from each lamp, but not nearly as much as from a gas-burner—one-fifteenth as much as from gas, the inventor says. The light was soft, mellow, and grateful to the eye, and it seemed almost like writing by daylight to have a light without a particle of flicker and with scarcely any heat to make the head ache. . . . The decision was unanimously in favor of the Edison electric lamp as against gas."

Language Arts Activity

The reporter who wrote the newspaper story observed details carefully and used them to write about an event—the first lights in his office. Look back at the story. Now write about the event as Edison would have told it to convince people to buy light bulbs and install electrical power systems. You could make an advertisement. Inform your readers about the product and persuade them to buy it.

Background

History Edison's mother loved to read and he adopted her love of reading. Before he was ten years old, his mother gave him a basic science book. He began performing the experiments in the book. Soon he was spending his pocket money on chemical supplies for more experiments. By the time he was 12, he got a job selling newspapers and candy to passengers on the train to buy books and supplies for the chemistry laboratory he built in the basement.

Solving Practical Problems

As he grew older, Edison worried that American students were not learning mathematics well enough. To motivate students, he suggested using problems that related to real-life situations. In 1925, when he was 78, he proposed these problems as recorded in his notebooks. Note that light bulbs were called *lamps*. Tungsten is a metal used in light bulbs.

PROBLEM 1
"American power plants now serve 9,500,000 homes. The estimated number of homes in the United States is 21,000,000. What percentage receives electric power?"

PROBLEM 2
"It needs about 280,000,000 tungsten lamps [bulbs] each year to supply the market today. And yet the first lamp factory in the world—the Edison Lamp Works. . .—was not started until 1880, and I was told it would never pay. The output for our first year was about 25,000 globes [bulbs]. How many times that figure would be required for the present market?"

PROBLEM 3
"A household using 21 lamps requires about 7 new lamps each year. What percentage is this?"

Math Activity

Solve the four math problems that Edison wrote. To solve Problem 4, use 1902 prices. That year, incandescent light bulbs (or lamps) cost $ .30 each.

PROBLEM 4
"If these lamps had been bought at the retail prices of the first year of the lamp factory, they would have cost $1.25 each. How much would the family save by the decreased prices of today?"

2 Facilitate

◆ If possible, bring to class some very old math textbooks. Have students examine the pages to see how rarely real-world problems were featured in such texts.
◆ Ask: **Do you think real-life problems would motivate students? Justify your answer.** *(Accept all thoughtful answers.)* Invite students to suggest other ways that math textbooks could motivate students to learn.
◆ Ask: **What do you think Edison would think of math books today?** *(Answers will vary. Samples: He would have thought they are much more colorful and lively; there are more questions that relate to real life)*

Math Activity

Point out that problem 2 has extraneous information (the year). Extraneous information is detail that you don't need to solve the problem Part of problem solving is learning what data you need and don't need. For problem 4, tell students to calculate how much the family would save per lamp.

To extend the activity, invite students to make a display of math questions that relate to real-life problems. Challenge students to write problems that they think would motivate others to learn math.

Teaching Resources The following worksheets correlate with this page: Can You Afford Candles?, page 124; Niagara Falls, Itaipu, and Light, page 125; and Analyzing Power Bills, page 126.

3 Assess

Activity Assessment

Answers:
1. 45.2%
2. 11,200
3. 33.3%
4. $.95 per lamp

Integrating Science and Technology
The incandescent light bulb is not the only type of lighting available. Electric discharge lamps were developed in the early 1900s. These lamps produced light by applying a voltage to two electrodes at either end of a tube filled with a small amount of a gas, such as mercury or sodium. Lights filled with mercury give off a bright, whitish blue-green light. These lights found use as street lighting in the early part of the 20th century in the United States. Lights filled with sodium vapor give off a yellow-orange glow. They are used to light streets, highways, and tunnels all over the world. Fluorescent lighting is another type of electric discharge lamp. Fluorescent lights are used as interior lighting in factories, schools, and office buildings.

2 Facilitate

♦ It is a common myth that Edison invented electric light. Clarify that Edison invented the first practical incandescent light bulb. Ask students: **If you lived in the 1920s, and were using only candles or gas lamps to light your home, would you go to the expense of installing electric lights? Why?** *(Accept all answers. Encourage students to weigh the advantages and disadvantages of this new kind of light.)*

♦ If possible, invite a representative from the local electric utility to talk to the class about how electricity is generated and distributed in the power grid.

Social Studies Activity

Have students compare this image to a map of the United States that is roughly the same size to help them judge which states have the most lights. Point out that Alaska and Hawaii are not shown on this map. Ask: **What do you know about the population in those areas? How bright do you think they appear at night?** *(Neither state is densely populated so they would likely not be brightly lit.)*

Teaching Resources The following worksheets correlate with this page: Want to Work for Edison?, page 127; and Light Pollution, pages 128-129.

Electrical Distribution

Electric lighting didn't begin with Edison's light bulb. Before the incandescent bulb, most electric lights were carbon arc lamps. An electric arc flashed between two carbon rods. Carbon arc lamps were used for public places such as railroad stations in both Europe and the United States. But they were too bright and too dangerous for most indoor uses.

Edison found a way to make indoor lighting practical. Along with the light bulb, he had to set up a system to distribute electricity to homes and business. That system included generators, underground cables, junction boxes, and meters.

Local power companies grew slowly. Laying cables to carry power was slow and expensive. In the 1920s, less than half the homes in cities had electricity. And less than 10 percent of rural areas had electricity. Only in 1935 was a program begun to bring power to the countryside.

Social Studies Activity

Look at the recent satellite photo of the United States at night. It shows how electric lights now light up the country from coast to coast. Using a map of the United States, identify the regions that are the brightest. What cities are located there? Which states have the most urban areas? Which have the least? Use an almanac to find out the population of 5 of the largest cities. Compare these data with the total United States population.

History of the phonograph

▼ This 1916 photo shows Edison with a disk-shaped record. Other improvements of the phonograph included a horn to project the sound.

▲ In 1878 Edison's first phonograph recorded sound on a rotating cylinder. A needle attached to a thin metal disk played the sound.

Background

Facts and Figures If street lights are visible from space, think of the great amount of light they give off. Light pollution is a problem faced by amateur and professional astronomers when gazing at the night sky. The amount of illumination from street lamps, buildings, billboards, and other light sources pointing toward the sky mask stars that should be visible.

Light pollution is caused by poorly designed or improperly installed light fixtures. It is estimated that in the United States, $1.5 billion per year in electricity bills is wasted on light going upward into the sky.

Because of light pollution, only a few hundred stars of the more than 320,000 stars that should be visible over North America can be seen in the night sky from most cities and towns in the United States.

As this satellite image shows, the glow of street lights is visible from space.

By the 1950s, phonographs used electric motors and electronic amplifiers. The quality of sound was better, and the volume could be much greater.

◀ 45 rpm records

▼ 78 rpm record

▲ $33\frac{1}{3}$ rpm record

Records played longer as the standard playing speed was reduced from 78 revolutions per minute to 45 and $33\frac{1}{3}$ revolutions per minute.

Compact discs are recordings, and they are shaped like phonograph records. But are they related to Edison's invention?

Tie It Together

Modern Times

Many of the inventions that came out of Menlo Park still affect things we do today. Work in pairs to research one of Edison's inventions. Or research another scientist's inventions. Find out how the device changed and improved in the 1900s. Write up your research and present it to the class. If the device is no longer used, explain what has replaced it. Here are a few inventions from which to choose. (Not all of them were Edison's.)

- ◆ stock ticker
- ◆ telegraph
- ◆ phonograph
- ◆ disk record
- ◆ voting machine
- ◆ electric pen and press
- ◆ typewriter
- ◆ telephone
- ◆ automobile
- ◆ radio transmitter
- ◆ vacuum tube
- ◆ mechanical music
- ◆ linotype

3 Assess

Activity Assessment

Students' answers may vary because it is difficult to judge where the state lines are on this image. Students are likely to note that, with the exception of coastal California and a few scattered cities, the eastern half of the country is more brightly lit than the western half.

According to the U.S. Census Bureau, the 1998 population of the United States was about 270 million. The top five cities in the 1990 census were: New York (7.3 million), Los Angeles (3.5 million), Chicago (2.8 million), Houston (1.6 million), and Philadelphia (1.6 million).

Tie It Together

Time 3 days (2 days to research; 1 day for presentations)

Tips Encourage students to choose any invention from Edison's time that interests them. Display a sheet in the classroom where students can record the invention they will research to ensure that all students research a different invention.

- ◆ Encourage students to make photocopies or flag the pages of books that show illustrations of the inventor, early versions of the invention, or other interesting graphics. Tell students to research enough material to be able to give a five-minute presentation.
- ◆ In the research stage, suggest that students visit a local historical museum to see some of these inventions firsthand.

Extend Students may wish to combine their research findings to make a classroom or hall display for the school.

Some students may wish to research the lives of other inventors who lived during this time period. Encourage these students to present their findings as biographies.

Suggest that students find out about present-day inventors by researching one of the organizations that help inventors. Students may also be able to find magazines published by these organizations for more information. These students should present their findings to the class.

Developing scientific thinking in students is important for a solid science education. To learn how to think scientifically, students need frequent opportunities to practice science process skills, critical thinking skills, as well as other skills that support scientific inquiry. The *Science Explorer* Skills Handbook introduces the following key science skills:
- Science Process Skills
- SI Measuring Skills
- Skills for Conducting a Scientific Investigation
- Critical Thinking Skills
- Information Organizing Skills
- Data Table and Graphing Skills

The Skills Handbook is designed as a reference for students to use whenever they need to review a science skill. You can use the activities provided in the Skills Handbook to teach or reinforce the skills.

Think Like a Scientist

Observing

Before students look at the photograph, remind them that an observation is only what they can see, hear, smell, taste, or feel. Ask: **Which senses will you use to make observations from this photograph?** *(Sight is the only sense that can be used to make observations from the photograph.)* **What are some observations you can make from the photograph?** *(Answers may vary. Sample answers: The boy is wearing sneakers, sport socks, shorts, and a tee shirt; the boy is sitting in the grass holding something blue against his knee; the boy is looking at his knee; there is a soccer ball laying beside the boy.)* List the observations on the chalkboard. If students make any inferences or predictions about the boy at this point, ask: **Can you be sure your statement is factual and accurate from just observing the photograph?** Help students understand how observations differ from inferences and predictions.

Inferring

Review students' observations from the photograph. Then ask: **What inferences can you**

Think Like a Scientist

Although you may not know it, you think like a scientist every day. Whenever you ask a question and explore possible answers, you use many of the same skills that scientists do. Some of these skills are described on this page.

Observing

When you use one or more of your five senses to gather information about the world, you are **observing.** Hearing a dog bark, counting twelve green seeds, and smelling smoke are all observations. To increase the power of their senses, scientists sometimes use microscopes, telescopes, or other instruments that help them make more detailed observations.

An observation must be factual and accurate—an exact report of what your senses detect. It is important to keep careful records of your observations in science class by writing or drawing in a notebook. The information collected through observations is called evidence, or data.

Inferring

When you explain or interpret an observation, you are **inferring,** or making an inference. For example, if you hear your dog barking, you may infer that someone is at your front door. To make this inference, you combine the evidence—the barking dog—and your experience or knowledge—you know that your dog barks when strangers approach—to reach a logical conclusion.

Notice that an inference is not a fact; it is only one of many possible explanations for an observation. For example, your dog may be barking because it wants to go for a walk. An inference may turn out to be incorrect even if it is based on accurate observations and logical reasoning. The only way to find out if an inference is correct is to investigate further.

Predicting

When you listen to the weather forecast, you hear many predictions about the next day's weather—what the temperature will be, whether it will rain, and how windy it will be. Weather forecasters use observations and knowledge of weather patterns to predict the weather. The skill of **predicting** involves making an inference about a future event based on current evidence or past experience.

Because a prediction is an inference, it may prove to be false. In science class, you can test some of your predictions by doing experiments. For example, suppose you predict that larger paper airplanes can fly farther than smaller airplanes. How could you test your prediction?

ACTIVITY Use the photograph to answer the questions below.

Observing Look closely at the photograph. List at least three observations.

Inferring Use your observations to make an inference about what has happened. What experience or knowledge did you use to make the inference?

Predicting Predict what will happen next. On what evidence or experience do you base your prediction?

---

make from your observations? *(Students may say that the boy hurt his knee playing soccer and is holding a coldpack against his injured knee.)* **What experience or knowledge helped you make this inference?** *(Students may have experienced knee injuries from playing soccer, and they may be familiar with coldpacks like the one the boy is using.)* **Can anyone suggest another possible explanation for these observations?** *(Answers may vary. Sample answer: The boy hurt his knee jogging, and he just happened to sit beside a soccer ball his sister*

left in the yard.) **How can you find out whether an inference is correct?** *(by further investigation)*

Predicting

After coming to some consensus about the inference that the boy hurt his knee, encourage students to make predictions about what will happen next. *(Students' predictions may vary. Sample answers: The boy will go to the doctor. A friend will help the boy home. The boy will get up and continue playing soccer.)*

Classifying

Could you imagine searching for a book in the library if the books were shelved in no particular order? Your trip to the library would be an all-day event! Luckily, librarians group together books on similar topics or by the same author. Grouping together items that are alike in some way is called **classifying**. You can classify items in many ways: by size, by shape, by use, and by other important characteristics.

Like librarians, scientists use the skill of classifying to organize information and objects. When things are sorted into groups, the relationships among them become easier to understand.

Classify the objects in the photograph into two groups based on any characteristic you choose. Then use another characteristic to classify the objects into three groups. **ACTIVITY**

Making Models

Have you ever drawn a picture to help someone understand what you were saying? Such a drawing is one type of model. A model is a picture, diagram, computer image, or other representation of a complex object or process. **Making models** helps people understand things that they cannot observe directly.

Scientists often use models to represent things that are either very large or very small, such as the planets in the solar system, or the parts of a cell. Such models are physical models—drawings or three-dimensional structures that look like the real thing. Other models are mental models—mathematical equations or words that describe how something works.

This student is using a model to demonstrate what causes day and night on Earth. What do the flashlight and the tennis ball represent? **ACTIVITY**

Communicating

Whenever you talk on the phone, write a letter, or listen to your teacher at school, you are communicating. **Communicating** is the process of sharing ideas and information with other people. Communicating effectively requires many skills, including writing, reading, speaking, listening, and making models.

Scientists communicate to share results, information, and opinions. Scientists often communicate about their work in journals, over the telephone, in letters, and on the Internet. They also attend scientific meetings where they share their ideas with one another in person.

On a sheet of paper, write out clear, detailed directions for tying your shoe. Then exchange directions with a partner. Follow your partner's directions exactly. How successful were you at tying your shoe? How could your partner have communicated more clearly? **ACTIVITY**

Classifying

 ACTIVITY

Encourage students to think of other common things that are classified. Then ask: **What things at home are classified?** (*Clothing might be classified by placing it in different dresser drawers; glasses, plates, and silverware are grouped in different parts of the kitchen; screws, nuts, bolts, washers, and nails might be separated into small containers.*) **What are some things that scientists classify?** (*Scientists classify many things they study, including organisms, geological features and processes, and kinds of machines.*) After students have classified the different fruits in the photograph, have them share their criteria for classifying them. (*Some characteristics students might use include shape, color, size, and where they are grown.*)

Making Models

 ACTIVITY

Ask students: **What are some models you have used to study science?** (*Students may have used human anatomical models, solar system models, maps, stream tables.*) **How did these models help you?** (*Models can help you learn about things that are difficult to study, either because they are too big, too small, or complex.*) Be sure students understand that a model does not have to be three-dimensional. For example, a map in a textbook is a model. Ask: **What do the flashlight and tennis ball represent?** (*The flashlight represents the sun, and the ball represents Earth.*) **What quality of each item makes this a good model?** (*The flashlight gives off light, and the ball is round and can be rotated by the student.*)

Communicating

ACTIVITY

Challenge students to identify the methods of communication they've used today. Then ask: **How is the way you communicate with a friend similar to and different from the way scientists communicate about their work to other scientists?** (*Both may communicate using various methods, but scientists must be very detailed and precise, whereas communication between friends may be less detailed and precise.*) Encourage students to communicate like a scientist as they carry out the activity. (*Students' directions should be detailed and precise enough for another person to successfully follow.*)

On what did you base your prediction? (*Scientific predictions are based on knowledge and experience.*) Point out that in science, predictions can often be tested with experiments.

Making Measurements

Measuring in SI

Review SI units in class with students. Begin by providing metric rulers, graduated cylinders, balances, and Celsius thermometers. Use these tools to reinforce that the meter is the unit of length, the liter is the unit of volume, the gram is the unit of mass, and the degree Celsius is the unit for temperature. Ask: **If you want to measure the length and width of your classroom, which SI unit would you use?** *(meter)* **Which unit would you use to measure the amount of matter in your textbook?** *(gram)* **Which would you use to measure how much water a drinking glass holds?** *(liter)* **When would you use the Celsius scale?** *(To measure the temperature of something)* Then use the measuring equipment to review SI prefixes. For example, ask: **What are the smallest units on the metric ruler?** *(millimeters)* **How many millimeters are there in 1 cm?** *(10 mm)* **How many in 10 cm?** *(100 mm)* **How many centimeters are there in 1 m?** *(100 cm)* **What does 1,000 m equal?** *(1 km)*

Length (Students

should state that the shell is 4.6 centimeters, or 46 millimeters, long.) If students need more practice measuring length, have them use meter sticks and metric rulers to measure various objects in the classroom.

Liquid Volume

(Students should state that the volume of water in the graduated cylinder is 62 milliliters.) If students need more practice measuring liquid volume, have them use a graduated cylinder to measure different volumes of water.

Making Measurements

When scientists make observations, it is not sufficient to say that something is "big" or "heavy." Instead, scientists use instruments to measure just how big or heavy an object is. By measuring, scientists can express their observations more precisely and communicate more information about what they observe.

Measuring in SI

The standard system of measurement used by scientists around the world is known as the International System of Units, which is abbreviated as SI (in French, *Système International d'Unités*). SI units are easy to use because they are based on multiples of 10. Each unit is ten times larger than the next smallest unit and one tenth the size of the next largest unit. The table lists the prefixes used to name the most common SI units.

Common SI Prefixes

Prefix	Symbol	Meaning
kilo-	k	1,000
hecto-	h	100
deka-	da	10
deci-	d	0.1 (one tenth)
centi-	c	0.01 (one hundredth)
milli-	m	0.001 (one thousandth)

Length To measure length, or the distance between two points, the unit of measure is the **meter (m).** One meter is the approximate distance from the floor to a doorknob. Long distances, such as the distance between two cities, are measured in kilometers (km). Small lengths are measured in centimeters (cm) or millimeters (mm). Scientists use metric rulers and meter sticks to measure length.

Common Conversions

1 km = 1,000 m
1 m = 100 cm
1 m = 1,000 mm
1 cm = 10 mm

The larger lines on the metric ruler in the picture show centimeter divisions, while the smaller, unnumbered lines show millimeter divisions. How many centimeters long is the shell? How many millimeters long is it?

Liquid Volume To measure the volume of a liquid, or the amount of space it takes up, you will use a unit of measure known as the **liter (L).** One liter is the approximate volume of a medium-sized carton of milk. Smaller volumes are measured in milliliters (mL). Scientists use graduated cylinders to measure liquid volume.

Common Conversion

1 L = 1,000 mL

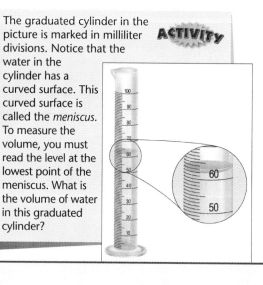

The graduated cylinder in the picture is marked in milliliter divisions. Notice that the water in the cylinder has a curved surface. This curved surface is called the *meniscus.* To measure the volume, you must read the level at the lowest point of the meniscus. What is the volume of water in this graduated cylinder?

Mass To measure mass, or the amount of matter in an object, you will use a unit of measure known as the **gram (g)**. One gram is approximately the mass of a paper clip. Larger masses are measured in kilograms (kg). Scientists use a balance to find the mass of an object.

Common Conversion

1 kg = 1,000 g

The electronic balance displays the mass of an apple in kilograms. What is the mass of the apple? Suppose a recipe for applesauce called for one kilogram of apples. About how many apples would you need?

ACTIVITY

Temperature
To measure the temperature of a substance, you will use the **Celsius scale**. Temperature is measured in degrees Celsius (°C) using a Celsius thermometer. Water freezes at 0°C and boils at 100°C.

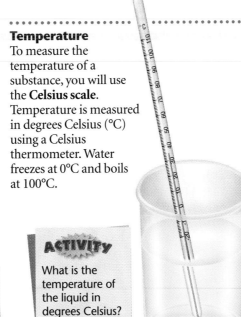

ACTIVITY
What is the temperature of the liquid in degrees Celsius?

Converting SI Units

To use the SI system, you must know how to convert between units. Converting from one unit to another involves the skill of **calculating**, or using mathematical operations. Converting between SI units is similar to converting between dollars and dimes because both systems are based on multiples of ten.

Suppose you want to convert a length of 80 centimeters to meters. Follow these steps to convert between units.

1. Begin by writing down the measurement you want to convert—in this example, 80 centimeters.

2. Write a conversion factor that represents the relationship between the two units you are converting. In this example, the relationship is *1 meter = 100 centimeters.* Write this conversion factor as a fraction, making sure to place the units you are converting from (centimeters, in this example) in the denominator.

3. Multiply the measurement you want to convert by the fraction. When you do this, the units in the first measurement will cancel out with the units in the denominator. Your answer will be in the units you are converting to (meters, in this example).

Example

80 centimeters = ____?____ meters

$$80 \text{ centimeters} \times \frac{1 \text{ meter}}{100 \text{ centimeters}} = \frac{80 \text{ meters}}{100}$$

$$= 0.8 \text{ meters}$$

ACTIVITY
Convert between the following units.
1. 600 millimeters = _?_ meters
2. 0.35 liters = _?_ milliliters
3. 1,050 grams = _?_ kilograms

Mass *(Students should state that the mass of the apple is 0.1 kilograms. They would need 10 apples to make 1 kilogram.)* If students need practice determining mass, have them use a balance to determine the mass of various common objects, such as coins, paper clips, and books.

ACTIVITY

Temperature *(Students should state that the temperature of the liquid is 35°C.)* If students need practice measuring temperature, have them use a Celsius thermometer to measure the temperature of various water samples.

ACTIVITY

Converting SI Units

ACTIVITY

Review the steps for converting SI units and work through the example with students. Then ask: **How many millimeters are in 80 centimeters?** *(Students should follow the steps to calculate that 80 centimeters is equal to 800 millimeters.)*

Have students do the conversion problems in the activity. (**1.** *600 millimeters = 0.6 meters;* **2.** *0.35 liters = 350 milliliters;* **3.** *1,050 grams = 1.05 kilograms)* If students need more practice converting SI units, have students make up conversion problems and trade with a partner.

Conducting a Scientific Investigation

Posing Questions

Before students do the activity on the next page, walk them through the steps of a typical scientific investigation. Begin by asking: **Why is a scientific question important to a scientific investigation?** *(It is the reason for conducting a scientific investigation and how every investigation begins.)* **What is the scientific question in the activity at the bottom of the next page?** *(Is a ball's bounce affected by the height from which it is dropped?)*

Developing a Hypothesis

Emphasize that a hypothesis is a prediction about the outcome of a scientific investigation, but it is *not* a guess. Ask: **On what information do scientists base their hypotheses?** *(Their observations and previous knowledge or experience)* Point out that a hypothesis does not always turn out to be correct. Ask: **In that case, do you think the scientist wasted his or her time? Explain your answer.** *(No, because the scientist probably learned from the investigation and maybe could develop another hypothesis that could be supported.)*

Designing an Experiment

Have a volunteer read the Experimental Procedure in the box. Then call on students to identify the manipulated variable *(amount of salt added to water)*, the variables that are kept constant *(amount and starting temperature of water, placing containers in freezer)*, the responding variable *(time it takes water to freeze)*, and the control *(Container 3)*.

Ask: **How might the experiment be affected if Container 1 had only 100 mL of water?** *(It wouldn't be a fair comparison with the containers that have more water.)* **What if Container 3 was not included in the experiment?** *(You wouldn't have anything to compare the other two containers to know if their freezing times were faster or slower than normal.)* Help students understand the importance of

Conducting a Scientific Investigation

In some ways, scientists are like detectives, piecing together clues to learn about a process or event. One way that scientists gather clues is by carrying out experiments. An experiment tests an idea in a careful, orderly manner. Although all experiments do not follow the same steps in the same order, many follow a pattern similar to the one described here.

Posing Questions

Experiments begin by asking a scientific question. A scientific question is one that can be answered by gathering evidence. For example, the question "Which freezes faster—fresh water or salt water?" is a scientific question because you can carry out an investigation and gather information to answer the question.

Developing a Hypothesis

The next step is to form a hypothesis. A **hypothesis** is a prediction about the outcome of the experiment. Like all predictions, hypotheses are based on your observations and previous knowledge or experience. But, unlike many predictions, a hypothesis must be something that can be tested. A properly worded hypothesis should take the form of an *If . . . then . . .* statement. For example, a hypothesis might be *"If I add salt to fresh water, then the water will take longer to freeze."* A hypothesis worded this way serves as a rough outline of the experiment you should perform.

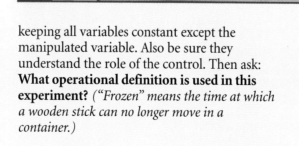

keeping all variables constant except the manipulated variable. Also be sure they understand the role of the control. Then ask: **What operational definition is used in this experiment?** *("Frozen" means the time at which a wooden stick can no longer move in a container.)*

Designing an Experiment

Next you need to plan a way to test your hypothesis. Your plan should be written out as a step-by-step procedure and should describe the observations or measurements you will make.

Two important steps involved in designing an experiment are controlling variables and forming operational definitions.

Controlling Variables In a well-designed experiment, you need to keep all variables the same except for one. A **variable** is any factor that can change in an experiment. The factor that you change is called the **manipulated variable.** In this experiment, the manipulated variable is the amount of salt added to the water. Other factors, such as the amount of water or the starting temperature, are kept constant.

The factor that changes as a result of the manipulated variable is called the responding variable. The **responding variable** is what you measure or observe to obtain your results. In this experiment, the responding variable is how long the water takes to freeze.

An experiment in which all factors except one are kept constant is a **controlled experiment.** Most controlled experiments include a test called the control. In this experiment, Container 3 is the control. Because no salt is added to Container 3, you can compare the results from the other containers to it. Any difference in results must be due to the addition of salt alone.

Forming Operational Definitions

Another important aspect of a well-designed experiment is having clear operational definitions. An **operational definition** is a statement that describes how a particular variable is to be measured or how a term is to be defined. For example, in this experiment, how will you determine if the water has frozen? You might decide to insert a stick in each container at the start of the experiment. Your operational definition of "frozen" would be the time at which the stick can no longer move.

EXPERIMENTAL PROCEDURE

1. Fill 3 containers with 300 milliliters of cold tap water.

2. Add 10 grams of salt to Container 1; stir. Add 20 grams of salt to Container 2; stir. Add no salt to Container 3.

3. Place the 3 containers in a freezer.

4. Check the containers every 15 minutes. Record your observations.

Interpreting Data

The observations and measurements you make in an experiment are called data. At the end of an experiment, you need to analyze the data to look for any patterns or trends. Patterns often become clear if you organize your data in a data table or graph. Then think through what the data reveal. Do they support your hypothesis? Do they point out a flaw in your experiment? Do you need to collect more data?

Drawing Conclusions

A conclusion is a statement that sums up what you have learned from an experiment. When you draw a conclusion, you need to decide whether the data you collected support your hypothesis or not. You may need to repeat an experiment several times before you can draw any conclusions from it. Conclusions often lead you to pose new questions and plan new experiments to answer them.

Is a ball's bounce affected by the height from which it is dropped? Using the steps just described, plan a controlled experiment to investigate this problem. **ACTIVITY**

Interpreting Data

Emphasize the importance of collecting accurate and detailed data in a scientific investigation. Ask: **What if the students forgot to record the times that they made their observations in the experiment?** *(They wouldn't be able to completely analyze their data to draw valid conclusions.)* Then ask: **Why are data tables and graphs a good way to organize data?** *(They often make it easier to compare and analyze data.)* You may wish to have students review the Skills Handbook pages on Creating Data Tables and Graphs at this point.

Drawing Conclusions

Help students understand that a conclusion is not necessarily the end of a scientific investigation. A conclusion about one experiment may lead right into another experiment. Point out that in scientific investigations, a conclusion is a summary and explanation of the results of an experiment.

Tell students to suppose that for the Experimental Procedure described on this page, they obtained the following results: Container 1 froze in 45 minutes, Container 2 in 80 minutes, and Container 3 in 25 minutes. Ask: **What conclusions can you draw about this experiment?** *(Students might conclude that the more salt that is added to fresh water, the longer it takes the water to freeze. The hypothesis is supported, and the question of which freezes faster is answered—fresh water.)*

You might wish to have students work in pairs to plan the controlled experiment. *(Students should develop a hypothesis, such as "If I increase the height from which a ball is dropped, then the height of its bounce will increase." They can test the hypothesis by dropping balls from varying heights (the manipulated variable). All trials should be done with the same kind of ball and on the same surface (constant variables). For each trial, they should measure the height of the bounce (responding variable).) After students have designed the experiment, provide rubber balls and invite them to carry out the experiment so they can collect and interpret data and draw conclusions.*

Thinking Critically

Comparing and Contrasting

Emphasize that the skill of comparing and contrasting often relies on good observation skills, as in this activity. (*Students' answers may vary. Sample answer: Similarities—both are dogs and have four legs, two eyes, two ears, brown and white fur, black noses, pink tongues; Differences—smooth coat vs. rough coat, more white fur vs. more brown fur, shorter vs. taller, long ears vs. short ears.*)

Applying Concepts

Point out to students that they apply concepts that they learn in school in their daily lives. For example, they learn to add, subtract, multiply, and divide in school. If they get a paper route or some other part-time job, they can apply those concepts. Challenge students to practice applying concepts by doing the activity. (*Antifreeze lowers the temperature at which the solution will freeze, and thus keeps the water in the radiator from freezing.*)

Interpreting Illustrations

Again, point out the need for good observation skills. Ask: **What is the difference between "interpreting illustrations" and "looking at the pictures"?** (*"Interpreting illustrations" requires thorough examination of the illustration, caption, and labels, while "looking at the pictures" implies less thorough examination.*) Encourage students to thoroughly examine the diagram as they do the activity. (*Students' paragraphs may vary, but should describe the internal anatomy of an earthworm, including some of the organs in the earthworm.*)

Thinking Critically

Has a friend ever asked for your advice about a problem? If so, you may have helped your friend think through the problem in a logical way. Without knowing it, you used critical-thinking skills to help your friend. Critical thinking involves the use of reasoning and logic to solve problems or make decisions. Some critical-thinking skills are described below.

Comparing and Contrasting

When you examine two objects for similarities and differences, you are using the skill of **comparing and contrasting.** Comparing involves identifying similarities, or common characteristics. Contrasting involves identifying differences. Analyzing objects in this way can help you discover details that you might otherwise overlook.

Compare and contrast the two animals in the photo. First list all the similarities that you see. Then list all the differences.

Applying Concepts

When you use your knowledge about one situation to make sense of a similar situation, you are using the skill of **applying concepts.** Being able to transfer your knowledge from one situation to another shows that you truly understand a concept. You may use this skill in answering test questions that present different problems from the ones you've reviewed in class.

You have just learned that water takes longer to freeze when other substances are mixed into it. Use this knowledge to explain why people need a substance called antifreeze in their car's radiator in the winter.

Interpreting Illustrations

Diagrams, photographs, and maps are included in textbooks to help clarify what you read. These illustrations show processes, places, and ideas in a visual manner. The skill called **interpreting illustrations** can help you learn from these visual elements. To understand an illustration, take the time to study the illustration along with all the written information that accompanies it. Captions identify the key concepts shown in the illustration. Labels point out the important parts of a diagram or map, while keys identify the symbols used in a map.

Blood vessels

Reproductive organs

Hearts

Brain

Mouth

Bristles

Digestive tract

Nerve cord

Waste-removal organs

Intestine

▲ Internal anatomy of an earthworm

Study the diagram above. Then write a short paragraph explaining what you have learned.

Relating Cause and Effect

If one event causes another event to occur, the two events are said to have a cause-and-effect relationship. When you determine that such a relationship exists between two events, you use a skill called **relating cause and effect.** For example, if you notice an itchy, red bump on your skin, you might infer that a mosquito bit you. The mosquito bite is the cause, and the bump is the effect.

It is important to note that two events do not necessarily have a cause-and-effect relationship just because they occur together. Scientists carry out experiments or use past experience to determine whether a cause-and-effect relationship exists.

> **ACTIVITY**
> You are on a camping trip and your flashlight has stopped working. List some possible causes for the flashlight malfunction. How could you determine which cause-and-effect relationship has left you in the dark?

Making Generalizations

When you draw a conclusion about an entire group based on information about only some of the group's members, you are using a skill called **making generalizations.** For a generalization to be valid, the sample you choose must be large enough and representative of the entire group. You might, for example, put this skill to work at a farm stand if you see a sign that says, "Sample some grapes before you buy." If you sample a few sweet grapes, you may conclude that all the grapes are sweet—and purchase a large bunch.

> **ACTIVITY**
> A team of scientists needs to determine whether the water in a large reservoir is safe to drink. How could they use the skill of making generalizations to help them? What should they do?

Making Judgments

When you evaluate something to decide whether it is good or bad, or right or wrong, you are using a skill called **making judgments.** For example, you make judgments when you decide to eat healthful foods or to pick up litter in a park. Before you make a judgment, you need to think through the pros and cons of a situation, and identify the values or standards that you hold.

> **ACTIVITY**
> Should children and teens be required to wear helmets when bicycling? Explain why you feel the way you do.

Problem Solving

When you use critical-thinking skills to resolve an issue or decide on a course of action, you are using a skill called **problem solving.** Some problems, such as how to convert a fraction into a decimal, are straightforward. Other problems, such as figuring out why your computer has stopped working, are complex. Some complex problems can be solved using the trial and error method—try out one solution first, and if that doesn't work, try another. Other useful problem-solving strategies include making models and brainstorming possible solutions with a partner.

Relating Cause and Effect

Emphasize that not all events that occur together have a cause-and-effect relationship. For example, tell students that you went to the grocery and your car stalled. Ask: **Is there a cause-and-effect relationship in this situation? Explain your answer.** (*No, because going to the grocery could not cause a car to stall. There must be another cause to make the car stall.*) Have students do the activity to practice relating cause and effect. (*Students should identify that the flashlight not working is the effect. Some possible causes include dead batteries, a burned-out light bulb, or a loose part.*)

Making Generalizations

Point out the importance of having a large, representative sample before making a generalization. Ask: **If you went fishing at a lake and caught three catfish, could you make the generalization that all fish in the lake are catfish? Why or why not?** (*No, because there might be other kinds of fish you didn't catch because they didn't like the bait or they may be in other parts of the lake.*) **How could you make a generalization about the kinds of fish in the lake?** (*By having a larger sample*) Have students do the activity to practice making generalizations. (*The scientists should collect and test water samples from a number of different parts of the reservoir.*)

Making Judgments

Remind students that they make a judgment almost every time they make a decision. Ask: **What steps should you follow to make a judgment?** (*Gather information, list pros and cons, analyze values, make judgment*) Invite students to do the activity, and then to share and discuss the judgments they made. (*Students' judgments will vary, but should be supported by valid reasoning. Sample answer: Children and teens should be required to wear helmets when bicycling because helmets have been proven to save lives and reduce head injuries.*)

Problem Solving **ACTIVITY**

Challenge student pairs to solve a problem about a soapbox derby. Explain that their younger brother is building a car to enter in the race. The brother wants to know how to make his soapbox car go faster. After student pairs have considered the problem, have them share their ideas about solutions with the class. (*Most will probably suggest using trial and error by making small changes to the car and testing the car after each change. Some students may suggest making and manipulating a model.*)

Organizing Information

Concept Maps

Challenge students to make a concept map with at least three levels of concepts to organize information about types of transportation. All students should start with the phrase *types of transportation* at the top of the concept map. After that point, their concept maps may vary. *(For example, some students might place* private transportation *and* public transportation *at the next level, while other students might have* human-powered *and* gas-powered. *Make sure students connect the concepts with linking words. Challenge students to include cross-linkages as well.)*

Compare/ Contrast Tables

Have students make their own compare/contrast tables using two or more different sports or other activities, such as playing musical instruments. Emphasize that students should select characteristics that highlight the similarities and differences between the activities. *(Students' compare/contrast tables should include several appropriate characteristics and list information about each activity for every characteristic.)*

Organizing Information

As you read this textbook, how can you make sense of all the information it contains? Some useful tools to help you organize information are shown on this page. These tools are called *graphic organizers* because they give you a visual picture of a topic, showing at a glance how key concepts are related.

Concept Maps

Concept maps are useful tools for organizing information on broad topics. A concept map begins with a general concept and shows how it can be broken down into more specific concepts. In that way, relationships between concepts become easier to understand.

A concept map is constructed by placing concept words (usually nouns) in ovals and connecting them with linking words. Often, the most general concept word is placed at the top, and the words become more specific as you move downward. Often the linking words, which are written on a line extending between two ovals, describe the relationship between the two concepts they connect. If you follow any string of concepts and linking words down the map, it should read like a sentence.

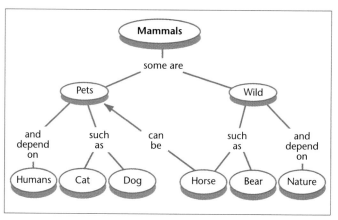

Some concept maps include linking words that connect a concept on one branch of the map to a concept on another branch. These linking words, called cross-linkages, show more complex interrelationships among concepts.

Compare/Contrast Tables

Compare/contrast tables are useful tools for sorting out the similarities and differences between two or more items. A table provides an organized framework in which to compare items based on specific characteristics that you identify.

To create a compare/contrast table, list the items to be compared across the top of a table. Then list the characteristics that will form the basis of your comparison in the left-hand column. Complete the table by filling in information about each characteristic, first for one item and then for the other.

Characteristic	Baseball	Basketball
Number of Players	9	5
Playing Field	Baseball diamond	Basketball court
Equipment	Bat, baseball, mitts	Basket, basketball

Venn Diagrams

Another way to show similarities and differences between items is with a Venn diagram. A Venn diagram consists of two or more circles that partially overlap. Each circle represents a particular concept or idea. Common characteristics, or similarities, are written within the area of overlap between the two circles. Unique characteristics, or differences, are written in the parts of the circles outside the area of overlap.

To create a Venn diagram, draw two overlapping circles. Label the circles with the names of the items being compared. Write the

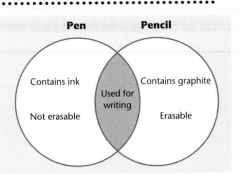

unique characteristics in each circle outside the area of overlap. Then write the shared characteristics within the area of overlap.

Flowcharts

A flowchart can help you understand the order in which certain events have occurred or should occur. Flowcharts are useful for outlining the stages in a process or the steps in a procedure.

To make a flowchart, write a brief description of each event in a box. Place the first event at the top of the page, followed by the second event, the third event, and so on. Then draw an arrow to connect each event to the one that occurs next.

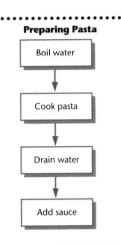

Cycle Diagrams

A cycle diagram can be used to show a sequence of events that is continuous, or cyclical. A continuous sequence does not have an end because, when the final event is over, the first event begins again. Like a flowchart, a cycle diagram can help you understand the order of events.

To create a cycle diagram, write a brief description of each event in a box. Place one event at the top of the page in the center. Then, moving in a clockwise direction around an imaginary circle, write each event in its proper sequence. Draw arrows that connect each event to the one that occurs next, forming a continuous circle.

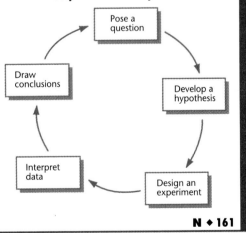

Venn Diagrams

Students can use the same information from their compare/contrast tables to create a Venn diagram. Make sure students understand that the overlapping area of the circles is used to list similarities and the parts of the circles outside the overlap area are used to show differences. If students want to list similarities and differences among three activities, show them how to add a third circle that overlaps each of the other two circles and has an area of overlap for all three circles. (*Students' Venn diagrams will vary. Make sure they have accurately listed similarities in the overlap area and differences in the parts of the circles that do not overlap.*)

Flowcharts

Encourage students to create a flowchart to show the things they did this morning as they got ready for school. Remind students that a flowchart should show the correct order in which events occurred or should occur. (*Students' flowcharts will vary somewhat. A typical flowchart might include: got up → ate breakfast → took a shower → brushed teeth → got dressed → gathered books and homework → put on jacket.*)

Cycle Diagrams

Review that a cycle diagram shows a sequence of events that is continuous. Then challenge students to create a cycle diagram that shows how the weather changes with the seasons where they live. (*Students' cycle diagrams may vary, though most will include four steps, one for each season.*)

Creating Data Tables and Graphs

Data Tables

Have students create a data table to show how much time they spend on different activities during one week. Suggest that students first list the main activities they do every week. Then they should determine the amount of time they spend on each activity each day. Remind students to give this data table a title. *(Students' data tables will vary. A sample data table is shown below.)*

Bar Graphs

Students can use the data from their data table above to make a bar graph showing how much time they spend on different activities during a week. The vertical axis should be divided into units of time, such as hours. Remind students to label both axes and give their graph a title. *(Students' bar graphs will vary. A sample bar graph is shown below.)*

Creating Data Tables and Graphs

How can you make sense of the data in a science experiment? The first step is to organize the data to help you understand them. Data tables and graphs are helpful tools for organizing data.

Data Tables

You have gathered your materials and set up your experiment. But before you start, you need to plan a way to record what happens during the experiment. By creating a data table, you can record your observations and measurements in an orderly way.

Suppose, for example, that a scientist conducted an experiment to find out how many Calories people of different body masses burn while doing various activities. The data table shows the results.

Notice in this data table that the manipulated variable (body mass) is the heading of one column. The responding variable (for Experiment 1, the number of Calories burned while bicycling) is the heading of the next column. Additional columns were added for related experiments.

CALORIES BURNED IN 30 MINUTES OF ACTIVITY			
Body Mass	Experiment 1 Bicycling	Experiment 2 Playing Basketball	Experiment 3 Watching Television
30 kg	60 Calories	120 Calories	21 Calories
40 kg	77 Calories	164 Calories	27 Calories
50 kg	95 Calories	206 Calories	33 Calories
60 kg	114 Calories	248 Calories	38 Calories

Bar Graphs

To compare how many Calories a person burns doing various activities, you could create a bar graph. A bar graph is used to display data in a number of separate, or distinct, categories. In this example, bicycling, playing basketball, and watching television are three separate categories.

To create a bar graph, follow these steps.

1. On graph paper, draw a horizontal, or *x*-, axis and a vertical, or *y*-, axis.
2. Write the names of the categories to be graphed along the horizontal axis. Include an overall label for the axis as well.
3. Label the vertical axis with the name of the responding variable. Include units of measurement. Then create a scale along the axis by marking off equally spaced numbers that cover the range of the data collected.
4. For each category, draw a solid bar using the scale on the vertical axis to determine the

appropriate height. For example, for bicycling, draw the bar as high as the 60 mark on the vertical axis. Make all the bars the same width and leave equal spaces between them.
5. Add a title that describes the graph.

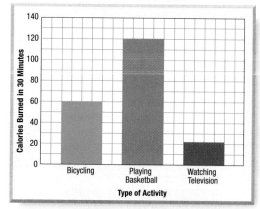

Calories Burned by a 30-kilogram Person in Various Activities

Time Spent on Different Activities in a Week				
	Going to Classes	Eating Meals	Playing Soccer	Watching Television
Monday	6	2	2	0.5
Tuesday	6	1.5	1.5	1.5
Wednesday	6	2	1	2
Thursday	6	2	2	1.5
Friday	6	2	2	0.5
Saturday	0	2.5	2.5	1
Sunday	0	3	1	2

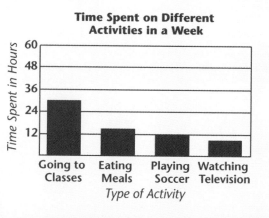

Time Spent on Different Activities in a Week

Line Graphs

To see whether a relationship exists between body mass and the number of Calories burned while bicycling, you could create a line graph. A line graph is used to display data that show how one variable (the responding variable) changes in response to another variable (the manipulated variable). You can use a line graph when your manipulated variable is *continuous*, that is, when there are other points between the ones that you tested. In this example, body mass is a continuous variable because there are other body masses between 30 and 40 kilograms (for example, 31 kilograms). Time is another example of a continuous variable.

Line graphs are powerful tools because they allow you to estimate values for conditions that you did not test in the experiment. For example, you can use the line graph to estimate that a 35-kilogram person would burn 68 Calories while bicycling.

To create a line graph, follow these steps.

1. On graph paper, draw a horizontal, or *x*-, axis and a vertical, or *y*-, axis.
2. Label the horizontal axis with the name of the manipulated variable. Label the vertical axis with the name of the responding variable. Include units of measurement.
3. Create a scale on each axis by marking off equally spaced numbers that cover the range of the data collected.
4. Plot a point on the graph for each piece of data. In the line graph above, the dotted lines show how to plot the first data point (30 kilograms and 60 Calories). Draw an imaginary vertical line extending up from the horizontal axis at the 30-kilogram mark. Then draw an imaginary horizontal line extending across from the vertical axis at the 60-Calorie mark. Plot the point where the two lines intersect.

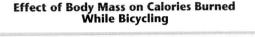

Effect of Body Mass on Calories Burned While Bicycling

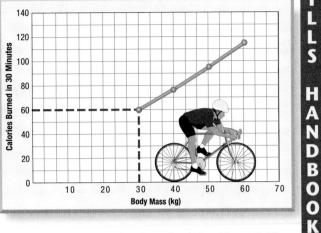

5. Connect the plotted points with a solid line. (In some cases, it may be more appropriate to draw a line that shows the general trend of the plotted points. In those cases, some of the points may fall above or below the line.)
6. Add a title that identifies the variables or relationship in the graph.

> **ACTIVITY** Create line graphs to display the data from Experiment 2 and Experiment 3 in the data table.

> **ACTIVITY** You read in the newspaper that a total of 4 centimeters of rain fell in your area in June, 2.5 centimeters fell in July, and 1.5 centimeters fell in August. What type of graph would you use to display these data? Use graph paper to create the graph.

Line Graphs

Walk students through the steps involved in creating a line graph using the example illustrated on the page. For example, ask: **What is the label on the horizontal axis? On the vertical axis?** (*Body Mass (kg); Calories Burned in 30 Minutes*) **What scales are used on each axis?** (*3 squares per 10 kg on the x-axis and 2 squares per 20 calories on the y-axis*) **What does the second data point represent?** (*77 Calories burned for a body mass of 40 kg*) **What trend or pattern does the graph show?** (*The number of Calories burned in 30 minutes of cycling increases with body mass.*)

Have students follow the steps to carry out the first activity. (*Students should make a different graph for each experiment with different y-axis scales to practice making scales appropriate for data. See sample graphs below.*)

Have students carry out the second activity. (*Students should conclude that a bar graph would be best to display the data. A sample bar graph for these data is shown below.*)

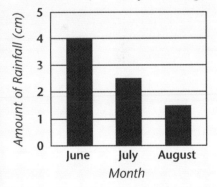

Rainfall in June, July, and August

Effect of Body Mass on Calories Burned While Playing Basketball

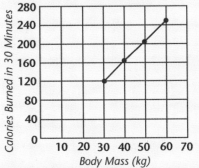

Effect of Body Mass on Calories Burned While Watching Television

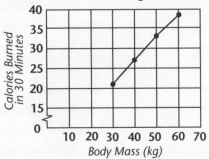

Circle Graphs

Emphasize that a circle graph has to include 100 percent of the categories for the topic being graphed. For example, ask: **Could the data in the bar graph titled "Calories Burned by a 30-kilogram Person in Various Activities" (on the previous page) be shown in a circle graph? Why or why not?** (*No, because it does not include all the possible ways a 30-kilogram person can burn Calories.*) Then walk students through the steps for making a circle graph. Help students to use a compass and a protractor. Use the protractor to illustrate that a circle has 360 degrees. Make sure students understand the mathematical calculations involved in making a circle graph.

You might wish to have students work in pairs to complete the activity. (*Students' circle graphs should look like the graph below.*) **ACTIVITY**

Circle Graphs

Like bar graphs, circle graphs can be used to display data in a number of separate categories. Unlike bar graphs, however, circle graphs can only be used when you have data for *all* the categories that make up a given topic. A circle graph is sometimes called a pie chart because it resembles a pie cut into slices. The pie represents the entire topic, while the slices represent the individual categories. The size of a slice indicates what percentage of the whole a particular category makes up.

The data table below shows the results of a survey in which 24 teenagers were asked to identify their favorite sport. The data were then used to create the circle graph at the right.

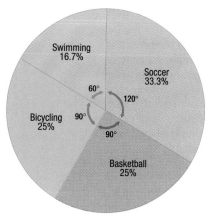

Sports That Teens Prefer

FAVORITE SPORTS	
Sport	Number of Students
Soccer	8
Basketball	6
Bicycling	6
Swimming	4

To create a circle graph, follow these steps.

1. Use a compass to draw a circle. Mark the center of the circle with a point. Then draw a line from the center point to the top of the circle.
2. Determine the size of each "slice" by setting up a proportion where *x* equals the number of degrees in a slice. (NOTE: A circle contains 360 degrees.) For example, to find the number of degrees in the "soccer" slice, set up the following proportion:

$$\frac{\text{students who prefer soccer}}{\text{total number of students}} = \frac{x}{\text{total number of degrees in a circle}}$$

$$\frac{8}{24} = \frac{x}{360}$$

Cross-multiply and solve for *x*.

$$24x = 8 \times 360$$
$$x = 120$$

The "soccer" slice should contain 120 degrees.

3. Use a protractor to measure the angle of the first slice, using the line you drew to the top of the circle as the 0° line. Draw a line from the center of the circle to the edge for the angle you measured.
4. Continue around the circle by measuring the size of each slice with the protractor. Start measuring from the edge of the previous slice so the wedges do not overlap. When you are done, the entire circle should be filled in.
5. Determine the percentage of the whole circle that each slice represents. To do this, divide the number of degrees in a slice by the total number of degrees in a circle (360), and multiply by 100%. For the "soccer" slice, you can find the percentage as follows:

$$\frac{120}{360} \times 100\% = 33.3\%$$

6. Use a different color to shade in each slice. Label each slice with the name of the category and with the percentage of the whole it represents.
7. Add a title to the circle graph.

In a class of 28 students, 12 students take the bus to school, 10 students walk, and 6 students ride their bicycles. Create a circle graph to display these data. **ACTIVITY**

Ways Students Get to School

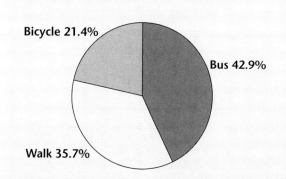

Laboratory Safety

Safety Symbols

These symbols alert you to possible dangers in the laboratory and remind you to work carefully.

 Safety Goggles Always wear safety goggles to protect your eyes in any activity involving chemicals, flames or heating, or the possibility of broken glassware.

Lab Apron Wear a laboratory apron to protect your skin and clothing from damage.

Breakage You are working with materials that may be breakable, such as glass containers, glass tubing, thermometers, or funnels. Handle breakable materials with care. Do not touch broken glassware.

Heat-resistant Gloves Use an oven mitt or other hand protection when handling hot materials. Hot plates, hot glassware, or hot water can cause burns. Do not touch hot objects with your bare hands.

Heating Use a clamp or tongs to pick up hot glassware. Do not touch hot objects with your bare hands.

Sharp Object Pointed-tip scissors, scalpels, knives, needles, pins, or tacks are sharp. They can cut or puncture your skin. Always direct a sharp edge or point away from yourself and others. Use sharp instruments only as instructed.

Electric Shock Avoid the possibility of electric shock. Never use electrical equipment around water, or when the equipment is wet or your hands are wet. Be sure cords are untangled and cannot trip anyone. Disconnect the equipment when it is not in use.

Corrosive Chemical You are working with an acid or another corrosive chemical. Avoid getting it on your skin or clothing, or in your eyes. Do not inhale the vapors. Wash your hands when you are finished with the activity.

 Poison Do not let any poisonous chemical come in contact with your skin, and do not inhale its vapors. Wash your hands when you are finished with the activity.

Physical Safety When an experiment involves physical activity, take precautions to avoid injuring yourself or others. Follow instructions from your teacher. Alert your teacher if there is any reason you should not participate in the activity.

Animal Safety Treat live animals with care to avoid harming the animals or yourself. Working with animal parts or preserved animals also may require caution. Wash your hands when you are finished with the activity.

Plant Safety Handle plants in the laboratory or during field work only as directed by your teacher. If you are allergic to certain plants, tell your teacher before doing an activity in which those plants are used. Avoid touching harmful plants such as poison ivy, poison oak, or poison sumac, or plants with thorns. Wash your hands when you are finished with the activity.

Flames You may be working with flames from a lab burner, candle, or matches. Tie back loose hair and clothing. Follow instructions from your teacher about lighting and extinguishing flames.

No Flames Flammable materials may be present. Make sure there are no flames, sparks, or other exposed heat sources present.

Fumes When poisonous or unpleasant vapors may be involved, work in a ventilated area. Avoid inhaling vapors directly. Only test an odor when directed to do so by your teacher, and use a wafting motion to direct the vapor toward your nose.

Disposal Chemicals and other laboratory materials used in the activity must be disposed of safely. Follow the instructions from your teacher.

Hand Washing Wash your hands thoroughly when finished with the activity. Use antibacterial soap and warm water. Lather both sides of your hands and between your fingers. Rinse well.

General Safety Awareness You may see this symbol when none of the symbols described earlier appears. In this case, follow the specific instructions provided. You may also see this symbol when you are asked to develop your own procedure in a lab. Have your teacher approve your plan before you go further.

N ◆ 165

Laboratory Safety

Laboratory safety is an essential element of a successful science class. It is important for you to emphasize laboratory safety to students. Students need to understand exactly what is safe and unsafe behavior, and what the rationale is behind each safety rule.

Review with students the Safety Symbols and Science Safety Rules listed on this and the next two pages. Then follow the safety guidelines below to ensure that your classroom will be a safe place for students to learn science.

◆ Post safety rules in the classroom and review them regularly with students.

◆ Familiarize yourself with the safety procedures for each activity before introducing it to your students.

◆ Review specific safety precautions with students before beginning every science activity.

◆ Always act as an exemplary role model by displaying safe behavior.

◆ Know how to use safety equipment, such as fire extinguishers and fire blankets, and always have it accessible.

◆ Have students practice leaving the classroom quickly and orderly to prepare them for emergencies.

◆ Explain to students how to use the intercom or other available means of communication to get help during an emergency.

◆ Never leave students unattended while they are engaged in science activities.

◆ Provide enough space for students to safely carry out science activities.

◆ Keep your classroom and all science materials in proper condition. Replace worn or broken items.

◆ Instruct students to report all accidents and injuries to you immediately.

Laboratory Safety

Additional tips are listed below for the Science Safety Rules discussed on these two pages. Please keep these tips in mind when you carry out science activities in your classroom.

General Precautions

◆ For open-ended activities like Chapter Projects, go over general safety guidelines with students. Have students submit their procedures or design plans in writing and check them for safety considerations.

◆ In an activity where students are directed to taste something, be sure to store the material in clean, *nonscience* containers. Distribute the material to students in *new* plastic or paper dispensables, which should be discarded after the tasting. Tasting or eating should never be done in a lab classroom.

◆ During physical activity, make sure students do not overexert themselves.

◆ Remind students to handle microscopes and telescopes with care to avoid breakage.

Heating and Fire Safety

◆ No flammable substances should be in use around hot plates, light bulbs, or open flames.

◆ Test tubes should be heated only in water baths.

◆ Students should be permitted to strike matches to light candles or burners *only* with strict supervision. When possible, you should light the flames, especially when working with sixth graders.

◆ Be sure to have proper ventilation when fumes are produced during a procedure.

◆ All electrical equipment used in the lab should have GFI switches.

Using Chemicals Safely

◆ When students use both chemicals and microscopes in one activity, microscopes should be in a separate part of the room from the chemicals so that when students remove their goggles to use the microscopes, their eyes are not at risk.

Science Safety Rules

To prepare yourself to work safely in the laboratory, read over the following safety rules. Then read them a second time. Make sure you understand and follow each rule. Ask your teacher to explain any rules you do not understand.

Dress Code

1. To protect yourself from injuring your eyes, wear safety goggles whenever you work with chemicals, burners, glassware, or any substance that might get into your eyes. If you wear contact lenses, notify your teacher.
2. Wear a lab apron or coat whenever you work with corrosive chemicals or substances that can stain.
3. Tie back long hair to keep it away from any chemicals, flames, or equipment.
4. Remove or tie back any article of clothing or jewelry that can hang down and touch chemicals, flames, or equipment. Roll up or secure long sleeves.
5. Never wear open shoes or sandals.

General Precautions

6. Read all directions for an experiment several times before beginning the activity. Carefully follow all written and oral instructions. If you are in doubt about any part of the experiment, ask your teacher for assistance.
7. Never perform activities that are not assigned or authorized by your teacher. Obtain permission before "experimenting" on your own. Never handle any equipment unless you have specific permission.
8. Never perform lab activities without direct supervision.
9. Never eat or drink in the laboratory.
10. Keep work areas clean and tidy at all times. Bring only notebooks and lab manuals or written lab procedures to the work area. All other items, such as purses and backpacks, should be left in a designated area.
11. Do not engage in horseplay.

First Aid

12. Always report all accidents or injuries to your teacher, no matter how minor. Notify your teacher immediately about any fires.
13. Learn what to do in case of specific accidents, such as getting acid in your eyes or on your skin. (Rinse acids from your body with lots of water.)
14. Be aware of the location of the first-aid kit, but do not use it unless instructed by your teacher. In case of injury, your teacher should administer first aid. Your teacher may also send you to the school nurse or call a physician.
15. Know the location of emergency equipment, such as the fire extinguisher and fire blanket, and know how to use it.
16. Know the location of the nearest telephone and whom to contact in an emergency.

Heating and Fire Safety

17. Never use a heat source, such as a candle, burner, or hot plate, without wearing safety goggles.
18. Never heat anything unless instructed to do so. A chemical that is harmless when cool may be dangerous when heated.
19. Keep all combustible materials away from flames. Never use a flame or spark near a combustible chemical.
20. Never reach across a flame.
21. Before using a laboratory burner, make sure you know proper procedures for lighting and adjusting the burner, as demonstrated by your teacher. Do not touch the burner. It may be hot. And never leave a lighted burner unattended!
22. Chemicals can splash or boil out of a heated test tube. When heating a substance in a test tube, make sure that the mouth of the tube is not pointed at you or anyone else.
23. Never heat a liquid in a closed container. The expanding gases produced may blow the container apart.
24. Before picking up a container that has been heated, hold the back of your hand near it. If you can feel heat on the back of your hand, the container is too hot to handle. Use an oven mitt to pick up a container that has been heated.

Using Glassware Safely

◆ Use plastic containers, graduated cylinders, and beakers whenever possible. If using glass, students should wear safety goggles.

◆ Use only nonmercury thermometers with anti-roll protectors.

◆ Check all glassware periodically for chips and scratches, which can cause cuts and breakage.

Using Chemicals Safely

25. Never mix chemicals "for the fun of it." You might produce a dangerous, possibly explosive substance.

26. Never put your face near the mouth of a container that holds chemicals. Never touch, taste, or smell a chemical unless you are instructed by your teacher to do so. Many chemicals are poisonous.

27. Use only those chemicals needed in the activity. Read and double-check labels on supply bottles before removing any chemicals. Take only as much as you need. Keep all containers closed when chemicals are not being used.

28. Dispose of all chemicals as instructed by your teacher. To avoid contamination, never return chemicals to their original containers. Never simply pour chemicals or other substances into the sink or trash containers.

29. Be extra careful when working with acids or bases. Pour all chemicals over the sink or a container, not over your work surface.

30. If you are instructed to test for odors, use a wafting motion to direct the odors to your nose. Do not inhale the fumes directly from the container.

31. When mixing an acid and water, always pour the water into the container first and then add the acid to the water. Never pour water into an acid.

32. Take extreme care not to spill any material in the laboratory. Wash chemical spills and splashes immediately with plenty of water. Immediately begin rinsing with water any acids that get on your skin or clothing, and notify your teacher of any acid spill at the same time.

Using Glassware Safely

33. Never force glass tubing or thermometers into a rubber stopper or rubber tubing. Have your teacher insert the glass tubing or thermometer if required for an activity.

34. If you are using a laboratory burner, use a wire screen to protect glassware from any flame. Never heat glassware that is not thoroughly dry on the outside.

35. Keep in mind that hot glassware looks cool. Never pick up glassware without first checking to see if it is hot. Use an oven mitt. See rule 24.

36. Never use broken or chipped glassware. If glassware breaks, notify your teacher and dispose of the glassware in the proper broken-glassware container. Never handle broken glass with your bare hands.

37. Never eat or drink from lab glassware.

38. Thoroughly clean glassware before putting it away.

Using Sharp Instruments

39. Handle scalpels or other sharp instruments with extreme care. Never cut material toward you; cut away from you.

40. Immediately notify your teacher if you cut your skin when working in the laboratory.

Animal and Plant Safety

41. Never perform experiments that cause pain, discomfort, or harm to mammals, birds, reptiles, fishes, or amphibians. This rule applies at home as well as in the classroom.

42. Animals should be handled only if absolutely necessary. Your teacher will instruct you as to how to handle each animal species brought into the classroom.

43. If you know that you are allergic to certain plants, molds, or animals, tell your teacher before doing an activity in which these are used.

44. During field work, protect your skin by wearing long pants, long sleeves, socks, and closed shoes. Know how to recognize the poisonous plants and fungi in your area, as well as plants with thorns, and avoid contact with them.

45. Never eat any part of an unidentified plant or fungus.

46. Wash your hands thoroughly after handling animals or the cage containing animals. Wash your hands when you are finished with any activity involving animal parts, plants, or soil.

End-of-Experiment Rules

47. After an experiment has been completed, clean up your work area and return all equipment to its proper place.

48. Dispose of waste materials as instructed by your teacher.

49. Wash your hands after every experiment.

50. Always turn off all burners or hot plates when they are not in use. Unplug hot plates and other electrical equipment. If you used a burner, check that the gas-line valve to the burner is off as well.

Using Sharp Instruments

◆ Always use blunt-tip safety scissors, except when pointed-tip scissors are required.

Animal and Plant Safety

◆ When working with live animals or plants, check ahead of time for students who may have allergies to the specimens.

◆ When growing bacteria cultures, use only disposable petri dishes. After streaking, the dishes should be sealed and not opened again by students. After the lab, students should return the unopened dishes to you. Students should wash their hands with antibacterial soap.

◆ Two methods are recommended for the safe disposal of bacteria cultures. *First method:* Autoclave the petri dishes and discard without opening. *Second method:* If no autoclave is available, carefully open the dishes (never have a student do this) and pour full-strength bleach into the dishes and let stand for a day. Then pour the bleach from the petri dishes down a drain and flush the drain with lots of water. Tape the petri dishes back together and place in a sealed plastic bag. Wrap the plastic bag with a brown paper bag or newspaper and tape securely. Throw the sealed package in the trash. Thoroughly disinfect the work area with bleach.

◆ To grow mold, use a new, sealable plastic bag that is two to three times larger than the material to be placed inside. Seal the bag and tape it shut. After the bag is sealed, students should not open it. To dispose of the bag and mold culture, make a small cut near an edge of the bag and cook in a microwave oven on high setting for at least 1 minute. Discard the bag according to local ordinance, usually in the trash.

◆ Students should wear disposable nitrile, latex, or food-handling gloves when handling live animals or nonliving specimens.

End-of Experiment Rules

◆ Always have students use antibacterial soap for washing their hands.

A

alternating current Current consisting of charges that move back and forth in a circuit. (p. 86)

ammeter A device used to measure current in a circuit. (p. 60)

amplitude The height of a wave from the center to a crest or trough. (p. 124)

amplitude modulation (AM) Changes the amplitude of the carrier wave to match the amplitude of the signal. (p. 124)

analog signal An electric current that is varied smoothly to represent information. (p. 113)

armature The moving part of an electric motor, consisting of dozens or hundreds of loops of wire wrapped around an iron core. (p. 81)

atom The smallest particle of an element that has the properties of that element. (p. 18)

aurora A glowing region produced by the interaction of charged particles from the sun and atoms in the atmosphere. (p. 28)

B

battery A combination of two or more electrochemical cells in series. (p. 102)

binary system A number system using combinations of only two digits, 0 and 1; used by computers. (p. 128)

bit Each binary digit, 1 or 0, in the binary system. (p. 129)

brushes The contact points connected to a current source and the commutator of a motor. (p. 81)

byte Arrangement of 8 bits. (p. 129)

C

cathode-ray tube (CRT) A sealed glass vacuum tube that uses electrons to produce images on a screen; picture tube. (p. 126)

central processing unit (CPU) Directs the operation of a computer, performs logical operations and calculations, and stores information. (p. 130)

chat room A network feature that allows two or more users to exchange messages. (p. 141)

chemical energy The energy stored in chemical compounds. (p. 100)

chemical reaction A process in which substances change into new substances with different properties. (p. 100)

circuit breaker A safety device that uses an electromagnet to shut off a circuit when the current becomes too high. (p. 71)

commutator A device that controls the direction of the flow of current through an electric motor. (p. 81)

compass A device with a magnetized needle that can spin freely; a compass needle always points north. (p. 24)

computer An electronic device that stores, processes, and retrieves information. (p. 128)

computer hardware The permanent components of a computer, including the central processing unit and input, output, and memory storage devices. (p. 130)

computer network A group of computers connected by cables or telephone lines that allows people to share information. (p. 138)

computer programmer A person who uses computer languages to write programs, or sets of operation instructions, for computers. (p. 134)

computer software A detailed set of instructions that directs the computer hardware to perform operations on stored information. (p. 134)

computer virus A program that can enter a computer, destroy files, and disable the computer. (p. 140)

conduction A method of charging an object by allowing electrons to flow directly from one object to another object. (p. 49)

conductor A material through which electrons move freely, forming an electric current. (p. 32)

conservation of charge The law that states that charges are neither created nor destroyed. (p. 50)

D

digital signal Pulses of current used to represent information. (p. 114)

diode A solid-state component that consists of layers of two types of semiconductors. (p. 116)

direct current Current consisting of charges that flow in only one direction in a circuit. (p. 86)

disk drive A device that reads information from a disk or enters information onto a disk for a computer. (p. 132)

diskette A plastic disk that holds information and can be removed from the computer. (p. 132)

dry cell An electrochemical cell in which the electrolyte is a paste. (p. 102)

electrical energy The energy of moving electrical charges. (p. 79)

electrical potential The potential energy per unit of electric charge. (p. 56)

electric charge A property of electrons and protons; electrons carry a negative charge, and protons carry a positive charge. (p. 30)

electric circuit A complete path through which electric charges can flow. (p. 32)

electric current The flow of electric charges through a material. (p. 31)

electric field The field around charged particles that exerts a force on other charged particles. (p. 47)

electric generator A device that converts mechanical energy into electrical energy. (p. 86)

electric motor A device that converts electrical energy to mechanical energy to turn an axle. (p. 80)

electrochemical cell A device that converts chemical energy into electrical energy. (p. 101)

electrode A metal part of an electrochemical cell, which gains or loses electrons. (p. 101)

electrolyte A liquid or paste that conducts electricity. (p. 101)

electromagnet A strong magnet that can be turned on and off; a solenoid with a ferromagnetic core. (p. 39)

electromagnetic induction The process of generating an electric current from the motion of a conductor through a magnetic field. (p. 85)

electromagnetic wave A wave made up of a combination of a changing electric field and changing magnetic field. (p. 123)

electron A negatively charged particle that orbits the nucleus of an atom. (p. 18)

electronics The use of electricity to control, communicate, and process information. (p. 112)

electronic signal A varying electric current that represents information. (p. 113)

electroscope An instrument used to detect electric charge. (p. 53)

element A substance in which all the atoms are alike; one of about 100 basic materials that make up all matter. (p. 18)

encryption A process of coding information so that only the intended user can read it. (p. 140)

energy The ability to move an object some distance. (p. 79)

ferromagnetic material A material that is strongly attracted to a magnet, and which can be made into a magnet. (p. 19)

freeware Software that the author has decided to let others use free of charge. (p. 141)

frequency The number of waves passing a given point each second. (p. 124)

frequency modulation (FM) Changes the frequency of the carrier wave to match the amplitude of the signal. (p. 124)

friction A force that is exerted when two substances are rubbed together; electrons are transferred by the rubbing. (p. 49)

fuse A safety device with a thin metal strip that will melt if too much current passes through a circuit. (p. 70)

galvanometer A device that uses an electromagnet to detect small amounts of current. (p. 79)

grounded Allowing charges to flow directly from the circuit to the ground connection. (p. 69)

hard disk The rigid magnetic metal disk that stays inside a computer and holds information that can be accessed any time the computer is on. (p. 132)

induction A method of electrically charging an object by means of the electric field of another object. (p. 50)

input device A device that feeds data to a CPU; a keyboard is an input device. (p. 130)

insulator A material through which the charges of an electric current are not able to move. (p. 32)

integrated circuit A circuit that has been manufactured on a chip (a tiny slice of semiconductor), which can contain thousands of diodes, transistors, and resistors. (p. 117)

intellectual property A story, poem, computer program, or similar product owned by the author. (p. 141)

Internet An international computer network that links millions of businesses, schools, and research organizations and that has millions of individual users. (p. 139)

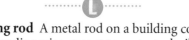

lightning rod A metal rod on a building connected to a grounding wire; meant to protect a building from lightning damage. (p. 70)

local area network (LAN) A set of computers connected in one office building or classroom. (p. 139)

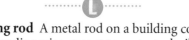

magnetic declination The angle between geographic north and the north to which a compass needle points. (p. 26)

magnetic domain A region in which the magnetic fields of all atoms are lined up in the same direction. (p. 19)

magnetic field The region around a magnet where the magnetic force is exerted. (p. 17)

magnetic field lines Lines that map out the magnetic field around a magnet. (p. 17)

magnetic pole The ends of a magnetic object, where the magnetic force is strongest. (p. 15)

magnetism The force of attraction or repulsion of magnetic materials. (p. 15)

magnetosphere The region of Earth's magnetic field confined by the solar wind. (p. 27)

mechanical energy The energy an object has due to its movement or position. (p. 79)

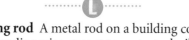

nonrenewable resource A natural resource that cannot be replaced if used up. (p. 91)

nucleus The core at the center of every atom. (p. 18)

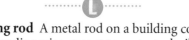

Ohm's law Resistance equals voltage divided by current. (p. 60)

optical disc A disc read by lasers that holds a great amount of information, even more than some hard drives. (p. 133)

output device A device that presents data from a computer; a monitor is an output device. (p. 131)

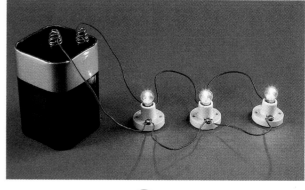

parallel circuit An electric circuit with multiple paths. (p. 66)

permanent magnet A magnet made of material that keeps its magnetism. (p. 20)

potential difference The difference in electrical potential between two places; measured in volts. (p. 57)

power The rate at which one form of energy is converted into another; the unit of power is the Watt; Watts = Volts × Amps. (p. 93)

proton A positively charged particle that is part of an atom's nucleus. (p. 18)

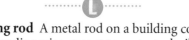

random-access memory (RAM) Temporary storage area for data while the computer is operating. (p. 131)

read-only memory (ROM) Permanent storage area for data in the computer; the CPU can read these data but not change them. (p. 131)

rechargeable battery A battery in which the products of the electrochemical reaction can be turned back into reactants to be reused. (p. 103)

renewable resource A natural resource that can be replaced in nature at a rate close to the rate at which it is used. (p. 91)

resistance The opposition to the movement of electric charges flowing through a material. (p. 34)

resistor A device in an electric circuit that uses electrical energy as it interferes with the flow of electric charge. (p. 34)

semiconductor A material that conducts electricity under certain conditions. (p. 115)

series circuit An electric circuit with a single path. (p. 65)

shareware Software that the author allows others to try out and use for a low fee. (p. 141)

short circuit An electrical connection that allows current to take an unintended path. (p. 68)

slip rings The parts of a generator that rotate with the armature and make contact with the brushes. (p. 87)

solar wind Streams of electrically charged particles flowing at high speeds from the sun; solar wind pushes against Earth's magnetic field and surrounds it. (p. 27)

solenoid A current-carrying coil of wire with many loops that acts as a magnet. (p. 39)

solid-state component The part of a circuit in which a signal is controlled by a solid material. (p. 116)

static discharge The loss of static electricity as electric charges move off an object. (p. 50)

static electricity A buildup of charges on an object. (p. 49)

step-down transformer A transformer that decreases voltage. (p. 95)

step-up transformer A transformer that increases voltage. (p. 95)

superconductor A material that has no electrical resistance. (p. 35)

terminal The part of an electrode above the surface of the electrolyte. (p. 101)

third prong The round prong of a plug which connects the metal shell of an appliance to the safety grounding wire of a building. (p. 69)

transformer A device that increases or decreases voltage. (p. 94)

transistor A solid-state component used to amplify an electronic signal or to switch current on and off. (p. 116)

turbine A circular device with many blades that is turned by water, wind, steam, or tides. (p. 87)

vacuum tube A glass tube from which almost all gases have been removed, and which contains electrodes that control the flow of electrons. (p. 118)

Van Allen belts Two doughnut-shaped regions 1,000–25,000 kilometers above Earth that contain electrons and protons traveling at high speeds. (p. 27)

voltage Potential difference; measured by a voltmeter. (p. 57)

voltage source Creates a potential difference in an electric circuit; batteries and generators are voltage sources. (p. 58)

voltmeter A device used to measure voltage, or potential difference. (p. 60)

wet cell An electrochemical cell in which the electrolyte is a liquid. (p. 102)

wide area network (WAN) A system of computers across large distances, with very large computers that serve as support connections. (p. 139)

World Wide Web Many computers connected over long distances; it allows the displaying and viewing of text, pictures, video, and sound. (p. 140)

Index

Acknowledgments

Illustration

Albert Molnar: 140
John Edwards and Associates: 26(t), 27, 98,
GeoSystems Global Corporation: 26(b),
Martucci Design: 162, 163, 164,
Matt Mayerchak: 42, 74, 144, 160, 161,
Morgan Cain & Associates: 17, 18, 19, 21, 38, 39, 40, 47, 48, 49, 53, 58, 59, 67, 125, 154,
Precision Graphics: 79, 80, 82, 84, 85, 86, 87, 95, 100, 101, 102, 108, 109, 112, 116, 123, 124t, 145
J/B Woolsey Associates: 29, 51, 57, 64, 65, 66, 75, 115, 121, 124b, 127, 130-131, 158,

Photography

Photo Research by Toni Michaels
Cover image Joseph B. Brignold/The Image Bank

Nature of Science
Page 8, 9t, inset, NASA; 9b, SPAR Aerospace/SPAR Space Systems; 10-11, 10t, NASA; 10b, Courtesy of Ellen Ochoa; 11, NASA.

Chapter 1
Pages 12-13, Dick Durrance II/The Stock Market; **14t,** Richard Haynes; **14b,** Marcello Bertinetti/Photo Researchers; **15t,** Paul Silverman/ Fundamental Photographs; **15b,** Russ Lappa; **16 both, 17l,** Richard Megna/Fundamental Photographs; **17r,** Phil Degginger/Color-Pic, Inc.; **18 both,** Richard Megna/Fundamental Photographs; **20t,** Russ Lappa; **20b,** Richard Haynes; **22,** Aaron Rezny/The Stock Market; **23 both,** Richard Haynes; **24t,** Russ Lappa; **24b,** Sisse Brimberg/National Geographic Image; **25,** National Geographic Society/NGS Image; **28,** Lionel F. Stevenson/Photo Researchers; **30t,** Russ Lappa; **30b,** Corbis-Bettmann; **31b,** Richard Megna/Fundamental Photographs; **31 all others,** Russ Lappa; **32,** Fred McKinney/FPG International; **33,** Corel Corp.; **33 inset,** Russ Lappa; **34l,** Russ Lappa; **34r,** Richard Megna/Fundamental Photographs; **35,** AT&T Bell Labs/ Science Photo Library/Photo Researchers; **36,** Kevin Cruff/FPG International; **37, 38t,** Richard Haynes; **38b, 39,** Richard Megna/ Fundamental Photographs; **40,** Applied Superconductivity Center at the University of Wisconsin-Madison; **41t,** Richard Megna/Fundamental Photographs; **41b,** Lionel F. Stevenson/Photo Researchers.

Chapter 2
Pages 44–45, Telegraph Colour Library/FPG International; **46t,** Richard Haynes; **46b,** Mark C. Burnett/Photo Researchers; **49,** Hank Morgan/ Rainbow; **50,** Russ Lappa; **51 both,** Richard Haynes; **52,** Richard Kaylin/TSI; **54, 55,** Richard Haynes; **56,** Russ Lappa; **57,** Bob Daemmrich/Stock Boston; **59, 60,** Russ Lappa; **61,** M. Antman/The Image Works; **62,** Mark Burnett/Stock Boston; **63,** Richard Haynes; **64,** James Dwyer/Stock Boston; **65, 66, 68,** Russ Lappa; **69t,** Joel Page/AP Wide World Photos; **69b,** Russ Lappa; **70,** Armen Kachaturian/Liaison International; **71l,** Russ Lappa; **71r,** M. Antman/The Image Works; **72,** Ross Harrison Koty/TSI; **73t,** M. Antman/The Image Works; **73b,** Russ Lappa.

Chapter 3
Pages 76-77, John Henley/The Stock Market; **78t,** Russ Lappa; **78b,** Jon Chomitz; **81, 83t,** Russ Lappa; **83b,** Telegraph Colour Library/FPG International; **84,** Richard Haynes; **88t,** Peter Menzel/Stock Boston; **88b,** Martin Rogers/TSI; **88 bkgd,** Peter/Stef Lamberti/TSI; **89t,** Adam Woolfitt/Woodfin Camp & Associates; **89m,** Roger Ball/The Stock Market; **89b,** Stephen J. Krasemann/Photo Researchers; **89 bkgd,** Manfred Gottschalk/Tom Stack & Associates; **91,** Alison Wright/Stock Boston; **92t,** Russ Lappa; **92b,** Frank Siteman/Stock Boston; **94l,** Toni Michaels; **94r,** B. Daemmrich/The Image Works; **95,** Russ Lappa; **96t,** The Granger Collection, NY; **96b,** Corbis-Bettmann; **97t,** The Granger Collection, NY; **97bl, br,** Corbis-Bettmann; **98,** Montes De Oca, Art 1998/FPG International; **99t,** Russ Lappa; **99b,** William Johnson/Stock Boston; **100,** J-L Charmet/ Science Photo Library/Photo Researchers; **103,** Jose Pelaez/The Stock Market; **104t,** David Barnes/TSI; **104b,** Russ Lappa; **105,** Richard Haynes; **106,** David R. Frasier/TSI; **107,** Peter Menzel/Stock Boston.

Chapter 4
Pages 110-111, Tim Davis/Photo Researchers; **113tl,** Bob Daemmrich/ Stock Boston; **113tr,** Bill Horsman/Stock Boston; **113b, 114b,** Russ Lappa; **114 inset,** Dr. Jeremy Burgess/Science Photo Library/Photo Researchers; **115t,** Russ Lappa; **115b,** Russ Lappa/Photo Researchers; **115 inset,** Dr. Jeremy Burgess/Science Photo Library/Photo Researchers; **116 both,** Russ Lappa; **117b,** Manfred Kage/Peter Arnold; **117 inset,** Charles Falco/Photo Researchers; **118,** Ken Whitmore/TSI; **119,** Russ Lappa; **120l,** B. Daemmrich/ The Image Works; **120r,** Camerique/Archive Photos; **122t,** Russ Lappa; **122b,** Richard Pasley/Stock Boston; **123b,** Craig Tuttle/The Stock Market; **123 inset,** Telegraph Colour Library/FPG International; **126,** I. Maier, Jr./The Image Works; **128t,** Richard Haynes; **128b,** L. Dematteis/The Image Works; **129,** Andrew Syred/Science Photo Library/Photo Researchers; **132t,** The Granger Collection, NY; **132b,** Corbis-Bettmann; **133t,** AP/Wide World Photos; **133b,** Camilla Smith/Rainbow; **134,** David Parker/Science Photo Library/Photo Researchers; **135, 136 both, 137,** Russ Lappa; **138,** Sanford/Asliolo/International Stock; **139tl,** AP Photo/Kamran Jebreili; **139tr,** Russ Lappa; **139bl,** Bob Daemmrich/Stock Boston; **139br,** AP Photo/Rick Bethem; **139m,** NASA; **141,** Russ Lappa; **142,** Andrew Oliney & TSI Imaging/TSI; **143,** I. Maier, Jr./The Image Works.

Interdisciplinary Exploration
Page 146t, Art Resource, NY; **146b,** The Granger Collection, NY; **147 all,** U.S. Dept. of the Interior, National Park Service, Edison National Historic Site; **148–149,** AP/Wide World Photos; **150l, m,** U.S. Dept. of the Interior, National Park Service, Edison National Historic Site; **150br,** Brooks/Brown/Photo Researchers; **151t,** US Geological Survery/Science Photo Library/Photo Researchers; **151bl,** Topham/The Image Works; **151br,** Michael Simpson/FPG International; **151 all others,** Russ Lappa.

Skills Handbook
Page 152, Mike Moreland/Photo Network; **153t,** Foodpix; **153m,** Richard Haynes; **153b,** Russ Lappa; **156,** Richard Haynes; **158,** Ron Kimball; **159,** Renee Lynn/Photo Researchers.